The 11th Alabama
Volunteer Regiment
in the Civil War

The 11th Alabama Volunteer Regiment in the Civil War

Ronald G. Griffin

McFarland & Company, Inc., Publishers
Jefferson, North Carolina, and London

The present work is a reprint of the library bound edition of
The 11th Alabama Volunteer Regiment in the Civil War,
first published in 2008 by McFarland.

LIBRARY OF CONGRESS CATALOGUING-IN-PUBLICATION DATA

Griffin, Ronald G.
The 11th Alabama Volunteer Regiment in the
Civil War / Ronald G. Griffin.
p.   cm.
Includes bibliographical references and index.

ISBN 978-0-7864-7158-4
softcover : acid free paper

1. Confederate States of America. Army. Alabama Infantry Regiment, 11th.
2. Alabama — History — Civil War, 1861–1865 — Regimental histories.
3. United States — History — Civil War, 1861–1865 — Regimental histories.
4. United States — History — Civil War, 1861–1865 — Campaigns.   I. Title.
E551.511th .G75   2012   973.7'461 — dc22   2007046128

BRITISH LIBRARY CATALOGUING DATA ARE AVAILABLE

© 2008 Ronald G. Griffin. All rights reserved

*No part of this book may be reproduced or transmitted in any form
or by any means, electronic or mechanical, including photocopying
or recording, or by any information storage and retrieval system,
without permission in writing from the publisher.*

On the cover: battle flag of the 11th Regiment of Alabama Volunteers
(Alabama Department of Archives and History, Montgomery);
Civil War musket rifles (iStockphoto/Thinkstock)

Manufactured in the United States of America

*McFarland & Company, Inc., Publishers
Box 611, Jefferson, North Carolina 28640
www.mcfarlandpub.com*

To Faye,
whose loving support helped
make this book possible

Table of Contents

Preface — 1

1. The Birth of a New Alabama Infantry Regiment — 3
    The Process of Raising and Organizing a Confederate Military Unit in 1861 — 3

2. The Organization of the 11th Alabama Infantry Regiment — 35
    The Companies Are Ordered to Rendezvous Camps — 35
    The Companies Are Mustered into Confederate Service — 48
    The Regiment Is Organized and Equipped at Lynchburg — 50
    The Regiment Is Furthered Organized and Equipped at Richmond — 52

3. A Whirlwind Week at Winchester — 56
    The Departure for Winchester — 56
    The 11th Alabama's Stay at Winchester — 57
    The 11th Alabama Departs for Manassas — 59

4. The Battle of Sickness and Boredom at Manassas — 63
    The Arrival at Manassas Junction — 63
    The Experiences and Developments Near the Lewis House — 64
    The Arrival Near Bristoe Station — 70
    The Encampment Near Centreville — 73
    The Encampment at Cub Run — 77
    A New Encampment Near Centreville — 81
    Winter Quarters Near the Lewis House — 84

5. A Baptism in Blood: The 11th Alabama in the Seven Days Battle — 90
    From Manassas to the Peninsula — 90
    The 11th Alabama's Position and Duties at Yorktown — 91
    From Yorktown to Seven Pines — 95
    The Battle of Seven Pines — 96
    From Seven Pines to Gaines' Mill — 101
    The Battle of Gaines' Mill — 101
    From Gaines' Mill to Frayser's Farm — 107
    The Battle of Frayser's Farm — 108
    A Summary of Regimental Losses During the Seven Days — 113

6. The Crippled 11th Marches into Maryland — 115

- From Frayser's Farm to Gordonsville — 115
- From Gordonsville to Manassas — 118
- The Battle of Second Manassas: August 29, 1862 — 120
- The Battle of Second Manassas: August 30, 1862 — 121
- From Manassas to Harpers Ferry — 122
- The Battle of Sharpsburg — 124

7. Bombarded at Fredericksburg and the Proud Day at Salem Church — 127

- The Stay at Winchester — 127
- From Winchester to Culpeper Court House — 128
- From Culpeper Court House to Fredericksburg — 130
- The Battle of Fredericksburg — 130
- Military Developments from Fredericksburg to Salem Church — 132
- The Passing of Time at Fredericksburg — 134
- Events Leading Up to the Battle of Salem Church — 136
- The Battle of Salem Church — 137

8. The Brave Charges at Gettysburg — 146

- Military Developments from Salem Church to Gettysburg — 146
- The Trip from Fredericksburg to Gettysburg — 147
- The 11th Alabama on the First Day of Battle: July 1, 1863 — 149
- The 11th Alabama on the Second Day of Battle: July 2, 1863 — 150
- The 11th Alabama on the Third Day of Battle: July 3, 1863 — 154
- The Casualties of the 11th Alabama at Gettysburg — 156
- The Prisoners of the 11th Alabama at Gettysburg — 158
- A Brief Evaluation of the Gettysburg Campaign — 160

9. The Lull Before the Storm — 161

- From Gettysburg to Orange Court House — 161
- The Encampment at Orange Court House — 163
- The Bristoe Station Campaign — 167
- Winter Quarters at Orange Court House, 1863–1864 — 168

10. The Conflict Fiercely Intensifies: The Wilderness and Spotsylvania — 175

- The Battle of the Wilderness: May 6, 1864 — 175
- The Battle of the Wilderness: May 7, 1864 — 178
- The Battle of Spotsylvania Court House: May 8–12, 1864 — 179

11. The Battles to the Trenches of Petersburg — 184

- The Engagement at Hanover Junction: May 24, 1864 — 184
- The Battle at Atlee's Station: June 1, 1864 — 186
- The Battle of Turkey Ridge: June 3, 1864 — 187
- The Battle of Wilcox Farm: June 22, 1864 — 188
- Skirmish Near Ream's Station: June 23, 1864 — 192
- Skirmish with Kautz and Wilson's Raiders: June 29, 1864 — 193
- The Battle of the Crater: July 30, 1864 — 195

The Battle of White's Tavern: August 16, 1864	202
The Battle of Davis Farm: August 21, 1864	205
The Battle of Ream's Station: August 25, 1864	208

12. The Desperate Struggle for Petersburg Is Lost — 210

Events Following the Battle of Ream's Station	210
The Battle of Burgess Mill: October 27, 1864	213
Events Between Burgess Mill and the End of 1864	215
Experiences in the Winter of 1865 to Hatcher's Run	217
The Battle of Hatcher's Run: February 6, 1865	218
Some Closing Scenes of the War	220
The Battle of Farmville: April 7, 1865	221
The 11th Alabama at Appomattox Court House: April 9, 1865	225
Some Closing Thoughts on the 11th Alabama	227

13. The Final Roll-Call of the 11th Alabama Infantry — 229

The Field Officers	229
The Officers and Enlisted Men of Company A	230
The Officers and Enlisted Men of Company B	233
The Officers and Enlisted Men of Company C	235
The Officers and Enlisted Men of Company D	236
The Officers and Enlisted Men of Company E	239
The Officers and Enlisted Men of Company F	240
The Officers and Enlisted Men of Company G	243
The Officers and Enlisted Men of Company H	245
The Officers and Enlisted Men of Company I	250
The Officers and Enlisted Men of Company K	253

Chapter Notes	257
Bibliography	263
Index	269

Preface

This book had its beginnings in the personal exploration of my family roots. I was able to trace my ancestors eventually to the years of 1861–1865. My Griffin family lived in old Perry County, Alabama. When the War between the States broke out in early 1861, my family, like hundreds of others in Perry County, willingly sent their sons off to fight. One of the companies raised in Perry County became known as the Independent Volunteers. Several of my ancestors signed up for service in this company, which eventually became a part of the 11th Regiment of Alabama Volunteers. It was this discovery which really provided the spark for the writing of this book. When I looked for additional information on this regiment, I learned that no definitive work had ever been written on this military unit. Even a superficial glance at the involvement of the 11th Alabama in the campaigns of the Army of Northern Virginia made it clear how pivotal their role was in the war. This knowledge only fueled my interest more in taking up the challenge of writing such a work.

The 11th Alabama Volunteer Regiment in the Civil War is a regimental history that seeks to trace a single military unit within the Army of Northern Virginia from its inception until its surrender at Appomattox Court House. From the beginning it has been my intent to focus primarily upon the regiment itself. It would be very easy to get caught up in the details on the brigade, division, corps, and army levels. This has not been my objective. I do touch on the relevant information as it directly bears on the regiment itself, or because note of it is taken from the regimental data. In keeping with this objective, then, I examine the 11th Regiment's story as it unfolds from 1861 to 1865. I look at the key leaders, the military organization of the individual companies, the movement of the regiment from 1861 to 1865, the battles fought, the men lost, and the personal stories that make all these details more vivid.

In order to carry out such a project it was necessary to examine a wide range of primary and secondary materials. A careful examination of the *Official Records* was absolutely indispensable. Along with the military reports, I discovered that knowledge of everything from military hospitals to railroad organization was necessary to complete a work like this one. Special mention needs to be made of two collections that proved to be most helpful in the construction of this book. The W.S. Hoole Special Collections at the University of Alabama holds what I have labeled the J.C.C. Sanders File. It contains many essential letters written by Gen. J.C.C. Sanders of the 11th Alabama. These detailed letters filled in what would have proved to be a lot of blanks in the historical reconstruction of the regiment. Added to these, note must be made of the 11th Alabama Regimental Files contained at the Department of Archives and History in Montgomery, Alabama. A wealth of information on the regiment is found in this holding.

I would not have been satisfied if this were all the information that could have been brought to bear on the subject. I didn't want this work to be an impersonal, uninteresting assemblage of military information. I wanted it to conform to the standards of academic scholarship, and yet at the same time to be personally interesting to read. This is sometimes a hard balance to strike, and only the reader can determine whether this writer was successful or not. To accomplish this balance, I sought as much information from the descendants of those who served in the 11th that I could find. I probed for copies of letters, diaries, photos, and personal stories that had been passed down to them. I am happy to say that a significant body of relevant material was received from my inquiries. These items have been interwoven into this regimental story of the 11th Alabama. In addition, I have written a final chapter that focuses exclusively upon the postwar years of the soldiers. What happened to the men after they stacked arms at Appomattox? I try to trace their lives as best I can. This will prove to be of great usefulness to those who have genealogical interests.

There is one final undertaking that made this work what it is. One cannot totally understand a regiment from written sources alone. One needs to go to where they encamped, where they fought, and where they died. Over the years of writing this history I traveled the same path as the companies did. I went to the railroad depots where they caught the trains to Virginia. I stood on the ground in Lynchburg where they were mustered into Confederate service. I retraced their steps all the way to Appomattox Court House. There are insights into a regiment that can only be obtained by taking such a journey.

Why is this work important? The production of a new regimental history has obvious historical importance. The information on the 11th Alabama had never been brought together and synthesized until now. This work will provide helpful information in the ongoing study and evaluation of the Army of Northern Virginia. There is now another significant body of information that can be brought to bear on the study of this Army, as well as the battles in which it was engaged.

In addition, this work aids in understanding of what was involved in the raising of a typical Confederate military unit in 1861. The dynamics involved in the raising of a military regiment are clearly embodied in the story of the 11th Regiment.

This work also contributes to the continuing dialogue of why the Southern soldier fought in the War between the States. It seems to this writer that the best way of knowing *why* the typical Southern soldier enlisted in the war, and why he was willing to die in the war, is to read what *he* himself said. The reader will hear in many places throughout this work the reasons why the men of the 11th Alabama were fighting this war.

It is my hope that this book will rekindle the pride that every Alabamian should have in his Confederate ancestors. The sacrifices they made, and the hardships they endured, should never be forgotten. These qualities of character are worthy of both admiration and continued emulation.

1

The Birth of a New Alabama Infantry Regiment

On April 29, 1861, President Jefferson Davis delivered an address to the Provisional Congress of the Confederate States of America (*Journal of the Congress of the Confederate States of America*, hereafter entitled *J.C.C.S.A.*, Vol. 1, 160–169). In this address he stated that Abraham Lincoln had declared war on the Confederacy. In light of this turn of events it became apparent to Mr. Davis that the military forces of the South needed to be mobilized as quickly as possible. Mr. Lincoln had issued the call for some 75,000 volunteers to join the Union effort; how was the South to respond to such a call? President Davis now delivered an appeal for 100,000 volunteers to fill the Confederate ranks. The new nation was then faced with the challenge of organizing these men in a hurry. In the pages to follow we shall look at the process involved in the birth of a Confederate military regiment in 1861; in particular, we shall look at the unfolding of this process in the raising of the 11th Alabama Infantry.

The Process of Raising and Organizing a Confederate Military Unit in 1861

A great deal has already been written about the method of raising and organizing a military company and regiment during the War between the States, and thus we offer here only a brief sketch of this process. It is hoped that through this analysis we will come to appreciate more of what was involved in the raising of the 11th Alabama. In order for a military company to be raised it was necessary that someone spearhead the effort. Certainly the entire process involved more than just a single individual, yet in many cases one particular person will often stand out. He might be a politician, a locally influential person, or an established military leader. Fortunately we have some information on the key persons involved in the raising of the 11th Alabama.

COLONEL SYDENHAM MOORE

Sydenham Moore was instrumental in the overall project of raising the 11th Alabama. One newspaper records the fact that Moore and Stephen F. Hale had been authorized by President Davis to raise a regiment of troops in Alabama (*The Alabama Beacon* [Greensboro], 7 June 1861). The article goes on to state that Moore had already been actively engaged in the raising of troops prior to his official commissioning by President Davis. Wheeler confirms that following secession Moore was promptly engaged in the organization of troops (Wheeler

1987, 713). Several of the individual companies of the 11th made mention of the fact that they tendered their services to Colonel Moore, who was at that time engaged in the raising of a regiment. For example, Capt. John B. Hughes of Co. G on January 4, 1865, mentions just how instrumental Colonel Moore was in the formation of the regiment in this late war report:

> On the 16th of June 1861 the services of the Company was tendered and received by Sydenham Moore, who was at that time raising a Regiment to serve three years—or war [11th Alabama Infantry Regimental Files, Alabama Department of Archives and History, Montgomery, Alabama, hereafter 11th Alabama].

Sydenham Moore was born on May 25, 1817, in Rutherford County, Tennessee (Owen 1921, 1236). Following his graduation from the University of Alabama, Moore read law at Huntsville and later practiced in Greensboro. In 1839 he moved to Eutaw in Greene County to practice law. Colonel Moore had military credentials prior to the outbreak of war in 1861. During the Cherokee and Indian War in 1838, Moore volunteered as a private in Captain Otey's Company. He also served in the Mexican War, and in 1846 he raised a company of volunteers at Eutaw (Butler 1998, xi). He eventually was made Brigadier General of militia in 1847. In 1857 Colonel Moore was appointed judge of the circuit court, and a few months later was elected as a Democrat to the Thirty-fifth and Thirty-sixth Congresses. He served in this capacity from March 4, 1857, until January 21, 1861. Moore left Washington along with his colleagues with the secession of Alabama from the Union (Owen 1921, 1236).

Moore was a well-known and respected legislator in Alabama. This would have contributed to his success as an organizer of an infantry regiment. In the June 6, 1860, issue of the *Linden Jeffersonian*, it gives a word of appreciation to the honorable Sydenham Moore for his provision of valuable congressional documents and speeches (*The Linden Jeffersonian*, 6 June 1860). Moore is called an able and popular representative of the Tuscaloosa district, one calm in manner, suave in temperament, and fair in debate (*The Alabama Beacon*, 28 September 1860). Brewer furthermore describes Moore in these words:

> Chivalrous, impulsive, generous, candid, Col. Moore "fear or falsehood never knew." Earnest and tenacious of purpose, he was yet courteous, obliging, and conciliatory. His sense of honor was delicate, his life upright, and his nature sociable and genial. His figure was slender and graceful, and his firmly-set jaw expressed undaunted resolution [Brewer 1975, 266].

He, along with his future Lieutenant Colonel, Stephen F. Hale, met with a concerned group of citizens on November 24, 1860, to discuss what action should be taken in the event of the election of Abraham Lincoln (*The Alabama Beacon*, 30 November 1860). It was the suggestion of Moore that the so-called Mobile Resolutions be adopted, that won the day. Among other things these resolutions included the right of Alabama to withdraw from the Federal Union in the light of Lincoln's election as president. One could list numerous references in the newspapers of the day which hold in high regard the

Sydenham Moore (Alabama Department of Archives and History, Montgomery, Alabama).

Sydenham Moore Home (Library of Congress, Prints and Photographs Division, Reproduction # HABS ALA 33 GREBO 5).

reputation of Sydenham Moore. This made his activities as an organizer of troops effectual in Greene, Tuscaloosa, and the surrounding counties.

STEPHEN FOWLER HALE

Colonel Moore's Greene County colleague, Stephen F. Hale, also assisted in the raising of the 11th Alabama. Colonel Hale has been described as being tall and lanky in appearance, and one who was rather eccentric in his manners (Brewer 1975, 267). Brewer has recorded some remarks made by Hon. Thomas H. Herndon regarding Hale at a meeting of the bar of Eutaw:

> His intellect was acute and analytical, rather than comprehensive; his perception quick and subtle. As a speaker he had but little grace of delivery, but he was lucid in statement and cogent in argument, and rarely failed to throw upon his cause all the elucidation of which it was susceptible.

Stephen Fowler Hale was born in Crittendon County, Kentucky, in 1816. After his graduation from Cumberland University he taught school in Greene County, Alabama (*Encyclopedia of the Confederacy*, s.v. "Hale, Stephen Fowler"). Hale's study of law in Lexington, Kentucky, served him well as he was elected representative to the Provisional Confederate Congress. He served as a committee member of Military Affairs, Judiciary, and Indian Affairs.[1]

He did not stand for election to the First Confederate Congress, but on August 28, 1861, his name was nominated for Lt. Colonel of the 11th Alabama (*J.C.C.S.A.*, Vol. 1, 434).

Colonel Hale was well admired by the very counties from which the 11th Alabama would eventually be drawn. One Carrollton newspaper gave a glowing review of a speech by Hale in February of 1860. These words capture some of the heartfelt feelings that were held for Colonel Hale:

> We admire the sterling Southern Rights sentiments and the independence of thought which characterizes this admirable speech.... As a lawyer and a man of intellect, not less than a pure patriot and a wise counsellor, the opinions of Mr. Hale are worthy of the attention of the people [*The West Alabamian* (Carrollton), 8 February 1860].

Eventually both Sydenham Moore and Stephen F. Hale were appointed by President Davis to raise a new infantry regiment (*The Alabama Beacon*, 7 June 1861). Hale was a natural choice to work together with Moore in the raising of a regiment. Hale had served in the same company with Moore during the Mexican War, and had also been politically active with Moore for some time (*ibid.*, 30 November 1860). Hale and Moore were considered by many to be leading lights in the battle for the preservation of southern rights (*The West Alabamian*, 21 March 1860). On September 1, 1860, Hale was to give a public address at Bridgeville in Pickens County. This is how Hale was described at the time:

> Col. Hale is well known to our people as a true and incorruptible Southern man, and as a pure and patriotic statesman whom no party prejudice can deter from supporting the cause of "truth, justice and the Constitution." Let all our people turn out on the day appointed and give Col. Hale a fair hearing—the time will be well spent [*ibid.*, 22 August 1860].

Stephen Fowler Hale (Alabama Department of Archives and History, Montgomery).

In an excerpt from the autobiography of Stephen F. Nunnalee, he states that Lieutenant Colonel Hale was in fact involved in the raising of the regiment:

> The war fever increased. We offered our services to the Government, and the army having been moved to Richmond and the Potomac, Capt. Moore and Hale were organizing a Regiment, and having organized, in June we were ordered to Richmond [11th Alabama].

On June 8, 1861, Hale was to appear at Carrollton as a member of the Provisional Congress, and as Lieutenant Colonel of a regiment being raised in conjunction with that of Col. Sydenham Moore:

> No better Southern man lives than Stephen F. Hale. His position, as member of Congress, will enable him to given information with regard to our public affairs, which will be of great interest to our people.... Hon. Sydenham Moore has been appointed Colonel in the Confederate States Army, and Stephen F. Hale Lieut. Colonel, and these gentlemen are now raising a Regiment for the war [*The West Alabamian*, 5 June 1861].

Major Isham Garrott

Isham W. Garrott of Perry County was the first Major of the 11th Alabama (11th Alabama). Garrott was born in Wake County, North Carolina, in 1816 (Owen 1921, 640). He studied law at the University of North Carolina, and eventually moved to Marion, Alabama, to practice in 1840. He formed a partnership with James Phelan, and became noted as a leading lawyer in the state. He was Perry County representative in the state legislature from 1845 to 1849, and eventually formed a partnership with Judge William M. Brooks of Marion. Garrett notes:

> He was fiery in his temperament, and bold and fearless in his political assaults. Few men in the Legislature carried more of mercury and bile in their organization, especially in discussing party measures.... When addressing himself to a political adversary, he was somewhat overbearing in his manner; but it was the result of temperament, and not malice [Garrett 1872, 434].

Following the secession of Alabama, Garrott was sent by Governor Moore to North Carolina to ask for the cooperation of their legislature in the continuing tide of the secession movement (Wheeler 1987, 411). A group of letters he penned during this time have been preserved (Howard 1961, 13–19). His first letter was written from Milledgeville, Georgia, on December 7, 1860, in which he reported on the secessionist fever in the state of Georgia. He observes that Governor Brown was a warm secessionist, and it was his opinion that Georgia would secede when its convention met on January 16. He arrived in Columbia, South Carolina, on December 8, and finally in Raleigh on December 10. He wrote Governor Moore two letters from Raleigh in which he reported on the political activity of that state. Garrott was convinced that North Carolina would go out of the Union, but the people of the state were moving slowly in this regard. Garrott's popularity and social influence no doubt were instrumental in his consideration as Major of the 11th Alabama. We were unable to find any evidence that Garrott was directly involved in the raising of troops for the regiment. It appears, however, that Garrott was the first choice for the rank of Major in the 11th Alabama (*The Alabama Beacon*, 5 July 1861).

Though the overall effort of raising a regiment was under the control of Moore and Hale, the job would never have been completed without the help of various local men. We now will turn our attention to the plethora of local men who helped with the raising of the individual companies of the regiment.

Young M. Moody and the Raising of Company A: The Marengo Rifles

Young Marshall Moody was born on June 23, 1822, in Chesterfield County, Virginia (Owen 1921, 1220). As a son born to Carter and Sarah Moody, Young was educated in the Richmond schools before coming to Marengo County, Alabama, in 1842 to teach school and sell merchandise. In 1856 he was appointed circuit clerk. He was also the proprietor of the Linden Hotel as early as January 12, 1859, as this notice appears in the *Linden Jeffersonian*:

> LINDEN HOTEL
> The Undersigned having become Proprietor of the LINDEN HOTEL, respectfully solicits the patronage of the Public — He will endeavor at all times to have his table well furnished with as good accomodations for the "inner" man as the Country can afford. Good and attentive Servants will always be in readiness to do the bidings of his guests. His Stables will be well supplied with Corn, Fodder, Oats &c., for Horses with careful and attentive Hostlers always on hand.
>
> Y.M. Moody
Proprietor

(*Linden Jeffersonian*, 17 May 1859)[2]

Cousins James Moody on the left, Young Marshall Moody on the right (courtesy Woodson Research Center, Fondren Library, Rice University, Houston, Texas).

Moody is described as having a soldierly bearing, about six feet tall, and rather slender and erect (Davis & Hoffman 1991, 179). He was to have a distinguished career in the Confederate military, eventually rising to the rank of General.

One note suggests that the Marengo Rifles had their genesis on January 17, 1861, in the town of Linden (11th Alabama). It does appear, however, that the company was not formally organized until May 4 of 1861. It was on that date that the company was organized for twelve months; afterwards, the terms of enlistment were changed to embrace the war. William C. Morgan in his diary states that he enlisted on June 18, 1861 (*The Mobile Press Register*, 13 May 1934). He writes of his feelings at the time of his enlistment:

> I volunteered for the war today; not expecting to find a soldier's life a pleasant one, but rather a "hard pill." I volunteered to save the south from the awful doom which appears to overshadow it — not because it will be an easy work, but because it is a duty which I owe to my country.

Needham B. Hogan, a teenage private in Co. A, has written of the beginnings of the unit. He states that it was composed of schoolboys from the Linden Academy as well as other schools from the county. As a boy of seventeen he recalls vividly the overwhelming spirit of pride the day he enrolled in the company:

> I well remember, on the day the Company was organized and as the boys, one by one, attached their signatures to the Company roll, while old man Jim Welch (my cousin) beat the long roll upon the old drum he had used in the Mexican war, how I was so thrilled with excitement that I trembled as I ascended the stairway of the old court house in Linden to place my autograph along with those who were offering their lives in defense of their homes and loved ones. I was just seventeen years of age, and the youngest member of the Company [*Confederate Veteran 1893–1912*, Vol. 4, 50].

Most of the men enlisted in the Marengo Rifles were from the Linden, Alabama, area, but Shiloh, Nanafalia, Jefferson, McKinley, and Clio also provided substantial numbers of recruits.[3] The following muster roll includes those men that were part of the original company enlisted by Captain Moody:

Officers

Young M. Moody, 39, Capt.
Thomas H. Holcomb, 27, 1st Lt.
John B. Rains, 31, 2nd Lt.
William B. Young, 18, Brevt. 2nd Lt.
Thomas M. Witherspoon, 23, 1st Sergt.
Thomas J. Adams, 23, 2nd Sergt.
John H. Adams, 22, 3rd Sergt.
Henry L. Bruce, 26, 4th Sergt.
Paul G. Shaw, 19, 5th Sergt.
Robert E. Allen, 26, 1st Corp.
John J. Carter, 24, 2nd Corp.
Reavis B. Woodson, 19, 3rd Corp.
Thomas H. Johnson, 21, 4th Corp.

Privates

Charles J. Adams, 25
Elisha B. Adams, 17
James H.E. Adams, 19
Barzella Beasley, 32
John T. Blackwell, 29
Henry Brame Jr., 26
Elias Braswell, 28
Jefferson Breckenridge, 37
Albert Brown, 31
James R. Bulloch, 37
Boaz W. Bush, 32
Samuel D. Carter, 19
James H. Cleland, 21
John R. Coats, 30
George J. Crawford, 30
Lucius W. Crawford, 24
Jesse W. Daniel, 20
George W. Doss, 21
Benjamin F. Dunaway, 18
Joseph A. Eskridge, 19
William Eskridge, 21
William J. Ethridge, 20
Henry P. Ford, 25
William R. Forniss, 21
Allen A. Gillmore, 20
Basil N. Gillmore, 26
William J. Griffith, 25
James P. Hankins, 26
John A. Hayes, 23
Thomas S. Heard, 25
Henry C. Heath, 23
Needham B. Hogan, 17
Alfred A. Johnson, 43

Merrit Morgan Johnson, 18	Moses Nichols	Frederick E. Solley, 21
John B. Jolly, 21	James L. Ogletree, 36	Jesse H. Steadman, 30
William Jolly, 23	Thomas J. Ogletree, 24	William H.H. Stephenson, 19
Wiley P. Jones, 23	Jesse S. Parker, 21	George P. Suggs, 20
James M. Kelly, 26	Stephen Pearl, 22	Daniel Tice, 41
James H.B. Lee, 25, a musician	Thomas Pearl, 19	James D. Tucker, 21
William T. Marshall, 19	Charles H. Phifer, 21	Thomas W. Tucker, 20
Benjamin E. McClinton, 18	John H. Phifer, 23	James H. Varner, 19
James T. McDonald, 21	George C. Post, 24	John R. Varner, 21
William A.D. McIntosh, 25	James E. Riggins, 23	Samuel Varner, 19
William A. McNeill, 18	Francis M. Rogers, 29	Alexander M. Waller, 20
Jesse B. Mobley, 22	William H. Rogers, 21	Alexander F. Wayne, 20
Alfred J. Morgan, 21	Thomas F. Ross, 21	Joseph J. Williams, 23
William C. Morgan, 26	Richard A. Sanders, 25	William C. Williams, 21
Lemuel Napier, 28	John G. Smith, 26	

At least ninety men were on the original roll for the Marengo Rifles who were organized in Linden. There may have been more, but based on the muster rolls we provide the above as the assured minimum.[4]

George W. Field and the Raising of Company B: The Greene County Greys

George Field was the son of Stephen G. Field and Harriet Wallace Field of Greene County, Alabama (Brownell 1878, 20). George was born around 1828 in North Carolina. His mother

Old Marengo County Courthouse, where the Marengo Rifles enlisted for the war.

was also born there, but his father hailed from Providence, Rhode Island. The name of George Field appears on the roll of the Eutaw Rangers commanded by Col. Sydenham Moore during the Mexican War (Butler 1998, 121). Field worked alongside his father as a hotel keeper in Eutaw Beat as early as 1850 (*Seventh Census* Roll 6, 289a). Prior to the outbreak of the war, Field served as Sheriff of Greene County, and it was a position that he did not formally resign from even after he left for Virginia with the company (*Alabama Beacon*, 26 April 1861). In a letter penned on September 11, 1862, to Secretary of War Benjamin, Governor Shorter of Alabama asks for a furlough on his behalf in order for him to resign as Sheriff and to attend to other pressing business matters:

> Hon. J.P. Benjamin   Executive Department
> Secretary of War   Montgomery, Jan 20th 1862
> Sir:
>   I have been requested to call your attention to the fact that George Field, Captain of Company B in the 11th Ala Regt. near Manassas Junction, is sheriff of Greene County, Alabama. In addition to the multiplied duties of his office which may be lawfully discharged by a deputy, he is *ex officio* Administrator of various estates in his county, and for the one administration of which his securities on his official deed are liable — He wishes to come to Alabama on a furlough to settle up his office and resign it, that he may return unincumbered to his regiment. This duty he owes to the State as well as to his bondsman — He informs me however that an application to the General commanding a furlough was refused on the ground that it was a personal matter. I am persuaded that the General did not fully understand the complication of Capt Field, & the relation he occupies to the State. A furlough of sixty days would enable him to return, close up his official business, report back to his command ... and [I] respectfully recommend that the same be allowed by your department, and if allowed that it be forwarded to him at his encampment in Virginia
>
>   Very Respectfully
>   Yr Obedt Sert
>   Gov Gill Shorter (CSR)

Owen mentions that Field was responsible for raising Co. B (Owen 1921, 430). It appears that the company was raised in the latter days of May at Eutaw, Alabama. The muster rolls consistently give May 27, 1861, as the date of the original enlistment for the men of Co. B; yet, we must go further back in 1861 in order to discover the very beginnings of what became the Greene County Greys.

The very beginnings of the company must be traced back to earlier unit named the Eutaw Rifles. We find the following reference to the Rifles in the *Alabama Whig*, published in Eutaw on February 14, 1861:

> The Eutaw Rifles received a letter from Governor Moore, on Tuesday last, requesting the company to volunteer for twelve months, unless sooner discharged. If, on an election, a majority of the members vote to tender their services to the state for the time specified, the Governor will at once order them into the service at Fort Morgan. We think the company will decide to go by a heavy vote. ... it will be necessary for the company to elect officers before they go into service.

It seems that Stephen F. Nunnalee was involved in the early efforts at organizing this company. He was born to Howell and Malinda Nunnalee on July 23, 1825, yet previous to this, his parents moved from Georgia to Monroe County, Alabama, around 1817 or 1818 (11th Alabama). Early in his life he demonstrated interest in journalism, and so by February of 1842 he had become an apprentice in the company of Houston and Davis, publishers of the *Eutaw Whig*. This opportunity would prove to be rather short-lived, for in May of 1846 he joined Sydenham Moore's company to do service in the Mexican War. He kept a journal of his Mexican War experiences, as did Captain Moore; finally, in 1902 he wrote his autobiography (11th Alabama).

Upon his return from the war a year later Nunnalee went back to work at Houston and Davis. The work was becoming more and more difficult for Nunnalee to bear, and so he made the decision to sell out to Mr. W.H. Fowler. After leaving Houston and Davis, Nunnalee began working as a clerk for Johnson and Bostick in Eutaw. On March 9, 1853, he married Miss Mary A. Murphy. Two years later Nunnalee started his own newspaper called the *Independent Observer*. This was the fourth newspaper in Greene County, the *Whig, Beacon,* and the *Democrat* being the other three in circulation at the time.

The Eutaw Rifles made themselves available to the service of the state of Alabama, as Nunnalee recalls:

> I was, in time, elected Captain of the Eutaw Rifles. I did not believe it would come to actual bloodshed.... Our Co. had tendered its services to the Gov. (Moore) of Alabama, we were accepted and ordered to Fort Morgan, where we drilled as Artillery. The order changing the terms of our enlistment to the Confederate States, the Co. determined to reorganize, and I was elected to a 2d Lieutenancy [11th Alabama].

It seems that at the earliest stages of the company's development Nunnalee was the elected Captain. Governor Moore requested that the Rifles volunteer their services for a period of not less than twelve months (*The Alabama Whig*, 14 February 1861). Their assignment was to include being stationed at Fort Morgan. The company took immediate action upon the recommendation of Governor Moore, as noted in the *Alabama Whig*:

> **Attention Eutaw Rifles**
> You are hereby commanded to assemble at Eutaw, on Saturday the 16th of Feb'y. 1861. This command includes all those who have withdrawn from the Company from its organization and who have not complied with the condition of their discharge.
> By order of Lt. Nunnalee, Comd'g
> G. FIELD, O.S. [*The Alabama Whig*, 14 February 1861].

It is interesting to note that George Field was at this point the Orderly Sergeant of the budding company. It was on February 16, 1861, that the Eutaw Rifles enlisted for twelve months of service (CSR).[5] A further note in the newspaper notifies the public that the uniforms of the Eutaw Rifles had been received the week before, and in the opinion of the writer, they lacked much to be desired in their appearance!

Under the leadership of Nunnalee the company proceeded to Fort Morgan, at which place it was drilled as an artillery unit (11th Alabama). The time of their departure appears to have been toward the end of February or the first of March. Upon their arrival at Fort Morgan they were to relieve the Greensboro Guards (*The Alabama Beacon* [Greensboro], 22 February 1861). On March 8 it is noted that the Rifles had departed from Eutaw for Fort Morgan. It also mentions the ceremony surrounding their departure:

> Before the Company was dismissed it was announced that Chas. P. Dexter, Esqr., had presented to the Company one hundred dollars. This was received with three rousing cheers for the donor. Messrs. Hubbard & Pollard presented fifty which was received with other three cheers. Then Dr. Constantine followed with twenty, received in like manner. It was also announced that Duncan Dew Jr., and Charles Hayes had given to the Company one hundred and fifty dollars, to be appropriated to the purchase of Fatigue Caps. This was received also with hearty cheers. We heard afterwards that D. Dew, Sr., had also given to the Company fifty dollars [*The Alabama Beacon*, 26 April 1861].

We know nothing of the Rifles' service at Fort Morgan other than the brief statement of Nunnalee that they drilled as artillery. Nunnalee indicates that when the order came which changed the terms of the company's enlistment, it was decided that the entire company would be reorganized. The time of this reorganization was probably in early April. We find that the *Beacon* notes a reference from the *Eutaw Whig* that the Rifles voted not to enlist in the service of the Confederate States, and were to be discharged and sent home (*The Alabama Beacon*, 12 April 1861). The Rifles arrived home on April 11 and were escorted from Trussell's Ferry into town (*ibid.*, 19 April 1861). The town presented the company with a public welcome on the 21st, at which time a public address was offered by Hon. Thomas H. Herndon. Captain Nunnalee responded to this kindness with an address of his own on behalf of the company.

In the days that followed the Rifles' return to Eutaw we can only assume that a great deal of reorganizing was taking place. In a note dated April 26, 1861, George W. Field is said to have joined a company being raised on the west side of the river (*ibid.*, 26 April 1861). This was no doubt a reference to the newly reorganized company that was to become the Greene County Greys. On May 3, 1861, we learn that this new company was now being headed by Capt. Sydenham Moore (*The Alabama Beacon*, 3 May 1861)! Stephen Nunnalee was elected 1st Lieutenant, R.E. Watkins 2nd Lieutenant, and W.M. Bratton 3rd Lieutenant. The company is said to have been composed of approximately ninety men. This new company is now labeled the Greene County Greys (*The Alabama Beacon*, 10 May 1861).[6] Due to his anticipated duties in the field, Nunnalee was compelled to sell out his interests in the *Eutaw Observer*:

> Mr. Nunnalee having sold out to Mr. Wm. O. Monroe, late of the *Whig*. The change, as appears from the retiring proprietor's Card, has been rendered necessary by the fact that he is about to engage in the stirring duties of the tented field. As a member —1st Lieutenant— of the "Greene County Grays," Captain Syd. Moore, Mr. Nunnalee will soon exchange the peaceful scenes of home, for the excitements and perils of war.

On May 24 it is reported that the Greys have disbanded on the grounds that they are unwilling to serve for the entire war (*The Alabama Beacon*, 24 May 1861). It seems then that the terms of enlistment for the Greys was originally only for one year; however, the article goes on to say that an effort was now underway to get up a company for the entire war. George Clark remembers that he and his father went down to the courthouse where a meeting was being held concerning the organization and equipping of a military company (Clark 1914, 11). It only took a few days for this reorganization to take place, for we read the following notice in the *Alabama Beacon* dated June 7, 1861:

> The "Green County Grays" is the name adopted by the Company that has been raised at Eutaw for the war. The following officers have been elected: George Field, Captain. Wm. Bratton, 1st Lieutenant. S.F. Nunnalee, 2nd Lieut. Geo. W. Clark, 2nd Lieut. R.P. Shoppert, Orderly Serg't. F.H. Mundy, 2nd Serg't. N.C. Norris, 3rd Serg't. David Scarborough, 4th Serg't. James J. Gordon, 5th Serg't. The Company went into Camp on Thursday of last week.

Based on the above notice, it was only one week after disbanding that the reorganization took place. The reorganized Greys went into camp on May 30, 1861. Based on the muster roll information that we have of this company it seems that May 27, 1861, was most likely the date when the reorganization of the unit for the war officially occurred.

Company B: The Greene County Greys

Most of the men enlisted in the Greys were from Eutaw, but Forkland, Union, Knoxville, Springfield, and Boligee also provided men for the company.[7] The following muster roll contains the names of those men that were originally enlisted by Captain Field:

Officers

George Field, 30, Capt.
William M. Bratton, 36, 1st Lt.
Stephen F. Nunnalee, 35, 2nd Lt.
George W. Clark, 19, 3rd Lt.
Robert P. Schoppert, 25, 1st Sergt.
Frank H. Mundy, 24, 2nd Sergt.
Martin C. Norris, 23, 3rd Sergt.
David P. Scarbrough, 21, 4th Sergt.
Anderson Crenshaw, 21, 1st Corp.
John A. True, 32, 2nd Corp.
Winfield S. Bird, 21, 3rd Corp.
John Cullin, 21, 4th Corp.

Privates

James F. Allen, 18
Thomas N. Avery, 18
Kindred P. Banks, 23
Pharis Bevill, 20
William P. Bird, 22
James D. Brassfield, 25
Calvin Brett, 30, Regimental Drummer
Henry P. Caulfield, 22
Joseph P. Clark, 24
John R. Collins, 44
Robert N. Crawford, 20
Stephens Croom, 21
Edward B. Deale, 36
Andrew J. Derby, 27
Peter F. Doub, 22
Calvin Edmiston, 24
James Edmiston, 23
Joseph E. Eubanks, 24
James R. Evans, 17
John W. Friend, 19
Thomas E. Fuller, 22
Charles Galloway, 21
James S. Gibson, 28
Alexander S. Gilbert, 23
Benjamin F. Gordon, 26
James J. Gordon, 21
Nathan K. Greenwood, 19
Jordan Hall, 26
Matthew P. Hamilton, 28[8]
Robert G. Hamlet, 25
John P. Hatter, 21
Isaiah S.. High, 25
Gabriel L. Hill, 26
William L. Hunter, 19
Francis J. Inge, 27
Thomas J. Johnston, 18
N. Henderson Jones, 27
William L. Kennedy, 23
James D. Kimbrough, 30
Thomas J. Knight, 30
John A. Knox, 19
Samuel P. Knox, 16
Robert H. Lamb, 21
James P. Lee, 23
D. Milton Little, 19
William P. Loyd, 19
Moody H. May, 33
William E. McCracken, 22
John S. McCulley, 26
Richard J. McCulley, 27
Henry McGee, 28
Patrick F. McGuire, 28
Alexander M. McIntosh, 40
Joseph S. Merrill, 24
Henry E. Monroe, 21
Robert Moore, 23
Spencer Green Moore, 39
William H. Moore, 28
William F. Morris, 22
Nicholas Neary, 40
John P. Parham, 22
Abner E. Patton, 26
Arthur M. Perry, 20
John W. Phares, 22
John H. Phillips, 22
John W. Pool, 20
John C.J. Ridgeway, 20
Francis M. Ried
Martin Van B. Roberts, 24
William P. Robuck, 26
John W. Skates, 20
Lemuel Tharp, 27
William F. Thetford, 21
Fleming W. Thompson, 25
William L. True, 25
Robert P. Tutwiler, 23
George Willis Webb, 18
Henry C. White, 18
Meady M. Williford, 25
Lowndes Womack, 21
Elisha Woods, 27
Joseph E. Wooten, 24

The original muster roll for Co. B was at least ninety-four.

J.C.C. Sanders and the Raising of Company C: The Confederate Guards

John Caldwell Calhoun Sanders was born on March 18, 1840, in Tuscaloosa, Alabama (Owen 1921, 1496). Sanders's father, Dr. Charles Peake Sanders, was a medical doctor who hailed from South Carolina. His mother, Elizabeth Ann Sanders, was also a native of South Carolina. The Sanders family removed first to Tuscaloosa County, Alabama, where John was born, and later to Clinton in Greene County. Dr. Sanders practiced medicine at this place for some twenty years. It was here that John Sanders was educated and began to manifest the qualities of character requisite for the military positions he eventually held. John's brother, William, who was to become the Surgeon of the 11th, recalls these qualities vividly in a speech delivered in Richmond in 1916 (Dr. Sanders's Papers, Alabama Department of Archives and History, hereafter, Dr. Sanders's Papers). John possessed a solidity of mind, a decisiveness of character, and a drive for accuracy from a very early age. He was a responsible and hard-working young man.

As he grew into a young man, Sanders showed an intense interest in military schools. It was as a sophomore that he entered the University of Alabama in 1858. He excelled in his studies, and was even given the privilege of delivering the valedictory address to the members of the prestigious Erosophic Literary Society. In the fall of 1860 the university had a military department attached to it. John became a cadet and served as an Orderly Sergeant of one of the companies. William, John's brother, wrote to him while he himself was studying medicine in Philadelphia (Clapp Papers, W.S. Hoole Special Collections Library, hereafter Sanders's File). William told John on November 1, 1860, that there was no telling how soon his military services might be needed due to the rising tide of national sentiment: "The Southern people ought to prepare for resistence and not think of submitting. I s'pose you are preparing yourselves for soldiers, and there is no telling how soon your services may be needed on the tented field [Sanders's File]."

John traveled with the cadets from the university to Montgomery in January of 1861. The trip was meant to impress upon the state lawmakers the value of the new system at the university. John wrote to his father a letter about military life while aboard a steamer bound for Montgomery. He speaks of such daily activities as: Reveille, Prayers, Surgeon's Call, Drill, and Taps. Cadets are in bed by 10:30 P.M., and up in the morning at 6:00 A.M. His final thought in this letter was his hope that the Governor would order them out for service. While at Montgomery John wrote to his parents asking for their permission to enter the ranks of active service:

> I am anxious to engage in active service and seeing no immediate prospect of doing so, by remaining with the Corps of Cadets, I now ask your permission to withdraw from the University. I have said nothing to any one of my intentions; but, should you give your consent, direct your letter to me at Mobile (as we return that way), and I will there withdraw and immediately proceed to Fort Morgan or Pensacola. I feel that my country calls for all her sons, and I, for one, cannot refuse her maternal voice [Sanders's File].

He wanted to leave prior to his graduation and join the service; nevertheless, at his parents' insistence, he returned to the university in order to complete his graduation. After the firing upon Fort Sumter, Sanders could wait no longer to fulfill his longing. He left the university in May and joined a military company in Clinton as a private.

The company, which was to become the Confederate Guards, was organized on April 26, 1861 (11th Alabama). The unit was initially raised for a period of only twelve months, but was reorganized to serve for the entire war. Dr. William H. Sanders kept in his possession a roll which appears to be a very early roll of the Guards. It is not dated, but the preface states that the undersigned list of men have volunteered their services to the Confederate States in the present war with the United States. The following list of men signed this document: W.H. Richardson, James F. Cross, J.B. Maxwell, Richard M. Kennedy, R.H. Gordon, Sam M. Hill, Harkness (probably J.C.B.), W.B. Harkness Jr., C.W. Sanders, John J. Steele, E.M. Richardson, W.H. Sanders, James H. Adams, R.N. Archibald, W.H. Bibb, James Breathwait, C.H. Bullock, J.W. Carnes, J. Collins, J. Dodson, F.M. Doss, N.J. Eatman, James F. Gandy, O.H. Goree, and J.M. Gordon. This roll may have only been partially preserved since it contains only twenty-five names. An *x* is placed beside the names of those who probably served as officers. Each man marked by an *x* was an officer at the time of the company's reorganization: James F. Cross, Richard M. Kennedy, Robert H. Gordon, Sam H. Hill, E.M. Richardson, and James F. Gandy. James F. Cross appears at the top of the list of officers on this roll. This probably suggests that Cross was an early organizer of this company. Cross was living in Eutaw, Alabama, according to the 1860 Census (*Eighth Census* Roll 10, 19). He was a wealthy planter from Tennessee. He was to eventually become the 1st Lieutenant of the Guards. It does not seem that the name of John C.C. Sanders actually appears on this early list. In any case, it was to this body of men that Sanders attached himself in May of 1861. Although he enlisted in this unit as a private, he was given the job of drilling the men. It was no doubt due to his military training that Sanders was eventually elected Captain of the company. The Guards are listed on June 7, 1861, with the following officers: John C. Sanders, Captain; Flem. Cross, 1st Lt.; Robt. A. Gordon, 2nd Lt.; B.T. Higginbotham, 3rd Lt.; R.M. Kennedy, Orderly Sgt.; C.L. Knox, 2nd Sgt.; S.M. Hill, 3rd Sgt.; W.R. Gathright, 4th Sgt.; H.M. Richardson, 5th Sgt.; J.J. Robinson, 1st Corp.; E. Clay Ellis, 2nd Corp.; Daniel Hooppaugh, 3rd Corp.; and Foster Gandy, 4th Corp. (*Alabama Beacon*, 7 June 1861). We have a letter written on June 15, 1861, by Josiah Collins in which he mentions the Guards and Captain Sanders:

> Capt Sanders,
> Dr. Sir
> If you will leave a roll of your company, where I can get it I will have an order made at the next County Commissioners Court — to place the same on the Record of the County, the name of the Regiment & Commanding officers to which you may be attached would I think be proper.
> Such a record I think would be desirable for future reference
> Respectfully
> Josiah Collins

[Sanders's File]

Most of the men were living in Clinton, Alabama, who enlisted in the Guards; however, both Union and Mt. Hebron provided substantial numbers of soldiers to fill the ranks.[9]

Company C: The Confederate Guards

The following is the list of men who joined the Confederate Guards:

Officers

John C.C. Sanders, 21, Capt.
James F. Cross, 32, 1st Lt.
Robert H. Gordon, 21, 2nd Lt.[10]
Benjamin T. Higginbotham, 34, 3rd Lt.
Richard M. Kennedy, 29, 1st Sergt.
Carlos La Fayette Knox, 21, 2nd Sergt.
Samuel M. Hill, 19, 3rd Sergt.
Wilson R. Gathright, 20, 4th Sergt.
Erlander M. Richardson, 20, 5th Sergt.
Jesse Robinson, 27, 1st Corp.
Evander C. Ellis, 19, 2nd Corp.
Daniel M. Hooppaugh, 23, 3rd Corp.
James F. Gandy, 18, 4th Corp.

Privates

James H. Adams, 20
Robert N. Archibald, 23
John B. Baines, 19
Albert Baldwin, 28
Moses H. Baskin, 28
William H. Bibb, 22
James Breathwait, 25
Charles H. Bulloch, 18
James F. Cameron, 20
John W. Carnes, 28
William B. Carpenter, 21
Erastus A. Chambers, 20
Thomas S./C. Childers, 27
Wm. H. Childers, 19
Wm. M. Chipman, 21
Wiley J. Coleman, 27
Josiah Collins Jr., 18
Thomas B. Colvin, 20

Francis M. Doss, 21
James O. Duncan, 16
Henry C. Dunlap, 17
Albert Eatman
Francis L. Eatman, 21
Newton J. Eatman, 18
Phelan Eatman, 18
Calvin Fason, 25
Willis Finch, 33
James M. Gordon, 21
Walter H. Gordon, 18
Orlando H. Goree, 22
John Greenwood, 20
David M. Grizzle, 18
James C.B. Harkness, 18
Wm. B. Harkness, 21
Rufus L. Harris, 19
Wm. O. Harrison, 18
John T. Hill, 21
Alexander P. Hitt, 18
James M. Hitt, 18
Andrew F. Hooppaugh, 21
James W. Horton, 20
Matthew A. Jolly, 25
John L. Jones, 27
Josiah J. Jones, 25
Thomas C. Jordan, 19
Lemuel H. Kelly, 24
Thomas H.P. Lanford, 22
Thomas A. Lowry, 21
Robert L. Lyon, 20
John H. Mahaffy, 21
John B. Maxwell, 22
John S.B. McCrackin, 16
Robert H. McLane/McClain, 22
William A. McMillian, 17
James E. Milner, 39
David M. Montgomery, 20
Thomas Moore, 23, musician
John Murphy, 27
Nathaniel Norwood, 19
James J. Paschal, 19
John G. Pierce, 28
Little Berry A. Pippen, 17
Wm. M. Prince, 21
Gilbert M. Reynolds, 32
Thomas B. Richardson, 24
William H. Richardson, 24
Charles W. Sanders, 20
William H. Sanders, 22, Surgeon
William H.H. Sanders, 18
Thomas J. Smith, 27
James R. Stafford, 18
Joseph P. Stallsworth, 17
Elmore A. Steele, 17
John J. Steele, 23
John A. Stewart, 18
George W. Story, 29
Thomas Sullivan, 28
Francis B. Tarr, 24
Robert J. Upchurch, 19
James I. Vaughn, 19
Robert L. Waller, 22
John A. White, 22
Joseph C. Whiteside, 20
Tescharner Williams, 20
William C. Williams, 22
Francis C. Wilson, 19
James H. Wilson, 24
William F. Wilson, 33
Thomas W. Winn, 23

There were at least 102 on the original muster rolls of Company C.

GEORGE E. TAYLOE AND THE RAISING OF COMPANY D: THE CANEBRAKE LEGION

George E. Tayloe was born on June 26, 1838, in Cloverdale, Virginia, in Botetourt County (11th Alabama). The farm on which Tayloe was born is now part of either the city of Roanoke or its suburbs.[11] His parents, Mr. George Plater Tayloe and Mary Langhorne, were native Virginians. George P. Tayloe was born at Mt. Airy in Richmond County, while Mary lived and eventually died in Roanoke County, Virginia. George E. Tayloe was educated in the noted Virginia Military Institute. Tayloe married the former Delia Willis, daughter of George Sallie Willis, at Wood Park in Orange County, Virginia. It appears that Tayloe moved to Alabama in order to reside on the Elmwood Plantation near Demopolis.

George E. Tayloe was a man of great character and dignity. Everything that remains in written form about the man only extols his virtues. William B. Young of Co. A spoke of Tayloe in these terms:

> He was a fine officer and a gallant and courteous gentleman. The men in the regiment called him "the game cock." Though I never met him until the regiment was organized we became very warm friends [11th Alabama].

Herman H. Perry was a staff officer with Tayloe after he was placed in command of the former Sorrel's Brigade of Georgians. Perry speaks glowingly of Tayloe in a letter dated July 2, 1893, to the son of the late Colonel:

> I learned to know this of your father; that as a soldier, true Southern gentleman and devoted son of the South, he had no superior and a limited number of peers....
>
> I have seldom known of any one of equal unflinching courage as he, without brute recklessness, and who had more self possessed coolness under the most trying moments, when danger was face to face. For this I at once conceived for him the greatest admiration. The soldiers were quick to find this out and were willing to trust to his courage and stand by him to the last [11th Alabama].

Tayloe's widow writes in fond recollection of her brave husband in a letter dated October 16, 1902. She recalls how he immediately responded to the call from the land he loved. He defended his country, and the rights he was convinced she had under the Federal Constitution (11th Alabama).

It has been noted that a company bearing the name, Canebrake Legion, goes back to the year 1840. Apparently it existed as an independent company within the Alabama militia system; however, the name and unit were reactivated in October of 1860 in Marengo County. In an early letter written to Governor A.B. Moore from Macon, Alabama, the reorganized Canebrake Legion make a request of the Alabama executive:

> We herewith transmit for your favorable comidation a roll of the rank and file of the Canebrake Legion as recruited under its old charter and respectfully solicit a position in the Volunteer force of the State under the Military act passed by the last legislature.
>
> And request to be furnished with Sabre pistols (revolver, such as furnished to U.S. Dragoons) and breech loading Carbines, so that our corps may efficient either as mounted, or troops on foot [A.B. Moore 1860–61].

This letter was signed by J.W. Tayloe, the brother of George E. Tayloe, as well as John H. Prince, who was later to become the 1st Lieutenant of Co. D.[12] It suggests that as early as October of 1860 a great deal of recruiting had been going on, and that this unit could function as either cavalry or infantry. At this juncture it appears that the company conceived of itself solely as one company which could, as needed, function as an infantry or cavalry force. In a letter dated November 7, 1860, formal commissions were issued to J.W. Tayloe as Captain, J.H. Prince as 1st Lieutenant, A.H. Hays as 2nd Lieutenant, and Thomas G. Steed as 3rd Lieutenant (A.B. Moore 1860–61). The Canebrake Legion is still at this point considered a single entity.

By December of 1860 some changes were already beginning to occur within the company. These changes are captured in an order from Governor Moore in which R.M. Campbell is commissioned as 2nd Lieutenant, and George E. Tayloe as 3rd Lieutenant of the Legion. These men replace both Hays and Steed, respectively, who resigned their commissions. From the end of the year 1860 until April of 1861, the Canebrake Legion was busy drilling and securing the necessary equipment they lacked. A neighborhood fund that raised some

George Tayloe (Alabama Department of Archives and History, Montgomery).

$4,000 provided the cavalry with both sabers and revolvers (11th Alabama). The people of the neighborhood would gather at the parade grounds to watch the cavalry charge over four-foot hurdles, while the infantry would double-quick around the racetrack of the fair grounds. In a letter dated April 20, 1861, we see how this company stood in readiness to be used in whatever manner the Governor saw fit:

> Sir
>   At a meeting of the Canebrake Legion of Marengo County held on the 20th day of April 1861 it was resolved unammously, that said Company offer themselves for actual service subject to your order. At a heavy expense said Company has been fully supplied with the best army saddles bridles, uniforms, and is as perfectly equipped as any cavalry Company in the Confederacy.
>   Should you decline to accept the Company as Cavalry, they tender their services on foot as light troops, but reques that you will allow them to resume thier position as Cavalry, as soon as Cavalry Companies shall be required in the service.
>   J.W. Tayloe = Capt. Canebrake Legion
>   Jno. H. Prince = 1st Lieut. "
>   Geo. E. Tayloe = 2nd Lieut. "
>   Jas. W. Strudwick = 3rd Lieut. "
>
> Macon Marengo Co., Ala–20 April, 1861 [A.B. Moore 1860–61].

THE CANEBRAKE LEGION COMPANY B

Not long after this letter reached the desk of Governor Moore it was determined to break the unit into two companies: one of cavalry, and one of infantry. This new order can be seen in a letter dated May 15, 1861, in which George E. Tayloe is now commissioned as Captain of the Canebrake Legion. In addition, John H. Prince is 1st Lieutenant, Walter E. Winn 2nd Lieutenant, and James W. Strudwick is elected Jr. 2nd Lieutenant. This would suggest that brother J.W. Tayloe was now in command of the cavalry company. The cavalry company took the designation A, while the infantry was labeled Co. B of the Canebrake Legion. This company was enlisted for twelve months of service (11th Alabama). June 8, 1861, is a date that frequently appears as the mustering date for Co. B. The following list contains the list of names on the original muster roll for Co. B, the Canebrake Legion, approximately sixty-nine in number:

Officers

George E. Tayloe, Capt.
John H. Prince, 1st Lt.
Walter E. Winn, 2nd Lt.
James W. Strudwick, 2nd Lt.

Privates

Walter J. Blunt
L.A. Breton
William Burgey
David C. Carter
James W. Cathey
Benjamin J. Chapman
H. Christian
John W. Cole
John D. Collins
P. Collins
Joseph Compton
James W. Deanes
T.J.L. DeYampert
James E. Dossett
William W. Duggan
William W. Ellington
A. Fritz
Richard B. Gullett
John M. Gulley
Nathan Y. Hankins
Benjamin T. Hart
T. Hendricks
William H. Hummell
John W. Jones
Benjamin F. Jordan
T.A. Kelly
George W. Law
J.H. Lee
William Leighton
Samuel B. Lomax
William H. Lyon
T.B. Manley
J.T. Mason
William T. McCauley
Charles McNeil
D. McNeil
George Michael
H.A. Mounier
Thomas W. Oakley
J. Parish

Robert A. Patterson
J.B. Pegues
William C. Pegues
Michael Phifer
Charles A. Poellnitz
James A. Peollnitz
Jeff Purcell
William H. Purcell

James M. Quinney
R.M. Robertson
John A. Sisson
John R. Sentell
John L. Skinner
James H. Stewart
Osmund L. Strudwick
David M. Talliaferro

D.S.P. Thompson
James W. Thompson
President F. Thompson
James E. Warthen
Needham G. Whitfield
Charles W. Williams
G. Williams
W.C. Willingham

Company D: The Canebrake Legion

Most of the men came from the Demopolis area, but both Dayton and Macon also provided a large number of recruits.[13] George E. Tayloe's Company was eventually enlisted for three years or the period of the war, and increased substantially in numbers:

Officers

George E. Tayloe, 22, Capt.
John H. Prince, 37, 1st Lt.
Walter E. Winn, 27, 2nd Lt.
Osmund L. Strudwick, 21, 3rd Lt.
David M. Talliaferro, 35, 1st Sergt.
John W. Cole, 26, 2nd Sergt.
Frank L. Glover, 19, 3rd Sergt.
William H. Hummell, 20, 4th Sergt.
Shubal Henry Bartlett, 24, 1st Corp.
John M. Gulley, 31, 2nd Corp.
Benjamin T. Hart, 27, 3rd Corp.
Warren A. Anderson, 19, 4th Corp.

Privates

Elijah T. Alvis, 20
Thomas C. Anderson, 24
Ruffin Y. Ashe, 24
William C. Ashe, 45
Hillard J. I. Askew, 24
Thomas W. Askew, 20
Franklin L. Bailey, 23
Andrew W. Barr, 24
Ralph A. Barton, 21
Edward D. Blunt, 21
James W. Blunt, 17
James Bradley, 21
Henry Bryant, 24
William Burgey, had not reported to Virginia by the end of June
Jesse L. Burton, 23
Henry C. Cabe, 19
Dewitt C. C. Carter, 23
John W. Cathey, 28
Benjamin J. Chapman, 21
John D. Collins, 20
Joseph L. Compton, 19
William H. Compton, 23
Henry Connor, 22
John W. Deans, 24
James E. Dossett, 23
William W. Duggar, 26
Leonidus Eddings, 22
David Elder, 23
William W. Ellington, 20
Pearson Elmore, 16, enlisted June 30
Robert Elmore, 18, enlisted June 30
William F. Frisby, 23
Richard B. Gullett, 25
Nathan Y. Hankins, 18
William J. Howell, 25
William H. Johnson, 28
Banbury Jones, 21
John W. Jones, 36
Benjamin F. Jordan, 21
Charles F. Kirker, 21, enlisted June 30
George W. Law, 24
William S. Leighton, 36
Columbus Lockhart, 17, enlisted June 30
Samuel S. Lomax, 20
William H. Lyon, 30
Payton B. Mason, 19
James McCarroll, 23
William F. McCauley, 23
Charles McNeill, 25
George Michael, 19, enlisted June 30
Jesse W. Mustion, 19
Calvin Noble, 26
Thomas W. Oakley, 18
Wyman A. Osborn(e), 19
Robert A. Patterson, 23
William C. Pegues, 22
Joseph H. Peoples, 24
William H. Percell, 22
Michael, Phifer, 31
Charles A. Poellnitz, 22
James A. Poellnitz, 21
Jeff Purcell, 45
James M. Quinney, 23
Simon H. Rawls, 24
Curtis R. Roane, 21, enlisted June 30
Richard M. Robertson, 29
Bernard Rooney, 43
Joseph N. Ross, 26
John E. Ruffin, 44, enlisted June 30
John Schirm, 26

John R. Sentell, 20
John F. Simmons, 22, enlisted June 30
John A. Sisson, 25
James L. Skinner, 59
Robert E. Springle, 21
James H. Stewart, 20
Edmund L. Strudwick, 22, enlisted June 30
Shephard T. Strudwick, 22

James W. Thompson, 31
Lewis L. "Independence" Thompson, 19
President F. Thompson, 19
James J. Tucker, 22
Sam Turner, 19
Thomas J. Waddell, 28
John Walker, 52
Needham Ward, 17, enlisted June 30

James E. Warthen, 22
Cornelius Watlington, 19, enlisted June 30
Needham G. Whitfield, 30
Charles W. Williams, 32
Carroll D. Williamson, 26
William H. Williamson, 23
Strudwick Young, 21, enlisted June 30

There was a total of ninety-two original members of Company D, with an additional twelve enlisting on June 30.

R.J. Fletcher and the Raising of Company E: The Yancey Rifles[14]

Not a great deal has survived regarding the raising of this company among the ranks of the 11th Alabama. It does appear that this company had its beginnings as early as May 14 of 1861. At this early date we have record of the company known as the Washington Sharpshooters. We do know that Richard J. Fletcher was the Captain of the Washington Sharpshooters, and so from the very beginning he was prominent in the organization of this unit. It may be that the Sharpshooters were a twelve-month company only. If this was the case, then upon its reorganization for the war the company became known as the Yancey Rifles. We have already noted this process with several other companies in the 11th. On June 11, 1861, the company was reorganized at St. Stephens, Alabama, as the Yancey Rifles. On June 16, 1861, the company offered its services to Colonel Moore and was received (11th Alabama).

Richard J. Fletcher appears on the 1860 census of Washington County, Alabama, along with his mother and siblings (*Eight Census* Roll 26, 10). Fletcher's mother, M.H. Fletcher, was, like himself, born in Virginia. Based upon the census record, Fletcher would have been born around 1834. Interestingly, he would return to live in his native state after the war was over. By January 24, 1869, Fletcher was living at Prospect Hill in Louisa County, Virginia (CSR).

Company E: The Yancey Rifles

In the following list, those names which originally were included in the Washington Sharpshooters muster roll are marked by *. You will also note that some men appear only on the muster roll for the Washington Sharpshooters. This indicates that they have no extant muster roll of service with the Yancey Rifles. In addition, I have placed + next to those names that also appear in a muster roll dated July 4, 1861, in the *Clark County Democrat*. You will notice that the muster roll of Co. E in the *Democrat* is substantially less than what we are offering below. The *Democrat* lists only seventy-seven men on the original muster rolls, while we are offering eighty-three. The difference between the two figures is based upon the additional data given to us in the official muster rolls. I have included those men who are listed in the National Archives Muster Rolls that are said to have enlisted in June of 1861.[15] The majority of recruits came from St. Stephens, Alabama. But in addition, Coffeeville, Pleasant Valley, and Bladon Springs also provided many soldiers.[16]

Officers

Richard J. Fletcher, 28, Capt. * +
John W. Baker, 35, 1st Lt. June 11, 1861 * +
William C. Hudson, 34, 2nd Lt. * (he was 2nd Lt. in the Sharpshooters) +
William C. Faith, 19, 3rd Lt. * +
John W. Atchison, 21, 1st Sergt. * +
Frederick B. Smith, 21, 2nd Sergt. * +
Levi J. Fetner, 22, 3rd Sergt. * +
Benjamin F. Porter, 18, 4th Sergt. *
Joseph M. Heard, 30, 1st Corp. * +
Arthur C. Smith, 18, 2nd Corp. * +
Walter Winstanley, 21, 3rd Corp.* +
Moses A. Rainwater, 19, 4th Corp. +

Privates

Levin Ainsworth * +
George Allen, 33
Egbert B. Ashe, 31 +
Henry C. Atchison, 18 * +
Henry L. Atchison, 18 * +
McKindie Barnes, 19 +
Thomas E. Bassett * (only appears with Sharpshooters roll, no muster roll found for Yancey Rifles)
Cato Bethea, 30 * +
Robert J. Brantley, 18 * +
John Brunson/Bronson, 26 +
Washington L. Carrington, 24 +
John Clements, 20
Daniel Walter Coleman, 30 +
John D. Curry, 21 * +
Calvin Davis, 22 +
James M. Deshazo, 28 +
William R. Deshazo, 29 +
Andrew Dollins, 23 +
John Doyle, 30 +
John Dykes * (only appears with Sharpshooters roll, no muster roll found for Yancey Rifles)
James A. Faith, 19 +
William L. Few, 44 * +
Matthew M. Fletcher, 16 * +
William H. Frazier * (only appears with Sharpshooters roll, no muster roll found for Yancey Rifles)
Doc Freeney +
Dewitt, Gayle, 33 * +
Benjamin Gilbert, 22 * +
Joseph R. Green, 21 +
Thomas H. Green, 19 * +
Thomas R. Grimes, 19 * +
J.W. Gunn * (only appears with Sharpshooters roll, no muster roll found for Yancey Rifles)
W.F. Gunn * (only appears with Sharpshooters roll, no muster roll found for Yancey Rifles)
Joseph Hall +
Benjamin Hannibal * +
Jacob B. Hardy, 27 +
Augustus F. Hooks, 16 +
Samuel Hooks, 18 * +
William D. Hooks, 21 +
Joshua Jackson * (only appears with Sharpshooters roll, no muster roll found for Yancey Rifles)
Charles James, 19 * +
Dan James, 25 *
John James, 24 * +
Albert J. Johnson, 24 +
George Jones
John A. Jones, 23 * +
William H. Jones, 20 +
John Keith, 23 *
Mastin W. Landrum * (only appears with Sharpshooters roll, no muster roll found for Yancey Rifles)
William Lewis *
Allen Loper, 21 * +
John Martin, 20 +
Thomas Martin, 30 * +
Joseph M. Mason, 40 * +
William McGill, 26 +
F.M. McKenzie * (only appears with Sharpshooters roll, no muster roll found for Yancey Rifles)
Thomas J. Michie, 24 * +
Robert Moseley, 20 * +
James Murphy, 32
Harrison Odum, 16 +
William Odum, 25 +
Wooten O'Neal, 23 * +
Levi J. Parks, 24 * +
Raleigh Pevy, 25 * +
James S. Pharis, 46 +
R.M. Pugh * (only appears with Sharpshooters roll, no muster rolls found for Yancey Rifles)
Leslie V. Rain, 17 * +
Edward Rainwater * (did not enlist with the Yancey Rifles until September 8, 1861)
George Roberts, 25 * +
George W. Searcy, 45
James Searcy, 28
Benjamin Sherwood, 20 +
Allen Shultz, 22 +
John R. Shultz, 20 +
Burrill Simmons, 25 +
A.Y. Simpson * (only appears with Washington Sharpshooters roll, no muster roll found for Yancey Rifles)
Jackson Simpson, 20 (only one Simpson listed in *The Democrat*, no first name)+
Lewis Simpson, 45 *
William M. Smith, 35 * +
John A. Sronce, 45 * +
Joseph B. Stokely, 22 * +

| James B./S. Stoker, 31 | John Martin Williams, 24 * + | Pleasant L. Worsham, 23 + |
| Wright Wall, 32 + | John B. Willis, 23 + | |

James L. Davidson and the Raising of Company F: The Bibb Greys

The first volunteers for the war from Bibb County became known as the Bibb Greys (Ellison 1984, 117). There is one brief note which suggested that the company was raised on April 23, 1861 (11th Alabama). James L. Davidson, a merchant from Centreville, was elected Captain of the unit. He was born in Centreville, Alabama, on February 14, 1837, and became a leading merchant in Centreville (*The Heritage of Bibb County Alabama* 1998, 104). He was the son of Samuel W. and Frances Stringfellow Davidson, and received his education at Somerville and Tuscaloosa Colleges. He married Fanny Barclay on January 27, 1864.

Company F: The Bibb Greys

Most of the recruits came from the Centreville area, but a sizable number came from both Randolph and Maplesville.[17] The following list constituted the original muster roll for Company F, which was approximately 101 men total.

Officers

James LaFayette Davidson, 24, Capt.
Joseph C. Caddelle, 26, 1st Lt.
William J. Suttle, 21, 2nd Lt.
Lucius A. Winship, 28, Brevt. 2nd Lt.
John S. Gardner, 20, 1st Sergt.
Daniel E. Lightsey, 23, 2nd Sergt.
David V. Sneed, 19, 3rd Sergt.
William W. Brown, 19, 4th Sergt.
George W. Woodward, 23, 1st Corp.
Daniel N. Corley, 21, 2nd Corp.
John W. Johnson, 19, 3rd Corp.
Benjamin F. Sanford, 17, 4th Corp. (one record states July 3, 1861 for appoint.)

Privates

Zachariah Abney, 25
Abney W. Alexander, 27
Elbert Arnold, 23
Arthur W. Avery, 28
Henry W. Avery, 23
Martin V. Barnes, 21
Richard Barton, 18
William R. Bowling, 19
Green Washington Brazell, 18
David Brown, 18
David L. Brown, 22
Richard M. Brown, 26
Benjamin F. Caddelle, 31
Robert Campbell, 18
Milton J. Carson, 25
William M. Childress, 21
James D. Chism, 29
David M. Corley, 19
Samuel W. Davidson, 26
Henry Davis, 19
John M. Davis, 26
John H. Digby, 21
Perry Edwards, 21
Oliver Fitts, 26
John B. Fondron, 24
Gillis Franklin, 25
Andrew J. Garner, 22
Brantley W. Garner, 20
Rufus G. Goodson, 21
Henry Clay Goodwin, 19
Martin G. Goodwin, 25
Fletcher J. Goss, 29
William N. Green, 27
William Griffin, 21
Samuel Harding, 37
John C. Henry, 26
Patrick C. Henry, 18
James Hill Jr., 31
Jordon Holmes, 18
Leslie L. Horn, 22
Adam F. James, 19
Carter Jarvis, 18
Oliver C. Johnson, 26
Barney H. Kornegy, 19
Wesley E. Latham, 19
Fulton M. Lee, 20
John C. Leopard, 19
David E. Lightsey, 24
Martin N. Lightsey, 31
Moses J. Lightsey, 25
Charles C. Lowry, 25
George L. Mayberry, 18
John D. McArthur, 30
James M. McCraw, 20
John McMillion, 20
Martin J. Moore, 22
William W. Morrow, 32
Marion Oldham, 32
Thomas R. Owen, 24
Pleasant L. Pearce, 52
James W. Person, 28

Willis D. Person, 35	William W. Scroggins, 23	Zemiah Stemson, 18
Thaddeus M. Phillips, 21	John H. Smelley, 20	James N. Suttle, 19
Henry R. Potts, 22	Cadir M. Smith, 18	George W. Taylor, 20
Newton Rasberry, 22	Charles Smitherman, 20	Lewis Taylor, 21
Richard F. Rasberry, 23	Newton H. Smitherman, 20	Elias M. Thomas, 21
William R. Rasberry, 20	Thomas J. Smitherman, 24	Columbus, Webb, 18
Thomas Rayfield, 22	William J. Sneed, 30	George F. Woodruff, 22
John C. Risinger, 20	Jasper Spinks, 18	Green B. Wooley, 18
Jesse J. Robertson, 20	Newton Spinks, 18	
Thomas F. Roper, 17	Asa A. Stanley, 18	

James McMath and the Raising of Company G: The Tuscaloosa Rifles

The desire for the raising of a military company in Tuscaloosa reaches back to at least November of 1859 (*The Independent Monitor* [Tuscaloosa], 26 November 1859). A meeting was held at the courthouse on December 12 of this same year to further discuss the matter (*ibid.*, 10 December 1859). Recruiting began in earnest in Tuscaloosa in April of 1861. The following notice appears in the *Monitor* on April 5, 1861:

> ATTENTION!!
> By order, I have opened a recruiting office in Tuscaloosa for the Army of Alabama. Men desiring to enlist will apply immediately. Service for three years, unless sooner discharged. $10 Bounty. Pay $11 per month — and soldiers in this country are better paid, fed and clothed than any in the world.
> Head Quarters at the office of John J. Harris, Esq. [*ibid.*, 5 April 1861].

A special meeting by the Board of Aldermen took place on April 25, 1861, in which a resolution was passed securing the necessary funds for raising a new military company (Hendrix n.d., 11). By May 10, 1861, a new company had been raised by James H. McMath for military service. We find this notice in a Tuscaloosa paper:

> The Tuscaloosa Rifles. This is another new company just gotten up in this city by Capt. J.H. McMath. The Captain has got his men very snugly quartered at the old paper mill, he has ninety-seven men [*The Independent Monitor*, 10 May 1861].

This would indicate to us that the organization of McMath's company took place in early May of 1861. McMath wrote a letter to Governor Moore dated May 4, 1861, in which he stated that his company was organized, but he wished that orders for the company not to be given yet (CSR). He wished to dismiss the company for three weeks with the understanding that they would be ready to report for duty at the shortest of notices.

There is a family story that has survived regarding private William Jesse Keeton of Co. G. According to the story, Keeton went to the store in town owned by Capt. James M. McMath, and he never returned home due to having been enlisted (Scarpinato 1999)! McMath no doubt used his store as a "recruiting office" for many of the young men of Tuscaloosa. His store was called Glascock and M'Math, and was advertised as having the best, largest, and cheapest stock of goods and groceries in the market (*The Independent Monitor*, 1 February 1861).

What do we know about the man who was instrumental in organizing this company? James Hillman McMath was born August 15, 1819, in Warren County, Georgia (Snyder 2000). He was the son of Elisha McMath and Frances Gorman McMath. James moved along with his family to Tuscaloosa County, Alabama, around 1821. McMath's father was a man of comparative wealth who owned a general store on the Tuscaloosa-Huntsville Road, and lived east of Tuscaloosa near the McMath Spring. James H. McMath married Mary Lavina Tannehill on May 1, 1837, in Tuscaloosa County.

There is another key development regarding this company that needs to be noted. We also learn from a May 10, 1861, notice that Abner Newton Steele had just recently organized a military company:

> North Port Rifles
> A new company just organized by Capt. Steele numbering some eighty men rank and file. They are now awaiting marching orders from the Governor. The company is made up of a hearty [illegible] and we venture to say that they will do good service. The following named gentlemen are the commissioned officers:
> A.N. Steele   Capt.
> Wm. T. Poe   1st Lt.
> J.B. Hughes   2nd Lt.[18]
> Jno. Howell   3rd Lt.
> J. Mayfield   OS [*The Independent Monitor*, 10 May 1861].

Steele was the son of Richard Griffith Steele and Isabella Reid Baskin (Mungo 2001). Abner was born around 1826, and married Eleanor Caroline Thomson (Thomson 1999). Steele was no doubt a very influential man as his name is listed as a candidate for Sheriff in January of 1860 (*The Independent Monitor*, 7 January 1860).

Thus we see that the two companies that would soon merge were raised at approximately the same time. The same problem affected the Tuscaloosa-based companies as it did many of the others that we have already examined. The terms of service were changed from twelve months to the war. This placed many of the companies in jeopardy when substantial numbers of men were not willing to comply with the Confederate government's request. In an editorial in the *Monitor*, the writer encourages the three Tuscaloosa-based companies to comply with the government's notice:

> Some three companies from this county, besides the Guards, having offered their services for twelve months, were in hopes they would have been received, and had their orders to march; but in this they have been disappointed, for in response to the offer of their services by their captains, they were informed that the government would receive no more troops except for three years or for the war. We are grieved to chronicle the fact that these companies have not responded to this requirement of the Department [*The Independent Monitor*, 31 May 1861].

Company G: The Tuscaloosa Rifles

It was no doubt partly in light of these events that the company raised by Steele, the North Port Rifles, was eventually united with the company led

Abner Newton Steele (courtesy Larry Thomson).

by McMath sometime in June of 1861. With the merger of the two companies, McMath remained the Captain while Steele was designated the 1st Lieutenant. The following list constitutes the original muster roll for the unit, 104 men in all. Most of the recruits came from Tuscaloosa, North Port, McMath, Woodstock, and Tryon.[19]

Officers

James H. McMath, 46, Capt.
A. Newton Steele, 36, 1st Lt.
Green M. Allen, 27, 2nd Lt.
John G. White, 36, Jr. 2nd Lt.
Thomas N. Hayes, 32, 1st Sergt.
Solomon A. Ward, 28, 2nd Sergt.
Robert S. Carroll, 19, 3rd Sergt.
John B. Hughes, 27, 4th Sergt.
James N. Hayes, 25, 1st Corp.
John W. Weaver, 29, 2nd Corp.
Joseph R. Britt, 22, 3rd Corp.
Joseph E. McMath, 19, 4th Corp.

Privates

William M. Adams, 23
Francis M. Adcock, 19
Joseph Adcock, 19
Ezekiel M. Anders, 20
William T. Ashworth, 21
Richard J. Barber
Stephen D. Barber, 37
William H. Barry, 25
David A. Bennet, 28
Henry H. Bennet
John H. Brent, 20
George W. Brewer, 17
Samuel G. Brown, 30
Searcy P. Brown, 22
George W. Bryson, 24
Joseph D. Bryson, 19
James G. Burns, 22
James R. Burrage, 19
Albert C. Burton, 23
Constantine J. Campbell, 21
Green H. Campbell, 20
Robert C. Carroll, 24
James T. Childress, 24
Thomas H. Clark, 23
Virgil J. Clark, 20
William M. Cole, 17
David C. Cox, 25
William S. Cox, 21
Josephus Durrett, 19
Andrew J. Ellett, 19
Frank/Frederick Englebert, 56, musician
Charles L. Farrington, 19
Thomas M. Finley, 26
William N. Ford, 19
Raleigh M. Gaddy, 17
Daniel C. Gallant, 19
William Gallant, 21
John Gibson, 20
Eli W. Goree, 21
William P. Gossett, 43
John P. Green, 26
William H. Green, 21
Thomas W. Hamner, 22
Alexander Harkey, 56
Benjamin F. Hasty, 23
Pleasant L. Hayes, 23
William S. Hayes, 19
James H. House, 36
Thomas B. Howell, 20
Basil M. Hughes, 17
William W. Hughes, 27
Allen H. Johnson, 26
Ivan H. Johnson/Johnston, 17
James N. Keeton, 19
Edward Kizziar, 37
James L. Lacy, 28
William H. Leopard, 20
Jackson Lindsey, 21
William J./A. McCain, 19
Alexander J. McCoy, 25
James McGee, 24
Wiley McGuire, 20
Malcom E. McPhatter, 25
William J. McTurk, 20
Andrew J. Mitchell, 22
Jeremiah Morrison, 58
John G. Morrow, 19
Thomas J. Nabors, 35
Thomas J. Oglesberry, 23
Thomas S. Otey, 21
George W. Pierson, 23
William A. Plummer, 45
John B.P. Poole, 19
John C. Powell, 19 (never mustered in with Co. G, but enlisted in Co. H, 24th Alabama on June 13, 1861)
Jesse Pumphry, 17
James Ray, 25
Joseph J. Ray, 22
Thomas Reeves, 21
James H. Renfro, 20
Joseph N. Richards, 16
John T. Rigsby, 20
William G. Ross, 30
Francis M. Rosser, 19
David Shamblin, 19
Joseph R. Shuttlesworth, 18
Jasper Smith, 29
David Snider, 20
Peter K. Thomson, 16
David A. Tibbs, 21
Samuel W. Vance, 17
Samuel O.P. Watson
George J.H.T. Weaver, 21
Henyard T. Williamson, 21

Reuben Chapman and the Raising of Company H: The Pickens County Guards

It is a joy to examine a military company's history when we have ample extant material to guide our steps. The Pickens County Guards have left behind a trail of evidence for us to reconstruct the paths it took leading up to the War between the States. Martin L. Stewart, who eventually became Captain of the company, pointed out that this unit had its inception in December of 1859 (11th Alabama). In the early days the company was known as the Carrollton Guards. The man behind this original band was Capt. Fergers McDowell. A note in one newspaper mentions the fact that this company had its origin some eighteen months earlier, and was one of the best-drilled companies in the entire state of Alabama (*The Pickens Republican* [Carrollton], 30, May 1861).

It was not until June 16, 1860, that the organization of the Carrollton Guards was finally reached. At this time a letter and muster roll were sent to Governor Moore. The letter is a precious treasure of this company's history:

> Dear Sir   Carrollton, Ala. June 16, 1860
> You will find above a Roll of the Officers and Members of the "Carrollton Guards," which has just been organized here.
> Our company desire the *Minnie* Musket, say *fifty* Guns, as other members will join the company.
> Please send us a blank bond, such as is required by the law, and we will have it filled up, and forward to you immediately.
> Our Company is in good earnest. We have already made up the money, and sent on for our uniforms, which we will receive by the 10th of July, and want our arms by that time if possible.
> Very Respectfully,
> Your Obd. servt.
> M.L. Stansel,
> Clerk of said Company (11th Alabama)

We have a copy of the original muster roll for the Carrollton Guards that was attached to the above letter. The names on the list do not appear in alphabetical order:

Officers

F. McDowell, Capt.
R. Chapman Jr., 1st Lt.
James F. Nabers, 2nd Lt.
M.L. Stewart, 3rd Lt.
R.H. Curry, Orderly Sergt.
Wm. Watts, 2nd Sergt.
James A. Latham, 3rd Sergt.
A. Henry, 4th Sergt.
A.B. Cohen, 1st Corp.
Ben Marler, 2nd Corp.
Jno. B. Latham, 3rd Corp.
Jno. W. Wiggins, 4th Corp.
L.P.S. Green, 1st Drummer
Jno. W. Sanders, 2nd Drummer
L.M. Shelton, Fifer
D. Jno. W. Wier, Surgeon
M.F. Cook, Ensign

Privates

Jno. F. Nabers
Newton L. Ferguson
Walter M. Gilkey
F.A. Gunter
W.S. Wier
W.L. McGraw
R.U. Huckaby
J.C. Shenod
A. Makamson
W.D. Smith
W.D. O'Daniel
H. Shepperd
E. Lee
John M. McKinney
Joel H. Puckett
T.S. Thomas
Jas. E. Lee
Jackson Adams
Thos A. Wier
Y.L. Naben, Esqr.
Wm H. Jones
A.B. Clitherall
E.D. Willett
M.L. Stansel
Jas. P. Ferguson
Jno. F. Shepperd
Jas. D. Wier
Thomas Peeks
L.A. Gilkey
John Crowell
John T. Terry

A. Wier	T.S. Owen	B.A. Hudgins
T.J. Cohen	S.F. Hill	F.F. Hudgins
R.G. Parker	B.C. Thomas	J.W. Taylor
Jn. M. Curry	N.F. Smith	Jas D. Keer
W.L. Lipsey	C.L. Stone	C. Eastland
W.L. Adams	J.W. Puckett	H. Ferguson
H.B. Latham	James T. Free	John Pratt
W.K. Wier	A.F. Nichols	Tom Stewart
Wm. M. Hill	Lee Mock	Wm G. Mustin
B.F. Wilson	John M. Sprowl[?]	J.A. Boothe
L.M. Stone	Wm Kilpatrick	

Governor Moore was next addressed in a letter dated March 15, 1861, by Reuben Chapman Jr. (A.B. Moore 1860–61). It is a letter filled with disgust for the manner in which the Carrollton Guards perceived that they had been treated at the governor's hands. It seems that another company within Pickens County had received orders from Governor Moore for service; it was a younger company, and less equipped than the Guards. Chapman takes the governor to task for this perceived injustice:

> In consideration of the facts that we were first organized, first willing, first ready to battle for our Country amidst its direst dangers we think that you should at least have given us the compliment of the first order from this county. But adversely to every principle of propriety which should govern you in your high civil position, you have ordered a company from this county younger than ours, unarmed and unequipped and have treated the Carrollton Guards with the utmost contempt.

Governor Moore responded to this letter on March 19 when he penned a correspondence to Captain McDowell. In this letter Governor Moore points out that the Carrollton Guards had failed to formally tender their services for twelve months as required by the law. He had not overlooked them, nor preferred another, it was simply a matter of carrying out the ordinances adopted by the state convention dated January 19, 1861. It was not long before this controversy was settled. In the *Pickens Republican*, notice is given of the acceptance of the Carrollton Guards into service by Governor Moore (*Pickens Republican* [Carrollton], 25 April 1861). The article notes that it was on April 20 when the company was mustered:

> The "*Carrollton Guards,*" having been accepted by the Governor, their rank and file being up to the full complement, mustered here last Saturday and presented a fine appearance. They had speeches from Hons LEWIS M. STONE and Wm. H. DAVIS, and a "basket dinner" from the ladies. There was a plenty of good cheer, music, banners, military display, and a patriotic spirit manifested throughout the day [*Pickens Republican*, 25 April 1861].

The Carrollton Guards had now tendered their services for twelve months and, had been readily accepted by Governor Moore.

As the Guards waited for their assignment for Alabama service they were dealt another blow: the terms of service were now being extended for three years or the war. The *Pickens Republican* ran an article on their quandary on May 30, 1861. It extols the virtues of the Guards: their discipline, their drilling, their desire to serve for twelve months under the old order, and their splendid officers. God forbid that the company should disband!

Listen to the situation as the writer saw it:

> The company is composed of such as are willing and able to leave their homes and business for one year. It is impossible for many of them to be absent any longer. They mustered here last

Saturday as usual, and when the alternative was put for three years, or stay at home, some eighteen or twenty only, were willing to volunteer on other terms than those of the original call. Who can blame them [*Pickens Republican*, 30 May 1861].

In this same issue of the *Republican* a notice is placed in the paper to all members of the Carrollton Guards. The following Saturday a vote would be taken to decide whether the company would volunteer for the entire war or not:

ATTENTION COMPANY
AT a meeting of the Carrollton Guards to be held next Saturday a vote will be taken to decide if the Company will volunteer for the war. A full attendance is required. As the ranks are not yet filled others who may desire to go are invited to attend. It is anxiously hoped that a company will go to the battle field from Pickens. An impacable enemy bent on our subjugation and destruction has invaded our soil and must be repulsed.
By order of the Captain.
R.H. CURRY, OS [*Pickens Republican*, 30 May 1861].

No doubt many voted to serve for the war, and yet this perhaps depleted their numbers for service. Many were not willing to serve under the new guidelines. It may perhaps have been for this reason that it became necessary for the Guards to be united with another company in order to fill up the ranks.

Another company in Pickens had been raised by Capt. Samuel H. Vanzant. This company was known as the Calhoun Guards (*The West Alabamian* [Carrollton], 18 July 1860). Many of the men who would eventually make up the Pickens County Guards were on the roster of the Calhoun Guards: James H. Moorehead, Joseph N. Bell, Franklin L. Smith, Elisha D. Duncan, Aaron Hawkins, Benjamin F. Bell, James E. Williams, James P. Shaw, Edward H. Keasler, Herbert P. Hawkins, and David U. Duncan.[20] Following the election of Abraham Lincoln the Calhoun Guards made a public declaration of their sentiments:

1. *Resolved*, That while we deeply deplore the condition of our federal government, and look forward with unfeigned sorrow to the dismemberment of our National Republic, we are unprepared, and are not willing as free men to ever submit to Black Republican rule.
2. *Resolved*, That the Black Republican doctrine has been set forth too clearly to admit of doubt that its tendency is, and ultimate result will be, negro equality, which is a doctrine we claim no fellowship with, and will forever fight against even to the spilling of blood.
3. *Resolved*, That we are ready to prove ourselves worthy sons of worthy ancestors, and will hail with joy the day that a Southern Confederacy is established.
4. *Resolved*, That these proceedings be sent to the county papers for publication, and that other military companies in this county and throughout the State be requested to speak out on this subject [*The West Alabamian*, 28 November 1860].

The Calhoun Guards were presented with a flag by the ladies near Providence, Alabama on February 22, 1861 (*ibid.*, 6 February 1861). The date of April 6, 1861, is given in the muster rolls as the time of the Guards' formal organization. This was probably the time they enlisted for twelve months. By May of 1861 more men had joined this company, which would eventually become the Pickens Guards: Robert J. Henry, Alfred Howard, Robert P. Davis, Jacob J. Funderburk, Josiah A. Allan, Adam F. Bennett, David Burgess, William A. Davis, John D.L. Fant, James B. Hodo, Daniel F. Johnson, W.C. McShan, Milus Morehead, C.M. Makamson, James E. Rudd, Joel Randall, William H.H. Sanders, D. Stoker, A.J. Self, A.J. Story, Jasper Wooten, John R. Woods, and A.S. Welch (*The West Alabamian*, 15 May 1861).

A very important notice reveals how these two companies came together to form the Pickens County Guards. On June 8, 1861, Colonel Hale was scheduled to speak at Carrollton. The editor encourages the members of both the Calhoun Guards and the Carrollton Guards to attend this meeting:

> We hope all the *Carrollton Guards* and the *Calhoun Guards*, will be present. Hon. SYDENHAM MOORE has been appointed Colonel in the Confederate States Army, and STEPHEN F. HALE Liet. Colonel, and these gentlemen are now raising a Regiment for the war. Col. Syd. Moore is just the man to lead our Pickens boys. Two better officers or more perfect gentlemen cannot be found in the country, and we would greatly prefer their regiment to any other it is proposed to raise [*The West Alabamian*, 5 June 1861].

Obviously from this meeting a merger of the two companies resulted under the leadership of Capt. Rueben Chapman. Vanzant was made 1st Lieutenant for his part in raising a company, and under this new reorganization the combined companies were styled the Pickens County Guards.

Company H: The Pickens County Guards

What do we know about the man who was elected Captain of this company? Reuben Chapman was born on May 25, 1833, at Madison Springs, Alabama (Owen 1921, 317). He was the son of Samuel and Mary Lucinda Chapman. Samuel Chapman was the elder brother of Governor Reuben Chapman of Madison County, Alabama (Dubose 1904, 91–92). Rueben received his early education at the Montrose Academy in Mississippi, and even spent two years at the Concord Academy in Caroline County, Virginia. He concluded his education under the tutelage of Dr. Henry Tutwiler at Greene Springs, Alabama. Chapman practiced law both before and after the war, after having been elected to the bar in July of 1856 (Owen 1921, 318). He opened a law office in Carrollton in January of 1857; the practice was known as Stone and Chapman, Attorneys at Law and Solicitors in Chancery (*The West Alabamian*, 6 February 1861). Captain Chapman was also a very influential member of the Carrollton community. As Elector for Pickens County he frequently spoke on behalf of Breckinridge and Lane (*ibid.*, 26 September 1860). He also made numerous public addresses on the issues facing the South at that time (*ibid.*, 12 December 1860). In March of 1860 Chapman was elected Justice of the Peace in place of J.M. Sprowl (*ibid.*, 27 March 1861). One can readily see that Chapman was a leading figure in Pickens County. Under his leadership some 116 men traveled to Lynchburg, most of whom hailed from Carrollton, Providence, Reform, Gordo, and Yorkville.[21]

Officers

Reuben Chapman Jr., 28, Capt.
Samuel H. Vanzant, 28, 1st Lt.
Martin L. Stewart, 25, 2nd Lt.
James H. Moorehead, 43, Jr. 2nd Lt.
Lonzo B. Cohen, 19, 1st Sergt.
Robert J. Henry, 27, 2nd Sergt.
Benjamin F. Marler, 25, 3rd Sergt.
Joseph N Bell, 26, 4th Sergt.
John W. Sanders, 27, 5th Sergt.
William T. Bryant, 24, 1st Corp.
Walter T. Palmer, 24, 2nd Corp.
Aaron Hawkins, 27, 3rd Corp.
Frank H. Black, 22, 4th Corp.

Privates

Joseph P. Acker, 22
Samuel M. Acker, 25
John C. Adams, 23
James H. Allen, 20
Josiah A. Allen, 32
David A. Ballard, 25
Thomas J. Ballard, 21
Benjamin F. Bell, 20
Adam F. Bennett, 26
Andrew J. Bostick, 21
David Burgess, 24
James Carson, 27
Thomas G. Carson, 26
David B. Chambers, 24
Isaac L. Cottles, 25
Alfred B. Cox, 20
George Craig, 17

James M. Davis, 21
Robert P. Davis, 24
William A. Davis, 23
David U. Duncan, 22
Elisha D. Duncan, 22
Alexander Dunlap, 24
Jacob M. Ergle
Joseph E. Everett, 23
John D.L. Fant, 20
James P. Ferguson, 23
Elijah J. Foster, 25
Jacob J. Funderburk, 27
Benjamin M. Gammill
Andrew J. Gannon, 18
Walter M. Gilkey, 19
Robert F. Gore, 21
John T. Hamiter, 19
John P. Hatcher, 25
Herbert P. Hawkins, 20
James S. Hemphill, 24
John W. Hodge, 26
Joseph W. Hodge, 24
James B. Hodo, 22
Alfred Howard, 21
Thomas J. Jay, 23
Daniel F. Johnson, 27
Elisha D. Johnson, 23
Edward H. Keasler, 25
Jefferson M. Kemp, 18
William J. Kerr, 18
Joseph M. Land, 35
James E. Lee, 27
Michael H. Linebarger, 24
Henry O. Love, 23
Calvin M. Makamson, 21
James H. McGraw, 19
Washington L. McGraw, 34
George A McKinney, 24
William C. McShan, 21
Robert P. Miller, 22
John A. Moore
Milus J. Moorehead, 19
Daniel A. Morgan, 22
Isaac M. Noland, 24
James E. Phillips, 35
James T. Phillips, 23
Elijah J. Pridmore, 25
James L. Randall
Joel R. Randall, 34
Hugh K. Read
James E. Rudd, 18
John D. Sanders, 22
John W. Sanders, 27
William H.H. Sanders, 21
Andrew J. Self, 28
James I. Seymore, 22
James P. Shaw, 20
Thomas W. Shaw, 24
William J. Shaw, 25
John T. Shepherd, 25
David C. Smith, 26
Franklin L. Smith, 27
Leroy H. Speed, 20
Wm. A. Speed, 23
Josiah G. Stewart, 27
Davidson Stoker, 26
Andrew J. Story, 19
Pleasant A. Sutton, 23
Moses W. Taggart, 17
Thomas R. Taylor, 25
Tristram S. Thomas, 21
Joseph C. Thompson, 20
James A. Turnipseed, 23
John W. Turnipseed, 21
Andrew S. Welch, 27
Samuel M. Wier, 23
Thomas A. Wier, 20
John A. Wilkins, 25
James E. Williams, 19
William J. Williams, 21
Charles S. Wilson, 23
Jason Wilson, 40
William F. Wilson, 19
John R. Woods, 23
Wiley B. Woods, 22
Jasper W. Wooten, 18

GEORGE TRAWEEK AND THE RAISING OF
COMPANY I: THE FAYETTE AND PICKENS RIFLES

George Traweek appears responsible for the organization of the company that was eventually named the Fayette and Pickens Rifles. One note affirms the difficulty he was having in raising the requisite number of men for a military company:

> Fayette Rifles. We had the pleasure of a call on yesterday from Capt. Georg Trawick of Fayette. The captain we learn has been at much trouble in getting up his company, but has now about eighty-five men, and is awaiting orders from Gov. Moore. Below we give a list of the officers of his company:
>
> Georg. Trawick   Captain
> W.T. Holland   1st Lieutenant
> James Sullivan   2nd Lt.
> Dr. S.F. Bell   3rd Lt. [*The Independent Monitor* (Tuscaloosa), 10 May 1861]

It should be noted that by May 10 of 1861, Captain Traweek had secured most of the men who eventually traveled to Lynchburg. As will be seen in the following list, we have counted at least ninety men in the original company. It is also worth noting that the company is called the Fayette Rifles in the May 10 notice, and they are awaiting orders from Governor Moore. This may indicate that they have enlisted for twelve months' service only. If this is true, then upon their reorganization for the war they changed their name to the Fayette and Pickens Rifles. The change in name may reflect the fact that a number of men from Pickens County joined in the reorganization effort. In any respect, for his organizational efforts George Traweek was elected the first Captain when the Fayette and Pickens Rifles were organized at the Fayette County Courthouse on June 11, 1861 (11th Alabama).

Company I: The Fayette and Pickens Rifles

Traweek was born in 1818 in Georgia, the son of Spencer and Margaret Traweek (Allison 2004). He married Roda Howell, and together they had one son named Nelson Traweek. By the outbreak of war in 1861 Traweek had become a successful farmer in the area. Most of the recruits for the company came from Fayette Court House, while a substantial number also lived in Palmetto.[22] The following ninety men constituted the original muster roll for Traweek's Company:

Officers

George Traweek, 46, Capt.
William T. Holland, 51, 1st Lt.
James H. Sullivan, 2nd Lt.
Stephen E. Bell, 32, 3rd Lt.
Abel A. Walden, 26, 1st Sergt.
Rufus H. Shelton, 20, 2nd Sergt.
William P. Jones, 21, 3rd Sergt.
Francis M. Hollingsworth, 19, 4th Sergt.
George L. Traweek, 23, 5th Sergt.
Robert L. Smith, 20, 1st Corp.
James A. Kirkland, 24, 2nd Corp.
John F. Bell, 24, 3rd Corp.
Lemuel Harris, 22, 4th Corp.

Privates

Prince W. Aldridge, 29
James W. Anthony, 24
Samuel A. Black, 23
Elbert F. Bolton, 25
Joseph A. Bolton, 27
Marshall C. Bolton, 20
Francis A. Brotherton, 21
John B. Burris, 18
Sterling D. Clanton, 20
James C. Clippard, 17
Moses J. Coleman, 18
George J. Collins, 22
Wm. J. Cranford, 18
Daniel J. Cribbs, 21
Henry C. Cribbs, 20
James A. Darr, 18
William T. Davis, 25
Nathan J. Dozier, 19
William H. Duckworth, 20
Aurelius W. Dumas, 27
James J. Falk, 19
Andrew J. Foster, 21
Jeremiah W. Gee, 23
Francis C. Gregg, 19
Henry C. Hollingsworth, 21
Thomas G. Hollingsworth, 17
Samuel H. Horton, 24
Ferguson Kelley, 48, drummer
Calvin R. Kirkland, 20
William F. Kirkland, 22
William F. Lane, 26
Esqr. C. Levingston, 16
Ephraim Long, 21
David A. Lowe, 19
William J. Lowe, 21
John T. Lowery, 21
Henry M. McCollum, 18
John W. Miles, 20
John A. Mixon, 22
Wiley H. Nall, 17
Philip M. Newton, 31
William H. Nunn, 26
James W. Oliver, 22
John K. Perkins, 23
William H.H. Phillips, 22
Ezekiel R. Powell, 39
John A. Prater, 21
Allen H. Propst, 20
Jackson W.J. Richardson, 23
Luther H.J. Richardson, 20
Henry L. Rodgers, 20
James N. Ross, 18
John W. Shelton, 28
Benjamin F. Smith, 29
Henry S. Smith, 19
James M. Smith, 18
Reuben J. Stewart, 31
George W. Strickland, 23
Jabez P. Sudduth, 27
Daniel P.M. Summers, 16
Charles A. Taylor, 21
James C. Terry, 25
William J. Thompson, 24
Preston W. Thornton, 20
Jesse Threat, 32
Simon P. Traweek, 21
Jesse M. Vaile, 17
Richard H. Wait, 21
George W. Walden, 21
Thomas A. Ward, 19
David E. Welborn, 17
Oran A. White, 27
Jasper Wilkins, 22
Henry T. Williams, 17
Thomas J. Wimberly, 18
Ignicious Wright, 19
Alexander F. Yearby, 20

Henry Talbird and the Raising of Company K: The Independent Volunteers

The Rev. Henry Talbird (Partee Center for Baptist Historical Studies, Missouri Baptist Historical Commission).

Henry Talbird was born November 7, 1811, on Hilton Head Island in Beaufort District, South Carolina (Owen 1921, 1641). His grandfather was John Talbird, a commissioned officer in the Revolutionary War. The Talbirds were one of the earliest and most prominent families to settle in South Carolina. After receiving his theological training at Madison University in New York, Talbird served in Alabama churches some ten years. In addition to his pastorates, Talbird was elected six times as president of the Baptist State Convention (Dill n.d., 76). Talbird was called as Professor of Theology at Howard College in Marion, Alabama, in January of 1852. At the end of his first year of teaching at Howard, Talbird was elected as President of the institution. His administration brought prosperity to Howard College, for not only was the endowment fund increased, but the college property was enlarged to the point that it became one of the most flourishing schools in the South (Talbird n.d.).

Company K: The Independent Volunteers

Talbird was over medium height and possessed a benevolent expression (Duncan 1882, 719). He was very polished as well as graceful in his manners, and was one who was devoted to study. While he was in no wise a recluse, he nevertheless did not engage himself often in social entertainments. He was a well-noted preacher who was both scholarly in his content, as well as convincing in his presentation. Talbird turned from his work at Howard with the outbreak of the war. He organized a military company that was composed of many of his Howard students (Dill n.d., 78). The 1st of June, 1861, was the approximate time of the organization of the unit in Marion, Alabama (11th Alabama). In one soldier's recollection the company was already organized in May of 1861 (Cooke, 1998). The early days of drilling for the company would most certainly have taken place on the grounds of Howard College. The following 112 men make up the original muster roll for Talbird's company, although five of these never mustered into service, while another deserted from the ranks. So approximately 106 went to Virginia. Most of the men recruited came from Marion, Pinetucky, Hamburg, and Morgan Springs.

Officers

Henry Talbird, 49, Capt.
Matthew M. England, 26, 1st Lt.
Walter C.Y. Parker, 21, 2nd Lt. Parker didn't report until July of 1861
James H. George, 20, 3rd Lt.
Thomas J. Weekly, 27, 1st Sergt.
Stewart Melvin, 35, 2nd Sergt.
Nathaniel P. Muse, 20, 3rd Sergt.
George W. Woodfin, 4th Sergt.
Beverly L. Waddell, 22, Ensign

John B. Trammill, 23, 1st Corp.
Henry Clinton Lea, 21, 2nd Corp.
John W. Guthrie, 25, 3rd Corp
John G. Brewer, 32, 4th Corp.

Privates

William A. Austin, 19
Richard Bailey, enlisted June 11, 1861, but never mustered into service
Newell Baker, 27
Thomas B. Ballard, 21
John J. Barge, 20
James L. Brazelton, 19
William W. Brazelton, 22
Patrick Brice, 24
William L. Brown, 20
Thomas Burk
Townsend D. Carter, 29
Peter Casey, 27
John W. Cochran, 20
David W. Colburn, 25
Henry Clay Cook, 16
James B. Cook, 22
William E. Couch, 21
James M. Crews
Aaron M. Curb, 18
Napoleon B. Curb, 18
David A. Cureton, 17
George A. Didlake, 25
Thomas Donnelly, 40
Austin P. Eskridge, 18
Frank M. Ezell, 18
James Faha, 25
Thomas Farrell, 28
George W. Given, 23
James W. Goff/Gaff, 24
Lysander J. Gray, 20
John R. Griffin, 23
Robert H. Griffin, 19
A.B. Harden, 28
Marcellus E. Harper, 21
William J. Hay, 18
Eli A. Heidt, never mustered into service
William F. Herman, 26
Williamson W. Hilton
Robert F. Holifield
Milton Holly, 40
William D. Hopkins, 19
James F. Horn, 19
John W. Horton, 20
Thomas B. Howell, 20
William L. Huff, 22
Archie M. Hunsucker, 19
William P. Hunsucker, 20
William G. Johnson, 30
John E. King, 34
William H. King, 20
Felix Kirk, 29
Andrew J. Langford, 25
Robert P. Lockhart, 19
Noah H. Lovelady, 31
Edward R. Lucas, 25
John Marlow, 20
William B. Massingale, 20
John McCormic/McCormick, 25
Bryant L. McInnis, 30
William B. McLaughlin, 18
Joseph W. Merriman, 17
William B. Miller, 21
Thomas L. Mitchell, 21
George W. Morton, 20
Owen Murphy, 28
William C. Muse, 23
George Nixon, 35
George Petty
William A. Phillips, 26
John T. Pollard, 22
Isham W. Pounds, 43
John M. Pounds, 20
William M. Price, 45
James H. Raiford
William H.H. Ratliff, 21
Robert M. Rea, 21
James B. Sellick, 27, never mustered into service
O. Shevernell, never mustered into service
John Smith, 27
M. Daniel L. Stewart, 23
James H. Tadlock, 20
William D. Tadlock, 24
James Thames, never mustered into service
Elias B. Thompson, 22
Joseph Thompson, 20
Shade C. Trammill, 22
John A.B. Underwood, 18; Doc Underwood also appears
George Updegrove, 25
John B. Wallace, 19
Ruffus B. Wallace, 19
William P. Walton, 20
John Ward, 23
Aaron Warren, 30
Marion Warren, 20
Andrew J. Washburn, 17
A.D. White, deserted on June 11–30 muster roll
Elihu E. Williams, 23
David S. Wood(s), 18
J. Thomas Worrell, 20

Ten new military companies had now been given birth in Alabama. The original number of men who enlisted in the companies which traveled to Virginia numbered around 975. The counties of Washington, Perry, Marengo, Greene, Fayette, Bibb, Tuscaloosa, and Pickens had offered some of their finest boys to the Confederate service. This was still the high tide of excitement for the men. They were all very anxious to get on with the business of fighting for Southern honor and independence.

2

The Organization of the 11th Alabama Infantry Regiment

Sydenham Moore now had his ten companies. He now had a regiment of Alabama volunteers. A great deal of work was still necessary to bring these diverse companies into a unified body of fighting men. There were positions yet to be filled and necessary camp equipage to be obtained. The companies needed to learn how to function as a regiment, and not just as individual companies. In this chapter we will look at how the individual units were organized into a complete military regiment in June and July of 1861.

The Companies Are Ordered to Rendezvous Camps

Each of the companies needed to be forwarded to a common rendezvous camp. No doubt that each day following the company's acceptance into the regiment this question was asked: "Will we be called today?" The companies passed the time in this interim period between their acceptance for service by Colonel Moore, and the time they were formally called to rendezvous, in fairly predictable fashion: they drilled, drilled, and drilled some more.

Hogan recalls that following the election of officers for Co. A the unit made preparations to go into camp (*Confederate Veteran 1893–1912* Vol. 4, 50). Many of the citizens of Marengo County provided financial assistance to buy both tents and other necessary camp equipage. The Rifles were also provided nice gray uniforms by the citizens as well as a beautiful silk flag. Some two miles east of Linden at Hogan Springs, the newly organized Rifles went into camp. Here Moody's company pitched their tents and began to learn military tactics under the tutelage of Lt. William B. Young. Due to Young's position as a military cadet at the University of Alabama, he, like John C.C. Sanders of Co. C, assumed a leading role in the training of the company.[1] Hogan recalls that the group marched twice a day to the drill ground.

George Clark, who enlisted in Co. B, recalls very briefly the passing of time before leaving for Lynchburg:

> In a course of a few days the company went into camp for the purpose of discipline and drill, but it happened that no officer of the company was sufficiently acquainted with war tactics, and at once I was elected, or rather placed in charge and conducted the drill operations for about two weeks, after which the company elected me third lieutenant [Clark 1914, 11].

It is interesting that some of these early companies really did not have competent military leadership at the beginning. Men were learning on the job. Clark apparently demonstrated to everyone's satisfaction that he was capable after several weeks to serve as an officer in the company. It was after his "probationary period" that he was elected to the position of 3rd Lieutenant. Clark points out how the drilling began just a few days after the recruiting had stopped, and continued up till the call came to leave for Virginia. We do know that Co. B went into camp on May 30, 1861, for the purpose of drill (*Alabama Beacon* [Greensboro], 7 June 1861).

The Canebrake Legion of Co. D speaks about some of the things they did prior to receiving the call to Virginia. The company stayed for a brief period of time at the Fairgrounds at Demopolis (11th Alabama). John H. Prince reminisces about this period in the following:

> ...we were bountifully supplied with rations of every kind. From the Fairgrounds we moved out into the Prairies about five miles from Demopolis where we remained encamped about one week and were abundantly supplied with rations by the citizens of the vicinity. Here we received a splendid Stand of Colors presented by Miss Mary Lewis of Marengo County.

The Prairies is probably a reference to the area near present-day Prairieville in Hale County. St. Andrew's Church is also located in Prairieville, which would seem to reinforce the likelihood that this was the general area in which the company had gone into camp. As we shall see, the Legion will have occasion to stop at the church on their way to Lynchburg.

This was a period where for the first time the men were subject to the camp life which they would long endure. They encamped close to the place where they enlisted and spent the time in military drill. As was the case with Co. D, the locals would present the company with their own stand of colors to take with them into battle. The locals would also be active in preparing the company food to eat during their encampment.

Present-day location of Gary Springs.

The Bibb Greys obtained some tents and went into camp at Brown Springs, which is the present-day Gary Springs (Ellison 1984, 117). Gary Springs is about five miles from Centreville. At this location the green recruits were drilled by a cadet named Captain Pettaway from the University of Alabama. Apparently this place was known for its mineral water which is still evident to this day.

THE COMPANIES TRAVEL TO MONTGOMERY: JUNE 17–20, 1861

The initial place of rendezvous for the individual companies was to be Montgomery (*The Alabama Beacon*, 21 June 1861). Montgomery was bustling with military activity in those days. A reporter with the *Charleston Daily Courier* gives a vivid description of what life was like in the capital in the spring of 1861:

> As a matter of course, with so many soldiers in the city, the streets must be particularly gay and lively. At all hours of the day you hear the *rata-ta-tat* of the drum, and hear the tramp of armed men. Every train that comes in or goes out — every boat that arrives or departs from the bluff is laden with its precious freight of men and muskets. No one thinks of anything but war [Jones & Rogers 1964, 78].

One newspaper makes mention of the fact that Colonel Moore's regiment was already on its way to Montgomery by June 21:

> Col. Sydenham Moore's regiment is now, I suppose, on its way to Montgomery, destined for the same point; it was to have moved by companies yesterday, I believe [*The Mobile Register and Advertiser*, 21 June 1861].

This notice also recognizes that the ultimate destination of the companies was to be Virginia. Colonels Moore and Hale left Greensboro together on the morning of Wednesday, June

Historic Newbern Presbyterian Church (1848), near the old railroad depot.

19, for Newbern, Alabama. It was here that they met with the Confederate Guards who had traveled down from Clinton (Sanders's File).

The Colonels would travel all the way to Montgomery with Sanders's men. Dr. William Henry Sanders of Co. C remembers well the rather unpleasant trip that was made on the railroad to Selma:

> The accommodations on the Rail Road to Selma were only tolerable the greater portion of the company having to ride in open top cars. Fortunately however for us they have quickened their speed on that road and we were only exposed to the sun three hours [Sanders's File].

At Selma the Guards met up with Capt. George Field's men from Eutaw. Both companies took the river boat *Faney* to Montgomery. It took a full sixteen hours to make the forty-mile trip to the Alabama capital. The two units docked at Montgomery at 2:00 P.M. on June 20, 1861. The Guards and the Greys marched out to the Fair Grounds at Montgomery located about a mile from town. Apparently there were sufficient buildings at this location to make the pitching of tents unnecessary. One reporter states that these buildings were spacious at the Fair Grounds, and the troops had easy access to the necessities of camp life (Jones & Rogers 1964, 79). These were the only two companies of the regiment that had arrived at Montgomery by June 20.

The Tuscaloosa Rifles may have left Tuscaloosa as early as June 16. The company raised by Capt. James McMath departed Tuscaloosa with great pomp. They were escorted through the city by the Cadets of the University of Alabama along with a volunteer infantry company. The company proceeded to march some twenty-five miles to the residence of James Hill. At this location they were well fed by the local citizens (11th Alabama). On Sunday, June 17, McMath led his men through the town of Centreville to Randolph. The old railroad depot at Randolph no longer stands; it was located across the tracks from the historic motel at Randolph. From here they left on the Alabama and Tennessee Railroad for Selma. Just when they arrived at Selma we are not told, but in all likelihood it was late on June 19, or even June 20 before they pulled into the Selma station.

While the Tuscaloosa Rifles were traveling to Selma, both Pickens County companies had begun their trip to Montgomery. June 18 is the date that both the Pickens County Guards and the Fayette and Pickens Rifles were said to have begun their journey east, first by heading west into Mississippi. After leaving the Fayette Court House that Tuesday, Traweek's men marched to Palmetto in Pickens County, where they encamped for the night (11th Alabama).

This first march would have been over fifteen miles as the crow flies, and would have constituted a substantial march for the new soldiers. Harris recalls having blistered feet at the end of the day (Harris 1861–1864). The day had a nice ending as the boys were treated to a fine supper by the local citizens of Palmetto. On the 19th the march continued to Columbus, Mississippi, with a brief stop for dinner at Millport, Alabama. Traweek stayed only three hours at Millport when he gave the order to continue the march. Harris recalls that they marched about ten more miles beyond Millport before bivouacking for the night. At 10:00 P.M. the next day they arrived at Columbus, where they were again supplied with abundance by the local citizens.

Even as the Rifles were marching toward Columbus, Mississippi, the Pickens Guards were marching toward the railroad depot at Brooksville, Mississippi. The old railroad depot no longer stands at Brooksville. A voucher states that on June 19, 1861, a total of 108 men[2] of Chapman's company were transported a distance of 205¾ miles from the Brooksville Depot to Mobile, Alabama (CSR). The unit was transported on the Mobile and Ohio Railroad.[3]

Present-day Palmetto, Alabama.

The two Marengo County companies were now on the march as well. We have previously noted that Captain Tayloe's men were encamped near Demopolis at the Fairgrounds where they were abundantly supplied with food. From the Fairgrounds the Canebrake Legion moved to the Prairies about five miles outside of Demopolis (11th Alabama).[4] It was at a plantation near Prairieville that Tayloe received an attractive silk flag made in Mobile.[5] On June 19 orders were received from Colonel Moore to move to Lynchburg. The company began the march toward the Uniontown railroad depot. The Alabama and Mississippi River's Railroad would take the company from Uniontown to Selma. After breaking camp in the afternoon, they marched until about sunset when they turned into the St. Andrews Churchyard. The boys were again treated to a fine dinner. One of the distinguished citizens, W.R. Bocock, addressed the troops on the church steps with very stirring words. Following Bocock's remarks, Captain Tayloe stepped to the front and delivered an address. What happened next has been recorded:

> Capt. Tayloe made a few forcible and feeling remarks in reply, and then in his prompt, martial manner, turning to this troop, gave the quick order, *Company, right face. Forward! March!* The echo of the command had not died away when from head to foot of the line, the strains of *Dixie* burst out from many voices, and down the broad, smooth, white road, with faces toward Virginia, this splendid body of young men passed, flanked by carriages, loaded with friends, and equestrians on either side bidding them God-speed [11th Alabama].

There is an interesting note in the historical account of Co. D of the 10th Alabama that needs to be considered. Bailey George McClelen recalls that on the way to Selma from Talladega County his company met up with the Canebrake Legion. Let us hear him tell it in his own words:

Old Brooksville railroad depot location. Note the Confederate monument in the center of the photograph.

> At some station on the road before getting to Selma [Alabama], our train was lengthened by taking on three more freight cars loaded with a company who called themselves "The Cane Breakers," after which we learned they were part of the 11th Alabama Regiment, and part of our Alabama Brigade [McClelen 1995, 7].

What are we to make of this statement? First of all, the time frame of this notation seems to be accurate given all the data. It was June 19 when Captain Tayloe received notice to move out, and they reached the churchyard around sunset of the 19th. We do not know where they eventually encamped for the night before reaching Selma on June 20. According to McClelen's memory, the train pulled into Selma a few hours before sundown on June 20. We see from this that companies from different regiments were running into one another on the way to their respective rendezvous camps.

As far as Captain Moody's company is concerned, Morgan states that the men took up the march for Dayton on June 20 (*The Mobile Press Register*, 13 May 1934). They left at 4:00 A.M. and arrived that day at 10:00 A.M. He writes about what took place after their arrival at Dayton:

> Watson, Clark and Barker delivered addresses to the volunteers, also made strong appeals to the citizens to use their greatest influence to sustain all who might take up arms in defense of the south. We left Dayton at 5 P.M. after paying our best respects to a good dinner which the citizens of Dayton presented us.

They arrived just outside of Uniontown at about sundown and pitched their tents at an old sawmill. On June 21 the Rifles finally marched into Uniontown. From Uniontown they

2— *The Organization of the 11th Alabama Infantry Regiment*   41

St. Andrews Church at Prairieville, Alabama.

took the train to Selma in order to join their sister company. One notice does suggest that they met up with the Canebrake Legion in Selma at approximately the same time (*The Clark County Democrat* [Grove Hill], 27 June 1861).

THE COMPANIES TRAVEL TO LYNCHBURG: JUNE 21–28, 1861

We have examined the troop movement from June 17 to 20, 1861. The Confederate Guards and Greene County Greys are now encamped at Montgomery, while the remainder of the companies are either at Selma, or en route to Montgomery. Only the Yancey Rifles, Independent Volunteers, and Bibb Greys have yet to break camp for Montgomery. We will now consider the remaining developments until all the companies finally arrive at Lynchburg.

The Confederate Guards left Montgomery on June 21 for Lynchburg. Dr. Sanders maintains that they were the first company to leave for the rendezvous at Lynchburg (Sanders's File). The company was in good spirits and anxious to get to the front. What the men would soon find out is that the train ride from Montgomery to Lynchburg would involve switching from one railroad company to another (Black 1998, 1–11). The Montgomery and West Point Railroad took them from Montgomery to West Point only; from West Point they chugged into Atlanta on the Atlanta and West Point Railroad. The Western and Atlantic Railroad carried the boys from Atlanta to Chattanooga, Tennessee, where the East Tennessee and Georgia Railroad brought the unit to Knoxville. From Knoxville it was the East Tennessee and Virginia up to Bristol, and from there to Lynchburg the Virginia and Tennessee finished the trip. The trip from Montgomery to Lynchburg took Captain Sanders five full days to make.

It was five o'clock in the morning on June 25 before the weary Guards pulled into the Lynchburg depot (Sanders's File). Lieutenant Colonel Hale may have traveled with the Guards to Lynchburg as he is mentioned in the letter of Captain Sanders dated June 27, 1861.

The Green County Greys left Montgomery on the morning of June 21, 1861.[6] An original document has survived in the file of Capt. George Field regarding their trip to Lynchburg. It is a document of the Western and Atlantic Railroad dated June 22, 1861 (CSR). It certifies that on this date George Field's company was transported from Atlanta to Dalton, Georgia, on the railroad. The company reached as far as Dalton when they had to be detained due to the lack of available cars (Croom Collection). Croom notes that they arrived at 2:00 A.M. on June 22 at Dalton.

The Greys were being kept at the depot at Dalton as they awaited the necessary cars to take them on to Lynchburg. As it turned out, they were able to leave Dalton that very same afternoon on June 22. Upon leaving Dalton, Field's company arrived at Knoxville, where they were again detained for ten hours. The one positive thing for the men was that when they left Knoxville they were placed on the much more comfortable passenger cars (Croom Collection). Croom notes that upon reaching Bristol they were once again detained for sixteen hours. The train bearing the Greys finally pulled into the depot at Lynchburg at 5:00 P.M. on June 25.

George Clark relates some personal recollections about the trip to Lynchburg in his book (Clark 1914, 11–12). He tells of the trip in exciting terms, for as he notes, this was the first long-distance trip many of the lads from Greene County had ever made:

> The trip was eventful to most of the company, as they were young men who had never traveled and most of them had never taken a trip on a railroad. Nothing occurred worthy of mention of this trip, except that when we reached Atlanta, a man by the name of William H. Hurlbut of New York was placed aboard our train and it was whispered that he had been arrested as a spy.

The old railroad depot at Dalton, Georgia.

He was a large, intelligent man and I believe was finally released after a few days' detention at Richmond.

Clark recalls another incident during their stay at Knoxville. Apparently William G. Brownlow was being confined to his home as a prisoner. Clark mentions that many of the boys from the unit went to visit him while they were at Knoxville. In any event, no mention is made of how long they were kept over at Knoxville.

Croom adds a great many details about the trip from Alabama to Lynchburg. One of the things that made an impression upon him was the poor appearance of the crops along the route (Croom Collection); however, the crops were much better in both Tennessee and Virginia. Listen to his description of the trip:

> All along the route crowds would gather about the depots and welcome us cordially, though they seemed to be a little distasteful. Some Louisiana troops lately came this way and behaved shamefully. A good many of the flags were in the hands of negroes, and often their cheers were as lusty as those of the whites [Croom Collection].

The Canebrake Legion appears to have been the next company to arrive in Lynchburg. At Selma the men boarded the steamer *Duke* for Montgomery, where they would be staying for some three days.[7] It was a forty-mile trip from Selma to Montgomery on the steamer (Black 1998, 155). Black notes the busy schedule of the steamers during this stage of the conflict:

> Stern-wheelers breasted the chocolate current of the Alabama River upon advertised schedules to connect the railroads at Selma with those entering Montgomery. The real trunk lines of Dixie in the spring of 1861 were steamboat lines [Black 1998, 38].

While at Montgomery the Canebrake Legion received eight knapsacks from the Ordnance Depot (CSR). The date of June 24 is attached to this ordnance supply, and the name of G.E. Tayloe, Captain commanding the Canebrake Legion, is written at the bottom. Captain Tayloe and company may have left this same day because we are told in their historical memoranda that after leaving Montgomery they arrived in Lynchburg on June 27 (11th Alabama). Needham Whitfield fell off the cars somewhere close to West Point (Croom Collection). He was run over by three cars leaving him paralyzed in one leg and both arms. He was taken to Lynchburg to Ms. Otey's, where he was expected to recover.[8]

The other Marengo County unit was expected to arrive in Lynchburg on June 28 (Sanders's File). Moody's company passed along with the Canebrake Legion through Selma on June 22 (*The Clark County Democrat* [Grove Hill], 27 June 1861). We also know that on June 25, 1861, they arrived at Knoxville (*The Mobile Press Register*, 13 May 1934). Morgan makes some personal observations about the city of Knoxville in his diary. He states that the town reminded him of a place that was built without "taste." In addition to this, he mentions that it appeared to have been scattered over two or three hills. How long they stayed here he does not say. Moody's company is probably the one referred to in Captain Sanders's letter dated June 27, and so we may affirm that they probably arrived at Lynchburg on June 28.

The Yancey Rifles did not leave St. Stephens, Alabama, until June 21 (11th Alabama). At St. Stephens Landing the men boarded the steamer *Rescue*. The steamer arrived at Mobile on the morning of June 22, and orders were waiting which instructed the Rifles to proceed at once to Lynchburg. We have no additional information regarding the trip from Mobile. The date was June 28 when the Yancey Rifles pulled into Lynchburg, Virginia, to join their sister companies.

The Bibb Greys left Centreville, Alabama, on June 21 (Ellison 1984, 117). The day prior

Mobile (center) as it appeared to the Yancey Rifles in 1861 (University of South Alabama Archives, Mobile).

to their departure was marked by great excitement. The company marched around the courthouse in the city square to the applause of the admiring crowds. Bettie Howard presented Private Thomas J. Smitherman of the Greys with a silk battle flag which had been ordered from Selma. One note states that the flag was presented on the porch of the Presbyterian church (*The Heritage of Bibb County, Alabama*, 9). Many locals accompanied the unit to the railroad depot at Randolph that June 21 in order to see the boys off. There was one very touching scene that was witnessed by Josiah McNeil Kennedy (*The Heritage of Bibb County, Alabama*, 9). This youngster was forbidden to join the Greys by his father, but followed the boys all the way to Randolph. This was his account of their departure that day:

> I went to Randolph with the Bibb Greys and witnessed some of the most affecting scenes when they were taking their leave that the State of Bibb ever beheld — women squalling and fainting, old men shaking hands with the volunteers and making private and public speeches to them, and shedding crocodile tears.

The company traveled on the Alabama and Tennessee Railroad to Selma, and from there took the steamer to Montgomery. Captain Sanders does mention that the company from Bibb County was expected on June 28 (Sanders's File). The regimental history of the Greys also gives June 28 as the date of arrival (11th Alabama).

On June 21 the Tuscaloosa Rifles departed from Selma for Montgomery aboard the steamer *Luke* (11th Alabama). On Monday, June 22, they reached the Alabama capital. The Rifles had a several-day layover in Montgomery since they did not leave until June 25, and did not arrive in Lynchburg until June 28.

Presbyterian Church in Centreville, Alabama.

Captain Chapman's company traveled to Montgomery on a steamer from the port in Mobile. We are given one interesting piece of information regarding their trip to Lynchburg. The following document is dated June 26, 1861:

> This is to certify that one company, commanded by Capt R. Chapman is from Pickens Co. Ala. and comprizing a portion of my Regiment numbering Commissioned and non Commissioned officers, (myself and servant? included) one hundred and seventeen men this day passed over the railroad from Atlanta to Dalton Georgia.
>
> Sydenham Moore
Col Comadg
Reg Ala
Vols
June 26, 1861 [CSR].

The company numbered only 108 when it departed from Brooksville Station in Mississippi, but now it had risen to 117. We also learn here that Colonel Moore joined with Captain Chapman at Montgomery. Based on this information, as well as the June 27 letter of Captain Sanders, we may safely say that the Pickens Guards did not arrive in Lynchburg until at least June 28.

The Fayette and Pickens Rifles left Columbus, Mississippi, at 2:00 P.M., June 21, for Mobile. It took the train the entire day and night to arrive at Mobile by 6:00 A.M. (Harris 1861–1864). The company remained most of the day in Mobile before departing on the *steamer Coquette* at 4:00 P.M.[9] Traweek's men arrived at Montgomery around noon on Tuesday, June 25, approximately one week since the time of their departure from the Fayette Court House.[10]

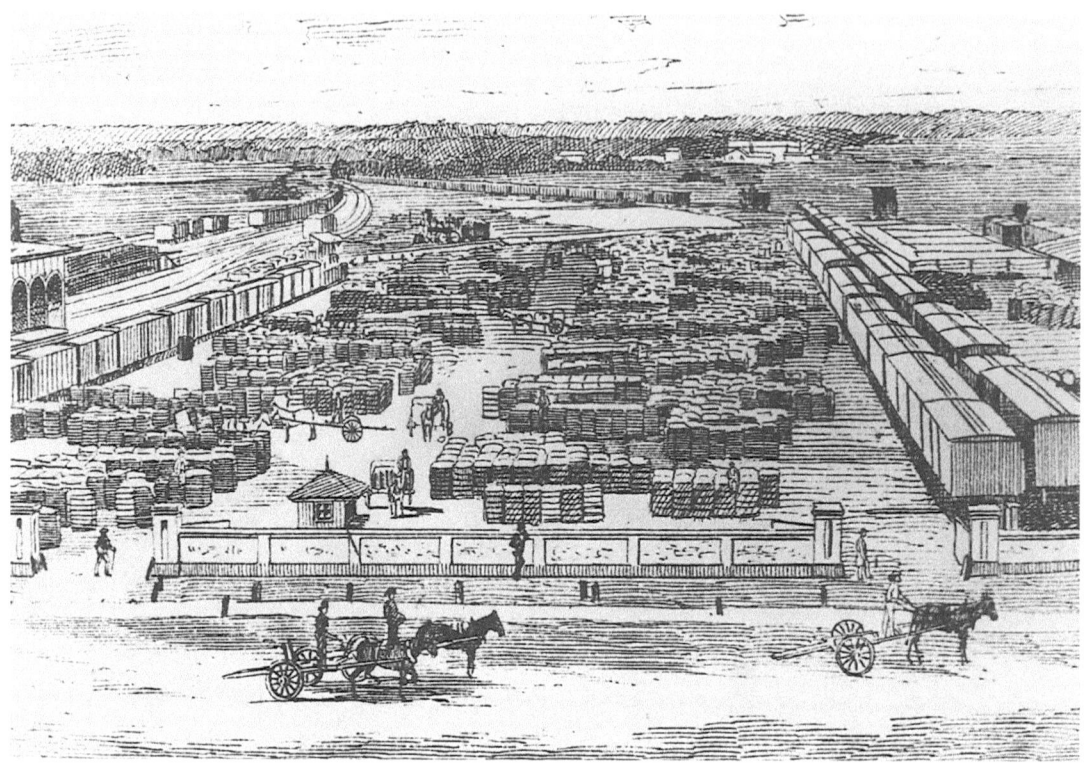

Mobile and Ohio Railroad Depot and Cotton Yard (University of South Alabama Archives, Mobile).

According to Harris, the men left Montgomery by 8:00 P.M. the same day, taking the train for West Point, Georgia. Harris gives us some interesting observations about the trip to Lynchburg that merits reading:

> If I had time I would try to give you a detailed account of my trip but it would be as long as the morrel law. suffice it to say we had a very rough time. no sleep nor rest the whole trip....
>
> The ladies were waveing there hakf [handkerchiefs] at us every hundred yard along the R road and throwing boquets at us. when a man could not fight for his Country amid such applause he ought to be drumed out of the country.
>
> There is beautifl senery all along the rail road. Mountians Rivers towns depots in abundance [Harris 1861–1864].

This description of Harris well captures the good and bad of the long trip to Lynchburg. Harris suggests that the company did not arrive at Lynchburg until July 1; this means that the Fayette and Pickens County Rifles were the last company to arrive in Virginia.

This leaves us with the Independent Volunteers under Dr. Henry Talbird. Captain Talbird's company left Marion, Alabama, on Friday, June 21. It appears that they took the Cahaba Marion and Greensboro Railroad out of Marion to Cahaba. At this juncture the railroad intersects with the Alabama and Mississippi Rivers Railroad which runs east into Selma. An unnamed soldier of Captain Talbird's company mentions their stay at Cahaba in a letter addressed to the *Marion Commonwealth* from Lynchburg (11th Alabama). Here the men were treated to a great feast at the Dallas Hall, and the soldiers did not fail to take advantage of the abundance spread before them. The men no doubt traveled on to Selma, picked up a steamer there, and disembarked at Montgomery. While at Montgomery they stopped at the

Old Lynchburg street scene from war times (courtesy the Jones Memorial Library, Lynchburg, Virginia).

Fair Grounds, where they were given nightcaps and canteen covers by the ladies of the city. This soldier praised the way the citizens of the Confederacy treated them all along the route to Lynchburg. Before arriving at Lynchburg on Friday morning, June 28, the men stayed a day and night at Dalton, Georgia.

The Companies Are Mustered into Confederate Service

Prior to the arrival of the various companies which would make up the 11th Regiment of Alabama Volunteers, Lynchburg, Virginia, had already become a major center for military companies. As Black notes:

> Although Lynchburg soon gave way to points like Manassas Junction and Centreville as a major place of assembly, full advantage continued to be taken of the railroad route which led through it from Knoxville, Chattanooga, and other points south and west, and its days and nights were filled with the rumble of trains [Black 1998, 59].

The strategic location of Lynchburg with its three railroads made it the logical dispatching center for Confederate soldiers (Morris and Foutz 1984, 11). Only days after the firing upon Fort Sumter, Jefferson Davis penned a letter to Governor John Letcher of Virginia (*The War of the Rebellion: A Compilation of the Official Records of the Union and Confederate Armies* Series 1 Vol. 2, 773, hereafter designated: OR).[11] In this letter dated April 22, 1861, President Davis informs the governor that some eight regiments would soon be arriving at Lynchburg. On May 1, Lt. Col. Edmund Kirby Smith is addressed by the Adjutant and Inspector General Cooper about the imminent arrival of two regiments from Alabama to Lynchburg (OR Series 1 Vol. 2, 792). It should be noted that E.K. Smith, the first brigade commander of the 11th Alabama, is at Lynchburg by direct order of the Secretary of War (*ibid.*, 798). He had been sent to Lynchburg on account of the large volume of troops being sent there to muster into the Confederate service. In a letter dated May 10, 1861, Smith writes to his mother about the swirl of activity going on at Lynchburg:

> Surrounded by military preparations, with troops arriving & departing daily, with the transfer of armed men and the rapid roll of the drum ringing hourly in my ear, I feel as if the realities of war were fast closing upon us [Edmund Kirby Smith Papers].

Smith was inspired emotionally by the fact that he saw planters, statesmen, and ministers all filling the ranks of the Southern army. In a letter to his mother dated May 16, 1861, Smith points out that the troops arriving at Lynchburg are generally undisciplined and uninstructed. General Smith's time of organization eventually came to an end as he notes in another letter five days later, for he was leaving on the morrow for Harpers Ferry to join Gen. Joseph Johnston.

After the companies arrived at Lynchburg they were all taken to a place that was called the Fairgrounds. George Clark of Co. B remembers that after his arrival they were marched out to this location some two miles from the heart of the city (Clark 1914., 12). It was at this spot that the 11th Regiment of Alabama Volunteers was given birth. The Fairgrounds was one of the two major locations for troop camping and drilling in 1861. The Fairgrounds was located west of the city on the top of a high hill on Fifth Street (Morris and Foutz 1984, 11–12). The Fairgrounds today is located at Miller Park. By the end of the first week in May more than 3000 soldiers were encamped here. This location lacked adequate shelter for the soldiers; in response to this need, sheds sectioned into stalls were erected on the north end of the Fairgrounds. Apparently these sheds allowed six men without tents to sleep in bunks.

2 — *The Organization of the 11th Alabama Infantry Regiment* 49

Miller Park as it appears today in Lynchburg, Virginia.

After all the companies finally reached Lynchburg, Virginia, in late June of 1861, the next step in the organizational process was the mustering and regimental organization of the groups. The evidence for the date of the mustering of the companies is quite clear. First of all, we must note that June 11, 1861, is the date for the birth of the 11th Alabama. This is the date from which Colonel Moore and the various captains of the companies were commissioned. It marks the time when a new Alabama regiment was given birth, and from that date the pay for the officers and men was calculated. It was also recognized that from June 11 the terms of enlistment were for three years or the war; however, June 11 was not the time when the various companies were mustered into Confederate service.

The evidence suggests that not all the companies of the 11th Alabama were mustered into service at the same time. The first company to be mustered into service was the Confederate Guards under Captain Sanders. Since they were the first company to arrive at Lynchburg, they also became the first company to muster into service on June 28 (11th Alabama). On Sunday morning, June 30, eight additional companies were mustered into service (Harris 1861–1864). The last company to be mustered in was also the last company to arrive: the Fayette and Pickens County Rifles. They arrived at Lynchburg on July 1, and were subsequently mustered into Confederate service on July 2. The mustering service was conducted by Major H.L. Clay, A.A.G. (11th Alabama). H.L. Clay had, interestingly enough, come to Lynchburg in the company of Edmund Kirby Smith (OR Series 1 Vol. 2, 798). In a note to the Secretary of War Walker dated May 8, 1861, it states that he is hard at work mustering in the troops just as fast as they arrive (OR Series 4 Vol. 1, 305). He is finding that many of the regiments that arrive at Lynchburg are deficient in such items as arms, accouterments, tents, and discipline! According to our present calculations there were approximately 975 men who were mustered into service at Lynchburg.¹² An important requisition by Colonel Moore has been preserved that is dated July 9, 1861 (CSR). In this document it states that the regiment consisted of 975 men, including ten captains, thirty lieutenants, and 935 privates. This number of Colonel Moore was given after the regiment had removed to Richmond. The rolls indicate that an additional twelve men were enlisted on June 30 by Lieutenant Prince; however, he did not rejoin the regiment until after the move to Richmond. He may have brought the recruits with him at that time. In addition, Lt. Walter C.Y. Parker, and Dewitt Gayle were not present at the time of muster (CSR). Of course absolute precision in determining the actual number of men who mustered into the ranks of the 11th Alabama may be beyond our reach today. But we may safely assume that somewhere around 975 men mustered into Confederate service at Lynchburg as the 11th Regiment of Alabama Volunteers.

The Regiment Is Organized and Equipped at Lynchburg

After the companies had been mustered into service there was still much that needed to be done by way of organization. We will now outline some of these developments as they occurred at Lynchburg. On July 1 the following regimental appointments were made: Thomas H. Holcomb of Co. A as Adjutant, Joseph P. Clark of Co. B as Sergeant Major, Jason Wilson of Co. H as Quartermaster Sergeant, and James Hill of Co. F as Commissary Sergeant (CSR). On June 30 Ruffin Y. Ashe of Co. D was appointed Hospital Steward, and finally on July 4, William C. Ashe was appointed the Regimental Surgeon. Other regimental appointments needed to be made but would wait until the regiment traveled to Richmond.

On the company level there were some developments at Lynchburg. Nathaniel P. Muse traveled to Lynchburg as Co. K's 3rd Sergeant; however, he refused to serve in that capacity and was replaced by Bryant L. McInnis on July 1, 1861. On July 3, Jabez P. Sudduth was sent from Co. I to Co. G in exchange for James H. Renfro. Walter C.Y. Parker arrived at Lynchburg on July 4 to take command as 2nd Lieutenant of Co. K. Beyond these particular shifts in personnel, there were men who never reported to the regiment for service at Lynchburg. Dewitt Gayle of Co. E was necessarily detained en route, and was unable to rejoin the company until after it had left Lynchburg. Other men who were absent in June of 1861 never returned to the army in Virginia.¹³ Some men were not at Lynchburg due to illness,¹⁴ while others had been given medical discharges.¹⁵

The Passing of Time at Lynchburg

What did the boys of the newly formed 11th Alabama spend their time doing at Lynchburg? All the companies needed to learn how to maneuver as a regiment. This meant that drilling would make up a large part of their days at Lynchburg. Even as Corporal Harris was penning his letter on July 3 his company was out on parade (Harris 1861–1864).

One of the things that is often mentioned in these early days of the war is the adjustment the men were making to military life. One member of Co. K makes light of the inability of many of the men to cook a tasty meal:

> It would please you to see the boys cooking. There is generally one man appointed from the different messes to do the cooking — take it time about. It is seldom you see a pone of bread that is not broken before it is taken out of the oven — the boys not yet having learned the "art" of cooking [11th Alabama].

Captain Sanders likewise mentions the cooking adventures of his men in a letter written to his father:

> It is rather strange to see them around the fires in the evening cooking their suppers, making bread, handling frying pans. Our rations consist of beef and meal one day, bacon and flour the next, coffee sugar molasses, the beef and bacon is very good [Sanders's File].

Harris notes some of the memorable experiences with Co. I at Lynchburg:

> I have so little money I can't write to very many person until I draw some money which will be two months as I learned yesterday from the Lieutenant Col. Allen....
>
> We have plenty to eat yet but such cooking you never did see in your life. we have little or no cooking vessels and what we have is made of sheet iron and they burn every thing in a minute [Harris 1861–1864].

Anderson Crenshaw of Co. B had some fond memories of this time at Lynchburg:

> Called on Mrs. Gen. Rhodes. Saw Mrs. Col. R. and Mrs. Martin of Tuscaloosa, had quite a good time while in the place:— drilling every day, though I managed to get to town whevever I wanted to. Mem. Corner of Church&— St. Girl with the beautiful eye [Crenshaw 1861–1862].[16]

Crenshaw may have seen Booker's Tobacco Warehouse, which eventually was turned into a hospital. It was also a time of visiting with friends and exploring the city itself. The city was flooded with soldiers (Morris and Foutz 1984, 12). The Lynchburg citizens were very hospitable to the soldiers, although extortion by local merchants was not unheard of. It was to be expected that visits to town would also result in behavior less than acceptable. Drinking

Booker's Tobacco Warehouse in Lynchburg, Virginia (courtesy the Jones Memorial Library, Lynchburg).

and the careless use of firearms were common complaints made by the people of Lynchburg against the soldiers (Morris and Foutz 1984, 14).

Stephens Croom was not at all impressed with the city of Lynchburg (Croom Collection). He regarded it as a rather dingy-looking place. In contrast with his perception of Lynchburg, Croom notes that the Greys' appearance was striking for all to see. They apparently were one of the better equipped companies in the regiment in those early days.

Morgan recalls a memorable day for him at Lynchburg on June 29, 1861 (*The Mobile Press Register*, 13 May 1934): "The rain fell in torrents; it ran in our tent to the depth of six inches. I sat on my knapsack with my oil cloth around me till daylight."

No doubt a major topic of discussion at Lynchburg was the question of when and where would they go. The men of the 11th were in good spirits, proud of their officers, and confident of military success. They were feeling anxious about waiting to fight, and many wished that if they had to do battle that it would be soon (Harris 1861–1864). All the news that the men were receiving at Lynchburg was good. They were told that every encounter with the Federals had met with success, and rumor had it that France recognized the independence of the South.

The Regiment Is Further Organized and Equipped at Richmond

The orders to depart for Richmond came on July 3,[17] and part of the regiment boarded the train on the evening of July 4. Six companies left Lynchburg in advance of the others.[18] Crenshaw mentions that there was a grand military demonstration at the time of their departure, and that the regiment arrived in Richmond by breakfast time on July 5 (Crenshaw 1861–1862).[19] The remaining four companies left on July 6 and arrived sometime in the morning on the same date (Sanders's File). The route often used by regiments traveling from Lynchburg to Richmond was the South Side Railroad (OR Series 1 Vol. 51, 151). The South Side took the men from Lynchburg to Burkeville; from Burkeville the Richmond and Danville took them all the way to Richmond. These trains ran this route from Lynchburg to Richmond on a daily basis (*The Daily Richmond Enquirer*, 1 July 1861).

The reason for the trip to Richmond was easy enough to understand: there was the need for further organization and equipping of the regiment. Many basic supplies and munitions of war were still lacking among the ranks. E. Porter Alexander remembers these days at Richmond:

> Richmond was very far from dull, for troops from all over the South were arriving every day & resigned Southern officers out of the old army were coming in from every territory ... arms and equipments were issued, & as fast as any body was organized & equipped it was sent forward [Alexander 1989, 37].

Upon their arrival at Richmond the boys were taken to a camp on the outskirts of Richmond (Clark 1914, 12). Crenshaw mentions that this camp was about a mile and a half from the train depot, and consisted of a large unshaded field in the neighborhood of a good water supply (Crenshaw 1861–1864). Apparently this new location was one of the hottest places that Captain McMath had ever seen (McMath Diary). Captain Sanders called this place an old field devoid of even a tree stump (Sanders's File). This new encampment was called Camp Clay (Croom Collection).

One of the first significant developments to take place at Richmond concerned the appointment of Isham Garrott. In a letter dated July 7, 1861, Captain Sanders mentions the fact that even though Garrott is presently at Richmond, there is some doubt about his appointment as Major (Sanders's File). There is little doubt that his appointment to Major was expected. One newspaper actually announces his appointment (*The Alabama Beacon* [Greensboro], 5 July 1861). Other evidence makes us question whether he was ever confirmed in this rank. For example, Major Garrott does not appear on any regimental staff muster rolls of the 11th Alabama. The only information that we have of Garrott's brief association with the regiment is a field and staff roster that simply states that Garrott resigned (11th Alabama). Perhaps he was himself debating whether to take the position, or return to Alabama in order to help raise another regiment. Whatever the reasons were, Major Garrott resigned this position in order to raise a new regiment for Confederate service.

Archibald Gracie Jr. was appointed July 12, 1861, as Major of the 11th Alabama. One muster roll states that he accepted this appointment on July 23 (CSR). He was eventually presented for confirmation before the Congress, which assented to his nomination on December 13, 1861 (*J.C.C.S.A.*, Vol. 1, 497). Gracie would rank as Major from July 12, 1861. Since he was Captain of a company in the 3rd Alabama from July 1 to 13, he could not have joined the 11th Alabama until they had reached Richmond. If he did not accept the nomination until July 23 as one roll states, Gracie may not have joined the regiment until it was encamped near Bull Run.

Archibald Gracie Jr. was born in New York on December 1, 1832 (Owen 1921, 686). He was trained and graduated from West Point in 1854, and served in Oregon with much success against the Walla-Walla Indians (Brewer 1975, 426). He worked with his father in Mobile as well as being active in a local militia group (*Encyclopedia of the Confederacy*, s.v. "Gracie, Archibald"). He was eventually made the Captain of the Washington Light Artillery, and it was this company that was ordered to seize the Mount Vernon Arsenal. This company later mustered into service as Co. E, 3rd Alabama Infantry Regiment; however, it was not with the 3rd Alabama that Gracie was destined to serve, but with the 11th Alabama (*J.C.C.S.A.*, Vol. 1, 434). With the departure of Garrott, Gracie was felt to be the most qualified to take his place. This was to be the beginning of a most successful service rendered for the cause of the Confederacy.

There were several additional appointments made in Richmond: Richard M. Robertson was made A.C.S., and John G. Pierce was appointed A.Q.M. on July 8 (CSR). Finally, John H. Prince, a Lieutenant with Co. D, reported for duty at Richmond after having been on recruiting duty since June 11.

The equipping of the companies was

Archibald Gracie Jr. (Alabama Department of Archives and History, Montgomery).

rather incomplete up to this point. Some, like the Canebrake Legion, had some issue of knapsacks already; while others, like the Fayette and Pickens Rifles, had no knapsacks whatsoever (Harris 1861–1864). Sanders made the observation that some of the companies have neither uniforms, tents, knapsacks, nor any camp equipage (Sanders's File). In addition, none of the boys appear to have been given muskets before arriving in Richmond. On July 7 the regiment drew the old altered muskets for their arms. Sanders was pleased with their polished appearance and was certain that they would do fine. Not everyone was pleased with the government issue of muskets. Morgan made this personal observation after being issued his musket: "We received our old muskets this morning. We hoped to get rifles, but were disappointed — some of us would prefer brickbats" (*The Mobile Press Register*, 13 May 1934).

July 11 appears to have been another important day for the reception of necessary regimental equipment. In this significant document we learn about the specific details of the individual requisitions that were made:

> Recd Richmond July 11 of Jno G. Pierce Q.M. of the 11th Ala Regiment. the following articles of camp equipage, for the use of our ... companies, each belonging to the 11th Ala Regiment — commanded by Col Sdh Moore
> Capt Talbird-14 canteens, 97 haversacks & 95 cap pouches
> H. Talbird Capt.
> Capt McMath 96 canteens, 90 Cap Pouches — J.A. McMath Capt.
> " Field 11 canteens, 90 " " George Field Capt.
> " Sanders, 24 " , 96 " " J.C.C. Sanders, Capt
> " Chapman 12 Haversacks, 6 canteens, 6 Knapsacks, 68 cap pouches
> RChapman Jr P.C.G.
> " Fletcher — 74 Haversacks, 74 cap Pouches — R J Fletcher Cap
> " Traweek — 84 cap Pouches 6 canteens-Capt
> " Tayloe — 14 canteens, 14 Haversacks & 95 Cap Pouches — GE Tayloe
> " Davidson — 6 canteens, 6 Haversacks, 1 knapsack & 93 Cap Pouches-
> J.L. Davidson — Capt
> " Moody-81 Cap Pouches Y M Moody Capt [CSR].[20]

Finally, on July 15, we also have record for the reception of needed wall tents by the commissary, adjutant, and quartermaster departments. They were beginning to look more and more like a regiment.

The Passing of Time at Richmond

What was it like for the men at Richmond? Obviously the unit continued its preparation through military drill at their new camp. George Clark of Co. B recalls his stay at Richmond as filled with drilling and the performance of diverse military duties (Clark 1914, 12). Captain Sanders felt that the Confederate Guards could hold their own with any of the companies in the regiment with respect to discipline and drill (Sanders's File). Some of the members of Co. C felt that Captain Sanders was too much of a disciplinarian. Many of the men signed and presented a petition calling for Sander's resignation (11th Alabama). As the story goes, Captain Sanders very calmly placed it in the fire and said that any more such papers would result in the arrest and court-martial of all signers. Later on the boys under his care realized that he was right, and they became loyally devoted to him. In an address delivered by Captain Sander's brother, Dr. W.H. Sanders, it is also noted how his firm discipline aroused early antagonism (Dr. Sanders's Papers). Dr. Sanders recalls that his brother strictly enforced discipline in the ranks; however, it was administered without his being any respecter of persons.

In addition to drilling, the boys also had opportunities to visit the historic city itself. McClelen of the 10th Alabama recalls his stay at Richmond with great pleasure. The men had access to written permits to visit the city every day (McClelen 1995, 11). He makes mention that one of the greatest attractions to the boys was a mammoth bovine! Anderson Crenshaw of Co. B also recalled with fondness the time they had at Richmond. He played billiards, engaged in interesting Richmond conversation, and saw some of the prettiest sites in the city (Crenshaw 1861–1862). This was his view of the sites of Richmond:

> Visited on the same day, the prettiest part of the city, seeing many beautiful, elegant, large tasteful buildings. The capitol buildings themselves are not so handsome but the grounds are delightfully elegant, shady, grass, slightly undulating, verticle, yet in the midst of the city, and much frequented.

He visited the cannon foundry at Richmond, and was able to witness the casting of cannon shells and balls. This particular foundry was casting two large eight-inch Columbiads per week. The penitentiary at Richmond was also on Crenshaw's list of visits. About 300 convicts were at that time housed at the penitentiary, and all were confined to very hard labor. Crenshaw mentions several other men of Co. B who were his companions during the Richmond stay: 2nd Sergeant Frank Mundy, Richard McCulley, and John Ridgeway. One particularly funny incident lodged in the memory of Crenshaw. It seems that he, along with Ridgeway and another unnamed man in the unit, got lost on the way back to camp from Richmond. It took them some six hours to find their way back to camp in the dark!

Captain Talbird received special recognition in the *Richmond Dispatch* for being a *fighting preacher*:

> Rev. H. Talbird D.D. President of Howard College, Alabama, one of the most distinquished Baptist clergymen of the State, has been for several days in this city as captain of a company [*The Mobile Register and Advertiser*, 20 July 1861].

The organization of the 11th Alabama was now for the most part complete. They had their arms, tents, accouterments, and other necessary camp equipage. Their company and field officers were now in place. They were beginning to come together as regiment on the parade field. At this point it appeared that the regiment would probably travel to Manassas Junction to reinforce General Beauregard (Sanders's File). Croom had heard by July 9 that they might even be sent to Martinsburg, where Johnston was being hemmed in by Patterson (Croom Collection). When the call to leave Richmond finally did arrive it was learned that Winchester was their destination. They were being called upon to reinforce Gen. Joseph Johnston rather than General Beauregard. It didn't matter to the men where they were going, just as long as they were going somewhere. They were now about to put all their military training to its first test.

3

A Whirlwind Week at Winchester

In this chapter we are going to look at the brief stay of the 11th at Winchester, Virginia. It was to prove to be a rather exciting week in several respects. First of all, the Alabamians became part of a brigade as well as an army. In addition, they experienced their first feelings of battle when they formed up in anticipation of a Federal attack. Finally, they experienced the anticipation of going directly into the fire of battle at Manassas. It was in the end, however, to be a whirlwind week at Winchester.

The Departure for Winchester

Trying to determine when the men left Richmond for Winchester proves to be a challenging exercise! If we take the various data at face value we would have to conclude that the companies left at different times for the front at Winchester. Corporal Crenshaw's diary gives the evening of July 12 as the time of departure for Co. B (Crenshaw 1861–1862). In confirmation of this date is the fact that Captain Field received a requisition at Richmond that is dated July 12 (CSR). It was the evening of July 12 when the company pulled out of Richmond, but it was Sunday morning of July 14 before they finally reached Strasburg. After resting for two hours at this location, they proceeded to make the eighteen-mile march to Winchester. Actually, Co. B stopped on the northwestern border of Winchester according to George Clark (Clark 1914, 12). According to one notice, Co. I left Richmond on July 12, and eventually marched into Winchester on the evening of July 14 (11th Alabama).[1] In the history of Co. A it states that they left Richmond on July 13. According to one record of Co. K, it asserts that Captain Talbird's company left Richmond on July 10; however, another notice offers July 14 as the date for Co. K's departure.[2]

The information that we gather regarding Co. G consistently affirms that they left Richmond on July 13.[3] They left Richmond on July 13, arriving at Strasburg on July 14. They proceeded to march from Strasburg to a point about one-half mile west of Winchester where they encamped for the night. The next morning they proceeded through Winchester to their permanent camp north of town. At the far end of the spectrum we have a note that states that Co. E left for Winchester on July 16 (11th Alabama).

It appears then from an examination of the evidence that not all the companies left at the same time for Winchester. It does seem that the companies left either on July 12 in the late evening, or early on July 13. One Pickens County Guard gave a very exact chronology of

Old Strasburg railroad depot.

the journey from Richmond all the way to Manassas Junction (*The West Alabamian* [Carrollton], 28 August 1861):

> In obedience to orders we took the cars at Richmond, Friday July 12th at 6 o'clock, P.M., arrived at Strasburg station Sunday 11 o'clock, A.M., and having slept but little overnight, made a halt of two hours to cook dinner and refresh ourselves. At 1 o'clock we formed a line and after a forced march of eighteen miles reached Winchester that night, and not having time to pitch tents slept upon the ground with knapsack for pillow, and blanket to protect our weary limbs from the heavy dew of the night.

The regiment was by July 15 relocated to their new encampment at a spot north of the town of Winchester.

The 11th Alabama's Stay at Winchester

It must have been a proud moment for the men as they marched into the beautiful city of Winchester that day. The people of Winchester responded liberally to the masses of Confederate troops entering her city limits (Delauter 1992, 8). The town offered food and drink, and even their very homes to the soldiers. But it was not all celebration at Winchester. There were military details to be worked out, and there was an enemy close by.

General Joseph Johnston's Army of the Shenandoah had four brigades prior to July 15: Jackson's Brigade, Bartow's Brigade, Bee's Brigade, and Elzey's Brigade. A fifth brigade was now formed by General Johnston in the effort to reinforce his small army. It was probably on July 15 that this new brigade was formed under the leadership of Brig. Gen. Edmund Kirby

Smith. The brigade consisted of the 9th, 10th, and 11th Alabama Regiments, the 19th Mississippi, the 38th Virginia, and Thomas Artillery of Virginia (Johnston 1959, 33).

General Edmund Kirby Smith was remembered by one officer of the 11th as a man who was not at all striking to look at (Clark 1914, 13). Notwithstanding his physical appearance, the men appear to have been satisfied with their new brigade commander. He was a West Point man who had seen active service as a Captain prior to the war (*ibid.*). Smith was born in 1824 in the town of St. Augustine, Florida, the son of Joseph Lee Smith. After his graduation from West Point in 1845, he saw action in Mexico as a Lieutenant from 1846 to 1848. Before the outbreak of the war Smith was stationed at Camp Colorado (Edmund Kirby Smith Papers). He resigned his commission in the old army on March 3, 1861, and was off to Montgomery to receive whatever orders the new government had for him. We noted earlier that Smith was sent to Lynchburg to help with the organization of the troops at that strategic location. By May 22 Smith was making preparations to report to General Johnston at Harper's Ferry. He felt that this assignment would place him in a position to be involved in the first decisive action of the war. In the first of many promotions to come, General Smith was given a brigade on July 15, 1861.

One private in the 38th Virginia recalls that the stay at Winchester was a rather pleasant one:

> I am in hopes that we will stay here for some time. We have elegant water and plenty of it and a plenty of good provisions so far and a fine chance of beautiful young ladies and the kindest that I ever saw in my life, and the most beautiful country that I ever saw [Gregory 1988, 7].

In contrast with the glowing report of this soldier, Private Croom of Co. B describes a different feeling at this time (Croom Collection). Everything was filthy! No matter how hard one tried, everything you possessed quickly became covered with dust and dirt. Listen to these sober words written in a letter from Winchester:

> The happy time is over now. There is no more waving of handkerchiefs and showering of bouquets. No more bright eyes to meet ours. No more pretty lips to encourage us. The enthusiasm and vanity of the journey is over now, and we have come down to the stern, hard discipline of the army.

On the morning of July 15 news was received that Union General Patterson was moving on Winchester with a force of over 30,000 men (McMath Diary). The intelligence that General Johnston had received at that time indicated that the Federal forces under Patterson were as high as 32,000 (OR Series 1 Vol. 2, 473). Patterson was reported to have advanced from Martinsburg, halting some nine miles from Winchester at Bunker Hill.

On July 16 the regiment was taken out to the battlefield that they might know where their position would be in the event of a Federal attack. This took about half of the day, after which time they were marched back to camp (Croom Collection). They had hardly been back to camp a half an hour when word came that Patterson was advancing toward Winchester some eight miles distant. In light of this urgent news, the regiment was ordered to return to the battlefield:

> There was confusion and excitement indescribable for a moment. But not a man appeared in the least scared and in a quarter of an hour the regiment was marching to the field. On the way a fine brass band was stationed to stir up the soldiers as they passed. And it had the desired effect [Croom Collection].

Gilkey recalls that the men marched forth with the Stars and Bars waving both gracefully and defiantly above their heads; indeed, the boys were eager for the fight, and anxiously awaited the attack (*The West Alabamian* [Carrollton], 28 August 1861). They remained in this position all night until about 9:00 the next morning. This was a very unpleasant night for the men since it rained heavily all evening long (Crenshaw 1861–1862). All the men had that night was their oil cloths, blankets, and straw. The regiment marched back to camp that morning, and the entire day passed with no further word of an advance by Patterson. That evening five prisoners were brought into camp (*Mobile Press Register*, 13 May 1934).[4] As the captured men passed they received a great many "French cheers" from the men. The men perceived that Patterson wanted nothing to do with the Confederates at Winchester. What would be Patterson's next move? They would find out the very next day.

The 11th Alabama Departs for Manassas

At approximately 1:00 A.M., July 18, General Johnston received a telegram regarding some alarming developments. His army was now needed at Manassas Junction:

> General J.E. JOHNSTON, *Winchester, Va.*:RICHMOND July 17, 1861
> General Beauregard is attacked. To strike the enemy a decisive blow a junction of all your effective force will be needed. If practicable, make the movement, sending your sick and baggage to Culpepper Court-House either by railroad or by Warrenton. In all the arrangements exercise your discretion.
> S. COOPER
> Adjutant and Inspector General [OR Series 1 Vol. 2, 478].

General Johnston determined to leave as early as possible that very morning to the Piedmont Station on the Manassas Gap Railroad. On the morning of the 18th the men from Alabama were told to strike their tents, prepare their baggage, and cook three days' rations (Clark 1914, 13). It was decided at this point not to tell the men the particulars of their mission. Clark recalls that the entire morning and afternoon was one of confusion and excitement. By noon the lead brigade commanded by General Jackson began the march to Piedmont (Johnston 1959, 36); however, not all the men of the 11th were going to leave Winchester. Sickness had already begun to take a toll on the men.

Estimates of the total number of soldiers left behind at Winchester range from 1,400 to 1,800.[5] One resident of Winchester noted in her diary the awful outbreak of measles among the troops (McGuire 1972, 33). Her entry for July 18 gives us some insight into the condition of the army at the time of its departure from Winchester:

Edmund Kirby Smith (Library of Congress, Prints and Photographs Division, Civil War Collection, Reproduction # LC-B8172–2013).

> But Winchester, what shall I say for Winchester that will do it justice? It is now a hospital. The soldiers from the far South have never had measles, and most unfortunately it has broken out among them, and many of them have died of it, notwithstanding the attention of surgeons and nurses [*ibid.*, 37].

Johnston recalls that measles and mumps so devastated the ranks that the average regiment was not larger than 500 in its effective strength (Johnston 1959, 33).

Colonel Moore's regiment was not immune from affliction with the measles, and several had to be left behind at Winchester. From Co. A we know that Henry L. Bruce, James H. Cleland, and James Devoy were left behind (CSR). Private John A. Wilkins of Co. H was left sick at Winchester on July 18, and was presumed dead on the September-October muster roll; however, Wilkins did not die at Winchester. We have record of his application for a Confederate pension in 1899.[6] Samuel A. Black, and John W. Shelton of Co. I were also unable to depart for Manassas, but both were later able to rejoin the unit. Henry S. Smith of Co. I died at Winchester on August 4.[7] Croom mentions that Co. B left four men at Winchester (Croom Collection). I have not been able to determine who these men were from the muster rolls. Many other soldiers were not feeling well when they left Winchester, but continued to force themselves to march on with their companies.[8] By the time these men reached Piedmont they were no longer able to go on.

The Trip to Piedmont

The 11th Alabama did not leave Winchester until 1:00 or 2:00 P.M. that Thursday (Harris 1861–1864; McMath Diary). The twenty-three-mile trip from Winchester to Piedmont took about a day and a half to make. This was obviously not good time by the standards of the day. In fact, General Johnston was very discouraged by the way the march was going. He attributed the *unbelievable* delays of the march to the inexperience of both officers and men (Johnston 1959, 36). The General was so discouraged that he even despaired that he would reach General Beauregard in time to be of service.

A mile or two from Winchester the men were given the news about their destination by Major Whiting (Clark 1914, 13). Clark recalls the reading of General Johnston's address:

> Reaching the outskirts of Winchester, General, then Major Whiting, who I believe was Inspector-General on General Johnston's staff, rode along on the line of the brigade and read General Johnston's address in a clear voice, telling us that we were on a march to relieve our brethren at Manassas and urging us not to complain during the heavy march that was before us.

This order of General Johnston had the desired effect of stirring the men on the long march before them that day. One soldier recalls the men cheered the order, and began marching as if they could complete the entire march that night.[9] After leaving Winchester the brigade would have passed through the town of Millwood before reaching the Shenandoah River. They would have marched by the Burwell Morgan Mill. This first day of marching brought the men of Smith's Brigade the thirteen miles necessary to reach the banks of the Shenandoah River. It was now midnight. The men were tired, and some of the companies rather disorganized by the time the march was resumed at 6:00 A.M. the next day (McMath Diary).

The first thing the men had to do the morning of July 19 was to take off their clothes (McClelen 1995, 15). The boys had to wade the currents of the Shenandoah River without getting their clothes and accouterments wet. Clark recalls that it was a very amusing sight to behold the men wading the cold waters with their drawers off (Clark 1914, 13). The final ten miles of the journey involved crossing the Blue Ridge Mountains at Ashby's Pass. By noon Colonel Moore's soldiers had arrived at Piedmont Station (McMath Diary).

Burwell Morgan Mill in Millwood, Virginia.

The Trouble at Piedmont

Although only thirty miles separated the men from the soon-to-be Manassas battlefield, it would prove to be a difficult distance to cover on the Manassas Gap Railroad. Shipments of the Confederate brigades took place regularly all afternoon, as Clark recalls, and the 11th expected to be conducted to Manassas the next morning (Clark 1914, 14). The next morning came and went, but no cars were available to transport the men to Manassas Junction. The men were led to understand that a train collision had prevented their arrival at Manassas until the day after the battle (Clark 1914, 14; and Freeman 1970, 52). In the long wait for transportation to Manassas the men encamped in a damp open field (Crenshaw 1861–1862). Crenshaw recalls that they had only their blankets for covering, and in addition they had little or nothing to eat. He recalls having a memorable foraging expedition while encamped at Piedmont:

> ...had a very pleasant time, went out to a lady's house and eat a snack, saw a beautiful girl, etc. Wrote a letter that day home, during the battle of Manassas, hearing the roaring of the cannon all the while.

Company B was placed on picket duty during this brief stay at Piedmont, and they remained so until the regiment departed on Monday (11th Alabama).

The regiment not only had to contend with the problem of the railroad at Piedmont, but they also had to attend to the problem of sickness. The measles were continuing to spread among the troops. The following men we can positively confirm took sick and were left at

Part of the old railroad depot at Piedmont Station (now Delaplane), Virginia.

Piedmont: Walter H. Gordon, Moses Baskin, Daniel Hooppaugh, James R. Stafford, William O. Harrison, John B. Baines, and James Cameron of Co. C; Henry C. White of Co. B[10]; Henry L. Bruce, James H. Cleland, and James Devoy of Co. A; Shade C. Trammill of Co. K; and six unnamed men from Co. F (CSR; and Sanders's File). Many of these boys were cared for in private homes around the Piedmont depot (Sanders's File). Walter Gordon was to live less than a week at Piedmont; he died on July 27, 1861 (CSR). Gordon was the first man to die in the regiment.

While the men were tending to their sick and the frustrations of the railroad delay, the first great battle of the war was raging thirty miles east of their encampment. It was not until Monday morning, July 22, that cars began to load up the anxious soldiers of Colonel Moore's regiment (11th Alabama). Many had to ride on top of the cars due to lack of space (Crenshaw 1861–1862). The men were looking for a battle at Manassas Junction that July 22 morning, but the battle that they would face proved to be of a different kind altogether. It is to this battle that we must now turn our attention.

4

The Battle of Sickness and Boredom at Manassas

In this chapter we are going to examine the long stay of the 11th Alabama at Manassas, Virginia. The men certainly never envisioned that they would have to stay at this place until March of the following year. Many months would pass before the men would get their first taste of battle, but in the meantime they had a very different battle to face — the battle of sickness and boredom.

The Arrival at Manassas Junction

Monday morning of July 22 the train bearing the 11th Alabama pulled into a buzzing Manassas Junction depot. Lieutenant Nunnalee recalls that it was about 9:00 A.M. when the regiment finally arrived (11th Alabama).[1] The depot was swirling with excitement over the battle fought the previous day. Crenshaw recalls that prior to their departure from the station he had already heard about a thousand different accounts of the clash (Crenshaw 1861–1862). The battle spoke for itself at the depot, since the bodies of the dead were lying about the station. Private Morgan recalls the powder-stained faces of the soldiers he saw, and the wagons full of dead and wounded that met his eye (*Mobile Press Register*, 13 May 1934). One of the most memorable things that the men relate about this moment was the horrendous weather that day. Private Walter M. Gilkey remembers that the rain was pouring down in torrents (*The West Alabamian* [Carrolton], 28 August 1861). The regiment had to stand in line prior to the march for camp for about an hour in this driving storm (*Mobile Press Register*, 13 May 1934). Notwithstanding the cloudburst, within an hour they had taken up the line of march for their first place of encampment. Crenshaw stated that the ground was so slick from the rain that it made the march almost intolerable (Crenshaw 1861–1862). Even though the march was only about six miles in length, it was made to seem like twelve. As the regiment was marching from Manassas they were met in the opposite direction by an ambulance carrying Gen. Edmund Kirby Smith (Clark 1914, 14). When the brigade was told that its commander was coming, they promptly opened ranks and presented arms. Clark remembers that General Smith responded by forcing his head up and saluting his troops. After this inspiring encounter the men trudged on toward their muddy encampment. Colonel Moore told his wife that by the time they reached the camp he was wet from his knees to his nose (Sydenham Moore Papers).[2] It was to be a place forever etched in their memories. It was a place that proved to be most disagreeable to the men.

The Experiences and Developments Near the Lewis House

The Lewis House was situated about a mile from the battlefield, and some six or seven miles from Manassas Junction. The house had been made General Johnston's headquarters. Here, on the edge of the woods, and without tents or blankets, the 11th Alabama went into camp. According to Dr. Sanders the encampment was in the woods (Dr. Sanders's Papers). The men were only a few hundred yards from the actual Lewis House. The boys scavenged for what brush they could find in order to cover themselves from the steady downpour of rain (*The West Alabamian*, 28 August 1861). Adding to their misery, it had been two days since they had drawn rations; the hungry soldiers simply made a fire and went to sleep on the wet ground (Clark 1914, 14). Even though the regiment only remained at the Lewis House for a few short weeks, there were many significant experiences and developments that we can describe in some detail.

While encamped near the Lewis House the men made their first priority a visit to the nearby battlefield. The sights and smells of that visit were never forgotten by the veterans. Clark describes his visit to the field:

> I went up the field of battle as we were camped very near it, and saw many evidences of the awful carnage that had taken place the day before. Most of the dead had been buried, though there were some corpses lying on the field. I went in the Widow Henry's house and found her lying dead on the bed. Dead horses were scattered over the field and it looked as if they were artillery horses as they were lying in groups. Altogether the scene was so terrible that I shall never forget [Clark 1914, 14–15].

Crenshaw is much more graphic in his depiction of the battlefield:

> On Wednesday I visited the battle field. A terrible sight it was. You could see where the battle had been hottest, at every half dozen paces the body of a mangled Yankee laying gory and

The old Lewis House.

putrifying, and otherwise extremely revolting. The majority of them seem to have been shot through the breast & belly and were lying on their faces. Horses, too, lay in abundance, and the millions of green flys that buzzed and blew over their swollen and putrid bodies render the scene truly disgusting & sickening [Crenshaw 1861–1862].

Private Gilkey of Captain Chapman's company recalls the cries for help among the wounded Yankees on the battlefield (*The West Alabamian*, 28 August 1861). Many of the wounded had not yet been attended to, and they were pitifully pleading for help from those passing by. To Colonel Moore the dead appeared to cover the ground for literally miles around:

> The dead lie thick on the ground of no great distance from us. In a quarter of a mile from where I am writing I counted many dead bodies on yesterday — 16 in one group & 6 horses by them & hundreds if not thousands all around for miles [Sydenham Moore Papers].

The dead soldiers in blue were being attended to as soon as possible. Colonel Moore states on July 23 that they were burying the Yankees in mass graves even as he wrote.

Private Morgan was as anxious as his fellow comrades to visit the scene of the war's first great battle (*Mobile Press Register*, 13 May 1934). In his own words he describes his feelings upon seeing the widespread carnage: "I thought I would feel sad or solemn when I would stand in the midst of thousands of dead Yankees, but not so; it had no more effect on me than the same number of dead rats." Not all the men had been buried nor attended to by July 23, 1861.[3] One of the most touching experiences of this visit to the battlefield involved a member of Co. B (Crenshaw 1861–1862). Corporal Crenshaw states that there was a member of Co. B who had a brother fighting in the Union Army. The day after the battle when they went over the field he found a roll of a company containing his brother's name on it; in addition, he found a belt with his brother's name on it! He offers no other details about what happened after this. It was not only bodies that covered the battlefield, but every imaginable article of war. Haversacks, pistols, swords, cannon balls, canteens, and muskets could be seen for miles. What a sight this must have been to the boys from Alabama!

During this encampment we are given some insight into the hopes of the 11th Alabama's future brigade commander, Cadmus M. Wilcox. During this present time Wilcox was the Colonel of the 9th Alabama Regiment. It is clear that he had aspirations to hold a higher position in the army, and in a letter dated August 1, 1861, he expresses some hopeful developments in this regard: "It may be that I will have good luck in this war, for I was told that Beauregard had telegraphed Jeff Davis to make me a Brigadier General & to place me in command of five Louisiana Regiments (Cadmus

General Cadmus M. Wilcox (Library of Congress, Prints and Photographs Division, Civil War Collection, Reproduction # LC-B8172-2153).

M. Wilcox Papers).[4] He goes on to say in this letter to his sister, Mary, that he never dreamed to have such an opportunity before, and had not even sought such. As we shall see later, Colonel Wilcox was destined to be appointed the new Brigadier General in place of the wounded Edmund Kirby Smith. This appointment would not be realized for several months from the time the brigade had settled in near the Lewis House. For now, Colonel Wilcox had only the hopes that he would receive the appointment.

THE MILITARY DEVELOPMENTS AT THE LEWIS HOUSE ENCAMPMENT

We will now consider some of the important military developments which took place at the Lewis House. Some of these developments took place on the company level, while others took place on the brigade level. Corporal Crenshaw of Co. B recalls the departure of Private Stephens Croom to the Brigade Headquarters (Crenshaw 1861–1862). Croom's appointment as brigade clerk came very soon after the arrival at the Lewis House, and was a source of disappointment for Crenshaw, who was fond of him. Croom was a prolific writer, often writing several letters a week to his parents back in Eutaw, Alabama. He was quite delighted in his appointment as clerk, and he in turn grew to be very fond of the temporary brigade commander, John H. Forney.

It was during this encampment that the first significant change in command took place. Capt. Henry Talbird of Co. K resigned his commission on August 6, 1861 (*Supplement to the Official Records of the Union and Confederate Armies* Vol. 1, 427, hereafter *OR Supplement*). Matthew England, the 1st Lieutenant of Co. K, was elected Captain in place of Talbird on August 20, 1861 (CSR). Dr. Talbird found that he could not endure the fatigues of military life. He resigned his captaincy and returned to teach at Howard College in Marion, Alabama (Dill 1938, 79). Upon his return to the lectern Dr. Talbird gave daily instruction in military tactics. Captain Talbird would not stay in military retirement for very long. He became involved in raising the 41st Alabama Regiment, and he served as its first Colonel. The 41st Alabama was mustered into service at Tuscaloosa on May 16, 1862 (Sifakis 1992, 111). One other development on the company level during this encampment needs to be mentioned. James H. Sullivan, 2nd Lieutenant of Co. I, tendered his resignation on August 1, 1861 (CSR). In his place, Stephen E. Bell, 3rd Lieutenant, was elected on the same date. Abel Walden, 1st Sergeant, would eventually be elected 3rd Lieutenant to replace Bell in September of 1861.

While encamped near the Lewis House the ranks of Co. A were swelled by additional recruits enlisted at Linden. On July 30, 1861, the following men were added to the muster rolls

Stephens Croom (Croom Collection, University of South Alabama Archives).

of Co. A: Nathan Daniel, Edmund Landrum, Joseph Gamble, John Heard, John Boozer, William H. Boozer, James Brady, Hugh Rogers, Ebenezer Breckenridge, Jesse Varner, Thomas Wade, William Wade, Arthur Corley, William Ethridge, James Gillmore, Benjamin Glass, Lucius Huckabee, William McLaughlin, Merrit Morgan, William Ross, James Singleton, Joseph Singleton, James Spiva, John Waller, James Wilkinson, and William Worthington (CSR).

The reign of General E. Kirby Smith as brigade commander of the 11th Alabama was a short one. Due to his wound on the Manassas battlefield he had to be replaced by a new commanding officer. Actually, Col. John H. Forney of the 10th Alabama Regiment had taken command of the Fifth Brigade back at Piedmont Station following General Smith's departure for Bull Run. The order has been preserved in the Official Records (OR Series 1 Vol. 51/2, 188–189). The date when Forney was placed in command of the Fifth Brigade is dated July 21, 1861, at Piedmont, Virginia. John Horace Forney was eventually to rise to the rank of Major General.

Forney hailed from Lincolnton, North Carolina (Evans 1987, 405). By the time he was six years of age his family had relocated to Calhoun County, Alabama. In 1848 Forney was appointed to the United States Military Academy, and he completed his graduation requirements in 1852. At the outbreak of the war Forney resigned his position as military instructor at West Point to offer his services to the Confederacy. He would begin his Confederate military service by traveling to Virginia as Colonel of the 10th Alabama Regiment. Forney would remain in temporary command of the brigade until late in October when Cadmus Wilcox would receive permanent appointment as brigade commander. The brigade included: 9th–11th Alabama Regiments, 19th Mississippi, 38th Virginia, and the Thomas Artillery of Richmond (Croom Collection). For the time being Col. John H. Forney was holding the reigns of the entire brigade at the Lewis House encampment. The brigade was now known as the 5th Brigade, 2nd Corps, the Army of the Potomac (not to be confused with the Federal army of the same name). This Corps would be commanded by Gustavus W. Smith by General Orders No. 31 dated September 25, 1861. Smith's command would include all those troops not under the command of the First Corps (OR Series 1, Vol. 5, 881).

Great Optimism and Hardships at the Lewis House Encampment

The men were highly optimistic at this stage of the war. One private notes that the men were in high spirits and anxious to dine in Washington (*The West Alabamian* [Carrollton], 23 August 1861)! The South had gained a great victory over the invaders, and this was cause for much excitement and boasting. Colonel Moore's sentiments reflect the mood of the entire regiment:

> It was a great battle — the greatest perhaps ever fought in America — and we gained a glorious victory....
>
> ... The Lincolnites were confident of success. It is said by some of the prisoners that they were told they w'd go on immediately to Richmond & that many of the (illegible) in Washington City — wives members & others all ready to go on as (illegible) our army was whipped. The Yankees fought harder then they have ever done before — indeed very well.... I heard yesterday that a wagon was found filled with hand cuffs. These were intended, it is said, for the prominent officers & the members of Congress ... to be carried in triumph, I suppose to Washington — after being taken prisoners [Sydenham Moore Papers].

Pride swelled in every southern boy's chest. The Yankees had been whipped soundly and sent reeling back to Washington. Certainly this battle would have a positive effect on the

European mind regarding the Confederacy. Crenshaw felt that this should have had the effect of showing the world that two great nations are battling one another (Crenshaw 1861–1862). This was not simply a rebellion by a small Southern contingent; yet, at the same time, there was a sense that this battle may have also awakened the Northern people to the magnitude of this struggle.

For all of the excitement stemming from the recent victory at Manassas, this was not a pleasant time for the regiment at this encampment. It was here that disease and sickness began to afflict the soldiers in earnest. For many of the men this was remembered as the most unpleasant time spent in the army (Clark 1914, 14). There were many reasons why this time was so disagreeable for the men. The obtaining of water proved to be a difficult task. Dead horses and men were actually in Bull Run Creek. The dead were visibly covered with maggots as they floated downstream (McClelen 1995, 17). The water had to be carried about a half of a mile to camp (Sanders's File). The creeks were muddy, and the springs were in very short supply.

The lack of tentage as well as necessary utensils added to the misery of the stay at the Lewis House. They had no blankets to lie upon or to cover up with (Clark 1914, 14). This was made even more miserable by the fact that it rained quite often as well. The lack of food, utensils, water, and shelter made for a very unpleasant time for the men. The foul odors emanating from the dead animals as well as the dead soldiers were well remembered. Crenshaw notes:

> Our proximity to the battle field made the camp ground a very disagreeable one owing to the horses and dead Yankees that lay unburied for many days. The shifting odors that would often assail our nostrils were perfectly intolerable as the unkind breeze constantly wafted it over from the decaying mounds of animal flesh [Crenshaw 1861–1862].

Another soldier in a letter home that dates from July 24, 1861, confesses how very unpleasant it was to be so close to the loathsome odors of the decaying flesh: "Our quarters is not very pleasant on account of the cent of the horses that were killed — all of the Enemy were not burried" (Harris 1861–1864). Literally every soldier who left behind a written record of their time at the Lewis House mentions the terrible odors of the battlefield. Hundreds of soldiers still lay unburied all across the war-torn landscape. Dr. Sanders believed that the foul odors brought by the winds proved to be injurious to the health of the regiment (Dr. Sanders's Papers). The extremely warm temperatures of those late July and early August days did not help matters either. These early weeks at Bull Run were considered to be the hottest that Crenshaw could ever recollect (Crenshaw 1861–1862). It also made the daily drills seem unbearable for the men.

Near the Lewis House the men began to experience the outbreak of the measles on a massive scale. Most of the sources make mention of how severe this epidemic became. One private writes that by late August only about 340 men in the entire regiment were physically able to drill (*The West Alabamian* [Carrollton], 23 August 1861). In a letter dated August 3, Colonel Moore reported that there were some 350 cases of sickness (Sydenham Moore Papers). Captain Fletcher's company was so hard hit by sickness that there were hardly enough well men to attend to the sick. Measles, typhoid fever, diarrhea, and pneumonia were attacking the men in every company. Clark was amazed that the stout country boys of the regiment seemed to be the ones who were afflicted more than the city boys (Clark 1914, 15). Lem Harris notes, "We have the measels in our Regiment but n[o] serious cases as yet we send them off to the hospital & the Diarhea has ben previlent especially when they have beef" (Harris

1861–1864). Captain Sanders was concerned that some would view him as responsible for the poor health of the men (Sanders's File). In a letter dated July 24, 1861, he states that it was his belief that the sickness was due rather to overeating, strong diet, and not properly caring for themselves. Some also believed that the foul water at Bull Run was the cause of the sickness (Crenshaw 1861–1862).

In light of the outbreak of sickness, the Lewis House was made into a hospital (Dr. Sanders's Papers). When the regiment left for its next encampment there would be some 140 left behind at the Lewis Hospital. Because it was thought in those early days that they could march at a moment's notice, many of the cases were sent off to Culpeper Court House. One notice makes mention of the fact that Culpeper Court House was playing a leading role in caring for the sick and wounded, and they now stood in dire need of nurses (*Daily Richmond Enquirer*, 22 July 1861). Two days after this notice, Capt. John Sanders wrote a letter home in which he affirms that the sick are now being sent to Culpeper Court House (Sanders's File). General Hospital at Culpeper was opened from June of 1861 until March of 1862 (Weaver, *Confederate Military Hospitals*). One writer visited this hospital and had nothing but praise for the facility (*Richmond Daily Dispatch*, 15, November 1861). There were eight well-ventilated hospital buildings at Culpeper, each of which could comfortably house between sixty and seventy-five men (*Richmond Daily Dispatch*, 6 December 1861). From June 7, 1861, until November 15, 1861, they had returned to the army some 3,000 convalescents. We know of several soldiers from the 11th Alabama who were sent to this hospital during the Lewis House encampment: Green Brazell of Co. F, and Tescharner Williams, William Williams, Tom Richardson, and James Horton of Co. C (Sanders's File; 11th Alabama).

Railroad crossing at present-day Bristoe, Virginia, not far from where the 11th Alabama encamped.

The first man to die in the 11th Alabama was Walter H. Gordon of Co. C. On July 27, 1861, he died of fever at Piedmont (CSR). Soon after Gordon's death many of the other companies experienced their first casualty of the war. On July 29 Co. F's Henry R. Potts died at Culpeper Court House, James Brassfield of Co. B died on August 6 or 8 at Orange Court House, Thomas S. Heard of Co. A died in Richmond on August 4, Henry S. Smith of Co. I died at Winchester on August 4 or 5, David Snider of Co. G died on August 8, and Nathan K. Greenwood of Co. B passed away at the Bull Run camp on August 8. Clark talked with Greenwood several times during his fight with the measles (Clark 1914, 15). He tried to encourage him that he would soon recover from the malady, but he was sadly called to his bedside during the last moments of his life. Martin Moore of Co. F died on August 8, and Newell Baker of Co. K died on August 9. The health of the regiment was not to show improvement for some time. The measles and related conditions were to follow the Alabamians on to their next encampment near Bristoe.

The Arrival Near Bristoe Station

On August 10, 1861, the boys left their camp near the Lewis House and traveled about six or seven miles to a new encampment near Bristoe Station.[5] The site was about two miles from Bristoe Station, but only about half a mile from the Orange and Alexandria Railroad (Croom Collection). The regiment pitched their tents on the left side of the tracks going north, and were approximately four miles from Manassas Junction on the road leading to the junction (Croom Collection; McMath Diary). The muster rolls often list this encampment as Broad Run due to the nearness of their location to that stream.

It didn't take the officers long to see that this was not an agreeable location. The ground was very low. After six or seven days of continuous rain the encampment was turned into a veritable quagmire (Dr. Sanders's Papers). On August 19, Colonel Moore and Dr. Ashe spent the day looking for a better spot for the regiment. It was difficult to find such a site due to the large volume of troops that already occupied the area. On August 26 the regiment moved about three quarters of a mile closer to Bristoe to a better location on high ground (McMath Diary). This was a pretty location nearer Bristoe, and the Colonel hoped that it would promote good health among the soldiers (Sydenham Moore Papers). Crenshaw recalls that even though it was a better location than the previous one, it still suffered from bad and scarce water (Crenshaw 1861–1862).

THE MILITARY DEVELOPMENTS NEAR BRISTOE STATION

One of the things that stands out about this encampment was the daily drilling of the troops. In several of the sources mention is made of how this was the habit of the regiment day by day at Bristoe Station. Colonel Moore makes note of this in a letter to his wife on September 13, 1861:

> I am kept constantly occupied all the day long, — drill, drill, drill — when without drilling I have always more work to do. Some cases to decide some order to give, or something to look after in the Reg't. [Sydenham Moore Papers].

During this time the rumors regarding attacks and possible movements of the army ran riot. Some rumors suggested that the Yankees would attack around Fairfax Court House, others stated that they had already crossed the Potomac some 10,000 strong, and finally some even hinted at the possible movement of the Confederate army into Maryland (Fleming W. Thompson Letters; Sydenham Moore Papers).

With the resignation of Henry Talbird as Captain from Co. K on August 6, 1861, the company now stood in need of substantial reorganization on the commissioned officer level. On August 20, 1861, many new appointments took place in the company (CSR). Matthew England was appointed the new Captain, Walter C.Y. Parker became the new 1st Lieutenant, James H. George became the 2nd Lieutenant, and Bryant L. McInnis became Junior 2nd Lieutenant.

Company I was without a 3rd Lieutenant due to the promotion of Stephen Bell to 2nd Lieutenant back on August 1, 1861. Abel Walden was elected 3rd Lieutenant of Co. I on September 8, 1861. William C. Hudson of Co. E resigned his commission as 2nd Lieutenant on August 31, 1861, and he was replaced by William C. Faith, the Junior 2nd Lieutenant. Other military developments at Bristoe included the appointment of Matthew Jolly of Co. C as an Assistant Surgeon, and Boaz W. Bush of Co. A as acting Assistant Surgeon. Finally, on August 28, 1861, President Jefferson Davis presented to the Confederate Congress as nominations for appointment in the Provisional Army the names of Sydenham Moore, Colonel; Stephen F. Hale, Lieutenant Colonel; and Archibald Gracie Jr. for Major (J.C.C.S.A., Vol. 1, 434).

The Hardships Near Bristoe Station

The period at Bristoe Station must be regarded as a real time of hardship for the regiment. There is little positive that can be said about it. Disease and death were daily visitors. It can rightly be said that at Bristoe the health of the regiment reached its lowest point. The measles outbreak which had begun at Piedmont now attained epidemic proportions. Corporal Crenshaw writes:

> The health of our reg. at this time is at its worst, from 15th to 30th of Aug. about one half or more being reported sick. The loss from the regiment up to this time will amount to over 25 or 30.... In our regiment Caufield Derby and several others are laying at the point of death [Crenshaw 1861–1862].

Dr. Sanders estimated that over the past two months there had been no less than 800 cases of sickness, and clearly half of these involved measles (Dr. Sanders's Papers). At this time is would not be unusual for 150 men to report to the surgeons with sickness, with another hundred too sick to leave their tents. Dr. Sanders noted that of the Confederate Guards, almost every single soldier who was liable to the disease either had had the measles, or was currently having them. On August 12, 1861, Walter Winn informed Juliet Opic Hopkins that between 400 and 500 men had the measles or typhoid fever (Bridges 2000, 89). Typhoid fever often followed closely upon the heels of the measles, and one private from Co. K spoke of his near-death experience from the dreaded malady (Aaron Monroe Curb Papers). Private Curb, along with many other boys from the 11th, was laid out on the floor of a nearby barn. Soldiers were dying everywhere. One morning a soldier lying at the end of the row where he lay was carried out dead. This was replicated the next morning, only this time it was the comrade next to Curb that was removed. Curb was sure that it would be his turn to die the next morning; however, the man on Curb's other side had died! Death had skipped over private Aaron Monroe Curb.

A medical board was established at Manassas before which all furloughs had to be obtained upon the certificate of a regimental surgeon (Dr. Sanders's Papers). Dr. Sanders was concerned that many of those who were going home to convalesce would not return to the ranks. It also seemed to encourage anyone who was sick to apply for a furlough. About twenty-five soldiers from the regiment were discharged during this encampment (CSR). There were certainly abuses of the furlough system; nevertheless the spread of disease was indeed a real one. One newspaper reporter gives his evaluation of the situation:

> The health of the camps is very bad indeed.... The prevalent diseases are measles, mumps, and a mild form of typhoid fever.... The lowness of the country, the great fall of rain, and the corruption of the atmosphere about Manassas ... and the extreme filth of the camps.... The water too, is bad, and its supply scant [*The Richmond Examiner*, 7 September 1861].

Surgeon Ashe received a requisition for a wall tent on September 14, 1861 (CSR). The tent was made into a hospital to care for the sick at Bristoe. It was a tremendous strain for the medical doctors of the regiment in those days. Many of the men from Co. G were appointed hospital attendants. On August 15, 1861, William H. Leopard, Thomas Clark, John P. Green, Constantine J. Campbell, and Green Campbell were all placed on extra duty in the hospital department (CSR).

In a letter written from Bristoe by Richard Kennedy of Co. C, he gives us a glimpse of the toll disease was taking. On August 16, 1861, Kennedy notes in his correspondence that on this day his company *only* had thirty-two men on the sick list (Kennedy Papers). When you consider that at this time Co. C had about one hundred men total on its muster roll, then you can begin to fathom the depth of the scourge of sickness at Bristoe. The death toll at Bristoe was high. Just to see the magnitude of the death rate among the ranks, I will list the men who died on a day by day basis: August 10: Albert Eatman, Co. C;[6] August 11: Green Brazell, Co. F; August 12: Calvin Davis, Co. E;[7] August 13: Andrew Welch, Co. H; August 14: David Sneed, Co. F; August 16: Columbus Webb, Co. F; August 17: James W. Person, Co. F; August 18: James Phillips, Co. H; August 19: Edward Deale, Co. B, and James Renfro, Co. I;[8] August 21: Andrew J. Ellett, Co. G; August 23: William Tadlock, Co. K, and Calvin Fason, Co. C; August 25: John Gibson, Co. G, Alfred Howard, Co. H, and Robert Holifield, Co. K; August 30: John Keith, Co. E; September 1: Benjamin F. Caddelle, Co. F; September 2: William Eskridge, Co. A; September 5: Charles Smitherman, Co. F; September 6: Jackson Richardson, Co. I, and Samuel Harding, Co. F; September 9: Ebenezer Breckenridge, Co. A; September 10: William J. Thompson, Co. I; September 11: James Ray, Co. G, and J. Thomas Worrell, Co. K; September 12: Eli Goree, Co. G; September 15: James M. Crews, Co. K, and Robert C. Carroll, Co. G; September 17: James M. Gillmore, Co. A; September 19: John F. Simmons, Co. D; and finally on September 20: James W. Horton, Co. C (CSR). The 11th Alabama lost thirty-two to disease while encamped at Bristoe in forty-two days. The men in the brigade were dying on an average of three a day, and Colonel Moore's men were the most unhealthy of all the regiments (Croom Collection). By September 12, 1861, the daily deaths of comrades were becoming so common that very little notice was being taken of them.

Life in Camp Near Bristoe Station

Judging from our previous look at the Bristoe encampment it might be thought that all was gloom and doom for the boys. For all the death and dying there were some experiences of a more positive nature that took place as well. In the *Alabama Beacon* mention is made of the Ladies Soldier's Aid Society of Greensboro (*Alabama Beacon*, 20 September 1861). This organization sent sixty-seven dollars for the relief of the 11th Alabama Regiment under Col.

Sydenham Moore. In addition, the young ladies of Clinton, Alabama, gave a concert on August 20, 1861, to help raise money for the benefit of the Confederate Guards (*ibid.*, 30 August 1861). This highly successful fund raiser was able to collect almost two hundred dollars for the cause. It was not only the locals back in Alabama who contributed to the supply of the men, but many in Virginia generously shared as well. Some six thousand dollars' worth of clothing was distributed to the 5th, 6th, 11th, and 13th Alabama Regiments from voluntary contributions (*Daily Richmond Enquirer*, 8 October 1861). In an August 19 letter Dr. Sanders mentions how helpful the ladies from different parts of Virginia had been in supplying needed hospital materials (Dr. Sanders's Papers). These contributions would especially prove to be beneficial as the long winter of 1861–62 approached.

In one letter from Bristoe, Dr. Sanders outlines the daily routine of the soldier during this time. He writes:

> It might be interesting to you to know precisely how we live, how we eat, sleep, and get our washing done. In the first place we sleep right upon the ground, sometimes with, oftener without any hay, and sleep sounder than we could on a feather bed — rise early and get down to breakfast prepared by_____, not ourselves. Our breakfast is generally comprised of bacon, beef or mutton, butter, & biscuit — sometimes is added sweet corn or Irish potatoes. For dinner we have about the same, with perhaps some addition of beets, milk or honey.

The enlisted men were of course divided into their messes. This did not stop the men from often going out into the surrounding homes to take meals. Soldiers could also find willing hands to do their laundry outside of the camp (Crenshaw 1861–1862). While eating with the locals the men discovered first-hand the character of the citizens of Bristoe. Some of the men felt that these Virginians were not as patriotic as Alabamians back home. It was believed by some that they were more interested in their own profit than the Southern cause. The prices they charged the soldiers for their goods was regarded as outrageously inflated. Notwithstanding these observations, it was acknowledged that many of the countrymen of Virginia were indeed helpful, patriotic, and caring people.

Many of the soldiers spent their time in camp either writing letters, playing cards, or just visiting around the campfire. In his September 5 entry, Corporal Crenshaw observes that there is a great deal of card playing and betting going on in camp. Richard Kennedy of Co. C was writing a letter on August 16 when a rather humorous accident occurred (Kennedy Papers). Lieutenant Higginbotham placed a rifled bomb shell in the fire, thinking the powder was all out of it. Soon the shell exploded, sending Higginbotham flying through the air! Amazingly enough, the stunned officer was unhurt. The shell rocketed out of the fire thirty yards before striking a rock. The twenty to thirty men gathered around the fire were all unhurt by the projectile.

The men also had the opportunity of attending religious services. Colonel Moore mentions on September 8, 1861, how religious services had been held in camp that very day (Sydenham Moore Papers). He notes that Mr. Kennedy and Mr. Phillips from Forkland conducted the services. William Kennedy of Co. B had just recently on August 24, 1861, been appointed as the regiment's chaplain. The other gentleman, John Henry Phillips, was also from Co. B.

The Encampment Near Centreville

On September 20, 1861, word filtered down that the regiment would march to a new encampment the next day (Crenshaw 1861–1862). The next morning found the boys on the march again for a site about fourteen miles away near Centreville.[9] Crenshaw records the details of this march in his diary:

> Took up my line of march for Centreville in company with Frank Inge pretty early in the morning, feeling very weary and sleepy, not having had two hours of sleep the night preceding. Our regiment marched considerably out of the way around by our old Camping gound near the battle field.... Frank and I left the main road and strayed out through the country. Visited several houses and had a good time generally, took dinner Grovertown. Got a bottle of whiskey, some sugar, tobacca etc. & set out about 2 o'clock, over took a carriage about a mile from Grovertown and rode to Centreville, raining like blazes all the time. Got there about five o'clock. Made a cup of coffee at the hotel. Ate a buisket & butter and set out to our camp ground in our shirt sleves about a quater distant, reached there wet & muddy and found every body also in the same plight.... Slept soundly & sweetly that night.

The new camp site was situated on the turnpike leading from Centreville to Fairfax Court House (Sanders's File). This location was about four or five miles south of Fairfax, a mile above Centreville on the south side of the road, fifteen miles from Alexandria, and an estimated twelve miles from the enemy (*The Pickens Republican* [Carrollton], 3 October 1861).[10]

The 11th Alabama lost thirteen men during this brief encampment near Centreville. The following men died: William Marshall of Co. A on September 24, John Rigsby of Co. G on September 27, Adam Bennett of Co. H on September 27, Thomas Otey of Co. G on September 30, John Hodge of Co. H on October 2, Joseph Eskridge of Co. A on October 4, Esq. Levingston of Co. I on October 4, Josephus Durrett of Co. G on October 10, William Carpenter of Co. C on October 11, Robert Gore of Co. H on October 11, John Barge of Co. K on October 13, Henry Ford of Co. A on October 14, and William Ethridge of Co. A on October 15 (CSR).

Military Developments Near Centreville

Not a great deal of change occurred during this third encampment of the regiment. Colonel Forney was still in charge of the Fifth Brigade, while the Alabamians were still under the command of Gen. Joseph Johnston, Army of the Potomac, in the 2nd Corps under Gen. G.W. Smith. According to one source, on September 25, 1861, the first brigade drill took place with Colonel Forney in command (Parker n.d., 24); in addition, on September 29, 1861, the brigade fell in for a full dress review. Crenshaw recorded what the typical days of drill were like for the regiment:

23rd	Had skirmish drill today....
24th	Skirmish drill by company, by Major Gracie.
25th	Brigade drill
26th	Brigade drill
27th	No drill, cold and raining
28th	Brigade drill with Artillery....
30th	Missed drill in morning. Drilling
Oct. 1st	Drill, Drill
" 2nd	Rain and no drill
" 3rd	Drill in the evening by Major Gracie (Crenshaw 1861–1862)

We also know that during this period talk began to emerge regarding Maj. Archibald Gracie. Crenshaw mentions in his diary on October 3, 1861, that Gracie has been acting Major General of the brigade, and will probably be appointed to that position (Crenshaw 1861–1862). Gracie was a distinguished officer, to be sure. It was just a matter of time before he would be promoted to a higher rank. This was not to come, however, until early in 1862.

The need for a 2nd Lieutenant was felt in Co. E since William Hudson had resigned on the last day of August. William Faith, who was 3rd Lieutenant of Co. E, was no doubt made 2nd Lieutenant, while John James was taken from the ranks and made 3rd Lieutenant on October 7, 1861 (CSR).[11] This must have been a confirmation of his skills as a soldier to be taken from the ranks and commissioned as an officer.

It seems that Colonel Moore had received many letters concerning his running for the Confederate Congress (*Alabama Beacon* [Greensboro], 11 October 1861). Moore felt compelled to stay in the field as long as the war might last. He endorsed the current candidate, Thomas H. Herndon, and thanked the people for their kind thoughts and support.

He writes:

> I cannot omit this opportunity, as it may be the last, of returning my most grateful acknowledgments to the noble constituency who have so highly honored me in the past....
>
> That our independence and liberties may be firmly established and perpetuated to our remotest posterity; and that peace and prosperity may ere long dwell within our borders, is the prayer of your obedient servant,
>
> SYDENHAM MOORE [Sydenham Moore Papers].

Some eleven men of the regiment were detailed on October 3 to work at Blackburn's Pond (Crenshaw 1861–1862). We found the following men detailed as teamsters in the month of October: John Lowery, Co. I; John Collins, Co. B; Thomas J. Waddell, Co. D; A.B. Harden, Co. K; Jesse Daniel, Co. A; William Chipman, Co. C; N. Henderson Jones, Co. B; James House, Co. G; and Jacob Hardy, Co. E (CSR). A two-hour march from camp brought them to the bridge. Here they worked until 10:00 P.M. carrying needed logs and dirt to the damaged bridge. The next day the work continued with the driving of spikes into the bridge, as well as fortifying it with dirt. By the end of the second day the detail had accomplished its mission, and the men proceeded to march back to their camp.

The regiment continued to be rather generously resupplied. On October 4, 8, and 10 mention is made of contributions being made to the 11th Alabama (*Daily Richmond Enquirer*). One B.L. Waddell is mentioned as contributing $1,300.00 worth of clothing for the regiment. This may refer to Beverly L. Waddell of Co. K. One J.J. Hutchinson contributed $6,000.00 worth of clothing to the 5th, 6th, 13th, and 11th Alabama Regiments, while S.D. Watson added $29,000.00 for the 3rd, 4th, 5th, 8th, 10th, and 11th Alabama Regiments.

All the men were still hungry for a fight (Sanders's File). Many believed that one good fight would make it possible for the men to spend Christmas at home. The feelings of the men ran high that a major battle was imminent. Private T.S. Thomas of Co. H wrote back home these words:

> We know very little of the military movement of our own army, or of the enemy, or about anything of the general affairs of the campaign, because everything is done and kept as secret as possible. There are said to be 150,000 men between the old battle gound at Bull Run and Alexandria [*The Pickens Republican*, 3 October 1861].

He goes on to note that the armies are very close to one another, and that occasionally they fire upon one another and take prisoners. Thomas believed that all the men wanted to fight real soon. Crenshaw also states that some 100,000 Yankees were said to have crossed the Occoquan (Crenshaw 1861–1862). He feels that a battle will soon take place, and this battle may include the Southern troops crossing the Potomac. On October 8, Crenshaw records the passing of the 19th Mississippi going out on picket duty. He adds that the constant roaring of cannon fire awakens them from their lethargy to the realization that war was imminent.

THE 11TH ALABAMA GOES ON PICKET

Little did Corporal Crenshaw know when he entered a note regarding the 19th Mississippi leaving for picket duty, that orders would come the next day for the 11th to prepare to leave as well. Colonel Moore wrote home to his wife on the evening of October 9, that he had just received orders to leave for picket duty the next morning (Sydenham Moore Papers). He had been told that they would travel to the advanced picket position, the exact location of which he did not know. As it turned out, the regiment proceeded to a location approximately ten to twelve miles from their present encampment (Sanders's File; McMath Diary). The regiment bivouacked on the banks of the Accotink Creek, some eight miles from Alexandria, and one mile southeast of Annandale; in fact, Clark recalls that they were situated at Ravenswood, where the lady of the house was in some way related to Gen. Robert E. Lee (Clark 1914, 16).

The regiment was able to leave camp at about 10:00 A.M. on October 10, 1861. All was astir in order to comply with the orders to prepare four days' rations (Sydenham Moore Papers). Corporal Crenshaw recorded some rather humorous details surrounding this march to the advanced picket (Crenshaw 1861–1862). He soon realized after the regiment had left for picket duty that he had forgotten his cup! In great haste he ran back several hundred yards to retrieve it. At this point the anxious Corporal ran into Lieutenant Clark. Lieutenant Clark proceeded to ask for Crenshaw to wait for him, as he was going directly to the picket in a nearer route than the one being taken by the regiment. After waiting more than half an hour, Crenshaw discovered that Lieutenant Clark was going in the company of Lieutenant Stealby.[12] This placed Crenshaw in the uncomfortable position of having to run in order to catch up with the rest of the regiment. By the time that he was ready to resume his march the men were already some three miles in advance. To add to Crenshaw's misery, the pair of shoes he had recently purchased were killing his feet as he crossed over innumerable hills and rocks!

The picket lines extended about one mile behind and to the right of Annandale (McMath Diary). It seems that Co. B formed the extreme right of the picket line on the Braddock Road (Crenshaw 1861–1862). Each of the companies was divided into squads in order to cover its assigned picket areas. Crenshaw remembers that one of the squads was near a large mansion owned by one Francis A. Dickens Sr. The place was a noble one with a fine grove, park, fountains, and beautiful orchard. The men were able to speak often with the Dickenses, and they in turn aided the soldiers with needed supplies. Before the first day on picket had come to an end it started raining in torrents! Of course the men had no shelters, and so they were completely soaked to the bone.

One night while Corporal Crenshaw was stretched out before his fire he began to reflect upon his situation:

> The night was beautiful beyond description; the nearly full moon shone forth in all its brilliancy upon our remantic situation....
>
> Beautiful Luna in all her bright elligence lighted up the scene to the lively music of the Yankee drums. Lying upon my bed of rails before a warm fire of glowing coals, I had time and opportunity, after all others had laid down to sleep, to reflect upon, and to realize the remance of my situation. I thought of the dear ones at home guessing what each one was doing at that hour,—wondering whether any fair one's thoughts were wandering up this far from home, settlling upon some one, perhaps, oh the joy, on myself, and she, too, wondering where I was and what doing. How I wished she, or anyone, could have had a birdseye view of our little square, as it then appeared. Thus I mused till sleep closed up my thoughts [Crenshaw 1861–1862].

One of the things that all of the soldiers remembered about this picket duty was the noises coming from the nearby Yankee camps. Drums and cannon fire were heard during the days and nights on picket. It appears that on October 14 the beating and firing took on an added intensity (Sanders's File). Most of the racket was coming from the direction of Mason's and Munson's Hill. On this Monday morning the camp was all astir with excitement about the intensity of the fire coming from the Union camp. The regiment was ordered into the line of battle in ditches to await the presumed enemy attack (Crenshaw 1861–1862; Sydenham Moore Papers). The Yankees never came. With the arrival of the 9th Alabama on October 15, the boys started the long march back to Centreville. It was around 11:00 P.M. when the tired soldiers of Colonel Moore's regiment reached camp. They were all anxious to crawl back into their tents for the night when new orders were received: the men must march to a new encampment!

The Encampment at Cub Run

At around 2:00 A.M. the weary soldiers from Alabama trudged some four or five miles to the Cub Run Bridge south of Centreville (CSR). After about a two- to three-hour march the men arrived at 4:00 A.M. (McMath Diary). The site was across the Cub Run, and so between Cub Run Creek and the Stone Bridge (Clark 1914, 16). According to Dr. Sanders, the rationale for this retreat was that it would prevent the enemy from a possible flanking movement (Dr. Sanders's Papers). It was in fact believed at this point that this was exactly what the Union forces were up to. At 8:00 A.M. the men were aroused for the purpose of finding another camping ground, but this effort proved to be futile (Crenshaw 1861–1862). Here at Cub Run Bridge the men would stay for a month.

THE MILITARY DEVELOPMENTS AT CUB RUN

The time at Cub Run was not marked by any momentous events for the regiment. The ordinary military routine continued: drilling, picket duty, and foraging. The feeling was still very high that a major battle could be fought at any time. This would have been reinforced by the brigade's removal in the efforts of reinforcing the flank. Colonel Moore's words to his wife on October 17 capture this expectancy:

> The enemy are advancing in large numbers and we expect to have a fight in a few days—It will no doubt be a hard fight—Many will fall on both sides & I do hope & pray we may gain such another victory as we did at Manassas—If I survive the battle, as I hope to do for your sake & that of the children, I will telegraph you as early as I can [Sydenham Moore Papers].

Colonel Moore in a letter written ten days later to his wife once again reflects the feeling that a battle was imminent:

> We are raise up now in large numbers & all closely packed together waiting for the Yankees who are reported to be coming to meet us.... Our generals & men all seem in fine spirits & confident of success.

Capt. John C.C. Sanders wrote his mother about this same time that the expectation was that a fight could commence at any moment (Sanders's File). They were told to be ready to march at a moment's notice, and to have rations cooked at all times. We have already noted that the withdrawal from Centreville to Cub Run Bridge was done because it was thought that the enemy might be in the process of flanking the army. Captain McMath recalled that many times during this encampment the men were ordered out to the entrenchments about a mile north of Centreville (McMath Diary). Consistent with the belief that a major offensive could be launched against them from across the Potomac, the army was busy throwing up entrenchments around Centreville.

It was during the time at Cub Run that Col. Cadmus M. Wilcox was appointed their brigade commander. Since First Manassas, Col. John H. Forney had been in command of the brigade, but with the appointment of Wilcox to Brigadier General on October 21, 1861, this was changed (CSR). On October 22, the 11th Alabama was assigned by the War Department to Longstreet's Division as the Third Brigade, in the Potomac District (OR Series 1 Vol. 5, 914). Gen. P.G.T. Beauregard was in command of this Potomac District, which was under the overall command of General Johnston in the newly designated Department of Northern Virginia. This brigade assignment was not to endure for very long. On October 26 the 11th Alabama became part of the Fifth Brigade, Second Corps, of the Army of the Potomac (OR Series 1 Vol. 5, 369). Now the brigade fell under the direction of Gen. Gustavus W. Smith. Amid all of these changes something stable had been created: Wilcox's Brigade. The regiment would stay in this brigade under Wilcox's command until August 13, 1863, following the battle of Gettysburg. Special Orders No. 461 gave Cadmus Wilcox the authorization to assume command of the brigade:

> Brig. Gen. Cadmus M. Wilcox, P.A.C.S., is assigned to the command of the Fifth Brigade, Second Corps, Army of the Potomac, and will be obeyed accordingly.
> By command of General Johnston [OR Series 1 Vol. 5, 922].

Cadmus M. Wilcox had tendered his resignation from Fort Fillmore, New Mexico, on June 8th, 1861 (Cadmus M. Wilcox Papers). At the time of his resignation he was a Captain in the 7th U.S. Infantry. As early as August 1, 1861, Wilcox had been under consideration for promotion to Brigadier General. General Beauregard had recommended him to the command of some five Louisiana regiments numbering between four and five thousand men (Cadmus M. Wilcox Papers). Wilcox had even been summoned to Beauregard's headquarters and told of his recommendation. By September 8th Wilcox had come to the conclusion that he would not receive the expected appointment. The Colonel's disappointment would be lifted on October 21, when he would receive the rank of Brigadier General. His thoughts on this turn of events are recorded in a letter to his sister Mary:

> I believe I wrote to you some time since that I had been made a Brigadier General, my appointment dates from the 21st of October, My Brigade is composed of 5 Regiments & one field battery of 4 guns, the Regiments are the 9th, 10th, 11th Ala' Regts, Col's Henry, Forney & Moore, the 19th Missi, Col Mott, and the 38th Va Regt, Col Edmonds, and Capt Stewards Battery (from Richmond). The Brigade is I believe the 2nd Strongest in this portion of the Army [Cadmus M. Wilcox Papers].

Wilcox's pride in his command comes shining through in these words. He told his sister he would work day and night to guarantee its success. No sacrifice would be too great to preserve the liberties of the Confederate cause.

Barely a week after Colonel Wilcox received his promotion to Brigadier General, Colonel Moore began to think hard and long about his own rank. On October 30, 1861, Colonel Moore wrote to President Davis regarding a promotion to Brigadier General (CSR). In this letter he mentions that even prior to active hostilities his name had been presented to the War Department for appointment to Brigadier General. Apparently this document, which had been signed by leading men from Alabama, had never been forwarded to the President. Colonel Moore writes:

> As Alabama has now over 20 Reg'ts in the field—11 of which are in Virginia, (besides several independent companies) it is presumed that other Brigadier Generals will be appointed, by your Excellency, from that State.
>
> I hope you will pardon me for requesting that my claims may be considered, when the names of others are presented for your consideration.

Colonel Moore goes on to make his case for the appointment. He reminds the President that he served in three different campaigns: three months as a volunteer in the Indian Nations, twelve months as a Captain in the Mexican War, and now over four months as a Colonel in the present conflict. Colonel Moore's desire for promotion was to go unfulfilled. Another appeal was made for his appointment on April 21, 1862, by William Yancey and C.C. Clay (McMillan 1963, 241–42). These two distinguished Alabamians strongly recommended Colonel Moore to President Davis for promotion to Brigadier General. No action was taken on their recommendation.

The rumors surrounding Major Gracie continued during this time. In a letter dated October 26, 1861, Croom mentions that Major Gracie had just recently received the authority to raise a new regiment from Alabama (Croom Collection). Gracie apparently told Croom that if he succeeded in this effort, he would get Croom an appointment of some kind. About a week later in a letter dated November 1, 1861, Croom mentions that Gracie had been approached about accepting the vacant Colonel's position in the 9th Alabama Regiment; however, Gracie no doubt had his sights set on raising a new regiment for the war.

On November 1, 1861, Capt. George Traweek's commission expired by virtue of his being court-martialed (CSR). Some light is shed on this turn of events in a letter dated February 9, 1862, by Lemuel Harris (Harris 1861–1864). He states that Captain Traweek had received hundreds of dollars to spend on the company, but he never used the money for its intended purpose. He swindled both the company and the Confederate government. This may have been part of the reason for his court-martial. Perhaps in response to this court-martial, 1st Lt. William T. Holland retired on November 1, 1861 (CSR). Now Co. I was without its two leading officers. It had lost its third ranking officer on August 1, 1861, when James Sullivan resigned. Stephen Bell was then promoted to 2nd Lieutenant. Bell would remain the ranking officer as 2nd Lieutenant until being elected Captain on January 1, 1862 (11th Alabama). Abel Walden was made 3rd Lieutenant on September 8, 1861. Company I would remain without an official Captain and 1st Lieutenant until January of 1862. For now, Bell and Walden were the ranking officers at Cub Run.

Help was being offered in various ways back in Alabama. Jackson Muse lived in Pinetucky, Alabama, in Bibb County. He wrote a letter to Governor Moore on Oct. 28, 1861, regarding the sending of supplies to Co. K (A.B. Moore 1860–1861). In this letter Muse mentions that it had been rumored that each military company would receive an appointed agent to help attend to the sick as well as forward needed supplies. He desired that appointment. He was ready to travel to Virginia with a fresh supply of clothing for the men. Whether he ever received that appointment is unknown.

Dr. Sanders mentions to his father the existence of a hospital relief fund (Dr. Sanders's Papers). This fund had been established by the good citizens of Clinton for use by the regiment. Dr. Sanders makes note of this and affirms that access to these funds should remain open for the future. Corporal Crenshaw made a notation in his diary on October 20, about the reception of boxes containing clothing, blankets, and other needed articles for the company (Crenshaw 1861–1862). All of these notices affirm that the companies of the 11th were being well supplied by the folks back home in their respective counties.[13]

There were many instances when official military court-martial proceedings were conducted. Dr. Sanders was told in a letter from home that many in the country were questioning the competency of some officers (Dr. Sanders's Papers). Sanders affirms that he is unwilling to deny all such allegations. Colonel Moore wrote a letter on November 12, 1861, during an actual court-martial proceeding (Sydenham Moore Papers). His observations are interesting:

> I am sitting here on a Court-Martial and while the proceedings are going on examing witnesses I will write a few lines to you....
>
> These Court Martials meet very often and some times they are very severe in their decisions. One of the Captains in my Reg't has been sentenced & dismissed — an old fellow from Fayette. One private in an Ala Regt (tho not mine) was sentenced to wear a ball and chain on his leg for months.

It should be noted that the Captain referred to by Colonel Moore was undoubtedly Capt. George Traweek.

On October 29, 1861, the regiment went out on picket duty again. Not much information is given about this time on picket. They took the main road to Centreville, and then proceeded about four more miles north of Centreville (Crenshaw 1861–1862). After reaching this point the regiment struck out in the woods off the main road about a mile or so. This would have placed them about halfway to Fairfax Court House. They were probably near B.S. Shop, or Mrs. Kidwell's place near the streams of the Piney Branch. Here they stayed until November 1, 1861, when they were relieved and returned to camp.

Hardships at Cub Run

Many men of were still at the sick camp at Bristoe during these days. It was a concern of Colonel Moore that those who could should be returned to the present encampment. In a letter dated October 18, 1861, Colonel Moore directs the Medical Director of Manassas to comply with his concerns:

> Dr. Williams
>   Med Director
>   at Manassas
> Dr Sir
>   I have many men at the sick camp near Bristoe who ought to be here — Can't you send off those really, sick & have the others join their Co? I hope you will have transportation for them today or tomorrow — or as soon thereafter as possible —
>   Respy'
>   Sydenham Moore
>   Col 11th Ala. Regt
>
> In camp near
> Centreville
>   Oct 18th 1861[CSR].

In compliance with Colonel Moore's wishes, the sick camp at Bristoe containing men from the 11th Alabama was broken up on October 24, 1861 (Crenshaw 1861–1862). Those who needed additional treatment were sent to Richmond, while the others were transported back to the Cub Run encampment.[14] Many of the 11th Alabama were now being sent to Richmond to the recently constructed hospital known as Chimborazo. As of November 1, there were 109 buildings at this location (*Richmond Daily Whig*, 1 November 1861).

With so many men being sent to Richmond, along with the steady rate of deaths among the ranks, it is no wonder Dr. Sanders wrote home about the need for continued recruiting (Dr. Sanders's Papers). Dr. Sanders notes that the ranks were being thinned by an enemy more terrible than the one facing them on the Virginia border. What was needed was the active recruiting of new members for the depleted companies.

During this time at Cub Run the following men died: Harrison Odum of Co. E on October 20, President Thompson of Co. D on November 1, William Williams of Co. C on November 1, Marshall Bolton of Co. I on November 2, James J. Tucker of Co. D on November 3, William Duckworth of Co. I on November 4, Austin Eskridge of Co. K on November 8, and John Clements of Co. E on November 10 (CSR). In addition to these deaths, the regiment had ten men either discharged or transferred at Cub Run: Aaron Hawkins of Co. H, Benjamin Sanford of Co. F, Leonidus Eddings of Co. D, James Thompson of Co. D, Jeremiah Morrison of Co. G, John Jones of Co. C, George Traweek of Co. I, William Holland of Co. I, Philip Newton of Co. I, and James Pharis of Co. E.

A New Encampment Near Centreville

On November 12, the very day Colonel Moore was writing home during a court-martial hearing, orders were received to move about a mile closer to Centreville (Sydenham Moore Papers). The site is described in some detail by Corporal Crenshaw:

> Pitched tents about a mile further on and about three quarters from the road in an old field formerly the camping ground of Gen. Tombs' brigade. Bad place. Wood & water hard to get. Muddy & nasty in wet weather. Besides it is far out of the way. Camp about 100 yards from the breastworks, near an old house with curious chimneys [Crenshaw 1861–1862].

It was here that the men would settle in for a month's time just prior to their going into winter quarters. We will now consider some of the significant developments during this encampment.

Military Developments Near Centreville

We have already examined how the 11th was placed in Longstreet's Division of Gen. G.T. Beauregard's Potomac District back on October 22, 1861. Four days after this they were then attached to the 2nd Corp of the Army of the Potomac under Maj. Gen. Gustavus W. Smith (Davis & Hoffman 1991, 178–179). A new directive was issued on November 16, 1861, by order of the Secretary of War (OR Series 1 Vol. 5, 960–61). The Wilcox Brigade was now the Second Brigade of the First Division commanded by Maj. Gen. Earl Van Dorn. As we shall see, this division alignment was to be rather short-lived.

One thing that becomes very clear during this period of time is the desire of Colonel Moore for advancement and relocation. He confides to his wife on November 27 the desire to relocate the entire regiment to Mobile (Sydenham Moore Papers). No doubt his own failing health at the time, coupled with the inclement weather, fueled this longing for the Gulf. In addition, he states plainly his desire to be Brigadier General, although he doubts that it will ever be realized. On December 11, 1861, he again takes up this subject with his wife. His poignant words on this matter deserve citation:

> Some of my friends have lately applied to the Pres't to appoint me a Brig. Gen'l. I do not know whether he will give it to me or not. He is very partial to West Pt men. Even if he sh'd it w'd be

very doubtful whether I w'd be tranferred to the Southern Coast. To be nearer home & on account of the mild climate. I w'd of course like it better, at least this winter — much more if I could take my Reg't with me. Like a good soldier I shall try to be content wherever I may be ordered whether I am promoted or not. Tho I confess I w'd like to be appointed a Brig Gen'l.

Colonel Moore goes on to note that Secretary Clay had written a very strong letter recommending him for the coveted appointment. By March of 1862 he begins to think that he will not receive the appointment, although he did believe that at one time the prospects were good.

It should never be forgotten that Lieutenant Colonel Hale had responsibilities in Richmond as well as Centreville. As a member of the Confederate Congress he was expected to be in attendance as much as possible. Sometime prior to November 27 Colonel Hale had gone to Richmond to sit at Congress (Sydenham Moore Papers). Then around December 8 or 9 he rushed to Centreville when it appeared that a fight was imminent. By December 22 Hale had already returned again to Richmond to resume his duties there (Dr. Sanders's Papers).

There were some medical developments that have been documented by Dr. Sanders (Dr. Sanders's Papers). On December 22, 1861, he notes that Dr. Clark had resigned his post as Brigade Surgeon. Upon the resignation of Dr. Clark the 11th Alabama's surgeon, Dr. Ashe, was up for promotion. According to Sanders this promotion was declined by Dr. Ashe for several reasons. Dr. Ashe was not fond of writing and keeping books, and both of these would have been important in this new position. In addition, this station involved no additional rank or pay, although it certainly did involve a great deal more labor. In light of these considerations, Dr. Ashe prevailed upon the surgeon of the 38th Virginia to assume this role.

It seems that a battle was still regarded as imminent during this encampment. We have already noted how Lieutenant Colonel Hale was summoned from Richmond in December in anticipation of a fight. We do know that some skirmishes did occur. Several minor skirmishes are noted in the Official Records at Annandale Station[15] and Burke's Station (OR Series 1, Vol. 5, 452; OR Series 1 Vol. 51/1, 49). No doubt the biggest clash took place on December 20, 1861, at Dranesville. The 11th Alabama was not involved in this battle; however, Drs. Ashe and Sanders assisted with the wounded among the boys of the 10th Alabama (Dr. Sanders's Papers). Colonel Moore in a November 18 letter states that he expects the Yankees to come, and that adequate preparations had been made to receive the expected attack (Sydenham Moore Papers). Samuel Wier of Co. H describes the feeling in this November 15, 1861, letter:

> We are expecting a fight at this place every day but it is useless for them to try to come through here. There are about 20 breast works thrown up around this point and large guns are being planted on them every day. Our regiment is placed behind a battery about ¼ of a mile long [*The Heritage of Pickens County, Alabama* 1999, 35].

General Wilcox was also confident that an attack was imminent (Cadmus Wilcox Papers). On November 26, 1861, he writes:

> I feel certain if McClellen will come & attack even with his vastly superior force we will repel him & possibly pursue them into Washington. We are strongly entrenched at this place, fear no attack, but are all eager for it.

On both November 14 and 29 the regiment was ordered out on picket duty. On November 14 they were stationed three miles above Centreville, and returned to camp three days later (Crenshaw 1861–1862). On November 29 the picket location was about two and a half miles west of Centreville (McMath Diary). Finally, on December 15 picket duty was again called for, and the regiment repaired some two miles northwest of their Centreville encampment. They returned to their tents on December 19.

On December 12, 1861, the Independent Volunteers lost their second Captain since being mustered into Confederate service. Captain Matthew M. England died in Richmond, according to Stephens Croom (Croom Collection). Croom makes some very kind remarks about him in a December 14, 1861, letter. He states that in his opinion he was one of the nicest gentlemen in the entire regiment. Tradition has it that England's body was returned to Alabama for burial, and that his body was buried along with the original Confederate flag presented to the Marion Rifles (*Alabama Portraits Prior to 1870* 1969, 425). Walter C.Y. Parker took over command of the company until his official appointment as Captain on January 1, 1862. Parker was born around 1839 in North Carolina, and was a single student living in Marion, Alabama, at the outbreak of the war (CSR). He began his military career as 2nd Lieutenant in the 8th Alabama, but was then transferred to Co. K on July 4, 1861.

Camp Life at the Centreville

The men were being exposed to the December temperatures of Virginia with only tents for shelter. Colonel Moore expresses his concern over this inadequate state of affairs in a letter to his wife: "Christmas is near at hand and we may look for snow & awful cold weather. I don't know what our poor soldiers are to do in open tents if they sh'd be kept in them" (Sydenham Moore Papers). Corporal Crenshaw makes a notation in his diary on November 15, 1861, which captures the soldier's plight during the winter of 1861:

> Cold, damp, muddy, and disagreeably windy. The great end that we all try to attain now is to keep warm without having our eyes put out with smoke & ashes. We first try the tent, which is dry & close, but our feet soon become too cold to stand it long unless we cover up, which we do until we become tired of lying down. We then go out and crowd around the fire, which imparts generally enough warmth for a score or more, but the cursed wind.... between cold and smoke we are worried & fretted so that our tempers about bed time are high enough to fight all the Yankees in Washington ten to one [Crenshaw 1861–1862].

Colonel Moore, in a letter dated November 27, 1861, gives a picture of what it was like during this winter:

> I went to my tent to write.... But the smoke drove me out the 1st time my chimney had smoked. ... am now writing with a sack of [illegible] for my seat & a plank in my lap for a table, with a bayonet sticking up by my shoulder ... as a substitute for a candle stick [Sydenham Moore Papers].

Colonel Moore's health suffered greatly during the month of December. In his letters to his wife Colonel Moore downplays his physical struggles. Yet on December 11 he states that this was the first day in more than a week that he felt well enough to even write (Sydenham Moore Papers). The doctors were advising him to secure shelter that would protect him from the cold weather. Dr. Sanders stated that as of December 22, the Colonel had been unable to command the regiment for more than two weeks (Dr. Sanders's Papers). The doctors were finally able to convince him to take lodging in a neighborhood house. Colonel Moore would eventually need to return to Alabama to fully recover.

Even though most of the boys did not receive the privilege of going home to Alabama for Christmas, the camp did have its share of the holiday spirit. Surgeon Sanders mentions how some preparations for Christmas had been made in camp (*ibid.*). He recalled how that turkey and whiskey were in high demand, and Captain Sanders himself had sent to Richmond for a keg of the latter. It seems that Captain Sanders wished to give his company a big "egg-nog." In keeping with the above mentioned activity, Corporal Crenshaw wrote in his diary of November 20 about a "pre-seasonal" celebration in the camp:

> Whole camp been on a general drunk for the last three days, first time I have seen Capt. drunk since left home. BIll Bird L.W., F.I., Mc I playing the principle parts. Night before last went down to Sutters tent and there joined all the captains in a champaign row. & & &. Adjutant had to disperse [Crenshaw 1861–1862].

December and the imminent arrival of Christmas did not prevent the resumption of the military routine. They drilled regularly twice a day, read the newspapers, went out on picket, and played cards. Overall the regiment was doing as well as could be expected under the circumstances. Cases of camp fever, jaundice, chills, mumps, and pneumonia were still being experienced (Dr. Sanders's Papers). Colonel Moore was anxious to go into winter quarters in order to protect the health of the regiment from the onslaught of pneumonia (Sydenham Moore Papers). Going into winter quarters would not prevent the regiment from saying goodbye to fifteen soldiers: Elijah Alvis, Co. D; Edmund Strudwick, Co. D; Isaac Cottles, Co. H; Joel Randall, Co. H; George Searcy, Co. E; John Sronce, Co. E; Samuel O.P. Watson, Co. G; Burrill Simmons, Co E; William Williams, Co. H; Mathew England, Co. K; William Hilton, Co. K; Jacob Ergle, Co. H; Levin Ainsworth, Co. E; William Cox, Co. G; and Robert Brantley, Co. E (CSR).

In addition to the fifteen soldiers lost to disease, a significant number were discharged during this cold winter. The following twenty-three men were sent home: Samuel and Jesse Varner of Co. A, Joseph N. Ross of Co. D, James Edmiston of Co. B, David Burgess of Co. H, Benjamin Hannibal of Co. E, Virgil Clark of Co. G, James Milner of Co. C, William Wilson of Co. H, John Smith of Co. A, James Devoy of Co. A, Shade Trammill of Co. K, David Smith of Co. H, Edward Keasler of Co. H, John R. Woods of Co. H, James Skinner of Co. D, John Knox of Co. B, William R. Ethridge of Co. A, John Gardner of Co. F, Martin Goodwin of Co. F, John W. Sanders of Co. H, S. Henry Bartlett of Co. D, and John Shepherd of Co. H (CSR).

Winter Quarters Near the Lewis House

The day after Christmas the men were moved back toward the Manassas battlefield one last time in 1861. As early as December 22 it was suspected that a location near the Lewis House would be the next stop for the regiment (Dr. Sanders's Papers). The most positive thing that could be said about this position is that the men would be close to General Johnston's headquarters at the Lewis House. Captain Sanders described the site as an old field covered with young pine trees (Sanders's File). The soil was easily muddied, lumber was scarce, and the water was bad. In fact, he felt that before the winter was over they would probably have to carry their firewood up to a mile away. By February of 1862 his suspicions regarding the post were confirmed as he notes:

> Our camp is very muddy and disagreeable. I can not get outside of my door without getting in mud over my shoe. The mud is from half shoe mouth to half leg deep all over the camp. The men have to carry nearly all their wood from ¼ to ½ mile through mud....
> Our water is very bad have no spring just seep holes the holes that we dug to set mud to daub the houses with a barrel put into them offered the best water.

It was at this rather desolate locale that they would stay through the winter of 1861–62. They began their stay near the battlefield, and now they were ending their stay near the battlefield.

Military Developments Near the Lewis House

From December 26, 1861, until March 8, 1862, one can detect many changes on the military level. Reorganization took place on the division, brigade, and company levels. The regiment moved to near the Lewis House as part of the 2nd Brigade, 1st Division, under the command of Maj. Gen. Earl Van Dorn. This had been ordered on November 16, 1861. On January 14, 1862, General Johnston ordered that the brigade of Wilcox — the 9th, 10th, 11th Alabama, 19th Mississippi, 38th Virginia, and Thomas Artillery (Virginia) — be designated as the 2nd Brigade of the 2nd Division under the command of Maj. Gen. Gustavus W. Smith (OR Series 1 Vol. 5, 1029). This assignment was slightly altered by General Order #22 dated February 5, 1862 (*ibid.*, 1061–62). Now the 11th was part of the 2nd Brigade of the 1st Division of the Army of the Potomac under the command of Maj. Gen. Gustavus W. Smith. The assignment would remain until the end of March in 1862.

We have already noted that substantial changes were being made within the Fayette and Pickens Rifles. Lemuel Harris reports the official election results for the company in several of his letters (Harris 1861–1864). The final tally of votes went as follows: Stephen E. Bell was unanimously elected as Captain; Lemuel Harris thirty-nine votes, and R.J. Stewart twenty-five votes for 1st Lieutenant; R.H. Shelton fifty votes, and G.L. Traweek five votes for 3rd Lieutenant; and William T. Davis thirty-seven votes, and William Kirkland thirty votes for 1st Sergeant.[16] The Fayette and Pickens Rifles now had an entirely different look as a company. Within seven months all the commissioned officers were replaced. A 3rd Lieutenant had now become Captain, the 4th Corporal had now been elected 1st Lieutenant, the 1st Sergeant had now taken on the bars of 2nd Lieutenant, and the 2nd Sergeant had now stepped into the shoes of the 3rd Lieutenant.

John W. Baker left for Virginia as 1st Lieutenant of the Yancey Rifles. On January 16, 1862, Lieutenant Baker tendered his resignation as an officer. In an attached letter that was penned on January 11, 1862, Surgeon Ashe in no uncertain terms suggests that Lieutenant Baker was unfit to be an officer in the Confederate States Army (CSR). Ashe states that Baker was incapable of carrying out or learning the rudiments of military drill; in addition, Ashe affirms that he would be confirmed in this judgment by all the field officers of the regiment — including Captain Fletcher. Baker's resignation was accepted upon the basis of both physical and mental disqualifications on January 24, 1862. Sadly, Baker returned home to Alabama only to die on May 30, 1862. On February 1, 1862, Thomas Michie was then elected 1st Lieutenant of the company.

The resignation of 2nd Lt. Stephen F. Nunnalee of Co. B was tendered to the Adjutant Inspector General's office on January 23, 1862 (CSR). In his resignation Nunnalee complained of suffering continuously from a rheumatism so severe that it impeded his ability to carry out his responsibilities. Dr. Sanders also recommended his discharge from the service. It appears that it was more than physical problems that led Nunnalee to his decision (11th Alabama). In his own personal reflections upon his actions, he maintains that Colonel Moore failed to carry out a promise he had made to him. Back in December of 1861 Colonel Moore had offered him the opportunity of going home on furlough. Nunnalee declined this offer, but with the assurance that come February he would be granted furlough to attend to his ailing wife. It became clear to the Lieutenant that his furlough had never been forwarded. This fact, coupled with his physical inability, led him to the decision to resign his commission. In his place George Clark was promoted on February 3, 1862, and James Gordon was then elected 3rd Lieutenant on February 9, 1862 (CSC).

Colonel Moore's December health problems continued to linger on as the new year began to dawn. Around January 3, 1862, Colonel Moore began the long trek back to Greene County.[17] One company captain thought that Colonel Moore might not be able to stand the rigors of camp life (Sanders's File). After the departure of Colonel Moore, the command of the regiment fell upon Major Gracie since Colonel Hale was in Richmond (Harris 1861–1864). Colonel Moore had every intention of staying at home for a week or so, but felt compelled after only three days to return to Virginia. The *Alabama Beacon* informs its readers of Colonel Moore's quandary:

> It was his intention to have spent a week or ten days with his family, but an apprehension that an advance movement might, in the meantime, be made by the enemy, and his great anxiety to be with his command, induced him to leave last Tuesday morning, after spending only three days with his family (11th Alabama).

The writer of this article was skeptical of the wisdom of Moore's decision of leaving so soon. It was his opinion that the Colonel's health had not sufficiently improved to merit such a quick return. On January 22, 1862, Colonel Moore tells his wife that he felt compelled to return to the regiment due to rumors of a Union advance (Sydenham Moore Papers). Moore soon discovered upon his arrival back to Manassas that there was no immediate danger of an enemy attack. This must have been a great source of discouragement to the Colonel, and apparently very soon thereafter preparations were made for his return home. It was around February 3–4, 1862, that Colonel Moore left again for home.[18] This time Captain Field and Lieutenant Clark accompanied Colonel Moore on this return trip. The extremely sad thing about this affair was that Colonel Moore never made it home. He got as far as Montgomery, but felt compelled again to return to Virginia (Sydenham Moore Papers). Upon his arrival at Montgomery he received reports that a large Federal force had crossed the Potomac. With great sadness he addressed his wife:

> My hope and expectation was when I left Manassas that I could remain at least 2 weeks at home. The very thought thrilled my heart.... Oh to be so near & yet to feel compelled to forgo the pleasure of seeing her & the torturing painfully so.

Moore finally arrived back near the Lewis House on February 19, 1862. Upon his arrival he was to discover once again that no present danger presented itself to the army.

On December 29, 1861, the regiment went out on picket. Corporal Crenshaw reports the events of his time on picket:

> Incidents at my post, burning the bunk, fighting mice, foraging. In going out had to pass old McMath's pickets, took my own time in coming back. The old fool got as hot as pepper, and spread out his sentinels to catch me. Bamboozled the old cuss [Crenshaw 1861–1862].

On January 13, 1862, the regiment again went out on picket duty north of the camp. It was a very unpleasant march through much water (McMath Diary). A big snow fell the first night along with rain and sleet. They were relieved of duty on January 17, 1862, and had to march back to camp through snow half way up their legs! Finally, we know that they went out on picket again on January 28, 1862, about six miles from their camp (Sanders's File).

Recruiting Service for the 11th Alabama

The Confederate Congress approved the act for recruiting the depleted troops of the army on December 19, 1861 (OR Series 1 Vol. 5, 1022–23). Recruiting was not to go beyond thirty days in the original neighborhoods of the various companies. The recruiting party was to include one subaltern, one non-commissioned officer or private. The new recruits had to be examined by a surgeon prior to leaving the state, and the funds for the entire endeavor were to be requisitioned from the Adjutant and Inspector General's Office.

Most of the companies of the 11th Alabama sent a Lieutenant, a Sergeant, and a private back home to recruit.[19] The muster rolls consistently give the dates of February 8–10 as the beginning time for the recruiting service, and mid to late March for its conclusion. James McMath's diary records his recruiting service journey back to Tuscaloosa (McMath Diary). McMath left the Lewis House camp for the War Department at Richmond on February 9, 1862. After getting all his papers organized for the recruiting service, he began the long trip back to Alabama. His trip would prove to be a very successful one. He would return to Virginia with an additional twenty-seven recruits.

Captain McMath was not the only one who was able to secure needed soldiers. All the company recruiters were successful in enlisting men for their respective ranks (CSR). We offer the following information with the realization that there may be names missing in the record. This is the only list that we can verify at present from the rolls. Company A added the following thirteen men: Anderson S. Crawford, Thomas J. Gillmore, James L. Heath, Thomas B. Jolly, J. Thomas McFarland, Thomas McGehee, Francis M. Norris, Wesley Norred, Benjamin Norred, James Pearl, Wm. H.F. Tice, Henry B. Tucker, and Nathaniel R. Walker.[20] Company B recruited at least the following ten men: Samuel B. Browne, William J. Caulfield, James B. Fuller, Milton A. Hamilton, Robert R. McCulley, Arthur B. Phillips, Wm. B. Skates, Albert Moore, John Monroe, and Joseph G. Williford. Company C enlisted the following eight men: James S. Brown, Joel A. Doss, John M. Doss, Beverly B. Pierce, George W. Williams, Joseph H. Harris, John Copp, and W.P. Massey. Company D signed up the following ten men: William Bryant, Thomas K. Cathey, Oliver D. Chapman, John C. Cade, Sillman McJinsey, John W. Norwood, Thomas M.C. Prince, Jordan W. Oakley, Asa Vaughan, and John R. Springfield.[21] The following seven men[22] were taken from Washington County: Joshua D. Bostick, Charles H. Griffin, Charles Cooper, John J. Robinson, James W. Henderson, William L. Cope, and Edwin A. Sherwood.[23] Captain Davidson brought back the following eighteen men from Bibb County: Richard Brown, William H. Brown, David A. Griffin, John L. Hill, Marion Hogan, Richard Hogan, Absalom H. James, Josiah H. Kennedy, Jacob D. Mayberry, John T. Moses, William R. Owen, General Marion Powell, Chesterfield Quinn, Ervin Stacy, Jacob J. Taylor, William W. Watkins, William J. Wilson, and Philip M. Vance. Thomas H. Thompson, James M. Waggoner and Pilgrim A. Espey were enlisted as substitutes early in 1862. From his store in Tuscaloosa, Captain McMath recruited the following twenty-seven men: John S. Allman, John T. Burchfield, Jesse H. Shackleford, John Carroll Sr., John Carroll Jr., Henry Champion, Enoch F. Erwin, Marion Gallant, Levi Young, George Wallace, John Hasty, John Dodds, Basil M. Hughes, Jesse Hughes, William Jesse Keeton, James M. Kent, James McMahon, Clement Clay McMath, James R. Moore, John Nabors, Benjamin W. Reese, John A. Redd, William W. Redd, Emanual C.B. Thrasher, Thomas Thrasher, Robert A. Watson, and Marion F. White.[24] Company H enlisted the following twelve men: Robert Henry, Benjamin Phillips, Thomas Hatcher, David Lawhorn, Charles Stewart, Thomas J. Bell, John H. Floyd, Calvin W. Free, George W. Hall, Joel J. Hamiter, John H. Richardson, and John W. Yateman. The following group went to Virginia from Fayette: Jefferson J. Morrow, D.W. Williams, Robert C. Mizell, Jeddiah H. Smith, Richard S. Sullivan, and William Wilson. Finally, from Perry County the following twenty-one men traveled to Virginia: Larkin Bagwell, John T. Church, Benjamin F. Gray, John A. Gray, Robert B. Griffin, John C. Harris, D.C.

Wallace, John Austin, Jesse J. Heard, Jesse M. Humphries, David C. Lovelady, Cumberland F. Lovelady, Allen Barnett, James Irwin, F.M. Morton, John Ratliffe, Little S.B.J. Ratliff, Benjamin F. Sanders, John D. Sanders, Malcomb D.C. Tadlock, and Meshack A. Turner.[25] If we add the total known men recruited in February and March of 1862 we come to a figure of 132 men. This new company of recruits was needed in the regiment. The battle of sickness and boredom would soon be replaced by a battle with muskets and artillery. The 11th Alabama needed all these troops for what would soon be faced in a series of battles around Richmond.

Camp Life Near the Lewis House

The weather began to take a turn for the worse following the move near the Lewis House. In a letter dated January 8, 1862, Lemuel Harris notes, "There has been snow on the ground for a week with no prospect of it melting soon and to night it has every appearance of falling weather" (Harris 1861–1864). By the end of January the roads had become unusable (Croom Collection). This weather was also hard on the animals. In one note dated February 15, 1862, it was stated that some seventeen horses and one mule had died in the service of the regiment (CSR). It was due to hard labor in the mud, disease, and want of sufficient protection from the weather.

One of the first tasks at hand following the move to the Lewis House was the construction of winter quarters. Captain Sanders describes the typical wooden cabin as measuring fourteen by sixteen feet, containing chimneys, and able to accommodate up to eight men (Sanders's File). He himself supervised the construction of ten such units for Co. C. The quarters were built of logs covered by boards, and then daubed to fill in the cracks (Croom Collection). By the last of January they had finally gotten into their new quarters for the winter. Harris was lamenting the fact that he had not gotten into his winter quarters as yet on January 16, 1862 (Harris 1861–1862). The walls were up, and the snow was over three inches thick on their tents!

Morale began to degenerate among some of the men. Captain Sanders was surprised at how quickly some of the men where resorting to every kind of means to avoid their work:

> To keep all hands at work so that each one might do his share is harder work probably than you would suppose. You can hardly have any idea what effect being in the army a short time has on some men. They will do anything and resort to every subterfuge to avoid their duty.... Some seem to lose all self pride and if they can get anybody to do their labor, rest perfectly quick. These men who do least duty and shirk it on every opportunity are more dissatisfied and complain more than any others [Sanders's File].

Croom recalls that the spirit of the men was way down. They all wanted to go home, get furloughs, and affirm that there was no fight coming (Croom Collection). Lieutenant Harris mentions that many of the men were imbibing on a regular basis (Harris 1861–1864). On January 16 he states that all is inactive except the quest for whiskey! Some of the men stayed out all night in the pursuit of the coveted spirits, only to return just in time for reveille the next morning. Harris notes that since Christmas, drinking had become more and more of a problem, and in his view something needed to be done about the dilemma.

Many of the men were not content to eat around the campfires near the Lewis House during that cold winter of 1861–62. They would frequently walk a mile or two to take dinner at a neighbor's home (Sanders's File). Captain Sanders observed that the entire county had become a public eating place. A soldier would go to a house, pay his half dollar, and journey back to camp. It was not unusual to observe a dozen soldiers at the same house.

During the encampment near the Lewis House from December 26, 1861, until March 8, 1862, the regiment lost eighteen men to disease. The following men never broke camp on March 8: James Maughan of Co. B, Francis Ried of Co. B, Columbus Lockhart of Co. D, Stewart Melvin of Co. K, David Welborn of Co. I, N. Henderson Jones of Co. B, Benjamin Chapman of Co. D, Andrew Dollins of Co. E, Robert Moseley of Co. E, Robert McLane of Co. C, James House of Co. G, Thomas Colvin of Co. C, Samuel Wier of Co. H, Joseph Singleton of Co. A, William Gallant of Co. G, John Pollard of Co. K, James McGraw of Co. H, and James Tucker of Co. A (CSR). To this list of soldiers we would add those twenty-seven men who were discharged at the Lewis House: Luther Richardson of Co. I, Richard Barber of Co. G, David Corley of Co. F, James Turnipseed of Co. H, Thomas Adams of Co. A, John Bronson of Co. E, Alexander Waller of Co. A, Joseph Peoples of Co. D, John Baker of Co. E, Milton Holly of Co. K, Green Wooley of Co. F, Frederick Englebert of Co. G, William Downey of Co. K, Gabriel Hill of Co. B, David Scarbrough of Co. B, Fletcher Goss of Co. F, David Wood of Co. K, William McLaughlin of Co. K, James Deshazo of Co. E, Stephen Nunnalee of Co. B, Thomas Smitherman of Co. F, William Morrow of Co. F, Ivan Johnson of Co. G, James Carson of Co. H, George Suggs of Co. A, David Brown of Co. F, and Andrew Derby of Co. B (CSR).

The order to move out from the Lewis House finally arrived on March 8, 1862. It must have been a relief just to go somewhere beyond the area surrounding Manassas Junction. Where were the men being ordered to go? The rumor was that North Carolina was their destination, and all indications seemed initially to substantiate this. Nevertheless, it would turn out to be a roundabout trip before reaching their final destination on the Peninsula.

5

A Baptism in Blood: The 11th Alabama in the Seven Days Battle

For almost an entire year the 11th Alabama had been spared from any direct engagement with the enemy. They had been shot at on picket duty, and drawn up in line of battle on many occasions; yet, they arrived a day late to participate in the first major battle of the war at Manassas Junction. This was soon to change. In this chapter we will follow the Alabamians from their withdrawal near Centreville until the battle of Frayser's Farm.

From Manassas to the Peninsula

Probably no one expected the stay at Manassas to last as long as it did. The men arrived on the battlefield of Manassas July 22, 1861, and they were not ordered to leave until March 8, 1862. The commanding general records the orders of withdrawal:

> The troops near Centreville and Manassas Junction were directed to march on the morning of the 8th; Smith's and Longstreet's divisions and Pendleton's reserve artillery by the Turnpike— to the south side of the Rappahannock—by the bridge near the Warrenton Springs [Johnston 1959, 103].

In a conference held with President Davis on February 20, 1862, General Johnston had indicated his desire to withdraw from Centreville (Johnston 1959, 96). He maintained that when the roads allowed it in the spring, McClellan's forces would most certainly invade Virginia, making it impossible for him to hold his present position. On March 5, 1862, General Whiting reported some unusual activity in the area opposite Dumfries, Virginia (*ibid.*, 102). This was a harbinger of the invasion that Johnston anticipated from McClellan; accordingly, he issued orders to be ready to march at a moment's notice (Sydenham Moore Papers). Colonel Moore recalls that the weather was cold, the snow several inches deep, and the mud deplorable. Yet for all these inconveniences Moore was ready to go anywhere other than stay where they presently were encamped.

In order to get south of the Rappahannock, and in a better defensive position to meet McClellan, the army moved down the Warrenton Turnpike in a southeasterly direction. By the end of the day on March 9, 1862, Longstreet's men had gotten to Gainesville before going into bivouac (OR Series 1 Vol. 5, 1096). The Wilcox Brigade bivouacked that first night at Groveton (Cadmus

M. Wilcox Papers). It would take the army several days to get south of the Rappahannock. Prior to crossing the river they encamped one night near New Baltimore. On March 10 they crossed the Rappahannock near Warrenton Springs. The following day they passed through Sulphur Springs before arriving at Culpeper Court House where they encamped for several days. Finally, on March 18 the brigade made their way to Orange Court House.[1] It was here, about a mile from the court house, that the boys rested for several days (Gregory 1988, 11–12). Croom penned a letter from Orange Court House on March 22, 1862, in which he speaks of the condition of the brigade at that time (Croom Collection). The men were without tents at this location, and the new recruits and furloughed men were slowly making their way back into the ranks. He himself was in a house a few miles from the old home of President Madison at Montpelier.

A Roundabout Trip to the Peninsula

While the men under Wilcox's command were resting at Orange Court House, General Johnston was trying to determine where they could best be stationed. The Confederate commander simply did not know for sure where McClellan intended to strike. In the meantime, General Wilcox's Brigade was ordered to proceed immediately to Goldsborough and report to Gen. Theophilus H. Holmes for duty. This special order was issued on March 24, 1862.

The regiment left Orange Court House on March 24, and proceeded by cars to Richmond (Croom Collection).[2] They arrived in Richmond on March 25. Colonel Moore was able to do some socializing during this brief stay in Richmond (Withers 1967, 160). After staying two days in the capital city, they proceeded to Petersburg, arriving on the morning of March 27, 1862. Colonel Moore wrote a letter that morning from Petersburg (Sydenham Moore Papers). He notified his wife that the regiment was to depart that afternoon for Weldon, North Carolina. After their arrival at Petersburg the men had marched through the streets looking rather muddy and worn. Colonel Moore asserted how proud he was of his men no matter how they looked on the outside. Moore noted that some one hundred new recruits joined up with the regiment at Petersburg. Captain McMath was among those who rejoined the regiment here (McMath Diary). Later that afternoon the men took the cars of the Petersburg and Weldon Railroad to Weldon, North Carolina.

It was immediately upon their arrival at this place that General Wilcox was ordered by way of telegraph to return to Petersburg (Cadmus M. Wilcox Papers). We know that the regiment returned to Petersburg and then proceeded to City Point, Virginia. After their arrival at City Point the men boarded steamers upon which they traveled to King's Mill on the Peninsula (11th Alabama). On March 29, 1862, General Lee informed General Magruder, who was in command on the Peninsula, that Wilcox's Brigade was leaving that day from City Point for the Peninsula (Dowdey & Manarin 1961, 140); however, the brigade may have left as early as March 28 for King's Mill.[3] On either March 28 or 29, 1862, a steamer bearing the boys of the 11th Alabama docked at King's Landing.

The 11th Alabama's Position and Duties at Yorktown

After disembarking at King's Landing, the men made their way across the Peninsula to a small church that lay halfway between Williamsburg and Yorktown (Clark 1914, 17). This no doubt refers to what was known as Lebanon Church (11th Alabama). The church was about nine miles from King's Landing, and the regiment was placed in some surrounding woods (Cadmus M. Wilcox Papers; McMath Diary). Records remain of various commissary requisitions for the 11th Alabama were made from Lebanon Church almost through the entire month of April (CSR).[4] The regiment remained at Lebanon Church until April 4, 1862.[5] Late in the afternoon of April 4 Colonel Moore's boys were marched to within three miles of Yorktown at a place called Lee's Mill (McMath Diary).

There were several interesting developments that took place during this time of encampment at Lee's Mill. When the 11th Alabama broke camp from Lebanon Church it did so as an incomplete regiment. General Wilcox notes that from April 3, 1862, until after the battle of Williamsburg on May 5, 1862, the regiment had one company detached under the command of Maj. Archibald Gracie (Cadmus M. Wilcox Papers).[6] Major Gracie's command included one company from both the 11th and 9th Alabama, and two from the 10th Alabama Regiment. The purpose of this detachment concerned the completion of the redoubts near Yorktown about two miles below Lee's Mill. Gracie's Battalion, some 276 strong, became part of Kershaw's Brigade under McLaw's Division (OR Series 1, Vol. 11/3, 480).

Not only was a single company from Colonel Moore detached to form Gracie's Battalion, but in fact the entire regiment was detached while on duty on the Warwick River. The remaining nine companies were placed under the command of Gen. Howell Cobb of Georgia (McMath Diary). Wilcox, on the other hand, commanded the 2nd Brigade of the 3rd Division in the Army of the Peninsula (Cadmus M. Wilcox Papers). This detachment from Wilcox's Brigade would last the entire stay at Yorktown.

What exactly was it like at Lee's Mill? General Wilcox describes the defensive position along the Warwick River in the following terms:

> Earth works were constructed at various points from Yorktown to Lee's Mill on the Warwick....
> The Warwick river rises near Yorktown flows in a south easterly direction into the James River below Mulberry Point. For several miles it is but a small stream a few feet wide, of little depth, runs through a low, flat, and in many places boggy soil, its banks being covered with a heavy forest and thick undergrowth.
> On this stream were two mills, Wynne's and Lee's, the former three or four miles from Yorktown, and the latter a like distance below it. A short distance below Lee's Mill the Warwick river ceased to be practicable for fords. The dams of the two mills, and three others constructed by Magruder, blocked the water causing it to expand over the soil, until it had in many places a width of 150 or 200 yards, and a depth that made it difficult if not impossible for infantry to ford. The enemy was confronted by newly made earth works at every point accessible to him on this stream, over the narrow wood roads that were not very numerous and of an indifferent order [Cadmus M. Wilcox Papers].

The Lee's Mill entrenchment appears to have been quite adequate for the men. The position is described as a large, well-protected breastwork of logs, covered with dirt (OR Series 1, Vol. 11/1, 394). The breastworks themselves were erected upon the crest of a hill some seventy-five yards away from the stream. In one Federal report regarding the disposition of Lee's Mill, it was noted that the batteries were constructed upon very rugged elevated points (OR Series 1, Vol. 11/1, 396). Coupled with the large timber obstacles surrounding it, and the strategic rifle pits within the battery, it made for an extremely formidable obstacle. The 11th Alabama spent most of this brief period at Yorktown in and around the Lee's Mill defenses.

Camp Life of the 11th Alabama at Yorktown

What was life like for the men of Colonel Moore's regiment at Yorktown? What significant developments transpired while they were encamped at Yorktown? Life at Yorktown proved to be very similar to what had been experienced over the previous year near Manassas. Colonel Moore had made the statement in a letter to his wife just prior to breaking camp at Centreville that he would be glad to move even if the place was just as muddy. He got his wish at Yorktown. Dr. Sanders described the land as swampy, low, flat, sandy, and the provider of malaria for the men (Sanders's File). These desperate conditions proved especially hazardous for the new recruits of the regiment. In a letter dated April 22, 1862, Dr. Sanders writes that only two recruits of Co. C remained in camp, while all the rest had been shipped to hospitals. One searches in vain for a pleasant description of the land at the Yorktown defenses. Mention is made here and there of some of the beautiful homes that dot the area, yet the defenses on the Warwick River were anything but satisfactory.

The weather also contributed to the miserable conditions at Yorktown. It was a naturally swampy lowland to begin with, but added to this was an almost incessant rain pattern. Early in the encampment time at Lee's Mill Dr. Sanders noted that the weather had been terrible, and the men were totally exposed without tents (Sanders's File). E.P. Alexander gives one of the most vivid pictures of the horrible conditions due to the weather that can be found. He writes:

> It rained almost incessantly. The trenches were filled with water. No fires could be allowed.... The best drilled regulars the world has ever seen would have mutinied under a continuous service of twenty nine days in the trenches, exposed every moment to musketry and shells, in water to their knees....
>
> The trenches, which were principally in the flat and swampy land bordering the Warwick, filled with water as fast as opened, and could not be drained. ... moreover, so hastily constructed, that they barely afforded room for the line of battle to crouch in. ... the crowds huddled together in the water they soon became offensive beyond description [SHSP Vol. 10, 35–36].

General Wilcox summed it up best when he stated that the discomforts at Yorktown could not possibly be too highly colored (Cadmus M. Wilcox Papers). It rained several days each week upon the wet, flat, and swampy peninsula.

There appears to have been an inadequate supply of rations for the men at Yorktown. The reduced supply of rations that made their way to Yorktown were cooked back in the camps behind the lines, and were often brought to the trenches at night for distribution (SHSP Vol. 10, 35–36). Items such as coffee, sugar, and even hard bread were in scant supply for the men. They subsisted by and large on salt meats and flour. This state of affairs would not be remedied until the army was moved closer to Richmond in May.

Military Developments at Yorktown

Skirmishing was a constant reality at Yorktown. Alexander noted that the artillery fire of the enemy was kept up night and day at Yorktown (SHSP Vol. 10, 35–36). He also mentions the deadly fire of the sharpshooters, who could find their mark at 250 yards. Dr. Sanders writes that attacks were expected all the time at Yorktown, and that skirmishing was experienced day and night all along the Warwick (Sanders's File). He recorded one incident that had taken place very early in April of 1862:

> Several days ago we were marched up in the direction of Yorktown and passed through an open field in full view and within range of a battery the enemy had planted on the other side of the creek. This was the first time we had been brought under the fire of the enemy and you would have been no little surprised and somewhat amused at the manner in which we acted.

Instead of going through the field in double-quick, the men walked along as leisurely as if the guns were not pointed at them and at each discharge of their pieces they would raise a defiant shout and break out into a ha! ha! All this while the shells were being thrown at them with remarkable precision and rapidity. They passed a little too high however and bursted first on the other side of the line. One fell about fifty feet short of the Regt and bursted on the ground. Another passed only about six feet over their heads and bursted just after it had passed.

The men were subjected to various skirmishes during their entire stay; however, it does not appear that any of them proved to be of a serious nature.[7] Captain McMath entered the following in his diary which was typical for the entire time:

Marched to the battie on the right of lees mills while there the enemy threw some shot at us. we then marched one mile to the right in rear of our pickets who was keeping up a brisk fire with the enemy pickets. we remained there about three or four hours awaiting the movements of the enemy. when the firing between the pickets had pretty much ceased we were then marched back in rear ... just behind Lees Mills & bivouacked for the night [McMath Diary].

The pickets didn't always fire at one another at Yorktown. Clark recalls that occasionally the boys would swim across the river to get things from the Yankees, and in return they would give things to them (Clark 1914, 17–18).

During the regiment's encampment at Lee's Mill some of the members of Co. C expressed their dissatisfaction with Capt. John C.C. Sanders. Forty-eight men of Sanders's company signed a petition asking for his removal as Captain (Sanders's File). Captain Sanders felt that he was not being supported by his highest ranking officers other than Lieutenant Higginbotham. The reason they gave for asking for his removal was that he was too cross! Sanders read the petition, tore it up, and paid no attention to it again. He later brought the matter up to Colonels Moore and Hale as well as Adjutant Winn. They were absolutely astonished by such a movement, and told Sanders that they considered him to be one of the best captains in the regiment.

Captain Davidson of Co. F was not in the best of health at this time. On March 29, 1862, he was in Richmond receiving payment for his recruiting services and appears to have stayed there for health reasons (11th Alabama). On April 10 he wrote from the American Hotel in Richmond stating that he had been sick for nearly two months before his attack with the fever. Four days later he received medical recommendation that he be given an additional thirty days' leave of absence to recuperate from his sickness.

Dr. Sanders informs us in a correspondence dated April 9, 1862, that Dr. Ashe had been thinking about resigning his present position as Surgeon of the regiment (11th Alabama). Apparently he had been contemplating it for some time, but Dr. Sanders had prevailed upon him to remain. Dr. Ashe agreed to stay until the present crisis had subsided. Dr. Ashe kept his word. On June 21, 1862, Dr. Ashe was relieved of his position as Surgeon of the 11th Alabama (CSR).

On May 1, 1862, the complexion of the brigade was changed when the 38th Virginia was transferred to Jubal Early's Brigade (Gregory 1988, 13). The 38th Virginia would be replaced in the brigade by the 8th Alabama (Hoole 1985, 3). On this same day Richard M. Robertson was officially appointed Major in the Commissary Department, while 1st Lieutenant Samuel Vanzant of Co. H died (CSR).

The death toll continued to rise among the ranks of the 11th Alabama at Yorktown. From the time the regiment departed from Manassas, until the withdrawal from Yorktown, the following men died: George Law, David Elder and Sillman McJinsey from Co. D; John Griffin, William Herman, Marion Warren, and Cumberland F. Lovelady from Co. K; James Chism of Co. F; Arthur Corley, Edmund Landrum, and Charles Adams of Co. A; Thomas Martin and James Henderson of Co. E; Levi Young of Co. G; Thomas Jordan, Jesse Robinson, W.P. Massey, and John Copp of Co. C; Isaiah High and Anderson Crenshaw of Co. B (CSR).

General Johnston never believed that the Federal army could be destroyed at Yorktown. The enemy could only be held temporarily by the Warwick River defenses. The best course of action was to abandon these defenses and move toward Richmond, where the Confederate army could be consolidated and fight on better ground (Johnston 1959, 118–119). Upon reception of information that the powerful Federal batteries would be capable of going into action in a day or two, General Johnston ordered the withdrawal from Yorktown on May 3, 1862. Longstreet and Magruder's Divisions were to travel by the Hampton Road to Williamsburg, while G.W. Smith and D.H. Hill's Divisions were to take the Yorktown Road to Williamsburg. At about 8:00 P.M., May 3, 1862, the men began the march down Hampton Road to Williamsburg.

From Yorktown to Seven Pines

As we have already noted above, the regiment began its withdrawal from Lee's Mill around 8:00 P.M. on May 3, 1862. The men arrived at Williamsburg the next morning after a grueling all-night march (McMath Diary). Clark recalls that on this first night of the march there was a great deal of straggling (Clark 1914, 18). He recalls how General Cobb tried to encourage the men to close up the ranks as he himself struggled to remain awake on his horse. It is to be remembered that the regiment was still detached from General Wilcox during this withdrawal. Around 2:00 P.M. on May 4, the men left Williamsburg by way of the New Kent Road and marched until midnight (McMath Diary). The next day found the boys back on the muddy road fighting against the rain which fell all day long. At the day's end, they encamped at Diascund Bridge (Johnston 1959, 125). It was not until May 7 that the regiment finally reached New Kent Court House some twelve miles from Barhamsville.[8] The records seem to indicate that they may have marched south on May 9 toward the Chickahominy River. McMath states that they marched for the Chickahominy and arrived within two miles of the river (McMath Diary); likewise, Colonel Moore wrote his wife on May 9 stating that they were then on the Chickahominy (Sydenham Moore Papers). McMath in his very accurate diary writes that between May 10–14 the regiment was marched back towards New Kent, and then marched to the left of that road in a series of movements (McMath Diary). On May 14, 1862, the 11th Alabama finally rejoined General Wilcox at the Long Bridge encampment.

One day after rejoining the Wilcox Brigade, the order was given to cross the Chickahominy River (Johnston 1959, 128). Johnston felt compelled to move the army closer to Richmond due to the attack on Drewry's Bluff that very day (OR Series 1, Vol. 11/1, 276). This new location was about six to seven miles from Richmond. The regiment then took up the march on May 16 and 17 until they reached a position about three miles from Richmond on the River Road (Cadmus M. Wilcox Papers). The line of the army was in front of the old redoubts that had been constructed in 1861. This position was very agreeable to Colonel Moore. He wrote his wife that they were near the James River, the land was lovely, and the people very kind and hospitable (Sydenham Moore Papers). At this location there were ample supplies of everything the army had lacked at Yorktown. Being part of Longstreet's Division,[9] the Wilcox Brigade formed the army's right covering the River Road, Hill's Division the center over the Williamsburg Road, and Magruder the left covering the Nine Mile Road (Cadmus M. Wilcox Papers).

The boys were soon moved again. On May 17, 1862, they reached the Charles City Road encampment. This location was some three and a half miles from Richmond (11th Alabama). While the regiment was in this encampment Assistant Surgeon Jolly was relieved of his duties.[10] In addition, Lieutenant Colonel Hale was placed in command of the 9th Alabama by special assignment.[11] Colonel Moore was lamenting in a letter dated May 24, 1862, that with Gracie in Mobile, and Hale assigned to the 9th Alabama, he was without a field officer (Sydenham Moore Papers).

McMath recalls that the regiment was sent out on picket on May 22, 1862, until May 24, 1862, at Drewry's Bluff (McMath Diary). Nothing worthy of note took place on this picket duty. McMath also wrote that they were constantly engaged in drilling. Here they remained until May 27 when Longstreet's Division moved near the Mechanicsville Turnpike.[12] This location was only about one and a half miles north of Richmond, and it was chosen in preparation for a strike on the Federal right, west of the Chickahominy (Longstreet 1992, 85). The Wilcox Brigade was the Fourth Brigade of Longstreet's Division, which now consisted of the 8th, 9th, 10th, and 11th Alabama regiments.

It should also be noted that from the time of the removal from the peninsula until the Battle of Seven Pines, there were more deaths in the regiment: William Cope and Edward Rainwater of Co. E, Richard McCulley of Co. B, Enoch Erwin of Co. G, Elijah Pridmore and Charles Stewart of Co. H, and Gilbert Reynolds and James Gordon of Co. C (CSR).

The Battle of Seven Pines

General Johnston wished to strike the Federal army while it was divided by the Chickahominy. Key's and Heintzelman's Corps were isolated from McClellan's right wing, north of the Chickahominy; while this state of affairs existed General Johnston determined to destroy this manageable portion of the Federal forces (Johnston 1959, 132–133). The three roads leading to the Federal army were the key to Johnston's plan of attack. D.H. Hill's Division was to deliver the main attack on the Williamsburg Road, Longstreet's Division was to march down the Nine Mile Road to attack on Hill's left, and Huger's Division would march down the Charles City Road to secure Hill's right flank. The attack was to be launched as soon as possible on May 31, 1862. It began to rain on the eve of the attack, and it rained torrentially all night long (Clark 1914, 18). In General Johnston's mind, this cloudburst was working in the South's favor since the Chickahominy would now be too swollen for any communication between the Federal army's two wings (Johnston 1959, 134).

The 11th Alabama's March to Seven Pines

The men arose to a soggy quagmire the morning of May 31, 1862. With rations prepared beforehand, the men broke camp around 6–6:30 A.M. Longstreet decided to send his forces down the Williamsburg Road rather than the Nine Mile Road.[13] In making their way over to the Williamsburg Road they encountered the flooded grounds around Gillis Creek (Longstreet 1992, 91). Due to this creek's swollen condition, the men were forced to build a bridge across it (Freeman 1970, 232). While this work on the bridge was being conducted, the men of Huger's division reached the scene on their way to the Charles City Road. The Wilcox Brigade passed over the Gillis Creek toward the juncture of the Williamsburg and Charles City roads. The Brigade reached this crossroads well before noon, and then waited some three or four hours in order to allow Huger's men to pass by them on to the Charles City Road (*ibid.*, 238). It was now about 3:30 P.M.

General Longstreet decided to send Wilcox's Brigade, along with Pryor's and Colston's, along the Charles City Road with Huger's Division as a support to them. General Wilcox was in command of three of these brigades which took up the rear of the march. After the march had gotten underway, Wilcox was then ordered to precede Huger's two brigades (Cadmus M. Wilcox Papers). After getting into position at the head of the column, General Wilcox received additional orders to countermarch, return to the Williamsburg Road, and to proceed in the rear of the troops on that road. The men had countermarched abut a mile toward the Williamsburg Road when orders were again received to continue down the Charles City Road! As they marched down the Charles City Road they were told to keep abreast with the firing that could be heard down the Williamsburg Road. Clark recalls the rather circuitous march of May 31:

> We marched and countermarched all morning, now taking one road, then reversing our steps and taking the other. Finally about noon the roar of cannon announced the opening of battle and we were marched steadily toward that point [Clark 1914, 19].

One final order came to General Wilcox as they trudged along the Charles City Road. In written form, Wilcox was ordered to proceed at once to the Williamsburg Road crossing over what paths and country roads were available (Cadmus M. Wilcox Papers). A guide was provided to assist their march across the divide between the two roads. The land between the two roads was low and flat, and of course very muddy due to the deluge the night before. At points the way was actually waist-deep in water. It was about a two-mile march through mainly swamp, but finally the men arrived on the Williamsburg Road about 5:00 P.M. General Longstreet was rather puzzled by the delay of Wilcox to the battle front. General Longstreet had his headquarters under a large tree, and it was here that the two generals engaged in a conversation about the route taken by Wilcox. General Wilcox recorded some of their conversation together:

> When the head of my column reached the Williamsburg road, Longstreet said, "you have taken good deal of time to reach this road," it was this question that caused me to report the orders and counter orders, the marches, and counter marches he had given and I had executed [Cadmus M. Wilcox Papers].

General Wilcox was not about to shoulder the blame for the tardiness of his arrival. He wanted Longstreet to know that he was only following orders.

THE 11TH ALABAMA ENGAGES THE ENEMY AT SEVEN PINES

Seven Pines was the first battle fought by the 11th Alabama. Colonel Moore was very anxious about getting into the fray, and probably told General Wilcox of his excitement. Clark over heard Wilcox and Longstreet talking about one commander who had been in several wars in the past, but had never been in a battle (Clark 1914, 19). It seems most likely that they were speaking about Col. Sydenham Moore. Little did they know that Moore's first battle would be his last. Some his last recorded words reveal his desire to engage the enemy:

> It is certain (I suppose) that a great battle must come off here very soon. It will be the greatest perhaps of the war. I hope to acquit myself well and also to survive it.... But I feel that I am doing my duty & battling for my wife & children & repelling a foe ... for my heart & mind & soul are enlisted in the cause [Sydenham Moore Papers].

General Wilcox reported that almost immediately upon their arrival to the front the leading regiment of the brigade, the 11th Alabama, was ordered to report to General D.H. Hill (Cadmus M. Wilcox Papers). The enemy had been driven from his first line of defense in an open field called Casey's Redoubts. Federal forces retreated back into the woods across the field from this first line of defense. Hill wanted to continue to drive the Federals, but he needed additional support to do so; accordingly, General Hill ordered the 11th to report to General Kemper (OR Series 1, Vol. 11/1, 986).

The first line of defense had been taken prior to the Alabamians' arrival. The first maneuver undertaken by the regiment was to cross the open field in front of this first line of captured redoubts. Colonel Moore led the way across the field, all the while the men were under torturous fire from the reformed Federal line in the woods beyond. Dr. Sanders records some thoughts about this first charge across the open field to Casey's Redoubts:

> Col Moore in front, we passed through an open field under a heavy fire in front of the enemy's works formed first behind a ditch then we moved just in front & sheltered ourselves by the enemy's works, they having been driven back into the woods.
>
> While passing through this field several of the regiment were killed & wounded Col Moore's horse was killed under him, several were also struck behind the ditch & while moving up to the enemy's works. Col Moore's watch was struck and completely shattered [Sanders's File].

The regiment was now crouched down behind the first line of redoubts, and were still under fire from the Federals' second line of defense in the woods. The men stayed in this position about a half an hour (McMath's Diary).

Clark recalls that about this time Colonel Gordon of the 6th Alabama asked him for three companies to go over and dislodge some sharpshooters on the right near a house in the woods (Clark 1914, 19–20). Clark told him he would need to speak with Colonel Moore. Moore told Gordon he could have the entire regiment if he needed it. Rather than ordering one of his company captains to lead these three detached companies, Colonel Moore led them himself.[14] Moving across the field at a run, Colonel Moore was shot in the leg just below the knee (Sanders's File).[15] N.B. Hogan of Co. A recalls the wounding of Colonel Moore:

Seven Pines marker. Here was McClellan's second line of defense that was broken with the aid of fresh troops sent in by General Longstreet.

When within fifty paces or less of the enemy's battery, which was flanked on either side by parallel lines of well-constructed earthworks, Col. Moore who, on foot, and near the right file of our company, threw his hand to his right side and staggered as if in the act of falling. Several of the boys rushed to him and gently laid him down. Soon afterwards he was taken to the rear where Dr. Ash, our regimental surgeon, dressed his wounds [*Confederate Veteran 1893–1912*. Vol. 10, 169].

Wilcox records that this action proved successful, but at the same time very costly. In a matter of some ten minutes it cost the regiment sixty-six in killed and wounded (OR Series 1, Vol. 11/1, 987). With the enemy now driven back from the woods toward their second line of defense, the stage was set for another charge.

McMath affirms that with the enemy in retreat the men formed up, crossed over the entrenchments, and drove the enemy from their position in the woods (McMath Diary). It is not clear from this description whether the entire regiment pursued the enemy into the woods, or whether it was the three detached companies. Clark gives the impression that only the three detached units actually charged the enemy, while the seven other companies were not under severe fire (Clark 1914, 19–20). General Wilcox clearly stated years later that the whole regiment was not engaged at Seven Pines, but only the small detachment under Colonel Moore (SHSP Vol. 6, 77).[16] What is very clear is that the 11th Alabama took part in what General Longstreet called some of the severest part of the work (SHSP Vol. 3, 278). The fighting in which the regiment was engaged contributed to deciding the day in the favor of the Confederates. The Federals were successfully driven from their second line of defense at Seven Pines. Longstreet commended Colonel Moore as well as General Wilcox for their gallantry and ability.

After this culminating breakthrough of the enemy's works the regiment was formed in line of battle again (McMath Diary; OR Series 1, Vol. 11/1, 987). No attack was ordered, nor was a Federal counterattack launched due to the late hour. At about 10:00 P.M. the regiment was ordered about a mile forward to their place of encampment for the night. General Wilcox describes this rather eerie march:

> In reaching this position we passed over the ground from which the enemy had been driven through two of their captured camps and bivouacked in a third. The night was intensely dark, and as the troops moved along the cries of the enemy's wounded were heard in the woods and swamps on the right and left, in many places the water being knee deep [*ibid.*].

It was around 1:00 A.M. before the men finally reached a spot that was tolerably suitable for sleeping. General Wilcox described this area as a open field some 300 yards wide and 1200 yards long. The boys found a sutler's tent full of food and champagne (Clark 1914, 20). They were able to treat themselves to some hard-won delicacies before bedding down for the night.[17]

The 11th Alabama on the Second Day at Seven Pines

June 1, 1862, opened with the firing of muskets from the enemy. The sounds revealed that the enemy was both in the front and rear of the brigade (OR Series 1, Vol. 11/1, 987). The regiments of Wilcox's Brigade were formed in line of battle in order to receive the anticipated attack. Some concentrated fire was felt by the 9th Alabama; therefore Captain McMath's Company was detached to lend support to that regiment (McMath Diary). General Wilcox recalls that although the battle began to heat up, he felt fully confident that a Federal repulse was imminent (Cadmus M. Wilcox Papers). It was at this point of the conflict that orders were received to withdraw.[18] The Federal forces did not pursue the retreating forces of Wilcox. The men were eventually withdrawn to the field near the captured Federal entrenchments at Seven Pines. The next morning on June 2, the Brigade returned to their encampments near Richmond (McMath Diary).

The 11th Alabama Casualties at Seven Pines

The only regiment of the Wilcox Brigade that was engaged on May 31 was the 11th Alabama (Cadmus M. Wilcox Papers). Of this regiment, Companies A, D, and F were the hardest hit. As I indicated earlier, this probably implies that they were the three detached companies led by Colonel Moore. At the top of the casualty list is Col. Sydenham Moore. General Wilcox gives Colonel Moore the highest commendation:

> Col. Sydenham Moore, Eleventh Alabama, an officer of great promise, yielding to an exuberance of courage, received two wounds, one of which proved mortal, while in command of but three companies of his regiment that had been ordered to dislodge the enemy from [an] advanced position held by them. The loss of such an officer must be seriously felt by both the service in general and his regiment, and to the former he [is] scarcely reparable [OR Series 1, Vol. 11/1, 988].

Colonel Moore was taken to Richmond. There was some hope that he might recover from his wounds (*The Alabama Beacon* [Greensboro], 13 June 1862). He was to linger on until August 20, 1862, when he finally succumbed to the wounds inflicted upon him in his brave charge at Seven Pines.

Company D, the Canebrake Legion, was hard hit at Seven Pines. They had five men killed, one missing, and at least eight wounded. Those killed were: Joseph Compton, Thomas W. Oakley,[19] Sam Turner, Benjamin F. Jordan, and William Williamson; those wounded were the following: Captain Tayloe, James W. Blunt (lost his left leg), Ralph Barton, Andrew Barr, William Compton, Nathan Hankins, Robert Patterson, and Robert Elmore. John Sentell was apparently captured (CSR). Captain Tayloe was shot in the foot and instep while leading his detached company under Colonel Moore. Dr. Sanders initially thought that he would probably lose his foot.

Company F, the Bibb Greys, also lost heavily at Seven Pines. Those killed were: Milton Carson (ball through the chest), William Childress, John M. Davis; those wounded were the following: John C. Henry (severely wounded in the right shoulder), Barney Kornegy (mortally wounded), George Mayberry (mortally wounded), Henry Davis, Fredrick James, Newton Smitherman, Jasper Spinks, James Suttle, George Woodruff, David Griffin, Richard Hogan, John Moses (severely wounded in both thighs), William N. Green (left arm), and William Brown (CSR; Sanders's File; 11th Alabama). Company F had at least seventeen killed and wounded.

Company A, the Marengo Rifles, was no doubt the third company, along with Companies F and D, that was detached for service under Colonel Moore. Those killed were the following: Anderson Crawford (he died from the effects of his wound in the bowels on June 13, 1862), Wesley Norred, and Benjamin Norred;[20] those who were wounded included the following: Henry Brame, James H.E. Adams, Jesse Parker,[21] and Capt. Thomas H. Holcomb. Holcomb had the third finger of his left hand shot off (Sanders's File). He was also in command of one of the detached companies under Colonel Moore.

The remaining companies had only slight casualties. Company I had Robert Smith, Aurelius Dumas, Richard C. Terry (left wrist), and Jesse Vaile wounded, and James Kirkland killed (11th Alabama). Company E had Walter E. Winstanley killed. He was the first man killed in Co. E. Company B had William Morris severely wounded, George Brewer of Co. G lost his right leg, and Milus Moorehead of Co. H was wounded. Finally, both William Phillips and Napoleon Curb of Co. K were wounded, while F.M. Morton was killed. If we take all the confirmed casualties of the 11th Alabama at Seven Pines and add them together we come up with thirteen killed, thirty-seven wounded or missing. The city of Richmond had literally been transformed into a hospital at this time. One reporter gives his description of the city:

> Every person in Richmond, male and female, is busily engaged in caring for the many wounded men now in the city. The hospitals are crowded, and at nearly every house can be seen evidences of hospital arrangements.... The stores are closed and the whole air of the town is very like that of a quarantined city [*Mobile Register and Advertiser*, 10 June 1862].

From Seven Pines to Gaines' Mill

The soldiers marched back to their camp near the Mechanicsville Turnpike the day after the battle of Seven Pines. They arrived in their camp by 8:00 A.M. on June 2, 1862 (McMath Diary). The very next day they were again ordered to return to the Seven Pines battlefield in anticipation of an attack. This proved to be a false alarm, and after a couple of days they again returned to Richmond (McMath Diary; Clark 1914, 21). Some time around June 10, the regiment marched to a new encampment across the Charles City Road about three quarters of a mile from its junction with the Williamsburg Road (Cadmus M. Wilcox Papers). This would remain the brigade's camp until the day of battle at Gaines' Mill.

There were a couple of minor movements of the regiment before Gaines' Mill that we need to note. The men were marched out from camp on June 13 in order to provide assistance for Jeb Stuart's re-crossing of the Chickahominy. They had no engagement with the enemy, and they returned to camp the next day. On June 25 there was a serious skirmish near Mahone's position. They moved to assist Mahone late that afternoon and then returned to camp that evening without incident.

We should also mention some needed leadership appointments. Samuel H. Vanzant, 1st Lieutenant of Co. H, actually died prior to the battle of Seven Pines (CSR). He had been admitted to General Hospital No. 18,[22] where he died with typhoid fever on May 1, 1862. James H. Moorehead was appointed 1st Lieutenant in Vanzant's stead on June 9, 1862. In addition, Alonzo B. Cohen was appointed 2nd Lieutenant of Co. H on May 30, 1862 (CSR). On June 10, 1862, Capt. Reuben Chapman of Co. H tendered his resignation from the service. He cited his physical problems that had made it impossible for him to carry out his duties in the field. Martin L. Stewart was made Captain in place of Chapman. On June 20, 1862, Capt. James Davidson of Co. F offered his letter of resignation. He also cited his physical inability to carry out his rigorous duties in the field. The day after Davidson's resignation as Captain, Dr. W.C. Ashe was relieved of his duties as the regimental surgeon. On June 2, 1862, William Brazelton of Co. K was appointed the new Sergeant Major; it proved to be a position he maintained throughout the remainder of the war.

In about one year's time the 11th Alabama had already gone through some major changes in command. Colonel Moore, Major Gracie, Captain Moody, Captain Davidson, Captain Chapman, Captain Traweek, Captain Talbird, and Surgeon Ashe were no longer a part of the regiment. The changes were far from over. The battle of Gaines' Mill would bring about some additional changes in command.

The Battle of Gaines' Mill

As the early morning hours dawned on June 26, 1862, the regiments of the Fourth Brigade commanded by General Wilcox began their march toward the Mechanicsville Turnpike (Cadmus M. Wilcox Papers). The Fourth Brigade of Longstreet's Division consisted of the 8th, 9th, 10th, and 11th Alabama Regiments, as well as the Thomas Artillery (OR Series 1, Vol. 11/2, 486). As the brigade came to a halt near the Mechanicsville Bridge, General Wilcox reflected upon the strategy of the battle which was to come. Lee hoped to hurl back the Federal right, which was now located to the north of the Chickahominy River. In order to accomplish this objective, Generals Jackson and A.P. Hill were to work in concert in driving the enemy from Mechanicsville. With this being accomplished, D.H. Hill and Longstreet's divisions could cross the Mechanicsville Bridge in support of Jackson and A.P. Hill (Dowdey & Manarin 1961, 199). Now the four divisions were to unite and proceed down the Chickahominy in a culminating sweep of the Federal right wing.

As the day began to wear away, so had the patience of A.P. Hill. He was not to cross the bridge before hearing from General Jackson. Around 3:00 P.M. Hill decided to wait no longer; he proceeded across the Chickahominy and soon was engaged with the enemy. The men of the 11th Alabama could hear clearly the firing of artillery and musketry, along with the shouts of soldiers engaged in the heat of battle (Clark 1914, 21). Another shout was heard by the men, but this was a shout of a different kind. The talk was of President Davis, and how he had been to the front and was now returning home. Sure enough, President Davis came riding by at full speed, hat in hand, to the shouts of the soldiers in the ranks. Soon after this the brigade reformed amidst the growing darkness and crossed over the Mechanicsville Bridge. Somewhere between the bridge and Mechanicsville, the men — now led by Stephen Fowler Hale — bivouacked for the night.

The morning of June 27 dawned with the resumption of artillery fire. Much of this shelling was very near the men's camp, and yet it did very little damage (Cadmus M. Wilcox Papers). After being ordered to come to the assistance of Pryor and Featherston's Brigades at Ellerson's Mill, and rendering needed artillery support, the Wilcox Brigade resumed the march along the Chickahominy. The Wilcox Brigade was on the extreme right while Pryor's Brigade was on the left. As they marched toward Gaines' Mill, three of the four regiments were in line of battle, while the fourth was in the center of the rear line. Before reaching the Gaines' House, Featherston's Brigade rejoined the continued march. Passing through a heavy pine forest the men finally reached the house of Dr. Gaines.

The attack against the enemy position had already been opened by General A.P Hill. General Longstreet informed Wilcox that he should prepare his men for an attack in support of A.P. Hill. The signal for the attack would be the opening of fire on their left. All the while the brigade was being formed they were under artillery fire from across the Chickahominy. Wilcox placed the 11th Alabama on the front line on the right, with the 10th Alabama on the left. Behind these lead regiments, the 8th and 9th Alabama regiments were aligned (Cadmus M. Wilcox Papers). Pryor's Brigade was on the left with Featherston's in reserve. General Wilcox recalls how bravely the boys conducted themselves at this most critical moment:

> It is proper to state that, while assigning the troops to their positions prepatory to the advance, the enemy's artillery on heights beyond the Chickahominy were directing upon them continous and brisk fire. The men of the three brigades behaved admirably under this fire, no confusion or disorder being perceptible in the ranks [Cadmus M. Wilcox Papers].

Lieutenant Clark recalls the moments just prior to the command to march (Clark 1914, 22). He was engaged in a conversation with Colonel Woodward of the 10th Alabama. While they were talking a courier arrived with a message for the Colonel. He was instructed to be sure and keep up with the line of the 11th Alabama. The Colonel replied, "The 11th Alabama had better look out or we will get ahead of them."

Soon the command was given to go forward over the crest of the hill leading down to the dried creek bed. Upon the reaching the crest of the hill they immediately came under blistering infantry fire. From this elevated position the men could see what they were up against: three lines of Federal breastworks. The first line, closest to the dried creek bed, served as a rifle pit. About halfway up the tree-studded slope opposite the creek bed was the second defensive line. This line, as well as the third at the crest of the slope, was well-constructed of

Part of the old Gaines' Mill battlefield as it looks today.

logs. The men faced the task of descending to the dried creek bed, and then ascending in the face of three lines of entrenchments. To say that the Federal position was a strong one is an understatement. One veteran of Co. A recalls this sight:

> Across a deep, open ravine some three hundred yards in front, we could plainly see three lines of Federal infantry — one at the base, one about midway up, and one near the top of the opposite hillside from where we lay. Each one of their lines was protected by an abatis of heavy timber, which had been felled for their protection.
>
> Looking across the Chickahominy, to our right and about three-fourths of a mile distant, we could see huge pieces of siege guns with their black muzzles pointing down our lines and blue-coated men standing ready for action [*Confederate Veteran 1893–1912* Vol. 6, 567].

Down the hill the men dashed in the face of the enemy's musketry. Many men were killed before they reached the bottom of the slope. Lieutenant Clark was shot in the arm as he reached the bottom (Clark 1914, 23). He determined to return to the field hospital in the rear of the lines. His words capture something of the awful nature of this bloody conflict:

> ...reaching a low wash at the foot of the hills, I was struck in the arm and the blood flowed freely, looking as if an artery had been severed. I at once retired and went back to the field hospital at Gaines Palm, and the route back was filled with wounded soldiers. The ambulance was in service carrying those who could not walk. When I reached the hospital my eyes never beheld such a spectable. There were thousands apparently wounded, and of all the groans, cries, curses and prayers that went from them! Surgeons were busy operating on them, taking off arms and legs [Clark 1914, 23].

Clark's wound was tended by a Catholic priest who also gave him a bottle of brandy. With his wound cleaned and dressed, Clark sat down and emptied the bottle into his stomach!

The men remained only briefly at the bottom of the slope before rushing forward to the enemy's first line of defense. From this rifle pit came close-range fire into the ranks of the 11th and 10th Alabama. The boys pushed their way over this first line, only to be blasted by the second and third lines of Yankees. There was some wavering among the men at this time. One report stated that General Wilcox threatened to behead the first man that hesitated (*The Alabama Beacon* [Greensboro], 20 July 1862). Quickly the 8th and 9th Alabama Regiments came to the support of the leading regiments. The gallant struggle is best captured in General Wilcox's own words:

> Nothing could surpass the firery valor, the irresistable impetousity of the men. They encountered the enemy in large force behind two lines of breastworks, the second overlooking the first, and from this as well as the first, a close and terrible fire of musketry was poured out upon them. The bed of the small stream directly in front of the first fortified line was used as a rifle pit, and from this also for a few minutes there was fire. Thus exposed to three lines of fire, they bravely confronted it all, pressing forward closed in upon the enemy. ... our men full of confidence, rushed on with irresistable force; and he was driven out of the stream over the first breastwork pell mell, and here vainly attempted to reform and then a bold front, but closely followed he yielded and was driven over and beyond his second log into the standing timber, and finally into the open field in rear [Cadmus M. Wilcox Papers].

The pursuit of the Federals was ended only by nightfall. Many prisoners and artillery pieces were taken by day's end.

Clearly the men of the 11th and 10th Alabama Regiments suffered the greatest in this charge. In retrospect, one veteran wondered how any of them ever escaped death climbing over that ridge (*Confederate Veteran 1893–1912* Vol. 8, 443). Several accounts of bravery need to be mentioned in connection with this charge. The Color Sergeant of Co. C, John B. Maxwell, had thirteen balls in his body when he fell at Gaines' Mill (Cadmus M. Wilcox Papers). Banbury Jones of Co. D picked up the colors from Maxwell, and very quickly his right arm was broken, then he held the colors with his left hand! Both of his legs were shot through, and then his left arm was wounded. The colors were then given to a third soldier over the protestations of Banbury. He complained to Lieutenant Winn in the following words:

> ...my arms are broken and I am shot through both legs but I can walk, and I asked them to tie the flag staff to my body and I would and could still carry it, and they would not do it [Cadmus M. Wilcox Papers].

Private Jones would be discharged on December 2, 1862, due to the wounds he received in the right arm and left hip (CSR). Fred Solley of Co. A provided the boys with a little humor in the midst of horror at Gaines' Mill (*Confederate Veteran 1893–1912* Vol. 6, 568). A Minié ball tore off the first joint of his right forefinger, and then it embedded itself into his thigh. He fell down with his feet and hands hoisted up in the air and yelled, "Boys, for God's sake don't tramp on me!" Finally, note should be made of the commendation paid to Surgeon Sanders by General Wilcox (Cadmus M. Wilcox Papers). Dr. Sanders is commended for the both prompt and efficient manner in which he attended to the many wounded at Gaines' Mill.

The Casualties of the 11th Alabama at Gaines' Mill

Lieutenant Colonel Stephen Fowler Hale was mortally wounded in the battle. He had taken over the command when Colonel Moore was mortally wounded at Seven Pines. Three balls pierced the body of Colonel Hale, breaking both his left arm and shoulder, as well as his left leg (Cadmus M. Wilcox Papers). The initial reports concerning Colonel Hale were mixed. Some of the early reports stated that he was doing well, while others stated that he was mortally wounded (*The Alabama Beacon* [Greensboro], 4 July 1862). Colonel Hale lingered on until July 18 or 19, 1862, before he died in Richmond (CSR).[23] Upon his wounding on the battlefield, Maj. George Field took command of the regiment.

In one report the total number of casualties sustained at Gaines' Mill by the 11th Alabama was 168 killed and wounded (Sanders's File). The following is the breakdown of casualties among the various companies of the regiment.[24] Company A had no one killed, but the following eleven men were wounded: John R. Coats, William Griffith (ball in leg), John Hayes, Lucius Huckabee (thigh), William Ross, Fredrick Solley, William Worthington (thigh), William Young, Alexander Wayne (right side), Thomas H. Johnson (shoulder), and Alfred Johnson (mortally wounded).[25]

Of the sixteen casualties in Co. B, three men were killed: Henry Caulfield, Robert H. Lamb, and James F. Allen. The following men were wounded: Joseph Clark (wounded in left arm; amputated), George Clark (wounded in the arm), Benjamin Gordon (wounded in leg), Robert Hamlet (wounded in hand), James Kimbrough (wounded in thigh), Cicero Kirksey (wounded in shoulder and leg), Joseph Merrill (wounded in head), Martin Norris (wounded in leg), Abner Patton (mortally wounded in lungs), William Robuck (wounded in side), Elisha Woods (wounded in head; ball still in head), Thomas Avery (wounded in hand), and Calvin Edmiston (wounded in head).

The Confederate Guards suffered twenty-four killed and wounded in the ranks. John Maxwell, Robert Archibald, John B. Baines, Francis Eatman, and Thomas Richardson were all killed. Wounded: Thomas Childers, Josiah Collins (mortally wounded), Robert Gordon (wounded in leg), Wilson Gathright (wounded in foot), Erlander M. Richardson (wounded in arm), James Breathwait (wounded in thigh), Moses Baskin (wounded in leg), James Duncan (wounded in arm), Rufus Harris, Thomas Lanford (mortally wounded; died August 17, 1862), Thomas Lowry, John Murphy (wounded in arm),[26] David Montgomery (wounded in arm),

Monument to Wilcox's Alabama Brigade for their part in the battle of Gaines' Mill.

James Paschal (wounded in hand), William H.H. Sanders (wounded in leg), Thomas Sullivan (mortally wounded in thigh), James Stafford (wounded in shoulder), Robert Waller (wounded in leg), and Thomas Moore (wounded in body). Company C shared with Co. F the distinction of having the highest number of men killed on the battlefield of Gaines' Mill.

Captain Tayloe's men suffered twenty casualties on June 27. James Dossett, Richard Gullett, and Franklin Wright were killed. Henry Cabe (wounded in arm), Thomas Cathey (wounded in hand), Banbury Jones (wounded in arm and leg), William Hummell (wounded in foot), Thomas Askew (wounded in leg and thighs), Jesse Burton (wounded in head), John Deans (wounded in hand), William Ellington (wounded in head), William Percell (wounded in hand), William Pegues (wounded in hip), Simon Rawls (wounded in face), James Stewart (wounded in breast), Strudwick Young (wounded in leg), Thomas Prince (mortally wounded in hip; died July 12, 1862), Nathan Hankins (wounded in hand), Charles Kirker (wounded in face), and Warren A. Anderson (wounded in thigh). Company E suffered the fewest casualties of all the companies at Gaines' Mill. The only man killed on the field was William Faith. Several men were mortally wounded, including Jack Simpson and Allen Shultz. Finally, John Jones and Dan James were wounded.

Twenty-one men were either killed or wounded in the ranks of Co. F. Andrew Garner, Newton Spinks, Lewis Taylor, Josiah Kennedy, and Jacob Taylor were all killed. The list of wounded includes: Robert Campbell (mortally wounded in the left thigh; died July 5, 1862), Daniel Corley, John Johnson, Henry Avery (wounded in left hand), Richard Brown, Oliver Fitts (mortally wounded in left thigh), Moses Lightsey, John McArthur, Marion Oldham, Fredrick James, John Digby, Pilgrim Espey (mortally wounded), David Lightsey, Benjamin Sanford, Absalom James (ball passed through his chest), and Cadir Smith.

The Tuscaloosa Rifles had Jesse Pumphrey killed, and Joseph Ray along with John Dodds mortally wounded in the leg (Ray died July 18, 1862, and Dodds died June 30, 1862). John Carroll, Joseph Britt, Charles Farrington, Thomas Finley (right thigh), Raleigh Gaddy, Thomas Hamner, Stephen Barber, William Gossett, Jesse Hughes, James McGee, Francis Rosser (leg), William Adams, and William Ashworth were all wounded.

Martin Stewart's men suffered more casualties than any other company at Gaines' Mill. Of the twenty-eight that are listed, Thomas Jay, John Sanders, and James Seymore were killed. Wounded: Reuben Thom, Martin Stewart (wounded in face), George Craig (wounded in shoulder), James Davis (wounded in thigh), William Davis (wounded in thigh and arm), Alexander Dunlap (wounded in hand), Benjamin Ferguson, Elijah Foster (wounded in foot), Calvin Free (wounded in head), James Hemphill (wounded in thigh), James Hodo (wounded in side), Robert Miller (wounded in left shoulder, hip, foot, and leg), Milus Moorehead (wounded in arm, thigh, and side), Horatio Nabers (wounded in thigh), Josiah Stewart (wounded in leg and arm; died July 2/5, 1862), Davidson Stoker (wounded in the left arm), Wiley B. Woods (had a leg amputated), Andrew Story (wounded in hand), John Wier (wounded in leg), William T. Bryant (wounded in foot), Frank H. Black (wounded in leg and head), David Ballard (wounded in hip), Joseph Everett, Daniel F. Johnson (wounded in head), and John Richardson (wounded and suffered amputation of his arm).

Company I had three mortally wounded: Thomas Hollingsworth, Andrew Foster, Jedidiah Smith. Two men were killed on the field: Oran White, and D.W. Williams. The wounded list includes: Abel Walden, Rufus Shelton, Lemuel Harris, Francis Brotherton, Samuel Black, Francis Gregg, Benjamin F.R. Harris (right leg), William Kirkland, Allen Propst, Reuben Stewart, James Terry (knee), Thomas Wimberly, James Oliver, and George Strickland.

James Goff was the only member of Co. K to be killed at this battle. John Austin, Peter

Casey (left foot), James J. Cook, James B. Cook, James George, Robert H. Griffin, John Guthrie, Felix Kirk (mortally wounded), William King, Henry Lea, George Morton (made totally deaf), William Massingale, and Thomas Ballard (mortally wounded). As we add together from all the companies the casualty figures it comes to a total of twenty-four killed, and 151 wounded or mortally wounded.

From Gaines' Mill to Frayser's Farm

The battered men of the 11th Alabama rested on the Gaines' Mill battlefield until the morning of June 29, 1862, when orders were received to move to a new location south of Richmond. With both ranking field officers incapacitated, Maj. George Field of Co. B was in temporary command of the regiment. Captain Sanders was also now acting as a field officer by virtue of his being the second ranking officer in the regiment (Sanders's File). There wasn't much time to ponder these regimental changes; General McClellan was now on the march for the James River. McClellan had decided to change his base to the James, and in order to do so it was necessary for him for cross the discouraging White Oak Swamp (OR Series 1 Vol. 11/1, 59–61). Lee's plan was simple: he wanted to intercept McClellan's army before it reached the safety of the gunboats on the James River. General Jackson was to assail the Federals' rear, Huger was to take the Charles City Road and attack the enemy's flank, and Longstreet along

Intersection of Nine Mile Road and the Richmond and York River Railroad as it looks today. The 11th Alabama passed through here on their way to Frayser's Farm.

with A.P. Hill's Division was to travel down the Darbytown Road and attack the Federal flank at Huger's right. Holmes was to attack on Longstreet's right proceeding down the New Market Road (Downey & Manarin 1961, 217–218).

The brigades of Wilcox's Division moved out from Gaines' Mill on the morning of June 29 and soon crossed over the Chickahominy at New Bridge (Cadmus M. Wilcox Papers). They marched down the Nine Mile Road over the York River Railroad, and reached the junction of the Williamsburg and Charles City Road around 2:00 P.M. After an hour's rest, the men continued down the Darbytown Road until reaching Mr. Atlee's Farm where they bivouacked for the night.

The Battle of Frayser's Farm

The battle was fought on June 30, 1862, and was to prove to be as bloody a conflict as the 11th Alabama would ever face. The men broke their camp near Mr. Atlee's Farm at around 6:00 A.M., and continued their march down the Darbytown Road (Cadmus M. Wilcox Papers). The Darbytown Road eventually intersects with the Long Bridge Road; upon reaching this junction the brigade turned left and started down the Long Bridge Road. After marching for about a mile the brigade was formed in line of battle to the left of the road. Kemper, Jenkins, and Pickett's Divisions were to the right of the road. The men stayed in this position only momentarily when it was ordered that they should take to the road and continue the march. Going about another mile or so they were again ordered to form on the left of the road. The boys could see an open field in front of them now as they stood at the edge of some woods. They would stay in this position about two or three hours.

At about 5:00 P.M. enemy artillery fire opened up upon the men in earnest (Cadmus M. Wilcox Papers). Wilcox placed one of his batteries on the road to respond to this development. This barrage continued for about an hour. Due to the thick forest round about them very little damage was done to the Confederate forces. At around 6:30 P.M. Kemper, Anderson, and Pickett's men were thrown forward on the right.

About a half hour after Pickett was ordered forward, Wilcox was ordered to form at right angles to the road and begin an advance. The men of the 11th, in concert with the other regiments of the brigade, advanced over the open field into the woods beyond. The woods and undergrowth were so dense that marching in the line of battle was impossible. Soon General Wilcox discovered that two of his regiments had become separated from the others. The 9th and 10th Alabama Regiments had veered off to the right of the Long Bridge Road. The 11th was next to the road on the left, while the 8th Alabama was to the left of the 11th.

With his brigade now divided, General Wilcox pressed forward to an unseen enemy in his front amidst artillery fire all around him. The land now descended somewhat and culminated at the crossing of a small steam. The men crossed this little stream and came to an open field in front of them. To the left of the field were dense woods, and some three hundred yards to the front, and one hundred yards to the left of the road, was a house. Beyond this house was seen a six-gun battery. The ground was level in front of the battery, and enemy fire was coming fast and furious from the woods on the left edge of the field (Cadmus M. Wilcox Papers). Now the decisive moment had come for the 11th Alabama. A charge was about to be ordered that would result in one of the most furious confrontations they would ever see as a regiment.

The 11th Alabama Charge Randol's Battery

While the 8th Alabama on their left became engaged with the Federal fire on the left, the 11th Alabama began a charge across the field toward the Randol Battery. Once the regiment came out into the open field they were immediately pelted with artillery fire from the battery. Here are General Wilcox's own words describing the charge:

> It continued to advance steadily and rapidly without firing until it came within a hundred yards when it made a rush for the guns cheering loudly at the same time. It halted for an instant and delivered a close fire upon the battery and the infantry supports in rear, and then charged successfully upon the battery and drove the infantry back [Cadmus M. Wilcox Papers].

Captain Holcomb of Co. A was killed by artillery as the men charged the battery (*Confederate Veteran 1893–1912* Vol. 1, 333–334). Lieutenant Alanson M. Randol in his report speaks of the charge made by the 11th Alabama (OR Series 1 Vol. 11/2, 255). He stated that when the regiment got to within thirty yards of the battery he ordered them to fire, but it was too late. The Alabamians rushed through the battery, driving out the cannoneers from their positions (*ibid.*, 256). General McCall remembers that the men rushed forward even though the muzzles of the guns were pointing in their faces (OR Series 1 Vol. 11/2, 391). The cannoneers were driven out, according to Lieutenant Randol, at the point of the bayonet. Joseph Williford was in Co. B at the time of this charge (Joseph G. Williford Letter). He lost an eye during this charge, and gives us a vivid description of what it was like for the men:

> ...this sad misfortune befel me the evening of the 30th June, while charging a batery of 8 guns directly in front of our company, with 8 more on our left and right, supported by three divisions of infantry, the cross fire on this occasion was never equaled before on earth. Thus you see we was in a hot place as our brigade was ordered in alone to make the first charge, but at the word charge boys, away we went with a spirit that rairly ever animates the soldiers brain and never did we stop until the enemy was driven from their position and the guns in our possessioin. ... as I was determined to go through or die in the attempt, this I was doing, going at a double quick looking to the left at an angle of 40 degrees when the ball came just missing my nose, slightly tuching the right corner of my eye destroying the sight of the eye, not bursting the ball, though the ball had to be extracted as it had swolen so much that it very much distracted my brain and would soon have taken my life.

The canister and grape that ripped through the lines of the charging men across that open field made many feel it necessary to retreat. George Field, who was the commander of the 11th during this battle, thought that retreat might be necessary and told Capt. Sanders to fall back (Sanders's File).[27] Captain Sanders replied, "No-sir, let's have those guns." The men were subject not only to fire from the battery and the infantry on the right flank, but also infantry fire from the left flank and immediately to the rear of the battery in the woods (OR Series 1 Vol. 11/2, 777).

Upon reaching the battery Charlie McNeill of Co. D mounted one of the guns with the regimental colors (*Confederate Veteran 1893–1912* Vol. 1, 333–334). He was immediately shot, but still waved the colors before the enemy. His nephew, William McNeill of Co. A, started toward his uncle in order to relieve him but was shot dead before he could get to him. The colors Charlie McNeill carried were taken by the Federals. In fact, the official reports claim to have taken two flags of the 11th Alabama (OR Series 1 Vol. 60/1, 719). Private Patrick Ryan and Private Isaac Sprinker of the Fourth Pennsylvania claimed the regimental flags. In addition, one Union flag was taken from the 11th Alabama (OR Series 1 Vol. 11/2, 421). This Union flag was taken as a prize by the 11th in their initial assault of the Randol Battery.[28]

The infantry driven out by the 11th Alabama was the Fourth Pennsylvania Reserves under Col. Albert L. Magilton, and the Seventh Pennsylvania (OR Series 1 Vol. 11/2, 421; SHSP Vol. 1, 69). They were positioned to the front and left of Randol's Battery during the charge. They lay in the grass hidden from the view of the charging Alabamians. In his report he states that they offered stiff resistance to the charging enemy but were finally forced to retire.[29] The men ran off into the woods to the rear of Randol's Battery. This was followed by a desperate struggle involving the sword and bayonet, as North and South clashed in the most arduous type of fighting that could ever be imagined. Wilcox wrote,

> ...from these woods under partial cover, a destructive fire was returned and from greatly superior numbers. With its ranks sadly thinned, it stood its ground heroically and returned an effective fire; the enemy confident from his numbers advanced against this small, isolated & unsupported regiment. The 11th overwhelmed by numbers, did not fly from this prize they had so hardly and deadly won; but with determination and courage unsurpassed, held their ground stubbornly, men and officers alike engaging in a most desperate personal conflict. The sword and the bayonet were freely used [Cadmus M. Wilcox Papers].

General McCall remembers the severity of this clash:

> It was here my fortune to witness one of the fiercest bayonet fights that perhaps ever occurred on this continent. Bayonet wounds, mortal or slight, were given and received. I saw skulls crushed by the butts of muskets, and every effort made by either party in this life-or-death struggle, proving indeed that here Greek had met Greek [OR Series 1 Vol. 11/2, 391].

Many experiences have been recorded of the bayonet and sword fighting on that day. Lieutenant Michie of Co. E received a ball in his right arm from the pistol of a Federal captain at the battery (*Confederate Veteran 1893–1912* Vol. 2, 268). What happened next has been recorded by N.B. Hogan:

> After receiving a ball from the captain's pistol in the right arm, a sword thrust in the cheek, and a cut which laid bare the skull bone on the crown of the head, Lieut Mickey made a desperate thrust with his bright and flashing sword which penetrated and passed clear through the body of the gallant captain, who staggered back and in a moment fell a lifeless corpse among the hundreds of slain who lay on the ensanguined field.

Lieutenant Michie fell over with a cut upon the head made by a saber from behind. He had three bayonet wounds to the face and two in his breast (OR Series 1 Vol. 11/2, 777). Captain Parker of Co. K distinguished himself at Randol's Battery. He encountered two Federal officers in succession, both of whom he killed with the sword; however, he himself was severed wounded by the enemy. He received two bayonet wounds in his breast, one in his side, and a ball in his left thigh. Frank Mundy of Co. B recalled that one of their officers, Winfield S. Bird, was attacked by two Federal officers (*Confederate Veteran 1893–1912* Vol. 2, 87). During this encounter he was impaled by a bayonet. The next day he was found to still be alive.

William McIntosh of Co. A had an experience that has been preserved by his comrade, Needham B. Hogan (*Confederate Veteran 1893–1912* Vol. 2, 268). McIntosh, along with the other survivors of the regiment, had just been forced back from the battery. McIntosh took shelter behind a tree about 75 paces from the battery. One Federal saw Bill behind the tree and made a lunge at him with his bayonet. Hogan records the rest of the incident:

> ...the Irishman missed his mark; but his bayonet became fastened between the cartridge box belt and the back of the Confederate, and, while trying to disengage it, McIntosh said: "Give me a fair show." "Be jabers, an 'Oi'll give ye a fair show;" and as the sentence was finished a puff of smoke from McIntosh's Enfield, and the Irishman's brains moistened the already crimson soil.

The battery was now in the hands of the 11th Alabama; however, the regiment was standing by itself totally alone. The boys of the 8th had remained in the rear, as they were being engaged by the enemy to the left in the woods. The 9th and 10th Alabama Regiments had much earlier veered off to the right of the Long Bridge Road, and they were not in a position to reinforce the 11th. The enemy soon realized that a single Confederate regiment was holding the battery—and he smelled blood. The enemy began to pour heavy fire into the depleted ranks of the 11th. Some of the reports seem to indicate that the bayonet and sword were also used during this time of trying to hold the battery (Cadmus M. Wilcox Papers).

In all the reports regarding the position of the men at Randol's Battery it is acknowledged that they were in an untenable situation. There was no way they could have held the battery since they were without reinforcements, isolated, in open ground, and under crossfire (SHSP Vol. 1, 69). In reflecting upon this situation, General Wilcox felt that it would not have happened had he been in charge of the other brigades on the field near him (Cadmus M. Wilcox Papers). He writes:

> Had the three brigades I commanded on the 27 been directed by me and at the same time it would have been better, there would not have been such a slaughter of the 11th Ala at the captured battery. It was a wrong inflicted upon that gallant little regiment to have been left it unsupported at such a time. My aid-de-camp when sent back after the battery had been asaulted, for Featherston's or Pryor's, found them over a mile in rear, at the point my brigade began the advance, and they never reached the field where the two batteries were captured by my brigade....

Being forced to retire from the fight around Randol's Battery, the 11th rejoined the other regiments of the brigade to the right of the Long Bridge Road near the captured Cooper's Battery (Cadmus M. Wilcox Papers). Here they encamped in the pines on the right of the road. The bravery of the men did not go unnoticed (OR Series 1 Vol. 11/2, 759–60). General Longstreet praised both General Wilcox and Captain Field for their gallantry and skill. General Wilcox praised all the officers and men of his brigade for their remarkable coolness and gallantry (*ibid.*, 778).

One last trophy of this battle for the 11th Alabama was the capture of commanding General George A. McCall. He accidentally rode into a body of Confederates and was immediately captured (*ibid.*, 404). According to Sergeant Mundy of Co. B, Private John Ridgway of his company was involved in the capture of General McCall (*Confederate Veteran 1893–1912* Vol. 2, 87).

The Casualties of the 11th Alabama at Frayser's Farm

The casualties suffered at Frayser's Farm were frightful. Sergeant Mundy only slightly exaggerated when he said that every field officer and captain present was either killed or wounded (*Confederate Veteran 1893–1912* Vol. 2, 87). Dr. Sanders gives the figure of 182 as the total number of men killed and wounded at Frayser's Farm (Sanders's File).[30] Another source gives a total of 181 casualties, including forty-nine killed, 121 wounded, and eleven missing (Fox 1889, 557).[31]

Major George Field was severely wounded in the battle, receiving wounds in both the leg and arm (Cadmus M. Wilcox Papers). Captain Sanders, who as we indicated earlier was acting as a field officer during this conflict, was also wounded in the leg (Sanders's File). A shell fragment tore away a substantial part of the flesh of his leg midway between the knee and ankle. He refused to leave the field, however, until after dark.

The Marengo Rifles lost their commander at Frayser's Farm: Thomas H. Holcomb. One report states that Captain Holcomb was killed by grape shot to the chest as they charged the Randol Battery (*Confederate Veteran 1893–1912* Vol. 1, 333–334). The following men were killed: George J. Crawford, William A. McNeill, and John H. Phifer. The following men were wounded: John J. Carter, Samuel D. Carter, John T. Blackwell, George W. Doss (mortally wounded), James P. Hankins, John B. Jolly, Benjamin H. Ogletree, Daniel S. Ogletree (leg and back), Thomas Pearl, Charles Phifer, Francis M. Rogers (shoulder), James Varner (mortally wounded, died July 6, 1862), Joseph J. Williams, and William C. Williams. In addition, the following men were reported missing: William C. Morgan, William H. Rogers, and William Wade. This gives a total of four killed, fourteen wounded, and three missing.

Company B had the following men killed: Captain William M. Bratton,[32] Thomas E. Fuller, Patrick McGuire, John W. Pool, and William L. True. The following men were wounded: Major Field, Kindred Banks (leg), Winfield S. Bird, Calvin Brett (right leg amputated), Samuel B. Browne (left leg amputated), Thomas J. Knight (mortally wounded in lungs, chest, and neck), John H. Phillips, John A. True (amputated right thumb), George W. Webb, and Joseph Williford. This amounts to five killed and ten wounded in Co. B.

The Confederate Guards had the following killed at Frayser's Farm: William H. Bibb, William Finch, John Greenwood, John T. Hill, William McMillian, William M. Prince, and Robert Upchurch.[33] In addition, the following were wounded among the ranks: Captain Sanders, Robert H. Gordon,[34] James Cameron, John W. Carnes, John M. Doss, Orlando Goree, Lieutenant Higginbotham (wounded and captured), John Mahaffy (foot), Nathaniel Norwood, James Paschal, Thomas J. Smith, Elmore Steele, and James Wilson. John Steward was captured along with Benjamin Higginbotham. Company C had a total of seven killed, thirteen wounded, and two captured.

The Canebrake Legion suffered the following deaths at Frayser's Farm: Charles McNeill, John Sisson, and Independence L. Thompson. This list includes the men wounded from Co. D: John Prince, who commanded the company at Frayser's Farm, Dewitt Carter, William F. Frisby, John M. Gulley (eye, right hand, left thigh), Charles Kirker, Jordan Oakley, and David Talliaferro. Two men were captured: John Sentell and Cornelius Watlington. Out of Co. D, three men were killed, seven were wounded, and two taken captive.

The casualty list of those killed from Co. E include: Benjamin Gilbert, Thomas Grimes, Benjamin Sherwood, James Warthen, and William Few. The list of wounded include: Thomas J. Michie (mortally wounded), Cato Bethea, Charles Cooper, Matthew Fletcher, Joseph R. Green (right hand amputated), Samuel Hooks (mortally wounded), Moses Rainwater (mortally wounded), George Roberts (mortally wounded in thigh; died July 6, 1862), John Shultz (left arm amputated), Frederick Smith (mortally wounded; died July 6/7, 1862), Joseph Stokely (right leg), and Pleasant Worsham. Finally, Joshua D. Bostick was taken prisoner. This totals to five killed, twelve wounded, and one missing.

The list of men killed in Co. F include the following: Charles Lowry, George Taylor, and Henry Goodwin. The wounded list entails the following: Abney Alexander, Patrick Henry, Marion Hogan, John Leopard (mortally wounded), Pleasant Pearce (mortally wounded; died July 22, 1862), General Marion Powell, Newton Rasberry (right leg amputated), William Rasberry, Jesse Robertson (mortally wounded; died July 1, 1862), Asa Stanley, William Suttle, Elias Thomas (leg), George Woodward, and Thomas Rayfield. Rufus G. Goodson and Richard Hogan were captured. Three men were killed, fourteen wounded, and two captured.

The Tuscaloosa Rifles' roll of men killed include the following: Captain James McMath,

James R. Burrage, Searcy Brown, William H. Green, William Jesse Keeton,[35] and Jasper Smith. Some 21 were wounded at Frayser's Farm including: Lt. Abner Steele (who died July 2, 1862), Joseph Adcock, George W. Bryson, Joseph Bryson (thighs), Albert Burton, Constantine Campbell, Robert C. Carroll, William M. Cole, William Ford (wounded in left thigh, hips), Basil M. Hughes, Alexander McCoy (mortally wounded in the abdomen; died July 2, 1862), Wiley McGuire (mortally wounded), Malcom McPhatter, William McTurk (mortally wounded), John Nabors, William Plummer (mortally wounded), William G. Ross (mortally wounded in both legs; died July 29, 1862), Jabez P. Sudduth (shoulder), David Tibbs, Solomon Ward (mortally wounded; died July 30, 1862), and George Weaver (abdomen). One man, Henyard Williamson, was captured. Company G lost six men on the field; an additional seven were mortally wounded. Altogether this company had some twenty-seven casualties, and one man taken prisoner.

The Pickens County Guards had the following men killed: William McShan, Daniel A. Morgan, Alonzo Cohen, and Thomas Taylor. On the wounded list were: Joseph N. Bell, George McKinney (mortally wounded; died July 20, 1862), Andrew Self (mortally wounded; died July 11, 1862), Charles Wilson, Wiley Woods (left ankle amputated), and William Speed as well as Thomas Wier were captured. The sum of casualties suffered by Co. H included four killed, five wounded, and two taken prisoner.

Company I lost the following men: Captain Stephen Bell, John F. Bell, William Jones, James Ross, Jeddiah Smith, George Strickland, Thomas Ward, and William Wilson. On the wounded list were: Sterling Clanton, Daniel J. Cribbs, Henry Cribbs, Jeremiah Gee (morally wounded in the left shoulder; died July 17, 1862), Henry Hollingsworth (mortally wounded; died July 27, 1862), William J. Lowe, John Perkins (mortally wounded), John Prater (mortally wounded with a compound fracture of the arm), Daniel Summers, Charles Taylor (mortally wounded), Jasper Wilkins, and Ignicious Wright. Eight men were killed, and twelve men wounded in Co. I.

The Independent Volunteers suffered the loss of the following men: Nathaniel Muse, John Trammill, George Updegrove, and Thomas J. Weekly. Company K's list of wounded included: Capt. Walter C.Y. Parker,[36] Patrick Brice (left thigh), Jacob J. Cook, Thomas Farrell (foot), George Given, John A. Gray, Lysander Gray, Marcellus Harper (mortally wounded in face and hip; died July 11, 1862), Robert Lockhart (thigh), William Muse (shoulder), John M. Pounds (mortally wounded), Jesse B. Shivers (arm amputated), Daniel Stewart, and Elihu Williams. Company K had four killed and fourteen wounded at Frayser's Farm.

I have been able to account for forty-nine deaths, 122 wounded, and thirteen missing. This comes to a total of 184 casualties suffered by the 11th Alabama at Frayser's Farm. Company G suffered the highest casualty total with twenty-seven, and Co. I had the highest number of men killed at eight.

A Summary of Regimental Losses During the Seven Days

How extensive were the losses of the 11th Alabama on the Peninsula? Statistically the breakdown looks like this. At Seven Pines there were thirteen killed and thirty-seven wounded. At Gaines' Mill there were twenty-five men killed and 151 wounded. Finally, at Frayser's Farm there were forty-nine men killed and 122 wounded. This is a grand total of eighty-seven killed and 310 wounded. The following is a statistical breakdown of the Seven Days by company:

Company A:	6 killed	30 wounded	36 total
Company B:	8 killed	24 wounded	32 total
Company C:	12 killed	32 wounded	44 total
Company D:	11 killed	32 wounded	43 total
Company E:	7 killed	16 wounded	23 total
Company F:	11 killed	44 wounded	55 total
Company G:	7 killed	37 wounded	44 total
Company H:	7 killed	31 wounded	40 total
Company I:	11 killed	33 wounded	44 total
Company K:	6 killed	29 wounded	35 total

Based upon these figures Co. C suffered the highest number of men killed on the Peninsula with twelve, but Co. F suffered the highest number of total casualties with fifty-five.

The fighting over the past seven days had been fast and furious. The men were exhausted and needed time to catch their breath. At least the danger of a Federal assault on Richmond had been averted for a while. The 11th Alabama had been involved in some of the hottest fighting in the battles around Richmond. They had already proved themselves to be hard fighters, and soldiers who were willing to charge into thickest of any enemy strength. They emerged from their baptism with blood as converted soldiers. They were immersed as fresh fish, and were raised as veterans.

6

The Crippled 11th Marches into Maryland

This chapter will follow the trail of the 11th Alabama from the days following Frayser's Farm until the battle at Sharpsburg. We will see that they marched to Manassas and into Maryland still smarting from the stinging losses of the Seven Days Battle. Major changes had to take place within the command structure of the regiment, and many more boys were buried or went home physically scarred for life.

From Frayser's Farm to Gordonsville

Following the battle fought at Frayser's Farm the 11th Alabama made their way back to their encampment site at Darbytown Road (Cadmus M. Wilcox Papers). Here the regiment remained near Atlee's Farm through the entire month of July and into early August. We want to examine some of the developments which took place during this brief period of encampment.

We have already noted that Capt. George Field had been appointed Major. He received this promotion by virtue of being the senior Captain in the regiment. Moody had resigned in the spring, and with the deaths of Colonels Moore and Hale the command of the regiment fell upon Field's shoulders. With Field's promotion to Major, George Clark was soon to receive promotion to Captain, while James Gordon was promoted to 1st Lieutenant. On July 21, Ruffin Y. Ashe received his promotion to Regimental Adjutant, while Frank Mundy would eventually be promoted to 2nd Lieutenant on September 22/23, 1862 (CSR).

Frank Henry Mundy was born on November 16, 1836, at Oxford, England, the son and grandson of professors at Oxford (*The Heritage of Greene County, Alabama* 2001, 171). After two years of college study Frank left for America on Christmas Eve of 1855. He found his way to Eutaw, Alabama, and what he found here was a thriving, cultured, and elegant community. Here Frank met, and stayed with, Alexander Jarvis and his daughter, Mary Elizabeth Jarvis. Jarvis owned at store on the Eutaw square when Mundy began working for him. After the war Frank would eventually marry Mary Elizabeth. Frank would prove to be a capable commander until his capture at Gettysburg.

We need to take a look at what the companies now looked like after the devastation of the Seven Days Battle. Company A had lost its Captain, Thomas H. Holcomb, on June 30, 1862. John Rains was now appointed Captain, with William Young and John H. Adams promoted to 1st and 2nd Lieutenants respectively (CSR). Company C still had John C.C. Sanders in command, but this would not be the case for much longer. He was appointed Colonel of the 11th Alabama on September 17, 1862, after the resignation of Major George Field. Some references give August 20, 1862, as the time of appointment; this would correspond with the death of Colonel Moore, and perhaps was the time from which he was to officially rank as Colonel. James Cross was still the 1st Lieutenant, while 2nd Lieutenant Robert Gordon would die from his wounds on July 29, 1862. Benjamin Higginbotham as Jr. 2nd Lieutenant rounded out the commissioned officer staff of Co. C.

With the death of Lieutenant Colonel Hale on July 19, 1862, the regiment stood in need of a replacement. Captain Tayloe of the Canebrake Legion stood in line for this appointment. He was commissioned at this rank on July 20/28, 1862.[1] John H. Prince was made Captain of Co. D on July 20, 1862. Osmund Strudwick and Frank Glover were also elected 1st and 2nd Lieutenants respectively on this same day.

The Yancey Rifles still had Richard J. Fletcher in command of the company after the Seven Days. John James was elected 1st Lieutenant on July 4, 1862. The record is silent regarding the election of a 2nd Lieutenant until February of 1863, when John Atchison was elevated to that post.

Company F promoted Joseph Caddelle to Captain on July 5, 1862, while William Suttle was made 1st Lieutenant and Lucius Winship 2nd Lieutenant. Lieutenant Winship took sick from Frayser's Farm until receiving furlough on September 15, 1862. He never returned to the ranks, finally succumbing to sickness on January 5, 1863. His absence led to Zachariah Abney's rising to Jr. 2nd Lieutenant in the company.

With the death of Captain McMath and 1st Lieutenant Steele, the Tuscaloosa Rifles stood in need of reorganization. Ranking officer, 2nd Lieutenant Green M. Allen, was eventually brought up on formal charges leading to his resignation on November 18, 1862. On November 7, 1862, John B. Hughes was elected the new Captain, with Hinyard T. Williamson as 1st Lieutenant, and James N. Hayes as 2nd Lieutenant.

Company H also required extensive changes in leadership. With the death of 1st Lieutenant Vanzant on May 30, 1862, along with the resignation of Captain Chapman on June 10, 1862, Martin L. Stewart was thereby made the ranking officer. Stewart was elected Captain on June 9, while James Moorehead was elected 1st Lieutenant. Walter T. Palmer was elected 2nd Lieutenant on October 10, 1862, and Reuben Thom the Jr. 2nd Lieutenant on the same day.

The Fayette and Pickens Rifles lost Capt. Stephen E. Bell at Frayser's Farm. Lemuel Harris, Abel Walden, and Rufus Shelton now became the ranking officers of the company. Finally, Co. K was experiencing some changes in command. Dr. Talbird had been the first Captain, he was followed by Matthew England, and he had been succeeded by Walter Parker. Parker was mortally wounded at Frayser's Farm, which resulted in the placing of James H. George in the position of ranking officer. The additional problem was that George had himself been severely wounded at Gaines' Mill, and on account of these wounds he would eventually be forced to resign his commission on June 1, 1863. James Brazelton was now the ranking officer in the company as Jr. 2nd Lieutenant. On September 4, 1862, he would be promoted to 2nd Lieutenant, and after the death of Captain Parker on May 25, 1863, he would be promoted to Captain on June 1, 1863.

On the brigade level some changes were experienced. Walter E. Winn was appointed Adjutant to General Wilcox on July 16, 1862. He had been functioning in this capacity for some time, and so he was actually to rank from June 23, 1862 (CSR). The Army of Northern Virginia was now divided into two wings under Generals Longstreet and Jackson (OR Series

Present-day Oakwood Confederate Cemetery in Richmond, Virginia.

1 Vol. 16, 547). General Longstreet was placed in command of the Right Wing while Jackson assumed control of the Left Wing of the army. The 11th Alabama was still in Wilcox's Brigade in the Third Division of the Right Wing, along with the 8th, 9th, and 10th Alabama, and Anderson's Battery. General Wilcox was placed in command of his own division as well. Wilcox's Division included: Wilcox's Brigade, Featherston's Brigade, and Pryor's Brigade.

The Depleting Ranks of the 11th Alabama

The changes were not just restricted to the command structure. Many of the boys wounded during the Seven Days either died, were still hospitalized, were furloughed, or were discharged from the service. Many brave soldiers were buried during the encampment on the Darbytown Road. The following group of men were buried at Oakwood Cemetery:[2] Alexander McCoy of Co. G on July 1/2, Abner Newton Steele on July 3, Thomas Knight of Co. B on July 4, Oliver Fitts of Co. F on July 5, George W. Roberts of Co. E on July 7, James Davis of Co. F on July 10, Sam Hooks of Co. E on July 10, John Pounds of Co. K on July 10, Marcellus E. Harper of Co. K on July 11, Thomas M.C. Prince of Co. D on July 12, George Doss of Co. A on July 12, William Plummer of Co. G on July 16, Thomas H. Wade of Co. A on July 18, Joseph Ray of Co. G on July 19, Robert Davis of Co. H on July 24, William G. Ross of Co. G on July 29, and Joseph Stokely of Co. E on August 9. Over in Hollywood Cemetery the 11th buried: James H. Varner of Co. A on July 6, Fredrick Smith of Co. E on July 8, Abner Patton of Co. B on July 14, John Murphy of Co. C on August 5, Benjamin Wilson Reese of Co. G on

August 5.³ These are not exhaustive lists of the soldiers who were buried at Hollywood and Oakwood cemeteries. These are only those we can verify during the time prior to the boys' departure from Richmond for Gordonsville. In addition, others died within the ranks and were taken back to Alabama for interment.

General Wilcox recalls that the brigade left Atlee's Farm on the afternoon of August 9 for Richmond, although in another note he states that formal orders to leave the city were not issued until August 10 (Cadmus M. Wilcox Papers). In any event, the stay nearer to Richmond was only for one night. The men boarded the cars of the Virginia Central Railroad for Gordonsville on August 11, 1862, and they arrived at the station that very evening.⁴ Captain Sanders was still not healed from his wounds at Frayser's Farm when he returned to command in the regiment (Sanders's File). In a letter dated July 21, 1862, his father mentions how Captain Sanders refused to take leave in order to fully recuperate. Although it would take his wound several more weeks to fully heal, Sanders felt too keenly the need of the regiment for his capable leadership. His wound would remain opened and unhealed during this entire Maryland Campaign.

The orders to proceed to Gordonsville were the combined result of the Federals' inactivity on the James River, and the observed buildup of General Pope's Army north of Richmond. General Lee did not believe that McClellan's forces on the James posed any threat to Richmond, but he saw that Burnside's Corps had reinforced Pope at Fredericksburg and moved up to the Rappahannock (OR Series 1 Vol. 16, 551–552). The Federals were also gathering at Culpeper Court House. Lee believed that Pope's army should be attacked before additional reinforcements arrived from McClellan (Longstreet 1992, 159). It was for these reasons that the orders for Gordonsville were issued.

From Gordonsville to Manassas

Very little information exists regarding the brief stay at Gordonsville. The records only indicate that the regiment camped near Gordonsville for a period of about five or six days. Around August 13 the brigade left Gordonsville to camp some four miles out (Cadmus M. Wilcox Papers). The very next day they boarded cars which took them to a camp three or four miles south of Gordonsville. They remained here an additional two days.

On August 16 Longstreet's Division began moving out from Gordonsville to Orange Court House (OR Series 1 Vol. 16, 563). It was not until the next day that the 11th Alabama began its march through Gordonsville (Cadmus M. Wilcox Papers). Lee was hoping to strike the Federal left since the enemy was stationed on the north side of the Rapidan all along the Orange and Alexandria Railroad towards Culpeper Court House (OR Series 1 Vol. 16, 552). In the meantime, General Stuart's cavalry was to move behind the Union rear in order to destroy the railroad bridge over the Rappahannock. This plan of attack was set for August 18, 1862. Unfortunately for Lee, Pope intercepted the dispatch to Stuart, and immediately withdrew from Culpeper Court House behind the Rappahannock (OR Series 1 Vol. 16, 552).

Passing through Gordonsville on August 17, the men, along with the other brigades of Wilcox's Division, encamped that night between Gordonsville and Orange Court House (Cadmus M. Wilcox Papers). By the end of the following day they had reached near their destination, and then bivouacked close to the town. Earlier in the day President Davis had delivered a powerful speech to the Confederate Congress in which he bristled with pride over the repulsing of the enemy from Richmond's door:

The vast army which threatened the capital of the Confederacy has been defeated and driven from the lines of investment, and the enemy, repeatedly foiled in his efforts for its capture, is now seeking to raise new armies on a scale such as modern history does not record, to effect that subjugation of the South so often proclaimed as on the eve of accomplishment [*J.C.C.S.A.*, Vol. 2, 226].

Lee gave orders for Longstreet's Wing to cross over the Rapidan by way of Raccoon Ford (Dowdey 1961, 259). Wilcox's Division marched toward the ford from Orange Court House on August 19 and bivouacked near a mill (Cadmus M. Wilcox Papers). The Rapidan was crossed the next day, and camp was made about five miles distant from Kelly's Ford (OR Series 1 Vol. 16, 596). On August 21 they continued on the road leading to Stevensburg until reaching a road that branched off toward Kelly's Ford to the right. About a mile and half later they crossed the small stream called Mountain Run, and then proceeded with the march towards Kelly's Ford. It was at Kelly's Ford that General Featherston's Brigade skirmished with Federal forces (OR Series 1 Vol. 16, 596). The Alabamians were not engaged in this skirmish. General Longstreet ordered Wilcox to take his division back across Mountain Run since the Federals were in force at Kelly's Ford. Longstreet needed to go further north to find a more suitable point to cross the Rappahannock.

Longstreet was ordered to move up the Rappahannock to Rappahannock Station on August 22, 1862 (OR Series 1 Vol. 16, 564). The soldiers encamped on August 23 near Brandy Station (Cadmus M. Wilcox Papers). After a brisk artillery duel with the Federals at the railroad bridge near Rappahannock Station, the march along the river continued on August 24. General Wilcox states that the brigade did not leave Brandy Station until August 25.[5]

The Wing crossed the Hazel River and bivouacked near Jeffersonton opposite Warrenton Springs. General Jackson was now dispatched to proceed to Manassas in order to strike General Pope's supply depot (Longstreet 1992, 168). Longstreet proceeded on August 26 to cross the Rappahannock six miles north of Waterloo at Hinson's Ford. By the end of the day they had reached a stopping spot near Orleans (OR Series 1 Vol. 16, 552). The boys moved from near Orleans on the 27th, and marched all day until reaching White Plains. The stage was now set for the Right Wing under General Longstreet to come to Jackson's aid at Manassas.

Early on August 28 the men began the march leading through Thoroughfare Gap, only to be checked by Rickett's Division about 3:00 P.M. (Longstreet 1992, 172). This gap was a rough pass through the Bull Run Mountains, which at times was no more than a hundred yards wide (BLCW Vol. 2, 517). On both sides of the gap the mountain rises several hundred feet, while the northern side is nearly perpendicular. The south side of the gap is less steep, and yet is covered with tangled mountain ivy and ominous boulders. General Longstreet became engaged with Rickett's men, who contested his passing through the gap. He decided to send General Wilcox some three miles to the left in order to strike the Federals from the rear (Longstreet 1992, 175). General Wilcox led his division back to the left over the rough and hilly road until they reached the Hopewell Pass (Cadmus M. Wilcox Papers). Wilcox was contemplating the possibility that the Federals might even be in force at the Hopewell Pass. Upon their arrival at the pass at 10:00 P.M., a regiment was detached in order to determine whether the enemy was present. After finding no presence of the enemy through the pass, Wilcox moved his division about one mile beyond to Antioch Church. Here the men bivouacked at about midnight.

The Battle of Second Manassas: August 29, 1862

The Hopewell Gap and Thoroughfare Gap roads converge some six miles beyond the mountains; it was at this intersection at about 9:30 A.M. that General Wilcox's Division was reunited with the remainder of the Right Wing (Cadmus M. Wilcox Papers). The noise of battle could be heard by the division even prior to reaching Gainesville (OR Series 1 Vol. 16, 564). General Longstreet recalls that as the sound of artillery become more pronounced, the step of the men involuntarily quickened on the march (Longstreet 1992, 180).

At Gainesville the men were turned onto the Warrenton Turnpike leading towards Groveton. General Wilcox's Division was in the rear of the advance as it headed down the pike. Up the pike they traveled an additional five miles to the sounds of artillery fire. At about a mile from Groveton they were formed in line of battle on the left, and at right angles to the pike (Cadmus M. Wilcox Papers). The crippled nature of the brigade is demonstrated by the fact that they were held in reserve the entire day (Sanders's File). Wilcox's Division was in support of Generals Hood and Evans at this point (Longstreet 1992, 180). Artillery fire was fast and hot on both sides of the battle lines. Somewhere around 4:00 or 5:00 P.M., word was received that a large Federal force was approaching from the direction of Bristoe Station threatening Longstreet's right (OR Series 1 Vol. 16, 556). D.R. Jones' Division, which formed the extreme right of Longstreet's line, was resting on the Manassas Gap Railroad. He would need to be reinforced if the information regarding the approaching Federal force was correct. General Wilcox's Division was moved over the turnpike to the right in order to support Jones at the Manassas Gap Railroad. Although some fire was given and received by the reinforced Jones, it proved to be of no real significance; however, things began to heat up back on the left of the turnpike. General Longstreet had ordered Hood and Evans to advance, but before they could do so the Federals had attacked first (OR Series 1 Vol. 16, 556–557). Wilcox's Division was quickly summoned back to reinforce Hood's advance on the left of the turnpike.[6] Wilcox's Division now advanced in the rear of General Hood's boys. General Longstreet recalls this movement in his official report:

> Wilcox's brigades were moved back to their former position, and Hood's two brigades, supported by Evans, were quickly pressed forward to the attack. At the same time Wilcox's three brigades made a like advance.... These movements were executed with commendable zeal and ability [OR Series 1 Vol. 16, 565].

It does not appear that the 11th Alabama was exposed to significant musketry in this advance (Cadmus M. Wilcox Papers). According to General Wilcox's recollections, by the time they reached their position in support of Hood very little musketry was heard; nevertheless, it should not be concluded that the boys were untouched by the battle of August 29, 1862. Dr. Sanders has pointed out the regiment's movements back and forth across the turnpike were in the midst of heavy artillery fire. He writes:

> The result was that we had to double quick over much of the field, exposed all the while to fire and frequently to a very heavy one. Not much damage was done however. About twenty-five men were struck. Only three of whom were killed [Sanders's File].

Following the end of the battle, Wilcox's men were withdrawn some seven or eight hundred yards in order to bivouac in some woods on a ridge (Cadmus M. Wilcox Papers). The men were weary from a long day of marching and countermarching. As they sat around their own campfires that evening, they could clearly see the campfires of the enemy to their left, front, and right (OR Series 1 Vol. 16, 598). The enemy was not going anywhere, and neither were the boys from Alabama.

The Battle of Second Manassas: August 30, 1862

The second day of battle opened very slowly for the men. Before 7:00 A.M., they formed in line of battle behind the brigades of Featherston and Pryor on the right of the turnpike (Cadmus M. Wilcox Papers). Featherston's Brigade connected with Jackson's right, while Pryor's Brigade rested on the pike itself. Hood was stationed to the right of the pike. As a supporting brigade Wilcox's men were in some woods in the rear (OR Series 1 Vol. 16, 598). As the men waited in this position the hours began to pass. Both artillery and infantry fire could be heard during most of the day, but it was not until around 3:00 P.M. that things began to heat up.

Sometime after 3:30 P.M., following the brave charge of the Federals over an open field in the teeth of Confederate artillery fire, General Wilcox ordered Featherston's Brigade to move down the slope. This movement intended to strike a line of Federals stalled in front of Jackson's position, and detached from their retreating comrades. All of Wilcox's Brigades swept forward in pursuit of the fleeing enemy. In their pursuit they passed into some woods which resulted in the disruption of their battle lines. Emerging upon the ridge at the wood's edge, they could see an open field followed by another set of woods beyond this. Enemy artillery fire was now directed upon them as they sought to reform the men into proper battle lines for the continued advance. General Wilcox recalls this time:

> It is proper that I should state that the field in which my command was now being formed was swept by a brisk artillery fire about 1,200 yards distant, the men being but indifferently protected by the ridge in front of them. This fire was borne by the men with great coolness, no disorder or embarrassment being perceptible [OR Series 1 Vol. 16, 600].

During the course of this reformation General Wilcox received orders to march his brigade to the right of the turnpike in support of General Hood. In order to fulfill his orders General Wilcox had to direct his men to the rear of the barking artillery, across the turnpike, and then on to the advanced position of the attack. All the while this maneuver was being carried out they were being subjected to heavy artillery fire (OR Series 1 Vol. 16, 600). General Wilcox had no one to instruct him as to the position of General Hood, so he just continued to advance in the direction of the heaviest firing. After crossing a deep ravine and ascending the opposite rising summit, the men could now see an open field before them. Over the field they marched, often at the double-quick, and down a slope beyond which descended to a small stream. Several enemy brigades were visible, and at one point the Federals stopped and fired a volley at the charging Confederates. The result of this volley was slight upon the brigade, and it did not stop them from their onward advance. After crossing the stream and passing through some additional woods, the boys changed direction to the left in order to connect with other positioned troops. Here in some woods they became engaged in some close musketry fire until darkness ended the day. It was in some woods at the base of the hill where Bee and Barton fell at First Manassas that the men bivouacked for the night (Cadmus M. Wilcox Papers). Their camp was on the side facing the Chinn House.

THE CASUALTIES OF THE 11TH ALABAMA AT SECOND MANASSAS

According to Dr. Sanders there were approximately twenty-five men wounded, and three killed (Sanders's File).[7] Company A's Reavis Woodson lost his arm (*Confederate Veteran 1893–1912* Vol. 4, 50). Additional causalities included: Henry White and John Cullin of Co.

B; John Steele, Erastus Chambers, and John White (left arm amputated) of Co. C; John Jones of Co. D; Charles Griffin and James Murphy (killed) of Co. E; David Brown, Patrick Henry, and Gillis Franklin of Co. F; John W. Weaver of Co. G (shoulder); Joseph Acker of Co. H (shoulder); Richard Terry (left hand, lost index finger) and James Terry of Co. I; and John Cochran of Co. K.[8] I have been able to identify only seventeen casualties from the 11th Alabama at Second Manassas. Of the above listed men, Gillis Franklin and James Murphy died as a result of their wounds.

One final word needs to be said regarding this battle of Second Manassas. Captain John Sanders appears to have acted in the capacity of regimental commander of the 11th. His admirable conduct in this role was not unnoticed by General Wilcox, who asserted that he acted in a manner that was "highly credible" (OR Series 1 Vol. 16, 601). Sanders displayed at Second Manassas the quality of leadership that would soon elevate him to the position of Colonel of the regiment.

From Manassas to Harpers Ferry

On the evening of the battle the brigade encamped at Sudley Springs (Cadmus M. Wilcox Papers). September 1, 1862, proved to be a very stormy day at Manassas, much like the day following the first battle fought here. Details were issued to bury the dead, to gather the supplies, and to collect the arms (OR Series 1 Vol. 16, 566). This same day the men began the march towards Chantilly by means of the Little River Turnpike. They had to trudge along the road in the middle of a rainstorm that only got worse the closer they approached Chantilly (SHSP Vol. 10, 505). On September 2 they encamped near Dranesville, and then crossed Goose Creek the next day before bivouacking that evening a mile or two beyond (Cadmus M. Wilcox Papers). On September 4 the men marched through Leesburg and made camp near the Potomac River. Dr. Sanders recalls that their camp was about two miles from the Potomac (Sanders's File). It needs to be mentioned at this point that the need for provisions was becoming critical for the army. One soldier recalls that by September 4 green corn was being passed out for consumption (SHSP Vol. 10, 507). By the time the men were marching into Maryland they were feasting upon a steady diet of apples and corn. This produced a great deal of sickness, as one would imagine.

September 5 found the men crossing at White's Ford, and then marching an additional eight or nine miles before resting for the night. It would be September 7 before the men of Wilcox's Brigade would bivouac in the vicinity of Fredrickstown (Frederick City). The regiment was about three miles out from town on the Monocacy (Cadmus M. Wilcox Papers). They were apparently close to the large iron bridge which spanned the creek (Hurst, 1863, 10; McClelen, 1995, 28). The boys would stay at this encampment until orders were received to travel to Harpers Ferry.

While the men rested near Fredrickstown, General Lee was planning his next move. Lee knew that the necessary provisions for his army could not be found in his present location. He either had to go into Maryland, or retreat further south into Virginia (Dowdey 1961, 293). Longstreet felt that the fields of Maryland would supply what the army needed to subsist upon (Longstreet 1992, 199). Another factor which led to the campaign into Maryland was the feeling that Marylanders would rally to the Southern cause. Dr. Sanders spoke about the liberation of the people of Maryland (Sanders's File). Although many thought that the Marylanders were just waiting to be liberated from the yoke of Northern oppression, it did not take long for them to realize that this was not the real state of affairs among the people. Even at Fredrickstown there was little enthusiasm for the Southern troops (SHSP Vol. 10, 508). In light of these enumerated beliefs, General Lee concluded that at the earliest possible time the army should continue into Maryland, and even possibly into Pennsylvania (Dowdey 1961, 294).

The Marching Orders for the 11th Alabama

In Special Order 191 General Lee gave the marching orders for all of his divisions (Dowdey 1961, 302). General Wilcox's Brigades were attached to General R.H. Anderson's Division, which was under the overall command of General Lafayette McLaws (OR Series 1 Vol. 27, 804).[9] The Alabama Brigade was to assist in taking the Maryland Heights. General Jackson was ordered to Harpers Ferry via Bolivar Heights to the south, General Walker by way of Loudoun Heights from the southeast, and General McLaws from the north through Maryland Heights. After securing this position, McLaws was to proceed to Harpers Ferry to confront the enemy.

On September 10, 1862, General Wilcox with his three brigades began the march toward Harpers Ferry down the Hagerstown Road (Cadmus M. Wilcox Papers). They were to follow General Longstreet as far as Middletown, and from there the road in the direction of Harpers Ferry. At the end of this first day of marching, the men made it about five miles beyond the turnoff at Middletown. The next day would be a difficult march entailing the crossing of South Mountain by means of the Brownsville Pass. General Wilcox had been sick for quite some time, and by the morning of September 11 he was too sick to continue the rigorous march. General Wilcox left his command on this day in an ambulance bound for Hagerstown (Cadmus M. Wilcox Papers).[10] He would stay at a hotel at Hagerstown for several days before leaving for Martinsburg on September 14. Here he would stay in bed for five consecutive days, but it would require an additional ten or twelve before his complete recovery. It would be September 22 before General Wilcox's health would allow him to rejoin his command.

While General Wilcox was riding towards Hagerstown, his command was proceeding to march down the road leading to Burkittsville. In many ways it was a sad march for the men in gray. Thousands of soldiers were without proper shoes at this time (Dowdey 1961, 293). General Wilcox himself stated that many men were left behind near Leesburg due to being barefooted (Cadmus M. Wilcox Papers). The men's clothing was also very rank and deteriorated. Many had not had a change of clothing since leaving Richmond over a month ago. It was no doubt due to these unsatisfactory conditions that straggling became a serious problem (SHSP Vol. 10, 507). This situation is best summarized by General Wilcox himself in a letter dated September 26, 1862:

> ...we have no discipline in our army, it is but little better than an armed mob, the wanton destruction of private property by our army is a shame & reproach ... marauding stragglers who leave their companies without authority, but not to desert, but come back voluntarily after being absent for a few days, but many go off and remain for weeks at home & some never do come back, but go to their homes & there they are among their friends & are safe & no danger of being taken up for desertion. The straggling along by the wayside has got to be such a vice as to be alarming [Cadmus M. Wilcox Papers].

Shoeless, without blankets, no change of clothes, and rations practically non-existent, the boys from Alabama crossed over the Blue Ridge through the Brownsville Gap and encamped for the night (OR Series 1 Vol. 27, 852). They were only about six miles from their objective on the Maryland Heights.

After dispatching brigades to cover the roads by which a Federal advance might be expected, McLaws proceeded with the rest of his command towards Harpers Ferry on September 12. Pleasant Valley is bounded on the west by the Elk Ridge, and on the east by the Blue Ridge. The southern tip of the Elk Ridge was known as Maryland Heights. There was only one main road in the valley that was capable of being used by the men as they marched towards the heights. One member of the Wilcox Brigade recalls the valley march well (McClelen 1995, 28). McClelen remembers that it was one of the most fertile valleys he had ever seen; in addition, it was literally gushing with streams of water from many directions.

On September 13 the main body had begun to assail Maryland Heights (OR Series 1 Vol. 27, 854). By 4:30 P.M. the Federal forces on the heights were driven off into Harpers Ferry below. There is no evidence that the 11th Alabama was directly involved in this affair at Maryland Heights. Since they were a part of the main force under McLaws, there is one muster roll which lists Harpers Ferry as one of its engagements (11th Alabama). The next day on September 14, as the men were cutting a road for the artillery on Maryland Heights, word was received of a Federal force approaching Pleasant Valley (OR Series 1 Vol. 27, 855). The enemy troops were seeking to enter the valley through Crampton's Gap, which was about a mile north of Brownsville Gap. This was the only gap that McLaws had failed to properly cover in his rear. Cobb was ordered to proceed to the gap and take command. He soon became engaged with the Federals. The Confederate forces were driven back in the afternoon, at which time McLaws dispatched the Wilcox Brigade, now under the command of Colonel Alfred Cumming (OR Series 1 Vol. 27, 855). According to all the battle reports of Crampton's Gap, the men of Wilcox's Brigade arrived too late to be involved in the engagement.[11] There is one soldier in the 11th Alabama, Alfred J. Morgan, who is listed as being captured on September 14 at the battle of Crampton's Pass (CSR). The next morning the men from Alabama were one of many regiments stationed in line of battle across the valley floor awaiting the anticipated Federal attack — but it never came (Longstreet 1992, 232).[12] As the men waited in line of battle the news arrived that Harpers Ferry had surrendered. This joyous news was made even more sweet by the growing realization that the Federals were not going to press through Crampton's Gap. The mission at Harpers Ferry had been completed, but now a new threat loomed near another Maryland town named Sharpsburg.

The Battle of Sharpsburg

Sometime later in the day of September 15, 1862, General McLaws received orders to proceed to Sharpsburg with his command (OR Series 1 Vol. 27, 856). The next day they marched over the pontoon bridge into the crowded streets of Harpers Ferry on the way towards Sharpsburg. The men marched until about 8:00 P.M., when they bivouacked near Halltown. All the men were tired, sleepy, and extremely hungry. They had been on the march since September 10, with sleep and food being in short supply. Just as they were settling in for the night, orders came for McLaws to march to Sharpsburg with all possible haste. One can only image the reaction of the men to this order! Many were no doubt already asleep, some were eating, while others were cooking their meal when the news came.

We are not given an exact time for the arrival of the 11th Alabama to the battlefield at Sharpsburg. One member of the brigade recalls that they crossed the Potomac at Shepherdstown around 9:00 A.M. (McClelen 1995, 29). Even as the men were crossing the swift current of the Potomac they could hear the rumble of cannon fire in the distance (Saunders 1969, 141). We can only suggest that it was probably around 10:00 A.M. or so when the brigade made its arrival at Sharpsburg. The men under the command of Colonel Cumming were no doubt very fatigued by the all-night march, and hunger must have added to their misery as they marched toward the fiery conflict. General McLaws reported to General Lee upon his arrival, and it was then that orders were received to send General Anderson's Division to the assistance of General D.H. Hill at the Confederate center (OR Series 1 Vol. 27, 858).

THE 11TH ALABAMA IN THE BATTLE AT SHARPSBURG

It is not clear from the records exactly how the regiment was employed during this horrific battle. General Wilcox was not there, so we do not have his usual detailed analysis of the battle; in addition, Gen. R.H. Anderson himself was severely wounded, and so we have no detailed account from his own pen. We have to piece together as best we can how the 11th was deployed during the bloody struggle at the Confederate center.

By the time the Alabama boys arrived General D.H. Hill had already repulsed a vicious Federal attack (OR Series 1 Vol. 27, 1023). General Hill's men were stationed in the old sunken road that afterwards was named "Bloody Lane." R.H. Anderson's Division was posted in the rear of D.H. Hill's men. After getting settled into their position, nothing is clear about what the regiment did from that point on. One member of the 9th Alabama recalls that they formed in line of battle in the cornfield around noon, and were then ordered to lie down (*Confederate Veteran 1893–1912* Vol. 10, 20). He goes on to state that they began to open fire upon the Federals, and were then blasted by heavy Yankee artillery. We do know that Gen. R.H. Anderson was seriously wounded at some point of the battle, and this in turn placed Gen. Roger Pryor in command. Freeman notes that after Pryor took command of the division it ceased to act as a unit (Freeman 1971, 211–12).

Longstreet recalls that at one point after the Federals had crossed the sunken road and were threatening the crest at the Piper House, that parts of the commands of General Pryor, Colonel Cumming, Posey, and G.T. Anderson came to the assistance of General D.H. Hill (Longstreet 1992, 253). Their efforts resulted in a checking of a heavy Federal advance at that time. Perhaps it was during this advance that many of the causalities of the 11th Alabama were sustained. One member of the regiment recalls that the color bearer was shot down, and the unit's battle flag was riddled with thirteen bullet holes (Cooke 1998). It appears that the division as a whole lacked direction and leadership after the wounding of General R.H. Anderson.

During this time of sporadic engagement around the Piper House the 11th was involved in some degree, and was exposed to Federal artillery and infantry. Henry C. Cooke of Co. K recalls that he was one of the nine men who were called to appear before Captain Sanders following the battle. Sanders was sitting on the ground at the time of Cooke's arrival. Sanders' cheek was bruised black from a shell fragment that had hit him under one eye (Cooke 1998). Cooke tells us what happened next in his own words:

> The Colonel made a short talk to us as we stood before him, saying that he had sent for us to go with the flag; that one of us must be color bearer. Realizing the danger in this service, he preferred that some one of the men should volunteer to carry the flag; otherwise, he would name the man to take the colors.... Seeing that no one appeared willing to volunteer to carry our tattered battle flag, which was lying on the ground at the feet of the Colonel, I finally stepped forward and ... offered to take the flag and carry it as far as I could [Cooke 1998].

Lemuel H. Kelly was the color bearer who was wounded at Sharpsburg (*Montgomery Weekly Advertiser*, 3 December 1862).

It seems that at some point during the battle Lt. James F. Cross of Co. C left the regiment (Sanders's File). He apparently returned to Greene County. On June 20, 1863, Cross enlisted in Co. B of the 7th Regiment Alabama Cavalry as a private (CSR). He was made a Sergeant in the company on July 28, 1863, and appears to have served in this unit until the surrender.

THE 11TH ALABAMA CASUALTIES AT SHARPSBURG

The list of wounded and dead of the 11th attests to the fact that the men were indeed exposed to severe fire at Sharpsburg: Co. A: John H. Adams (wounded), William H. Boozer (wounded), John Coats (mortally wounded), Joseph Gamble (killed), William A. McIntosh (severely wounded), and William C. Ross (severely wounded and disabled). Company B: Jordan Hall (killed), Joseph S. Merrill (mortally wounded), Fleming W. Thompson (wounded), and Lemuel Tharp (missing).[13]

Company C: Henry Dunlap (killed), Lemuel Kelly (wounded), and John C.C. Sanders (wounded). Company D: William Ellington (wounded). Company E: Richard Fletcher (wounded) and Benjamin F. Porter (captured). Company F: Abney Alexander (killed), William W. Brown (wounded), Thomas R. Owen (killed), and Asa Stanley (wounded). Company G: Benjamin F. Hasty (severely wounded, hand amputated), John B. Hughes (wounded), and John Poole (wounded). Company H: John T. Hamiter (wounded), William J. Kerr (wounded), Calvin M. Makamson (wounded), and Benjamin Phillips (killed). Company I: John W. Miles (shot through the right ankle, and thus disabled from infantry service),[14] James W. Oliver (wounded), William H.H. Phillips (wounded), Richard H. Wait (wounded and disabled), and Jasper Wilkins (wounded). Company K: James Bounds (wounded), George Didlake (killed), and Thomas L. Mitchell (shell tore off large portion of his left hand). The casualty figures total some thirty-five killed and wounded.[15] Seven soldiers were killed, and twenty-seven were wounded at Sharpsburg. This exceeded the casualty totals of Second Manassas, but fell far short of those of the Seven Days Battle.

The men would now have a couple of months to recuperate. They needed it. Except for July, the regiment had fought a major battle in every month from May to September. They had indeed marched into Maryland crippled from the Seven Days. But now the limp in their step was even more pronounced following Second Manassas and Sharpsburg.

7

Bombarded at Fredericksburg and the Proud Day at Salem Church

In this chapter we will trace the movements of the 11th Alabama from the time immediately following the battle at Sharpsburg, to its bombardment at Fredericksburg, until the proud moment this regiment had at Salem Church. Although some of the muster rolls and sources omit any mention of involvement of the brigade in the battle of Fredericksburg, it is clear by virtue of the bombardment they had to endure that they deserve to be mentioned in connection with this major engagement.

By the early morning of September 19, 1862, the 11th Alabama had made its way to the other side of the Potomac near Shepherdstown (Dowdey 1962, 322). Late on the evening of September 19, orders were received to travel to Martinsburg (Hurst 1863,12). The road from Martinsburg to Winchester was a firm one, but it was also very rough. The brigade arrived at Martinsburg on September 21, and would remain here until September 27. It goes without saying that the men were sorely in need of rest as well as clothes and shoes. General Wilcox paints a rather bleak picture of the army at this time:

> Our men are sadly in want of clothing especially shoes, many of our poor men have not changed their clothes since they left Richmond, and not less than 5000 are almost useless now for the want of shoes. ... we have no discipline in our army, it is but little better than an armed mob, the wanting destruction of private property by our army is a shame and reproach, when our army marches and camps desolation follows, they burn fences, pillage orchards, steal the green corn, kill beef, sheep, hogs and poultry [Cadmus M. Wilcox Papers].

Many stragglers had left the ranks of their companies, sometimes returning, and sometimes not. In spite of the straggling and physical condition of the men, on the morning of September 27, 1862, the brigade was on the move again. It was around this time that Frank Mundy was appointed 2nd Lieutenant of Co. B, and William H. Richardson was transferred to Co. C as 2nd Lieutenant (CSR).

The Stay at Winchester

General Wilcox records that after leaving Martinsburg the brigade traveled to Bunker Hill on the Winchester Road some eight miles distant (Cadmus M. Wilcox Papers). They stayed here a few days before moving on to within six miles of Winchester on the south side of the road.¹ This was an excellent location for a camp with plenty of wood and water. There are several things of note that occurred while the regiment was encamped near Winchester.

One of the most significant developments to take place at Winchester was the reorganization of the Confederate Army into corps. On September 5, 1862, the government set forth the organization of the army into corps to be commanded by Lieutenant Generals (SHSP Vol. 46, 42). It was determined that the army should consist of two corps, the first to be commanded by General Longstreet, the second by General Jackson. The First Corps under Longstreet included the divisions of McLaws, Anderson, Walker, Hood, and Longstreet. The brigade of Cadmus Wilcox was part of Anderson's Division of the First Corps. Wilcox had the First Brigade in the division, consisting of the 8th, 9th, 10th, and 11th Alabama.

There were some additional military developments on the regimental level at Winchester. In Co. E, John James was promoted to Captain on September 30, 1862 (CSR). On this same date Thomas Witherspoon of Co. A was elected 2nd Lieutenant, Osmund Strudwick 1st Lieutenant of Co. D, Frank Glover 2nd Lieutenant of Co. D, and Carlos Knox 2nd Lieutenant of Co. C.² Some additional changes took place in October. Winfield S. Bird of Co. B was appointed Jr. 2nd Lieutenant on October 9, Walter Palmer was made 2nd Lieutenant of Co. H on October 10, 1862, and Reuben Thom Jr. 2nd Lieutenant of Co. H on October 15 (CSR).

Dr. William Sanders penned a letter on October 4, 1862, while the regiment was encamped at Winchester (Sanders's File). He noted how quiet things were now that they were settled in at their new home. It was a far cry from the excitement of battle they had been experiencing since they marched into Maryland. The weather was dry, and the men were wearied. They had not had a change of clothes in over a month. One man in Co. A, Thomas McGehee, died on October 7, 1862, and was buried in Hollywood Cemetery in Richmond (*Register of the Confederate Dead* 1869, 69). Joseph Merrill of Co. B probably died on October 31, 1862, and was buried the next day in what is now called the Stonewall Cemetery in Winchester (Kurtz & Ritter n.d., 2). Dr. Sanders also mentions former 1st Lieutenant of Co. C, James Fleming Cross. He asserts that Cross had left suddenly while the battle of Sharpsburg was going on. He had heard that he had gone to Richmond, spreading discrediting reports about the company. Cross never returned to the ranks of the 11th Alabama. As we have already noted, he would eventually join the 7th Regiment of Alabama Cavalry back in Greene County on June 20, 1863.

From Winchester to Culpeper Court House

Toward the end of October the Federal army was observed moving toward the direction of Warrenton (OR Series 1 Vol. 19/1, 152). In response to this development, Lee ordered Longstreet to march by way of Front Royal through the Chester Gap to Culpeper Court House. This movement began on November 2,³ 1862, and by November 5 the entire brigade of Cadmus Wilcox was encamped within two miles of Culpeper (Cadmus M. Wilcox Papers). It was a difficult march from Winchester to Culpeper, and Dr. Sanders gives us some of the details:

> The distance is about sixty-five or seventy miles and you must know that the march was a severe one, at least to our army, many of whom are bare-footed and poorly clad. Take into consideration also that we had to stop once on the road and cook rations, and had to cross several rivers, all of which consumes time [Dr. Sanders's Papers].

General Wilcox expected that the army would do battle with the enemy at this location, but instead the Federals would begin another march to Richmond (Cadmus M. Wilcox Papers).

There were several significant military developments that took place while the regiment was encamped near Culpeper. Some of these developments took place on the brigade level, while others concerned the regiment alone. On November 10, 1862, the 14th Alabama Regiment was added to the brigade of General Wilcox (Cadmus M. Wilcox Papers). The brigade now consisted of five infantry regiments: the 8th, 9th, 10th, 11th, and 14th Alabama Regiments. It was also at Culpeper that General Wilcox expressed his frustration at being passed over for promotion to Major General. Both General Pickett and General Hood were his juniors, and they had just recently been promoted to that coveted rank. In response to this, General Wilcox penned a letter asking to be relieved of command and assigned to the command of Gen. Joseph E. Johnston. Fortunately for the soldiers in his brigade, General Wilcox was not reassigned to the western army. He was persuaded to remain at his post pending his own advancement, which was to come in the not too distant future.

Promotions came to several members of the Tuscaloosa Rifles at Culpeper. The most important of these concerned the election of a new Captain. John Bell Hughes was officially made Captain of Co. G on November 7, 1862. The Rifles had been without an official Captain since the death of James McMath on June 30, 1862. The election of Hughes to this post would prove to be a fruitful one, for he served the company for the remainder of the war.

The Hughes Family, from left to right: William Riley Hughes, Capt. John Bell Hughes, Joseph Hughes, Nancy Hughes, Jesse Hughes, Basil Hughes, Anthony Hughes, and Francis Albert Hughes (courtesy Herschel Kelly).

John was born on February 6, 1834, in Alabama (Johnson n.d.). He was the son of Daniel and Charlotte Bell Hughes. John had two brothers, Basil M. and Jesse Hughes, who also served in Co. G. John began his service as 4th Sergeant of the Rifles, but was eventually promoted to 2nd Lieutenant of the company. He was present at the first battle of the regiment at Seven Pines, but was absent sick the remainder of the Seven Days. In the battle at Sharpsburg, Lieutenant Bell was wounded and sent to the Alabama Hospital in Richmond. In addition to the promotion of John B. Hughes, Henyard T. Williamson was made 1st Lieutenant, and James N. Hayes 2nd Lieutenant of Co. G (CSR). Richard M. Kennedy was elected 2nd Lieutenant of Co. C on November 15, 1862, while William Johnson of Co. K was appointed Chaplain of the 11th Alabama on November 17, 1862.

From Culpeper Court House to Fredericksburg

The stay at Culpeper would prove to be a rather short one for the regiment. On November 20, 1862, according to the report of General Wilcox, the men left Culpeper for the environs of Fredericksburg (Cadmus M. Wilcox Papers). It took about three days for the boys to arrive at their new camp outside of the historic city.[4]

Anderson's Division was posted to the left of the Plank Road at Fredericksburg (SHSP Vol. 39, 149). Anderson's Division was to the left of General McLaws, and the extreme left of Anderson's position was occupied by the Wilcox Brigade. The men recall their encampment being near a Dr. Taylor's house (Cadmus M. Wilcox Papers). Their left ended at the river by a waterworks dam. A canal which ran in front of Dr. Taylor's house is also mentioned by the men.

General Wilcox asked General Longstreet to allow his brigade to do all the picketing on the Rappahannock (Cadmus M. Wilcox Papers). Longstreet gave his assent to this request, and so the men of his brigade, including the 11th Alabama, were involved in constant picket duty from the time of their arrival until the battle broke out on December 13. In addition to their picket duty, the men were engaged in constructing batteries at different points along the line from the Taylor House to the Plank Road.

From their position in front of Dr. Taylor's house, the men could clearly see the batteries of the enemy across the river. Wilcox recalls that during their encampment leading up to the battle, they were able to literally observe the constant buildup of enemy troops facing them. Day after day brought more Union troops to view as well as new batteries being constructed. The enemy batteries at many points were in tiers extending from the river upward on the banks of the Rappahannock. Both armies could have easily fired upon one another, but no such action was taken until December 11, when enemy fire woke the men from their sleep around 4:30 A.M.

The Battle of Fredericksburg

The battle at Fredericksburg is officially recorded to have taken place on December 13, 1862; however, a prelude to this clash actually took place two days earlier on December 11. Somewhere around 4:30 A.M. the signal guns of the brigade were fired, waking everybody up in the camps (Cadmus M. Wilcox Papers). As the men were scurrying about, the enemy guns began to pour fire upon the town of Fredericksburg. It was at this point that the people remaining in the town began a great exodus before the raining shells of the enemy. At this

Hill near Taylor House, where Wilcox's Brigade was stationed at Fredericksburg.

time, and even before the shelling began, people were streaming out of Fredericksburg (Clark 1914, 27). Captain George Clark had these sad recollections:

> I remember a number of women and children came along. The night was intensely cold and the ground was frozen. The children and some of the women were crying. Some of them had on very scanty clothing, and our boys took off their overcoats and gave them to the women and children.

While the helpless at Fredericksburg were hastily evacuating their homes, the men from Alabama were being formed in their brigade. General Wilcox formed his brigade in line of battle under the cover of the forest near the edge of the open field which fronted the Rappahannock River (Cadmus M. Wilcox Papers). All day long on December 11 the boys waited and watched anxiously in line of battle. General Wilcox reported that on this day his men received enemy fire in the woods occupied by his troops. It was at this time that one man was killed, and four others wounded from the 11th Alabama.

Who were the men killed in the regiment? General Wilcox offers a total casualty list on December 11 of five. From our study of the muster rolls and other sources, it appears that the exact total of killed and wounded was actually seven. I do not know whether five of this total occurred on December 11, while the remaining two took place on December 13. In any case, the following men were casualties from the 11th Alabama at Fredericksburg: William Owen and John D. McArthur of Co. F were wounded, Moses Baskin and Orlando Goree of Co. C were both mortally wounded, David Tibbs of Co. G was wounded, Henry C. Cook[5] of Co. K was wounded, and Daniel P.M. Summers of Co. I was killed (CSR).[6] Moses Baskin, Orlando Goree, and Daniel P.M. Summers were all buried in the Fredericksburg-Spotsylvania Confederate Cemetery (*Fredericksburg/Spotsylvania Civil War Cemeteries*).

Basil Hughes of Co. G recalls the aftermath of this terrible day of shelling on the town of Fredericksburg (Strawbridge 1998). He remembers that after the long day of shelling took place the men lay in line of battle all that night in the snow. The snow was what he called "half log deep," and this was made the more uncomfortable by the fact that the men had no bed, cover, or fire for warmth.[7] Thus ended the first day in the battle of Fredericksburg. As it turned out, it was a day of bombardment for the 11th Alabama resulting in both death and permanent disability among the ranks.

The Conclusion of the Battle of Fredericksburg on December 13, 1862

On December 12 the entire brigade remained under arms expecting an attack at any moment from the Union troops (Cadmus M. Wilcox Papers). During this day there was the occasional shot and shell from the enemy, but this proved to be entirely ineffectual. The men slept under arms again on December 12, having no idea of the carnage that would occur the next day. The 11th Alabama remained in line of battle along with the rest of the brigade on December 13. They would once again come under Federal bombardment although not engaged during the bloody charges by the enemy troops.[8] General Wilcox gives the following evaluation of why an attack was not made against his brigade on the left:

> I was with my brigade on the extreme left resting on the river. My command was not engaged, we were under fire but not musketry. I had ten men killed and wounded. The enemy intended to attack the extreme left, but after crossing they found that there was a canal in front of the left which they would have to cross under fire, this caused them to change their plans and thus I had but little part in the fight [Cadmus M. Wilcox Papers].

The brigade was held in readiness by General Lee, and could have been moved to any part of the line should it become necessary to do so. As it turned out, the services of the brigade were not needed this day.

Captain Clark was in charge of a skirmish line on the canal the day of the battle, and he has some recollections of the Federal bombardment:

> I remember the enemy had a cannon about Falmouth, the like of which I never encountered again during the war. With an ordinary cannon we could see the puff of smoke and get cover before the shot or shell reached us, but with this one the shots seemed to have come instantaneously [Clark 1914, 28].

Thus ended the battle of Fredericksburg. Although one may say that the boys were not technically engaged in this historic battle, it would not be true to say that they had no part to play. They held the left flank of the army at Fredericksburg, and were exposed to murderous artillery fire for three days. They had men killed, and they had men wounded. They were indeed bombarded at Fredericksburg.

Military Developments from Fredericksburg to Salem Church

We will begin by looking at the developments that occurred on the officer level within the ten companies. In Co. A the same command structure had been in place since the middle of 1862: John B. Raines was Captain, William B. Young served as 1st Lieutenant, John H. Adams was 2nd Lieutenant, and Thomas Witherspoon occupied the Jr. 2nd Lieutenant role (CSR).

There were some significant changes made in Co. B during this period of time. George Clark was still Captain, but the position of 1st Lieutenant saw a change of personnel. James Gordon was dropped as 1st Lieutenant on April 27, 1863, by Special Order #102/9. He was apparently charged with being absent without leave. He submitted his resignation on April 9, 1863, prior to being officially dropped. Interestingly, he appeared before Justice of the Peace William Brooks in Mobile on July 29, 1863, to contest the charges that he had in fact been absent without leave (CSR). In his place, Frank Mundy was promoted, and Winfield S. Bird likewise received promotion to replace Frank Mundy as 2nd Lieutenant. The Jr. 2nd Lieutenant position remained open until August 5, 1863, when Robert P. Schoppert was elected to that position.

Company C was settled entering into the new year of 1863 with Benjamin Higginbotham as Captain, William H. Richardson as 1st Lieutenant, and Richard M. Kennedy the 2nd Lieutenant. The only vacancy was that of Jr. 2nd Lieutenant, which was filled on January 14, 1863, by James C.B. Harkness (CSR). The Canebrake Legion was fairly settled with officers John H. Prince as Captain, Osmund Strudwick as 1st Lieutenant, and Frank Glover as 2nd Lieutenant. Cornelius Watlington was elected Jr. 2nd Lieutenant on February 28, 1863.

The company from Washington County was suffering on the officer level at this time. John James was Captain of Co. E, while John W. Atchison was made 2nd Lieutenant in February of 1863 (CSC). I have found no reference to attest to the promotion of Atchison to 1st Lieutenant of Company E. We might, however, infer this from the notice that by July 3, 1863, Egbert B. Ashe was in fact the 2nd Lieutenant of Co. E when he was captured in Pennsylvania (CSR).

Joseph C. Caddelle was still Captain of Co. F, and William J. Suttle was serving as 1st Lieutenant. On January 5, 1863, Lucius Winship died at Orangeburg, South Carolina, of sickness. The 2nd Lieutenant's body was brought back to Centreville to be buried in the Centreville Memorial Cemetery (McCord 1979, 273). Zachariah Abney was elected 2nd Lieutenant to replace Winship, while Philip Vance was elected Jr. 2nd Lieutenant on January 24, 1863, to fill the vacancy created by Abney's promotion.

The Tuscaloosa Rifles' command structure included: John B. Hughes as Captain, Hinyard T. Williamson as 1st Lieutenant, James N. Hayes as 2nd Lieutenant, and Joseph R. Britt was made Jr. 2nd Lieutenant on January 17, 1863. There was no change in Co. H during this period. Martin L. Stewart was serving as Captain, James H. Moorehead as 1st Lieutenant, Walter T. Palmer as 2nd Lieutenant, and Reuben Thom as Jr. 2nd Lieutenant. In Co. I, William T. Davis was elected Jr. 2nd Lieutenant on January 12, 1863 (CSR). With the election of Davis to Jr. 2nd Lieutenant, the officer structure for Co. I now consisted of Lemuel Harris as Captain, Abel Walden as 1st Lieutenant, and Rufus H. Shelton as 2nd Lieutenant.

Our final unit to consider is Co. K. Captain Walter C.Y. Parker lingered on from his wounds received at Frayser's Farm at his uncle's residence in Warrenton, North Carolina, until May 22, 1863. The *Alabama Beacon* has these things to say about Captain Parker:

> Captain Parker, though only 22 years of age when he received the wounds which finally terminated his existence, had established for himself the reputation of being a most efficient and valuable officer. The writer of his obituary says, "Recklessly brave, insensible to fatigue, filled with a passionate thirst for adventure, Walter Parker was a thorough soldier." He fell at the head of his gallant command, after receiving seven wounds. Though some of his wounds were

of a most dangerous character, and his life for several months despaired of, he finally commenced to improve, and was removed from Richmond to the residence of his uncle in Warrenton, N.C., where he lingered for some 5 or 6 months more, and where he died on the 22nd ult., aged 23 years. The deceased was the son of Dr. King Parker, of Marion, well known in this community [*Alabama Beacon*, 26 June 1863].

James H. George, 1st Lieutenant of Co. K, had also not been well since his wounding at Gaines' Mill. Finally, just days before the death of Captain Parker, he tendered his resignation as 1st Lieutenant due to his impaired heath:

> Genl,
> Richmond, Va
> May 18, 1863
> Having received an appointment as an Artillery Officer to Ordinance I respectfully tender my resignation as 1st Lt. Company K of the Eleventh Regiment of Alabama Volunteers. I am [illegible] this step due to wounding in the Battle of Gaines Mill which renders me unfit for infantry duty according to the opinion of the Surgeon in Charge.
> Very Respectfully
> Your Most Obdt. Servt
> James H. George
> 1st Lieut Co. K
> 11th Ala. Regt [CSR].

Due to the fact that Captain Parker died around the same time that 1st Lieutenant George resigned, James Brazelton probably was never formally promoted to 1st Lieutenant, but jumped from being 2nd Lieutenant to Captain. In fact, on June 1, 1863, Brazelton was formally made Captain of Co. K. On this same day Edwin R. Lucas was promoted to 1st Lieutenant.

In a letter dated February 10, 1863, Colonel Sanders reflected upon his feelings about why General Wilcox was in his opinion being passed over for promotion to Major General. He was being passed over in favor of some who were junior to General Wilcox. He seems to suggest that some boast about themselves, but words mean very little. What really matters is how one conducts himself on the battlefield: "I have learned that the professions of men are not always to be trusted, they are to be judged more by their actions than their words" (Sanders's File).

The Passing of Time at Fredericksburg

Early in 1863 General Lee allowed the men of the Army of Northern Virginia furloughs. Two privates and one officer from each company were being allowed a short leave of absence (Sanders's File). This had a very positive effect upon the morale of the men. Dr. Sanders mentions in a letter dated January 17, 1863, that Captain Higginbotham of Co. C had just returned to camp from a furlough. He was disappointed that he had not been successful in bringing back a single conscript for the Clinton company. Nevertheless, Dr. Sanders states that since the regiment is now full of veterans, they don't particularly desire a fresh infestation of every conceivable camp disease that comes with new recruits. Colonel Sanders states how happy the men were about the furlough system, and that he was hoping to have thirty days as well once Major Fletcher returned from his furlough.

General Wilcox had some things on his mind in early 1863. He wrote his sister Mary, on April 24, 1863, in which we hear the heart of the General regarding the northern abuses toward his country:

> Our enemies seem to be maddened with hate ... goated on by the most vindictive & fiendish spirits seem bent on our total destruction or subjugation. The many atrocities that are daily commmitted in the parts of the country where they are in possession would not be believed if not seen. They steal, rob, enter houses take any thing that they want before the eyes of the master and mistriss of the house, they will break open trunks, burals & help themselves ... of clothing & even what they do not want they destroy. Silver knifes, forks, spoons, and they always take every horse, corn, sheep, hog, poultry, even oats, flour, actually (illegible) people to the point of starvation & then insulting them by telling them that they will sell them what they want if they will take the oath of allegiance [Cadmus M. Wilcox Papers].

Camp life was still fairly good for the men while encamped at Fredericksburg. Fleming Thompson makes some very personal observations regarding camp life:

> Our rations is rather short though we are not in a starving condition by any means, we drew plenty of flour, but little of anything else. We are expecting a big fight here as soon as the roads & weather gets good. Five men deserted from our Regt night before last, they were from the Tuscaloosa company.... I hope they both get drowned in crossing the River, for I think there wives would be better off without them than with them [Fleming W. Thompson Letters].

From these observations it appears that the men had the essentials to eat while they were encamped, but that some had become disheartened and gone back to Alabama.

We have already noted that picket duty was delegated to the men of the Wilcox Brigade. One soldier mentions that since the river alone separated the two armies, it was not uncommon for them to make needed exchanges with one another (Honnoll Family Papers 1861–1865). In a March 6, 1863, letter, Daniel J. Cribbs of Co. I states that they often spoke with one another, and exchanged tobacco for coffee with the Yankees. In their conversations with the Yankees he stated that they seemed very anxious for peace. They felt very confident of victory should the Yankees advance across the river, and the men were generally in good health.

Captain Clark echoed these sentiments of Cribbs. He believed the ranks were renewed, had perfect confidence in their gallant commander, and were ready for action regardless of the disparity in numbers (Clark 1914, 30). Colonel Sanders also affirms his belief in the good spirits of the army (Sanders's File). He believed that the spirit of the Yankee army was very low by way of contrast. He believed it was so low that if the Confederates attacked them right now the war would be over. He relates one story that bears repeating:

> A few nights since a yankee band just opposite our camp struck up "Dixie" at the conclusion our regiment cheered, then struck up "Yankee Doodle" and the yankees cheered, they struck up "Home" and both our men and the yankees cheered lustily, it was so good that the yankees had to repeat it. This shows that they are getting anxious to return to their homes.

On a lighter note, we have Fleming W. Thompson's letter from a Richmond Hospital. He was still in the hospital in January of 1863 recovering from his Sharpsburg wounds (Fleming W. Thompson Letters). He mentions seeing Major Fletcher just recently. Apparently the Major was seeking clothing for the men of the regiment. He makes some rather humorous remarks about the possibility of returning to the regiment:

> I have formed some acquaintences in the City since I came here. I have formed the acquaintence of some very nice young ladies. They say that I must not go to the Regt. until Spring, as there is nothing doing there but freezing. I am pretty near of there opinion.

On April 23, 1863, there appeared in the *Mobile Advertiser and Register* a nice article about the 11th Alabama Infantry (*Mobile Advertiser and Register*, 23 April, 1863). In this article it gives an overview of the regiment's engagements to date, and then affirms that this regiment had not been given its just due in recognition: "This imperfect notice is given because full justice never has been done the 11th Alabama. It will be seen that it has shared all the hard fought battles in Virginia, and one in Maryland, and now numbers only one-third of its original number." It certainly would have been gratifying for the men to have read these encouraging words.

Events Leading Up to the Battle of Salem Church

We have noted that the 11th Alabama was stationed on the extreme left of the Confederate forces at Fredericksburg. The boys from Alabama also had the responsibility of guarding Bank's Ford some two and a half miles above Fredericksburg (Cadmus M. Wilcox Papers). A break in this daily routine was soon to come as the month of May dawned in 1863. On May 1, 1863, General Lee directed all but the Wilcox Brigade of Anderson's Division to remove in the direction of Chancellorsville. This movement was necessary in light of the enemy advancement in that direction (OR Series 1 Vol. 25/1, 854). Wilcox was under orders to remain at this position unless developments warranted his removal to Chancellorsville to aid the main body (Cadmus M. Wilcox Papers). It didn't take long before their services were needed.

At about 10:00 A.M. on May 1, 1863, Wilcox was ordered to advance up the Plank Road in order to meet the enemy advance. Pickets were left behind from Bank's Ford to the Taylor House, while Wilcox was ordered to report to General R.H. Anderson. While proceeding up the Plank Road the brigade came under long-range artillery fire (Parker n.d., 50). Upon reaching the junction at the old turnpike, Wilcox was then ordered to take the old turnpike and report to General McLaws. The Alabamians were then ordered to the right on the Mine Road, where a battery was then placed. After the Lewis Battery was in position, the enemy fire began to diminish; the brigade was then formed in line on the right of General Perry's Brigade. At this point the Alabama regiments occupied part of a line of rifle pits which ran from Bank's Ford to within a few hundred yards of the Mine Road (OR Series 1 Vol. 25/1, 855).

At 6:30 P.M. Wilcox was ordered to advance once again, but the going was made extremely difficult due to the dense forest in their path. By the time darkness had set in, the command had reached near Duerson's Mills on Mott's Run only three quarters of a mile from the Rappahannock River. At this point a detachment of two companies under the command of Capt. Benjamin Higginbotham was sent out with a view to ascertaining whether the enemy had come to occupy the River Road near Decker's House. The detachment returned after several hours along with some Federal prisoners who were making their way toward the United States Ford.[9] Around 10:00 P.M. new orders were received to return to the old turnpike, and encamp in the rear of the advanced troops on that road. The Alabama boys marched until 2:30 A.M., when they reached a suitable position to bivouac; however, upon reaching this location, General Jackson issued orders for the brigade to return to Bank's Ford to prevent a Federal force from crossing which was believed to be threatening that place. The boys reached Bank's Ford at around daylight the morning of May 2, 1863. May 1, 1863, proved to be an all-day affair of marching for the 11th Alabama. It was also a rather puzzling day for the men (*Confederate Veteran 1893–1912* Vol. 17, 125). Captain Clark relates that they puzzled their brains out trying to figure out why they had been isolated from the rest of the army they knew was concentrated at Chancellorsville. As it turns out they had the whole of May 2 to debate this puzzle, for the brigade remained stationed at Bank's Ford the entire day without incident.

They observed some enemy movement across the river, but nothing of consequence (Cadmus M. Wilcox Papers). This was a needed day of rest in light of both the all-night marching of May 1, and what the regiment was going to be facing the next day near a little brick church.

The Battle of Salem Church

It is appropriate to begin our consideration of the 11th Alabama's involvement at Salem Church by making mention of the activity of General Wilcox on the morning of May 3, 1863. Early on the morning of May 3, General Wilcox was up and about visiting his picket lines, as well as observing any change in the enemy's position or strength (Cadmus M. Wilcox Papers). It was at this point that the General ascertained that the enemy's strength had been depleted, and that from all appearances they were ready to leave at a moment's notice. He came to this conclusion based upon the fact that the remaining Union pickets had on both haversacks and knapsacks. This was a very unusual thing for a picket force to have on, and it suggested that they would soon be departing to join the main body at Chancellorsville.

General Wilcox was now of the opinion that there was no real threat of the enemy crossing at Bank's Ford. The evidence suggested that the Federals were concentrating at Chancellorsville. It seemed that the time had come to move in support of the main body. The pickets were called in, and the order given to make ready for a departure to aid General Lee. General Wilcox decided to leave about fifty men and two pieces of artillery at Bank's Ford, but the rest of the brigade would be marched to Chancellorsville. Colonel Sanders mentions that Companies A, F, and D were at this time stationed in the rifle pits just below Bank's Ford (Sanders's File). Several from Co. B were captured while on picket here: Henry E. Monroe, Albert L. Moore, and Fleming Thompson (CSR).

Wilcox had no idea that General Sedgwick had some 30,000 men opposite Fredericksburg (Herbert 1977, 97). He was unaware that Sedgwick had crossed the river and was taking Marye's Heights by successfully driving off both Barksdale and Hays' Brigades of Early's Division. He would soon find this out.

While Wilcox was waiting for his pickets to rejoin their regiments, some of the men on picket informed the general that the enemy was advancing up the road between the canal and the river. General Wilcox then deployed a small force of some twenty men as skirmishers on the crest of the hill that was in front of Dr. Taylor's house; in addition, he placed two rifled pieces of Huger's Battery across the road from the same position (Cadmus M. Wilcox Papers). After seeing the skirmishers, and being shelled by Huger's Battery, the enemy stopped its movement. Wilcox was of the opinion at this point that this was simply a strategy of the enemy to keep the Confederate forces at Fredericksburg rather than reinforce General Lee at Chancellorsville.

A new report came to General Wilcox that the enemy was in force in and below Fredericksburg. Not knowing the exact strength nor position of the enemy, Wilcox ordered his men into the ravine opposite Dr. Taylor's until he could determine what his next move should be. The boys appeared to take cover in the rifle pits that had been used in the battle back in December (*Confederate Veteran 1893–1912* Vol. 18, 125). The 11th Alabama was placed in position to the right of the 10th Alabama in the rifle pits (Sanders's File). An aide from General Barksdale's staff came to Wilcox requesting the aid of a regiment (Cadmus M. Wilcox Papers). General Wilcox immediately dispatched the 10th Alabama Regiment in the direction of

Marye's House, and rode along with them to evaluate the situation. Soon he saw General Hays' Brigade moving in the direction of the Plank Road. He discovered at this time that Marye's Hill had been taken by the enemy, that General Hays had been ordered to retreat to the Telegraph Road, and that Wilcox needed to do the same. General Wilcox had other ideas.

The Skirmishing Begins at Stansbury Hill

It is well to hear the words of General Wilcox himself at this point. Here we catch a glimpse of the determination and foresight of this great general. He was determined not to give up without offering a stubborn resistance to the enemy:

> Finding myself alone on the left of the Plank road, with the enemy in full view on the crests of the first range of hills in rear of Fredericksburg, and with three times my own force clearly seen and in line, I felt it a duty to delay the enemy as much as possible in his advance, and to endeavor to check him all that I could should he move forward on the Plank road [OR Series 1 Vol. 25/1, 856–57].

After making this decision, General Wilcox deployed his brigade in line of battle along the crests of the hills that ran near the Stansbury House at right angles to the Plank Road. The 11th Alabama was positioned to the left of the 10th Alabama at this point (Sanders's File). Colonel Sanders ordered Captain Clark to deploy some thirteen men as skirmishers to cover the regiment. Captain Clark recalls that upon reaching this position the entire earth seemed to be covered with Federal troops (*Confederate Veteran 1893–1912* Vol. 18, 125). With skirmishers deployed in his front, and the two pieces of Lewis's Battery in position, Wilcox began shelling the enemy's advance. The skirmishers were on the incline of the hill, and they were successful for some time in delaying the enemy advance.

It was not until it was reported that the enemy had moved on line with the brigade's right flank that the men were ordered to withdraw. Wilcox was being cut off, and he had to act quickly. It seems that when the withdrawal first began, the brigade marched in common time, but as soon as they were out of sight of the enemy they marched at the double-quick (Hebert 1977, 97). Hebert notes that they double-quicked for a point on the Plank Road about three quarters of a mile beyond where the enemy was. The brigade came to a stopping place on the River Road about a half of a mile in the rear of Dr. Taylor's House (OR Series 1 Vol. 25/1, 857). General Wilcox estimated that some three men were killed and twenty wounded by the enemy skirmishers. Captain Clark recalls that this reforming, falling back, and reforming every couple hundred yards was repeated quite often before reaching Salem Church (*Confederate Veteran 1893–1912* Vol. 18, 125).

The skirmish resulted in casualties from most of the regimental companies. From Co. A: Lucius Huckabee was captured, and John B. Jolly was missing. Company B experienced high losses at Stansbury Hill due to the fact that they were one of the skirmishing companies deployed. The following were the casualties of Co. B: John Cullin (wounded severely in the thigh), Benjamin F. Gordon (wounded slightly in the foot), Matthew P. Hamilton was captured, John S. McCulley (wounded slightly), Albert L. Moore (captured), Henry E. Monroe (captured), Thomas J. Johnston (missing), Nicholas Neary (wounded and taken prisoner), Martin Norris (wounded slightly in hand), William P. Robuck (loss of little and left ring finger), Fleming W. Thompson (captured), and William Thetford (wounded slightly in hand). Thomas Cathey of Co. D was the sole casualty at Stansbury Hill when he was captured by the enemy. From the ranks of Co. F we have the following losses: John W. Johnson, David Griffin, John McArthur, and Cadir Smith were all missing. The Tuscaloosa Rifles had the following casualties: Albert C. Burton (missing), Thomas H. Clark (captured), Charles Farrington (captured), Raleigh M. Gaddy (wounded severely in hand, finger amputated), Thomas W. Hamner (wounded and captured), Basil Hughes (captured), and Jesse H. Shackleford (captured). The men lost from Co. H included: William A. Davis (wounded slightly in hand), Andrew J. Gannon (captured), and Abner Knight (captured). Company I lists John Burris (captured) and Jesse Vaile (captured). Finally, Co. K lists the following casualties: David W. Colburn (captured), William A. Phillips (missing), and John Ward (captured). If we total the casualties for the skirmish at Stansbury Hill we come up with: twenty-six captured and missing, and ten wounded. Two of those captured were also wounded. So we have a total of thirty-four casualties.

Fighting at the Toll Gate

After resting a few minutes on the River Road, General Wilcox determined that the brigade would retire to the red church where a stand could be made. He was confident that with the aid of reinforcements the enemy advance could successfully be stopped. The command then moved down the Plank Road to Salem Church. After hearing that the skirmishers he had left behind at the River Road had successfully checked the enemy advance, Wilcox decided that he would make a stand at the Toll Gate. This stand would in addition provide more time for reinforcements to arrive from General Lee (Hebert 1977, 98). The brigade was recalled from Salem Church and placed in line of battle behind the Toll Gate. The Toll Gate

Near Salem Church looking down in the direction of the Toll Gate on the Plank Road as it appears today.

was on the Plank Road about twelve hundred yards or so from Salem Church (Hebert 1977, 98). The batteries were in position, and skirmishers placed out in front. The enemy artillery now began to shell the Alabamians at the Toll Gate. Colonel Sanders mentions that the 11th Alabama had one man killed at the Toll Gate (Sanders's File). As the fighting began to intensify, General Wilcox was informed that General McLaws had sent three brigades to support the Alabama Brigade, and that they should be arriving shortly (OR Series 1 Vol. 25/1, 857). The brigade was ordered back to the church.

The records list several casualties at the Toll Gate. John Wesley Boozer (wounded severely in the leg), William Henry Harrison Boozer (wounded slightly in the arm), and Joseph J. Williams (wounded slightly in the shoulder) were all casualties of Co. A at the Toll Gate (CSR). From the ranks of Co. B the casualties were: Frederick Merrill (wounded slightly), and Martin Van B. Roberts (killed with an abdomen wound).[10] Two soldiers: Simon Rawls (wounded severely in the left leg) and Wyman Osborn (wounded slightly in the shoulder) were casualties of Co. D. The Bibb Greys had only one casualty at the Toll Gate: Brantley Garner (wounded slightly in the thigh). Altogether, the 11th had about eight casualties at the Toll Gate. Some of the casualty reports may not have included those wounded at the Toll Gate; therefore, this can only be an approximate figure at best.

The Gallant Stand at Salem Church

With the hard-fought successes at Stansbury Hill and the Toll Gate, General Wilcox felt confident in his men's ability to withstand the enemy attack that might come at Salem Church. The battle lines were formed at right angles, and they reached all the way from the church across the Plank Road. The 14th and 11th Alabama Regiments were placed on the left of the road, with Semmes Brigade and Mahone to the extreme left. The 10th and 8th Alabama Regiments occupied the right side of the line, with the 10th Alabama's left resting on the church. The 9th Alabama was placed in the rear of the 10th Alabama, except for one company stationed inside the church itself. Kershaw's Brigade and Wofford's Brigades made up the extreme right of the line (Hebert 1977, 99).

Captain Clark recalls that the men of his company were sheltered somewhat behind a brush cedar fence which extended from the Plank Road to the river (*Confederate Veteran 1893–1912* Vol. 18, 125). These were the Confederate defenses when the battle of Salem Church began.

A field battery of the enemy preceded their advance and began to open fire upon the Confederate battery near the church around 4:00 P.M. (Sanders's File). This artillery duel continued for some twenty minutes before the Southern boys had exhausted their ammunition. Federal artillery fire continued to fall both to the left and right of the church without much effect. Around 5:00 P.M. the enemy artillery fire finally ceased with the advance of their skirmishers. Brisk fighting between the Alabama skirmishers and the enemy skirmishers continued for another fifteen minutes before the Confederates fell back to their lines at the church.

From the Toll Gate the blue infantry advance began which included some three lines in all (OR Series 1 Vol. 25/1, 858). Open fields awaited the Federal advance from the Toll Gate until about 250 yards from Salem Church, when a thick small growth of woods began a slight ascent leading up to the small brick building. Needham B. Hogan of Co. A recalls being stationed behind a thin brush fence about waist high waiting for the enemy to arrive (*Confederate Veteran 1893–1912* Vol. 2, 51–52). Upon reaching the woods, the enemy gave three cheers and rapidly charged the Confederate position. It was an impressive scene to Needham Hogan to view the approaching Federals:

Old Salem Church.

> ...a magnificent scene burst upon our view in the open field beyond the skirt of timber in our front. The ground in our front sloped gently from us, and up this gentle slope approached the dense columns of blue with steady tread, with banners fluttering and shining steel glimmering in the sunlight. Three columns deep this array pressed upon the small band of heroes before them, little dreaming that in a few moments they would be hurled back with fearful havoc....

The Federals charging on the Confederate right were the 5th Maine, 16th New York, 121st New York, 96th Pennsylvania, 2nd New Jersey and the 23rd New Jersey; while charging the Confederate left were the 1st, 2nd, and 15th New Jersey, 95th Pennsylvania, 119th Pennsylvania, and the 16th New York (Hebert 1977, 100).

The Alabamians did not open fire until the boys in blue were less than eighty yards away, and when they did, it was a terrible slaughter of the front line of advance. Hogan recalled being ordered not to fire until they saw the white of the enemy's eyes (*Confederate Veteran 1893–1912* Vol. 2, 51–52). Lt. Colonel William Henry Jr. of the 1st New Jersey Regiment filed a report of the battle that day (OR Series 1 Vol. 25/1, 576). This regiment would have been one of the Federal units facing the 11th. In his own words he writes about the fierceness of the fighting on the left side of the Plank road:

> We advanced at a double-quick, then the action became more general, and we attacked the enemy, who was strongly posted behind brush, fence, and entrenchments in a wood on the right and left of the road, from which position a destructive musketry fire was kept up on us. After severe fighting, we were relieved and fell back, having lost 105 in killed, wounded, and missing, besides the loss of our colonel, M.W. Collet, who was killed while the regiment was retiring [OR Series 1 Vol. 25/1, 576].

Despite this devastating first volley, the first line of Federals didn't retreat (*ibid.*, 101). The Federals wavered, some gave way, but the enemy pressed on still with its second line of infantry. During the heat of the battle Needham Hogan tells a story that is quite touching (*Confederate Veteran 1893–1912* Vol. 2, 51–52). His own Captain, John B. Rains, was constantly patting the men on the shoulders, encouraging them to fire as rapidly as possible. At this point a Yankee officer mounted on a horse came racing along the Plank Road. The cry rang out, "Shoot the man on the horse." Several turned and fired upon the officer causing him to fall dead on the Plank Road. After the battle was over Captain Rains and the others returned to the spot where the officer lay. Captain Rains burst out into tears upon examining the officer. He turned out to be an old friend and schoolmate of his at the Philadelphia Law School.

With the advance of the second Federal line the Alabama battle line appeared ready to break. The 10th Alabama began to fall back on the eight companies of the 9th Alabama behind them, while the men of the 9th Alabama in the school house were captured. The 121st New York actually passed the left of the 8th Alabama Infantry (Hebert 1977, 101). It was at this point that Capt. Walter Winn of the 11th Alabama played a significant role. In a report dated December 27, 1863, Colonel J.H. King of the 9th Alabama penned a letter of commendation for Captain Winn's efforts at helping to save the day on the right side of the Plank Road (CSR). He writes:

> When Capt. Winn galloped to them on his horse & while the battle was raging fiercly with the assistance of the Col. comdg suceeded in arresting the further retreat of the disorganized men. And by noble example and coolness returned many to their former position. While this was being done, the Capt was exposed to a heavy fire and had his horse shot under him while rallying and organizing the men. Again when the enemy had been repelled and had commenced to fall back, the Capt. brought the order to move forward and was one of the leaders in the charge which drove the enemy back from our front and won the day.

With the encouragement of Captain Winn, the 9th Alabama, in the rear of the 10th, sprang forward in order to restore the broken lines. This began a rally all along the lines, resulting in a charge by the Alabama regiments even without a direct order from General Wilcox to do so. Another enemy battle line was formed on the right and left of the road, but this too gave way to the charging soldiers of the Wilcox Brigade. The charge of the enemy continued until reaching the Toll Gate, where heavy reserves were awaiting the men. The Confederates were at this point halted, reformed, and due to the descent of darkness, marched back to the Salem Church line of defense. Captain Clark gives his recollection of the charge:

> ...when a sheet of flame burst from our lines, mowing down hundreds, when the brigade leaped forward to the charge apparently without orders, and the chase began. Down through the brush and thicket the brigade rushed, encountering a second line of the enemey, which gave way precipitately, and on and on went the boys, until the entire force of the enemy was driven beyond the red house [*Confederate Veteran 1893–1912* Vol. 18, 125].

Colonel Sanders's perspective on the 11th Alabama's charge of the Federal forces is found in his official report:

> We had exchanged but a few rounds (the enemy's fire being too high, doing but little damage) before I received the order from Gen'l Wilcox, and extended it to the regiment on my left (14th Alabama, Co. C Pinkard) to charge the enemy, which was done in gallant style; officers and men leaping the small bush fence in our front and rushing to the charge with a shout. The enemy's first line fell back upon his second and it again upon his third. We charged through the wood, an open field, across a lane and into the field beyond, driving the enemy before us [Sanders's File].

This charge continued until stiff resistance was received by the brigade, and then they proceeded to retire. The 11th along with the 14th Alabama retired to a lane about 200 yards ahead of their original position at the church. They remained here until the enemy advanced to within 200 yards of Sanders's front, and one hundred yards of the men's left flank. At this point they were unprotected, and so determined to return to their original position at Salem Church.

General Lee heaped praise upon the Wilcox Brigade for their gallant stand at Salem's Church:

> The enemy then began to advance up the plank road, his progress being gallantly disputed by the brigade of General Wilcox, who had moved from Banks' Ford as rapidly as possible to the assistance of General Barksdale; but arrived too late to take part in the action.... Brigidier General (now Major General) Wilcox is entitled to especial praise for the judgment and bravery displayed in impeding the advance of General Sedgwick towards Chancellorsville, and for the gallant and successful stand at Salem Church. To the skillful and efficient management of the artillery, the successful issue of the contest is a great measure due [SHSP Vol. 3, 242].

In addition to the praise heaped upon the Alabamians by General Lee, the 11th Alabama's own Colonel at dress parade on May 11, 1863, had the following commendation read to the entire regiment:

> The Colonel commanding desires to express to the officers and men of the Regiment his warmest appreciation of their conduct in the recent battle.... We witnessed with much pride the soldierly manner in which Capt Clark and his subordinate officers executed the order to deploy their company at Stansbury Hill, and the boldness with which the men confronted the enemys' extended line of skirmishers, within easy range of his main line of battle, thus checking by a well directed fire his rapid advance. He would also express his admiration of the intrepidity with which the officers and men of Company A, when advanced as skirmishers in our front, sustained a severe fire from the enemys' batteries.
>
> Their position was firmly held until the opposing lines of battle approached within musket range, when they retired without confusion, and resumed their places on the right.
>
> When ordered to the final charge you leaped forward with a shout, and swept thrice your numbers from the field. Prisoners, guns, accoutrements, baggage were your trophies.
>
> Soldiers let us not forget to shed tears of deep sorrow over the fresh graves of our comrades, who purchased victory with death. Cherish their names with eternal fidelity, and strive to emulate their virtues and their valor!
>
> A merciful Providence has spared our lives....
>
> By Order:
J.C.C. Sanders, Colonel,
>
> R.Y. Ashe, Adjutant
> [Sanders's File].

THE CASUALTIES OF SALEM CHURCH

We are placing as casualties from the 11th Alabama all those not otherwise designated as casualties at either Stansbury Hill or the Toll Gate. As we have already noted, it is possible that others were wounded at those places, but since they are not so designated we are placing them as casualties at Salem Church proper.

From the Marengo Rifles: John H. Adams (wounded slightly in the head), Basil N. Gillmore (wounded slightly in the arm), Thomas J. Gillmore (wounded severely in leg, leg amputated; he died June 13, 1863), and Merrit Morgan Johnson (wounded dangerously through the body; was eventually detailed). Colonel Sanders mentions the heroics of James N. Kelly of Co. A, who seized the colors after the fall of James M. Davis of Co. H (Sanders's File).

Captain Clark's company had the following casualties: Arthur B. Phillips (killed), and George Willis Webb (killed). From Co. C we have the following men: Charles H. Bulloch (flesh hip wound), Thomas Childers (killed), Josiah Jones (wounded in the head), Lemuel Kelly[11] (head wound, mortally wounded), John A. Stewart (wounded), Thomas Smith (wounded in the head), Joel Doss (wounded in muscles of the lumbar region), Newton J. Eatman (left leg amputated), Wilson Gathright (wounded slightly in the hand), Robert Lyon (wounded dangerously in the lung), George Williams (wounded severely in the hand), and Capt. Benjamin T. Higginbotham (wounded severely in the left arm). Captain Higginbotham had a ball pass out of his arm without harming the bone (Sanders's File).

The Canebrake Legion lost Lieutenant Osmund L. Strudwick on the field, Thomas Anderson was severely wounded in the right arm, and Asa Vaughan was wounded and captured. In his official report Colonel Sanders has many noble things to say about the death of Lieutenant Strudwick:

> While nobly charging the enemy, Lt. O.L. Strudwick Co. &c received his fatal wound, fell and expired on the field, a martyr to our cause. In him the country has lost a devoted soldier, and the regiment, a gallant officer. After having participated in several hard fought battles, it was reserved for him to fall with the enemy flying before him [Sanders's File].

The Washington County company had the following casualties: Benjamin F. Porter (wounded slightly in the right arm), Henry L. Atchison (leg amputated; later died), A. Fletcher Hooks (wounded slightly in the thigh), Leslie Rain (wounded slightly in the head), Charles Cooper (wounded slightly in the thumb), Albert J. Johnson (slightly in head), John A. Jones (wounded in head; killed), and Edwin A. Sherwood (wounded severely in the arm).

From the ranks of Co. F the following were casualties at Salem Church: Daniel Corley (mortally wounded in left shoulder; died May 15), Zack Abney (wounded), Martin Barnes (wounded in the left thigh), Richard Hogan (wounded severely in the thigh), Leslie Horn (wounded slightly in the thigh), Marion B. Ashworth (shot in abdomen; killed), Newton Smitherman (wounded slightly in the arm), and Asa Stanley (wounded slightly).

The Tuscaloosa Rifles reported the following casualties: James N. Hayes (wounded slightly in the hand), Joseph R. Britt (wounded slightly in the arm), Constantine J. Campbell (wounded slightly in the hand), William M. Cole (wounded slightly in shoulder), Clement Clay McMath[12] (shot in abdomen; killed), Joseph E. McMath (shot in toe), Andrew J. Mitchell (killed), Joseph R. Shuttlesworth (wounded slightly in the arm), and Jabez P. Sudduth (wounded slightly).

The Pickens County company noted these casualties: Andrew J. Bostick (wounded slightly in shoulder and captured), Elijah J. Foster (wounded slightly in the foot), Jacob J. Funderburk (wounded slightly in arm), Joel James Hamiter (wounded severely in the thigh), John Tyler Hamiter (wounded dangerously in thigh), James E. Lee (wounded slightly in side), James T. Phillips (wounded), James P. Shaw (wounded severely in right side below the ribs), John Wesley Turnipseed (wounded severely in the arm and head), and James M. Davis was killed. A word needs to be said about James M. Davis. James was the color bearer of the regiment. Colonel Sanders takes note of the bravery of Davis when he wrote these words: "The color-bearer James M. Davis, Co. H, fell while gallantly bearing the colors in the charge, and expired without a groan, a hero in the fight" (Sanders's File).

The men who were casualties from Co. I were: James Anthony (killed), F.A. Brotherton (slight wound in the head), George J. Collins (wounded), James A. Darr (severely wounded in lower jaw and neck), Nathan J. Dozier (shot in abdomen; killed), Francis Gregg (severely wounded in forearm), Robert Mizell (right arm amputated), Benjamin F. Smith (both thighs severely wounded), Preston Thornton (severely wounded in left arm; amputated), and Thomas Wimberly (severely wounded in ankle).

Finally, from the company raised from Perry County we have this list of casualties from Salem Church: James L. Brazelton (wounded slightly in foot), Aaron M. Curb (wounded severely in leg), David A. Cureton (shot in abdomen; killed), Robert B. Griffin (wounded slightly in the side), Robert H. Griffin (killed), William J. Hay (wounded severely in hand), John Marlow (wounded severely in arm and leg), Joseph W. Merriman (killed), William H.H. Ratliff (wounded in the shoulder), M. Daniel L. Stewart (wounded slightly in hand), Malcomb D.C. Tadlock (shot in leg), Ruffus B. Wallace (wounded severely in hand), and William P. Walton (wounded severely in arm).

The total casualties for just the Salem Church battle were: fifteen killed with four mortally wounded, along with sixty-four wounded and two captured. Company K appears to have had the most casualties at Salem Church with three killed and ten wounded. If we then add together the totals from the skirmish at Stansbury Hill, the Toll Gate, and Salem Church we come up with these figures: sixteen killed, four mortally wounded, eighty-one wounded, and twenty-eight captured or missing. This give us a total number of casualties of 129 within the ranks of the 11th Alabama.

The battle fought at Salem Church by the 11th Alabama was a pivotal one. For the success at Chancellorsville was in part made possible through the stand at Salem Church. It was a proud day for the Alabama boys. For their gallant stand, a monument still stands on the battlefield. The tribute paid to the Alabama Brigade comes from their equally brave opponents that day: the 23rd New Jersey Regiment. The words of the monument read: "To the brave Alabama boys, our opponents on this field of battle, whose memory we honor, this tablet is dedicated."

8

The Brave Charges at Gettysburg

In this chapter we are going to examine the developments of the 11th Alabama from the time after the battle at Salem Church, to the events leading up to and including the battle of Gettysburg. This particular chapter will mark a definite change in the character of the war for the men who served in the ranks of this hard-fighting regiment. Salem Church in many ways was a high point for both the regiment and the Army of Northern Virginia.

Military Developments from Salem Church to Gettysburg

After the death of Stonewall Jackson the Army of Northern Virginia stood in need of reorganization. It was determined to divide the army into three corps. Longstreet would command the 1st Corps, Richard Ewell the 2nd, and A.P. Hill the 3rd Corps (OR Series 1 Vol. 27/2, 288). The 11th Alabama was now placed in the new corps commanded by A.P. Hill.

There were quite a number of men from the 11th who were captured at Salem Church and subsequently taken to prisoner of war camps. We know that the following men were taken to Washington, D.C., and then on to Ft. Delaware following the Battle of Salem Church: Asa Vaughan, Co. D; John Ward, Co. K; Abner Knight, Co. H; Lucius Huckabee, Co. A; William A. Phillips, Co. K; John D. McArthur, Co. F; Nicholas Neary, Co. B; David Colburn, Co. K; Jesse Vaile, Co. I; Jesse Shackleford, Co. G; Basil Hughes, Co. G; Matthew P. Hamilton, Co. B; Henry E. Monroe, Co. B; Albert L. Moore, Co. B; Thomas H. Clark, Co. G; David A. Griffin, Co. F; John B. Burris, Co. I; Cadir M. Smith, Co. F; Charles Farrington, Co. G; Thomas K. Cathey, Co. D; Andrew J. Gannon, Co. H; Fleming W. Thompson, Co. B; John W. Johnson, Co. F; Thomas Hamner, Co. G; Andrew J. Bostick, Co. H; and Albert Burton, Co. G (CSR).

Many soldiers were taken from Salem Church to Ft. Delaware located on Pea Patch Island about one mile east of Delaware, City (*Encyclopedia of the Confederacy*, s.v. "Fort Delaware Prison"). By June of 1863, there were some 8,000 prisoners on the island. It is estimated that over 2,400 Confederates died at Ft. Delaware. Some 2,436 of these are buried in the Finn's Point National Cemetery across the Delaware River in New Jersey. The fort was commanded by Brigadier General Albin Francisco Schoepf, and the conditions there were deplorable. The water was especially bad in the prison. Water for cleaning came from the ditches, and the river was polluted by the fort's sewage. Drinking water had to be brought in by boat from a nearby creek. The prison was very damp due to its being barely above the water level of the river. Typhoid fever would break out in the camp in September of 1863, resulting in the deaths of about 327 men.

Finn's Point National Cemetery Monument (courtesy Carol Yates Wilkerson).

One Confederate soldier recalls the daily regiment of meals he had at Ft. Delaware. For breakfast, a cup of warm water called coffee (made from the grounds used in the Yankee hospital, redried, and given to them), one and a half hardtack, and one-fourth of a pound of beef or pork (Burrell 1997, 123). Dinner consisted of hardtack and about one pint of "soup" made sometimes from potatoes, cabbage, or carrots. A few of these were thrown into a kettle of water in which some beef or pork had been boiled.

There were several soldiers who died between Salem Church and the battle of Gettysburg. John S. Waller of Co. A died at Chimborazo from the effects of pneumonia on May 9, 1863. Daniel N. Corley of Co. F died at Richmond from the effect of wounds received at Salem Church on May 15, 1863. Corley was buried at Oakwood Cemetery, Grave #17, Row 25, and Division D (Oakwood Cemetery Register). Thomas J. Gillmore of Co A died on June 10, 1862 (CSR). Finally, William M. Price of Co. K died of disease in July of 1863.

On June 15, 1863, John Fondron of Co. F was transferred to Co. F of the 44th Alabama Regiment of Volunteers. He had been appointed 3rd Sergeant in Co. F back in September of 1862. After his transfer he was brevetted 2nd Lieutenant of Co. F on June 18. Fondron would eventually rise to be Captain of this company on November 29, 1864.

The Trip from Fredericksburg to Gettysburg

The 3rd Corps moved out from Fredericksburg on June 14, 1863, making its way toward Culpeper Court House (OR Series 1 Vol. 27/2, 613). They stopped for the night near Chancellorsville, and then came within four miles of Stevensburg the next day after a two-hour delay at the Rapidan. They crossed the Rapidan at Germania Ford (Patterson 1966, 104–108). Culpeper Court House was reached by June 16, and then it was a twelve-mile march to Hazel River the following day. After encamping on the 18th at Flint Rock, the division arrived at Front Royal on June 19. At Front Royal they arrived early in the day and began to make preparations to go into camp; however, at 4:00 P.M. they were ordered to resume the march towards the Shenandoah, which they crossed late that evening. After wading across the river they were able to bed down for the night. All the wagons of the division did not make it across until the next day, June 20, at which time the march was continued until reaching a point about two miles beyond White Post (OR Series 1 Vol. 27/2, 613). The next day's march brought them as far as Berryville, while bivouac on June 22 took place on the road to Charlestown at Roper's Farm. The last stop before crossing the Potomac was Shepherdstown on June 23, and then the next day the men reached Boonsborough before going into camp. One soldier recalls that the water of the Potomac was about three or four feet deep at the crossing (Patterson 1966, 109). While at Shepherdstown, Merrit J. Morgan of Co. A wrote a letter to his sister back in Alabama (Bragg Vol. 3 n.d.). It contains some of the enthusiasm that filled the hearts of the men as they journeyed north:

> ...we are on our way to the land of roasting ears and green apples again, as the boys call Maryland.... We have just passed through the garden spot of the Southern Confederacy, the finest lands and houses, the prettiest girls that ever lived inhabit the Valley of Virginia. Although the Yanks have had possession of their homes for a long time they still cheer the Rebels as they pass, and express their sympathy with Secessionism.... I am very tired and my feet are

City square near the spot where General Lee conferred with General Hill at Chambersburg, Pennsylvania.

blistered, but that is nothing when compared with a country's liberty. We have marched over 150 miles and waded 5 rivers in the last ten days.

June 25 found the men at Hagerstown, June 26 two miles beyond Greencastle, Pennsylvania, and then on June 27 the boys marched through Marion and Chambersburg to Fayetteville (Patterson 1966, 111). Here the regiment would stay until the morning of July 1, 1863.

General Wilcox notes an interesting account that took place as they passed through Chambersburg on the way to Fayetteville (Cadmus M. Wilcox Papers). General Wilcox writes:

> As we passed through Chambersburg riding at the head of my column, I saw in advance of me, a line of school girls stretched across the street from curbstone to curbstone, and as I approached near, I heard them singing, and when quite near it heard to be old "John Browns soul's a marching along." In rear of them were three sour looking old spinsters. Thinking they would like to be made martyrs, and not caring to encourage them, I ordered one of my staff to remain there, and make the troops incline to the left, on to the side walk and not to notice the singing girls. I rode on and soon the Staff officer rejoined me, I asked why he left so soon, he replied that when about two regiments had passed them without paying any attention to them, they quit singing & left the streets....

General Wilcox doesn't record any hostile actions from any of the Pennsylvania natives, but stories like these demonstrate that they were not *welcomed* by any means.

In another interesting story General Wilcox reveals to us the character of the men of his brigade. Once again, let us hear the story in the General's own words:

> While some of my men were getting water at a pump on the road side near a house, a woman standing in the doorway came out and addressing one of the men said "you have my son's knapsack on," the man replied, "how do you know?" she said "because I see his initials and the letter of his company, and the number of his regiment." She then asked him if he would give it to her, he replied "certainly," took it off & handed it to her. The man had gotten it at the fight at Salem Church [Cadmus M. Wilcox Papers].

Fleming Thompson of Co. B remembers that there were many interesting things that happened along the march into Pennsylvania (Fleming W. Thompson Letters). One story, which he did not elaborate on, was that he came very near falling in love with a Pennsylvania girl!

The 11th Alabama on the First Day of Battle: July 1, 1863

After being stationed for some three days at Fayetteville, the men finally received the order to move down the Chambersburg Pike in the direction of Gettysburg (OR Series 1 Vol. 27/2, 616). It was at an early hour of the morning when the regiment took to the pike, and at about the noon hour they arrived at the little village of Fairfield (Clark 1914, 34). Around 2:30 P.M. the sound of distant artillery could be heard by the men in the direction of Gettysburg. At this point near Cashtown the brigade was moved off the pike to the right, and remained here in some woods for about an hour. After this delay the march was again resumed toward Gettysburg. Soon prisoners and wounded began passing them along the way to the rear (Cadmus M. Wilcox Papers).

After passing over a stream on a stone bridge the men filed off to the right of the Chambersburg Pike (OR Series 1 Vol. 27/2, 616). They then marched along Marsh Creek for about a mile until stopping at a mill. This probably refers to Weigle's Mill. The miller's wife gave General Wilcox and three of his staff officers a good supper (Cadmus M. Wilcox Papers). They were formed at right angles to the right flank of the division at this place (OR Series 1 Vol. 27/2, 617). Pickets from the regiment were posted further down the stream for the night at the Black Horse Tavern (Longstreet 1992, 360). Captain Clark affirms that the 11th Alabama was involved in throwing out these pickets (Clark 1914, 35).

The first day of battle at Gettysburg had now come and gone. The men of Wilcox's Brigade had not been engaged in the fighting of July 1. As it turned out, they would indeed need the rest they received this night near Marsh Creek. July 2, 1863, would prove to be a very long and arduous day of fighting for the entire brigade.

The 11th Alabama on the Second Day of Battle: July 2, 1863

The second day at Gettysburg was the hardest day of fighting for the 11th Alabama. It is easily broken into two separate engagements; the first was more of a skirmish near the Pitzer's Woods, while the second was a furious battle around and beyond the Emmitsburg Road.

THE SKIRMISH NEAR PITZER'S WOODS

At 7:00 A.M. on July 2, 1863, the regiment moved up from its position near the Marsh Creek in order to rejoin the division (Cadmus M. Wilcox Papers). After passing through a field to their front, the men descended a slope before crossing a road and stream. This was probably Willoughby's Run. The men were then confronted with another open field, to the right of which were woods of large oak trees. This was the Spangler's Woods. The right of Wilcox's Brigade was adjoining these woods, with the extreme left against a stone wall

Looking out from the Pitzer's Woods toward the open fields in the direction where the Alabama regiments would have come.

running obliquely from the woods across an open field. It was determined that Wilcox should extend the Confederate right by advancing toward the slope leading to Pitzer's Woods. What was unknown at this point was whether the enemy had already occupied the woods themselves. In fact, Colonel Hiram Berdan and his sharpshooters were already in this same patch of woods (OR Series 1 Vol. 27/1, 514). Colonel Berdan had the 3rd Maine Regiment as his support as they traveled down the Emmitsburg Road in search of the enemy. They crossed over the Emmitsburg Road and on into Biesecker's Woods (Pfanz 1987, 98). From here they made their way northward into Pitzer's Woods. General Wilcox ordered the 10th Alabama, with the 11th on its left, to occupy the woods.

In his official report he states what developed next:

> The regiments, being proceded by skirmishers, were ordered to advance, the Eleventh to its position in line in rear of a fence, and the Tenth to keep on a line with the Eleventh, to protect it from the enemy's fire should he be found in the woods, the remaining regiments being held in rear till it should be ascertained if the enemy were in the woods.
>
> The Eleventh advanced more easily than the Tenth, being in the open field. Having moved forward about 300 yards, this regiment received a heavy volley of musketry on its right flank and rear from the enemy, concealed behind ledges of rock and trees in the woods on its right. The Tenth Alabama moved forward promptly, and soon encountered a strong line of skirmishers. These were driven back upon their supports, two regiments of infantry—the Third Maine and the First new York (U.S.) Sharpshooters [OR Series 1 Vol. 27/2, 617].

The 11th Alabama started out across an open wheat field with the 10th Alabama to its right (Clark 1914, 36). The 10th soon began to lag behind since they were making their way through the woods that ran along the right of the field. Eventually the 11th came up to and passed the waiting Berdan in the Pitzer's Woods. Colonel Berdan decided to open fire on the unsuspecting Confederates. This first blast hit the 11th at both the right flank and rear. Colonel Berdan recalls seeing the Alabamians changing direction by the right flank in the rear of the woods (OR Series 1 Vol. 27/1, 514). The regiment may have simply been wheeling to the left after reaching their assigned position (Pfanz 1987, 99). In any event, in light of this devastating volley, the men were forced to retreat back to their original point of movement behind the fence adjoining Spangler's Woods (Clark 1914, 36). No doubt Maj. Richard M. Fletcher was shot off his horse at the time of this volley.

While the 11th was reeling from the Sharpshooters' volley, the 10th Alabama came to the rescue on the right flank. The 10th Alabama was successful in driving back Berdan's men, who had been reinforced by this time with the 3rd Maine boys. By the time the Maine regiment arrived on the scene, it had turned into a heated contest in which the Alabamians were gradually pushing their way successfully forward (OR Series 1 Vol. 27/1, 507).

This skirmish was hard felt by the men of the 11th Alabama. It appears that they lost some seventeen men wounded (OR Series 1 Vol. 27/2, 617). It was at this time that the regiment lost Maj. Richard J. Fletcher to a serious leg wound. This wound would result in the loss of the Major's right leg, and ended his career in the Confederate Army.

THE CHARGE OVER THE EMMITSBURG ROAD

It was still early in the morning of July 2 when the skirmish finally came to end. General Wilcox recalls that it was about 9:00 A.M. when the brigade once again retook its position on the extreme right of the division (Cadmus M. Wilcox Papers). The 11th Alabama appears to have been in an open field during this time of waiting. Wondering what the next move would be, they were made to endure a blazing Pennsylvania sun. Captain Clark had vivid recollections of this time:

> Here we remained almost the entire day and until four P.M. The sun was fiercely hot and there was no shade or other protection for the men. Here they sweated, sweltered and swore, when the engagement began on the right about four o'clock [Clark 1914, 36].

It was during this time that General Wilcox informed his regimental commanders of the plan of attack. The attack would be by echelon, beginning with the right of Longstreet's Corps, and then extending to the left, thereby bringing each brigade into action (Clark 1914, 36). General Wilcox recalls his orders:

> My instructions were to advance when the troops on my right should advance, and to report this to the division commander, in order that the other brigades should advance in proper time. In order that I should advance with those on my right, it became necessary for me to move off by the left flank so as to uncover the ground over which they had to advance [Cadmus M. Wilcox Papers].

It was around 4:00 P.M. when the cannon could be heard opening up on the right of the Alabama Brigade. It would not be long now before the men would be making their charge. The first order was for the men to move by the left flank. This was necessary in order to clear the way for the Mississippians on their right to make their charge without impediment. As the men moved by the left flank to the low ground between the Spangler Woods and farmyard, they encountered many obstacles along the way: stone and plank fences (Pfanz 1987, 362). After they had moved to the left for some 400–500 yards, the command was then issued to face by the right flank and advance. Over an open field the men moved up the slope toward the Emmitsburg Road. Each step that was taken was being showered with grape and canister, courtesy of Lt. John G. Turnbull's Battery, Third U.S. Artillery, and Lt. Francis W. Seeley's Battery, Fourth U.S. Artillery. As if this weren't enough, there was also plenty of enemy musketry. During this movement a shell burst a little over the General's head, as well as his staff officers, resulting in the death of the courier Ridgeway (Cadmus M. Wilcox Papers). The men had to endure this terrible fire for the 250 yards that it would take to reach the Emmitsburg Road. One veteran of the 10th Alabama Regiment recalls that during this charge they were in support of the 11th Alabama (McClelen 1995, 42). They began the charge about seventy-five yards to the rear of the 11th, but it was not long before the two regiments became mixed together.

The musketry came from the enemy skirmishers who were lined behind a fence west of the Emmitsburg Road. The men drove these skirmishers back beyond the road, but then they faced a wall of blue formed in line of battle. These were men of the 12th New Hampshire and 16th Massachusetts, and they fought bravely, and very stubbornly. Captain Matthew Donovan of the 16th Massachusetts recalls the battle that day:

> At 8 A.M. were ordered into line of battle; lay down behind the stacks; skirmishing going on in front. At 4 P.M. we were ordered to advance in line of battle to an orchard; lay down under the crest of a hill. Soon after, the battle commenced in earnest. We were attacked in front and on the flank. Our men stood it bravely until overpowered by numbers; were forced to fall back a distance of 300 yards, when they again rallied, and drove the enemy back to their original lines. Our regiment lost, in killed, wounded, and missing, 81 officers and men [OR Series 1 Vol. 27/1, 551].

Here at the Emmitsburg Road, Blue and Gray fired upon one another for several minutes (Cadmus M. Wilcox Papers). As the report of Captain Donovan makes clear, the Federals were overwhelmed by the Confederates and fled down the slope to the rocky ravine of Plum Run. General Wilcox had struck the Federal line running between Seeley's Battery and the Klingle house to the right, and to the Rogers house on its left (Pfanz 1987, 374).

With the Federals in retreat, several artillery pieces now fell into Confederate hands; however, as Captain Clark recalls, little time was spent on the road. The regiment proceeded to chase the fleeing Federals without even stopping to reform their now rather jumbled lines (Clark 1914, 37). After crossing the pike the ground descended toward the base of Cemetery Ridge. General Wilcox visualizes what the Confederates saw from the top of the Emmitsburg Road:

> On the far side of the pike the ground was descending for some 600 or 700 yards. At the bottom of this descend was a narrow valley, through which ran a rocky ravine or stream, fringed with small trees and undergrowth of bushes. Beyond this, the ground rose rapidly for some 200 yards, and upon this ridge were numerous batteries of the enemy [Cadmus M. Wilcox Papers].

As the boys from Perry, Washington, Marengo, Greene, Tuscaloosa, Fayette, Pickens, and Bibb counties began to descend, they immediately came under artillery fire from both the front and the flanks. In addition to the artillery fire, the men were exposed to the muskets of the Federals now posted in this ravine. Confederate strength was, however, too overwhelming for the Unionists in the ravine. The remaining Federals were now driven from the bottom, and additional artillery pieces were captured by the Wilcox Brigade (Cadmus M. Wilcox Papers).

By the time the ravine was secured, and all the men had arrived on the scene, things were pretty much a chaotic confusion of regiments (Clark 1914, 38); nevertheless, although the brigade was in disarray and constantly exposed to enemy artillery, an attempt was now made to reach the top of Cemetery Ridge. Captain Clark recalls the heat of this charge up the slope:

> The air was thick with missiles of every character, the roar of the artillery practically drowning the shrill hiss of the Minnies. In spite of every obstacle and confusion the practically disorganized mass of Confederates pressed on up the incline, only to be forced again to drop back, until at last, becoming nearly surrounded and no re-enforcements coming to their aid, the retreat sounded and the Confederates withdrew, many being captured and the others being subjected for a distance to a destructive fire from the enemy [Clark 1914, 38].

It seems that the men were met on the way up the ridge by the 1st Minnesota Regiment. General Wilcox recalls a line of infantry descending in the front at the double-quick to support the fleeing Federals (Cadmus M. Wilcox Papers). Three times this last Federal line of support sought to drive the Alabama boys away without success. In the meantime, no signs of reinforcements for General Wilcox were in sight. Without such reinforcements the Confederates had absolutely no chance of taking the heights of Cemetery Ridge in their front. In order to save his men from utter destruction, the order to retreat back up the slope to the Emmitsburg Road was given. General Wilcox felt that the day could have been won were it not for the lack of reinforcements during this crucial part of the battle:

> I dispatched my adjutant-general to the division commander, to ask that support be sent to my men, but no support came. Three times did this last of the enemy's lines attempt to drive my men back, and were as often repulsed. This struggle at the foot of the hill on which were the enemy's batteries, though so unequal, was continued for some thirty minutes. With a second supporting line, the heights could have been carried. Without support on either my right or left, my men were withdrawn, to prevent their entire destruction or capture [Cadmus M. Wilcox Papers].

Wilcox's Brigade came charging from the direction of these woods when they met the 1st Minnesota Regiment.

This brought to an end the fighting for the 11th Alabama on July 2, 1863. It was a hard day of fighting that began with a skirmish, and ended with a gallant charge up Cemetery Ridge. The boys bivouacked for the night in their original position at the beginning of the day (OR Series 1 Vol. 27/2, 619).

The 11th Alabama on the Third Day of Battle: July 3, 1863

On the morning of July 3, 1863, the 11th was ordered along with the rest of the brigade to a position behind Colonel Alexander's artillery to the rear of Seminary Ridge (Clark 1914, 38). The artillery was still in the process of formation when the brigade took up its position in their rear about 200 yards to the west of the Emmitsburg Pike (Cadmus M. Wilcox Papers). As the men waited in this position trying to make themselves as comfortable as possible, the talk began to spread about what their role was to be in the coming battle. General Wilcox made his appearance before the men as he surveyed the enemy's position (Clark 1914, 38). Captain Clark recalls that some of the men were feeling skeptical about what might be coming their way:

> There were ominous shakings of the heads among the boys as to the wisdom of the move, and expressions were heard on all sides to the effect the Old Billy Fixin (the Brigadier's nickname), was not satisfied with having lost half his brigade the day before, but was determined to sacrifice the "whole caboodle" today [*ibid.*, 39].

According to the plan of battle for this day, the Alabama Brigade was to be in a position to render assistance if needed, and to take advantage of any success that might be gained by the assaulting column (OR Series 1 Vol. 27/2, 615). Around 10:00 A.M., the brigades of

General Pickett's Division took position immediately to the rear of General Wilcox's brigade (Cadmus M. Wilcox Papers). This is how the men remained for about five and a half hours. It was around 3:20 P.M. that the great artillery battle began, and along with that, the steady stream of Confederate casualties.

The men suffered no little damage during the artillery duel that day. General Anderson stated that of all the brigades in his division the brigade of Wilcox had the worst of it (OR Series 1 Vol. 27/2, 615). Listen to Captain Clark's description of the action at this point:

> After hours of waiting the bombardment opened with a fury beyond description. The earth seemed to rise up under the concussion, the air was filled with missiles, and the noice of all was so furious and overwhelming as well as continuous that one had to scream to his neighbor beside him to be heard.... Men could be seen, especially among the artillery, bleeding at both ears from the effect of concussion [Clark 1914, 38].

General Wilcox recalls that during this bombardment his men suffered terribly (OR Series 1 Vol. 27/2, 620). The solid shot and shell dropped in among the brigade, resulting in the wounding or death of about a dozen men. Captain Clark reflected back upon this time, and came to the conclusion that the "wisdom" of this charge was demonstrated by the terrible fire they received during this hour (Clark 1914, 39). The shelling the brigades received was a harbinger of what was to come.

THE POSITION OF THE 11TH ALABAMA DURING PICKETT'S CHARGE

After about an hour of this reciprocal artillery battle, Pickett's Division moved forward toward the enemy's position (Clark 1914, 39). According to General Wilcox's report, it was only about twenty minutes after Pickett's men began their charge that he was then ordered forward in support (OR Series 1 Vol. 27/2, 620). The men moved forward in this order from right to left: the 9th, 10th, 11th, 8th, and 14th Alabama Regiments.

The brigade was ordered to move by the right flank, according to Captain Clark, but the men soon had to move slightly to the left in order to cover the ground over which Pickett's men had traveled. Captain Clark appears to have recollections of seeing General Pickett's men for a time as they moved forward in support; however, it seems that Pickett soon moved by the left oblique and thereby passed out of Clark's view (Clark 1914, 39). General Wilcox states that as the brigade moved forward he could not see a single man he was being sent to support (OR Series 1 Vol. 27/2, 620).

It is clear from Captain Clark's recollection that many doubts were being expressed by the men about the wisdom of this charge. Listen to Clark's words:

> What such an absurd movement meant was never known to the officers then, nor has it ever been satisfactorily explained since. It was rumored afterwards that orders had been issued to stop our movements, but were not delivered. The whole affair is involved in mystery even until today. Be that as it may, the brigade moved forward rapidly, but one could hear frequent expressions from the men to the effect, "What in the devil does this mean?" [Clark 1914, 40].

This lack of certainty among the men was no doubt quickly reinforced by the canister and shower of missiles bursting all about them. They braved their way through this storm of cannon fire until they reached a scrubby timbered drain not far under the enemy's position. The men never got any further than this place, and it was here that Captain Clark himself was wounded by grape shot (Clark 1914, 40).

While in this position near the enemy, General Wilcox observed two lines of Federal infantry in a flanking movement toward the rear of his own left. He felt that reinforcements were their only hope of success at this point. He rode back for artillery support, but in the end discovered that none had ammunition capable of threatening the enemy's strength. In light of this hopeless situation, General Wilcox made the following decision:

> After some delay, not getting any artillery to fire upon the enemy's infantry that were on my left flank, and seeing none of the troops that I was ordered to support, and knowing that my small force could do nothing save to make a useless sacrifice of themselves, I ordered them back. The enemy did not pursue. My men, as on the day before, had to retire under a heavy artillery fire. My line was reformed on the ground it occupied before it advanced [OR Series 1 Vol. 27/2, 620].

As the men made their way back amidst the storm of artillery fire, Captain Clark was left behind due to his wound (Clark 1914, 40). As he was lying there contemplating what his fate would now be in the hands of the enemy, his mind also began to critically evaluate the foolish charge that had just been made. This charge, as he later reflected, was repudiated by every officer from the rank of 3rd Lieutenant to the commanding General. The day ended well for Captain Clark, however, for after the regiment was reformed it was discovered that he was missing. This prompted about four or five men to return in search of their absent Captain. Once he was found the men picked him up on a litter, and then carried him off the field of battle.

The Casualties of the 11th Alabama at Gettysburg

As we have examined together the 11th Alabama's involvement in the Gettysburg campaign, it has been discovered that there were three separate occasions when they were engaged. First, the skirmish on the morning of July 2; second, the charge over the Emmitsburg Road on the afternoon of the same day; finally, their supportive charge of Pickett's Division on the afternoon of July 3. We will now try to isolate the casualties as best we can within these three divisions of battle.

The casualties of the 11th Alabama in the skirmish of July 2, 1863, were not at all insignificant. Fleming W. Thompson notes that in the skirmish the regiment lost some fifteen men to wounds (Fleming W. Thompson Letters). The most noteworthy casualty of this skirmish was Maj. Richard Fletcher. His right leg was amputated on this same day. Major Fletcher never returned to duty in any capacity for the Confederacy following his wounding. General Wilcox reported that the 11th Alabama lost seventeen men in this skirmish, with some six or eight severely wounded (OR Series 1 Vol. 27/2, 617). What other men were wounded in this skirmish on the morning of July 2 cannot be determined from the existing materials.

In the charge over the Emmitsburg Road the casualties were also extremely heavy. As we have already noted above, since we cannot be sure for the most part who was wounded in the skirmish or this charge, we have opted to simply place the remainder of those known to have been wounded under this engagement. We do know for a fact that Colonel Sanders was wounded in this charge, and that privates Ridgeway (killed), Robert Crawford (mortally wounded), and John Hatter (arm wound) were wounded as well (Fleming W. Thompson Letters). Thompson writes graphically of his wounded comrades in this charge:

> The loss of our Company in this fight was one killed (Mr. Ridgway) & poor Bob Crawford was mortally wounded he was shot through the bowels with a musket ball, it entered his right hip bone and came out, or was cut rather, near his left hip joint, he walked about one hundred yards back to a house after he was wounded and stayed there until the fight was over, when

the Ball struck him he threw his hand up to his breast and said boys I am ruined, as soon as the fight was over, I went to him, help him off of the field to the field hospital and stand there with him until he was sent of to the Brigade Hospital, he told me he was mortally wounded & requested me to write to his Papa as soon as I could, if I came out of the fight safe.... Bob told us that he was willing to go as it had fallen to his lot, told me to write to his Pa & tell them that he was not afraid to die [Fleming W. Thompson Letters].

The following is a breakdown of the men who, according to the Confederate Service Records, were wounded or captured on July 2, 1863. From Co. A we have: Barzella Beasley wounded and captured (wounded in the right hip and left thigh), Henry Brame Jr. wounded, Henry L. Bruce wounded, Needham Hogan captured, James S. Singleton killed, Frederick E. Solley captured, Jesse Steadman wounded, William H.F. Tice wounded, and Solomon Tucker captured. From the ranks of Co. B we have: Robert Crawford mortally wounded, John P. Hatter wounded, William H. Moore wounded (no date is given), William F. Morris wounded (no date is given), John C.J. Ridgeway killed, and Lt. Frank Mundy captured. Colonel Sanders's old Co. C had the following casualties: Charles H. Bulloch wounded in the groin (no date), James F. Cameron killed, Rufus L. Harris wounded in the shoulder, Thomas A. Lowry wounded, Little Berry A. Pippen wounded, William H. Richardson wounded (no date), and Thomas W. Winn wounded. Company D listed the following men as casualties: Hillard Askew wounded in thigh, Andrew W. Barr wounded (no date given), Oliver D. Chapman killed, William F. Frisby wounded (no date given), William H. Johnson wounded (no date given), George W. Jones wounded and captured (no date given), Wyman Osborn wounded (no date given), William Percell wounded (no date given), and James H. Stewart wounded (no date given). Major Fletcher's old Co. E lists these men as casualties: Richard Allen captured, Charles Cooper wounded, James A. Faith captured, Thomas H. Green wounded, and William H. Jones killed. John James was admitted to the hospital on August 2, 1863, with a wound to the right ankle, which may indicate that he too was wounded at Gettysburg. The company from Bibb County lists these men as wounded or captured: Richard M. Brown seriously wounded in the left foot, William W. Brown captured, Henry Davis wounded (no date given), John H. Digby wounded (in the left hip), Lafayette W. Frasier captured, William Griffin wounded, Wesley E. Latham wounded (no date given), Moses J. Lightsey wounded (no date given), James McCraw captured, Thaddeus M. Phillips wounded and captured (fractured skull, left side), Asa A. Stanley wounded (no date given), Thomas H. Thompson wounded (no date given), and George F. Woodruff captured. Out of Co. G these men fell wounded or captured: Steven Barber wounded, Samuel G. Brown captured, Constantine J. Campbell severely wounded (in the hip, no date given), Thomas H. Clark wounded (left thigh), Daniel Gallant severely wounded (in leg), Marion Gallant severely wounded (left arm amputated, no date given), Thomas Hamner wounded, Basil Hughes wounded, Jesse Hughes captured, George Pierson wounded, John B.P. Poole wounded, and Jabez Sudduth severely wounded (in the arm). The wounded and captured from Co. H included: Andrew J. Bostick killed, William A. Davis wounded, John Francis Duncan wounded (right leg amputated July 29), John P. Hatcher captured, Benjamin F. Marler wounded (no date given), James H. Moorehead wounded (no date given), Horatio Nabers wounded (right leg amputated July 3), Thomas W. Shaw wounded July 2 (left arm amputated), Moses W. Taggart severely wounded (no date, left arm amputated), and Reuben Thom wounded (no date given). Company I's casualties included: Prince Wm. Aldridge wounded (in the arm), Daniel J. Cribbs wounded (no date), Francis M. Hollingsworth captured, William F. Kirkland wounded, David A. Lowe wounded, William J. Lowe wounded and captured (wounded in the face, no date given), Allen H. Propst wounded, Rufus H. Shelton wounded (in the left leg), Robert L. Smith wounded (in the ankle, no date given), Jasper Wilkins severely wounded (in the arm, right hand, two fingers amputated), and Ignicious M. Wright missing (supposed dead). Finally, the Independent Volunteers listed the following casualties: Patrick Brice wounded, John W. Cochran wounded (no date given), Elias Crews wounded (in the leg), Williford Curb wounded, Joe N. Eskridge captured, Frank Ezell wounded, John W. Horton captured, William H.H. Ratliff captured, Benjamin Sanders wounded, and Andrew J. Washburn wounded. If we total these together, we come up with seventy-one wounded, and seven killed. In addition, about eighteen were definitely captured on July 2. Surgeon Lafayette Guild, the Army Medical Director, lists the casualties of the 11th Alabama at six killed, and sixty-nine wounded (OR Series 1 Vol. 27/2, 332). Our lists may in fact be one and the same if we left off one of the men who was mortally wounded, and Ignicious Wright of Co. I who was missing and supposed dead.

THE CASUALTIES OF THE 11TH ALABAMA IN SUPPORT OF PICKETT'S CHARGE

The following group of men are listed as casualties of Co. A: Elias Braswell wounded, James M. Kelly captured, William A. McLaughlin captured, Alfred Johnson Morgan captured, Thomas W. Tucker captured, James P. Hankins captured, and Alexander F. Wayne captured. Company B had Thomas Avery wounded (right forearm), Capt. George Clark wounded, Calvin Edmiston killed, Henry McGee captured, and John Henry Phillips captured. No men from Co. C or Co. D were lost on July 3. From Co. E we find that Egbert B. Ashe was captured, along with Levi Parks and Edwin A. Sherwood. No casualty was reported from Co. F, but from Co. G, George W. Bryson was mortally wounded (he died July 10), John T. Burchfield wounded, Thomas H. Clark captured, William M. Cole wounded, and John B. Hughes wounded (in the left hand). Samuel M. Acker from Co. H was absent and supposed killed, David A. Ballard was captured, Thomas J. Ballard was captured, Jacob J. Funderburk was captured, Henry O. Love was wounded severely and captured, and Tristram S. Thomas was captured. Company I casualties were William F. Lane captured, William H.H. Phillips captured, William J. Lowe captured, Ephraim Long wounded, and George L. Traweek captured. From the ranks of Co. K the following men were casualties of the charge: Jacob Cook wounded, Noah H. Lovelady killed, and William B. Miller killed. This comes to a total of about ten wounded, including one mortally wounded, nineteen captured, and four killed. The 11th had almost as many killed on July 3 as they did on July 2.

The Prisoners of the 11th Alabama at Gettysburg

I think it is interesting to take note of what happened to many of those who were taken captive at Gettysburg. What became of the men who were either captured in battle, or who were left behind and eventually taken to prisons? The men captured at Gettysburg who were not seriously wounded probably experienced the following scenario (Burrell 1997, 121–123). Following Pickett's charge the prisoners were taken to the rear of the Union army, and placed in a camp strongly guarded by both infantry and cavalry. On the morning of July 4 they were formed into line for the march. It is possible that they may have been able to reach this same day the town of Westminster, Maryland. Here the prisoners were placed into an open field surrounded by a high fence under close guard. There was no shelter or blankets, and it then began to rain in buckets. Here they remained, sleeping in the mud.

On the morning of July 5 they were boarded on cars for Baltimore, Maryland. At just about dark they would have reached Baltimore, and from there the march would have continued to Fort McHenry. Fort McHenry was about two miles below Baltimore guarding the mouth to the city (SHSP Vol. 8, 77). Fort McHenry, in the summer of 1863, served as a rendezvous point for Confederate soldiers who were on their way to other permanent prisons like Fort Delaware. Not every soldier who was captured in the 11th Alabama was sent to Fort McHenry, according to the muster rolls. Those soldiers who were sent there found themselves being placed in open ground around the fort with no food or shelter. No rations were issued, and they once more had to endure sleeping in a driving rain. On the morning of July 6 rations were finally given: coffee, hardtack, and meat. On the morning of July 7 they were placed on a steamer bound for Fort Delaware. Before the day was out they reached their destination.

Frank M. Mundy (*Confederate Veteran* Vol. 5, 481).

Confederate Monument at Johnson's Island Cemetery.

A brief note is in order regarding Lieutenant Mundy of Co. B. He was taken prisoner at Gettysburg on the second day. His destination would eventually prove to be the Johnson's Island Prison near Sandusky, Ohio. This was a 300-acre island within Sandusky Bay that was uninhabited in 1861 (Johnson's Island Prison 1862–1865). At first the island received all ranks of Confederate prisoners, but by June of 1862 only Confederate officers were shipped to the bay. It was at this prison facility that Lieutenant Mundy would remain for the duration of the war. Soon Mundy would be joined by a former soldier in Co. B: Alexander Gilbert. Gilbert had risen to the rank of 2nd Lieutenant in Co. F, 28th Alabama Infantry (CSR). He was captured at Chattanooga and sent to Johnson's Island on November 24, 1863.

Many of the wounded men were too critical to be moved with the other prisoners. A substantial number were cared for at the Camp Letterman General Hospital at Gettysburg. Apparently Dr. Jonathan Letterman, the director of the Medical Department of the Army of the Potomac, gave the order to establish a large general hospital in the area (OR Series 1 Vol. 27/3, 620 ff.). A suitable site was located by July 14, 1863, yet the necessary tents for the hospital were as yet unavailable. Around July 20, 1863, Camp Letterman began receiving patients from the local field hospitals around Gettysburg (Camp Letterman History: July 1863). It was one mile east of Gettysburg on the York Road. The exact location appears to have been on the farm of George Wolf.

We know that the following were either left behind or captured, and then treated at Gettysburg: Barzella Beasley, Co. A; Rufus Harris, Co. C; Basil Hughes, Co. G; Marion Gallant, Co. G; Horatio Nabers, Co. H; George Jones, Co. D; Thaddeus M. Phillips, Co. F; Moses Taggart, Co. H; Henry O. Love, Co. H; Thomas J. Ballard, Co. H; Thomas W. Shaw, Co. H; John F. Duncan, Co. H; and Daniel J. Cribbs, Co. I (CSR).

A Brief Evaluation of the Gettysburg Campaign

In a letter dated October 27, 1863, to his sister Mary, General Wilcox expressed the feeling that Gettysburg was not the disaster that many thought it was (Cadmus M. Wilcox Papers). He states that they left behind around 6,500 wounded, sick, cooks, and surgeons; nevertheless, they brought back with them about 1,500 wounded. For every one killed they had seven or eight wounded. They took 6,000 prisoners from the Union army, yet paroled 1,500 on the field at Gettysburg. As he analyzed the Confederate losses with the Union losses, he concluded, "So you will see that Gettysburg was not a failure by any means. And in fact in all our battles we inflict generally three times the loss upon the enemy than he does upon us" (Cadmus M. Wilcox Papers). Even though this was a positive assessment by General Wilcox, he was also realistic in his view of the terrible losses the Confederacy endured. In a letter dated July 16, 1863, General Wilcox stated that the enemy could afford to lose the great number they had, but by way of contrast, the South could not afford such high casualties.

For some of the soldiers in the 11th Alabama, Gettysburg was their final battle in support of the Southern cause. James Kelly of Co. A, and William H.H. Phillips of Co. H, both swore the oath of allegiance to the United States and joined the U.S. 3rd Maryland Cavalry (CSR).

9

The Lull Before the Storm

In this chapter we will examine the developments within the 11th Alabama from the time immediately following Gettysburg, until the fierce fighting in the spring of 1864. In many ways this period can be characterized as a "lull before the storm." It proved to be the last substantial period of time of relative quiet for the regiment before the intense battles began leading to the siege of both Richmond and Petersburg.

From Gettysburg to Orange Court House

The day after Pickett's Charge the heavens opened up and the rains fell for most of the day (Cadmus M. Wilcox Papers). Pickets had been posted, but the Federals offered no fresh attack on the hurting armies of the South. On the evening of July 4, the Army of Northern Virginia began its long and arduous march toward the friendly confines of Virginia. The withdrawal took place by way of Fairfield. They were able to make some twelve miles before bivouacking for a few hours. The march was then resumed down a little-used old road which intersected the Hagerstown and Emmitsburg Turnpike near a large summer hotel called Monterey. Here the men turned to the right, and descended the mountain which led into a small village below (Cadmus M. Wilcox Papers). They left this small village around 5:00 P.M. on July 5, and were able to come within a few miles of Hagerstown on July 6. They remained in camp at Hagerstown for a couple of days. The men marched through Hagerstown on July 8 before camping a few miles outside of town. It was on July 9 that the weary soldiers were forced to take a position in line of battle near St. James College. General Wilcox identified this as Fountain Rock. He recalled that there was an enormous spring of cold water located here as well as the Old Ringgold Manor. Skirmishers were sent forward to probe the enemy, but no attack was made against the brigade.[1] On July 12 the army began its movement again toward the Potomac, where they crossed near Shepherdstown around July 14.[2]

Captain Clark recalls some personal details of this withdrawal from Gettysburg (Clark 1914, 41). He remembers that the line of wagons and ambulances which pulled out of Gettysburg must have been twenty-odd miles long. He writes:

> I was in a wagon fitted up as a kind of ambulance and my companions were Colonel John C. Saunders and Major R.J. Fletcher. We went back to Fairfield and then turned left and south, though over what roads we passed, or what towns we went through I do not know. I only know that all the night our steps were dogged by Kilpatrick's Federal cavalry which would frequently cross ahead of us, dash into our lines and cut down some ambulances and escape.

Upon arriving at the banks of the Potomac, Captain Clark recalls finding thousands of wagons and ambulances already there and unable to cross due to the high waters. In addition to the high waters, there was only one ferryboat that was obtainable at that time. This made for an extremely frustrating transition, but at long last they were able to get their ambulance across to safety (Clark 1914, 42).

Before reaching Orange Court House the men had a brief encampment midway between Martinsburg and Winchester, Virginia, near Bunker Hill (Sanders's File). On the way to Bunker Hill, General Wilcox became engaged in a conversation with General Early, and later with General Lee (Cadmus M. Wilcox Papers). In his conversation with General Lee, the subject of the letter General Wilcox had written to him surfaced. This no doubt referred to the desire of General Wilcox to be relieved of command in the Army of Northern Virginia. General Lee assured Wilcox that he would respond to his request, but that the Gettysburg campaign had consumed all his attention up to this point.

By July 16 the army was bivouacked at Bunker Hill (Sanders's File). Colonel Sanders was taken on to Winchester due to the leg wound received at Gettysburg. He remained at Winchester during the regiment's encampment at Bunker Hill, but left to rejoin his command after it moved on to Culpeper Court House. As the story goes, Colonel Sanders made it to Culpeper on his horse by propping his leg on a pillow.

The men had the feeling that this stay at Bunker Hill would prove to be very brief (Sanders's File). In fact, Dr. Sanders believed that they would be leaving the very next day. The men were here long enough to write some letters home, but by July 21 they were on their way toward Culpeper Court House (Cadmus M. Wilcox Papers). General Meade had crossed the Potomac and was moving along the eastern flank of the Blue Ridge. General Longstreet was ordered on July 19 to move by way of Front Royal to Culpeper Court House (Cadmus M. Wilcox Papers; Dowdey 1961, 554). On July 21 General Wilcox marched his forces through Winchester and Front Royal before bivouacking at Flint Hill on July 22. The next day they passed through Gaines Cross Roads to Newby's Cross Roads where they encamped on the Hazel River. It was July 24 when the men finally reached what was to be their new home for about a week at Culpeper Court House.

One soldier recalled that this was a splendid place for a camp (Wood and Jackson 2000, 44). William Thomas Jackson of Company A, 8th Alabama Infantry, wrote of this camp:

> We have a splendid place for campes & the cars run right to Culpeper. So we have a good way of getting transportation to Richmond. We marched very hard for the last three or four days. We averaged from fifteen to 20 miles a day. The Yankee cavalry attached us a Friday as we came on & delayed us some but we received but little or no damage.... Our brigade was not in it. Our division was.

As we mentioned above, Colonel Sanders rejoined his command while they were encamped at Culpeper. Since his leg had not as yet healed, he arrived at camp with his leg propped up on his horse. He had always found it difficult being away from his command for any length of time. In spite of his unhealed wound, Sanders would not allow himself another day away from his duties.

On August 1, 1863, rumor circulated that the enemy was approaching from the Rappahannock near Brandy Station (Cadmus M. Wilcox Papers). General Wilcox marched his men in that direction for several miles, but it only turned out to be Federal cavalry. On August 3 they moved toward the Rapidan and crossed at Barnett's Ford. Here two lines of Federal infantry were seen to be moving by the left flank of Wilcox, and the General ordered the men to hold their ground. He had no artillery support to engage the enemy with, and thus felt compelled to retire under heavy artillery fire. The brigade lost some 204 killed and wounded in this engagement.

The men moved southward now across the Rapidan toward Orange Court House. General Lee felt that the army needed to be located south of the Rapidan in order to be in a better position to engage the enemy (Dowdey 1961, 568). This location would also prove to be more advantageous in the event of a possible Federal decision to march towards Fredericksburg. The new camp at Orange Court House was situated upon a high ridge in a nice grove of trees (Cadmus M. Wilcox Papers). They were about six and a half miles from Orange Court House on its east side, and very near to the railroad. The men would call Orange Court House their home until the outbreak of the spring campaign of 1864.

The Encampment at Orange Court House

The biggest news to hit the brigade since the appointment of Cadmus M. Wilcox as brigade commander was the news that he was now departing by reason of promotion to division commander. General Wilcox recalled that after locating to Orange Court House, General A.P. Hill came to his headquarters with the news that he would soon be promoted to division commander (Cadmus M. Wilcox Papers). Wilcox told General Hill that he was not of the same opinion, and when Hill questioned him concerning his doubts, Wilcox responded that it didn't seem to him that he should be any closer now to promotion than he was at Gaines' Mill, Williamsburg, or Salem Church. Wilcox went on to tell General Hill that he thought very little about it just now, and that he was in hopes of being relieved from the army.

On August 13, 1863, Wilcox was in fact promoted to Major General and given Pender's old division (Freeman Vol. 3, 202; OR Series 1 Vol. 29/1, 401). It seems that this promotion was to date from around August 3, 1863 (OR Series 1 Vol. 27/3, 1061). From August 4, 1863, onward, the brigade fell under the command of Colonel J.C.C. Sanders (OR Series 1 Vol. 29/2, 685). Wilcox tried unsuccessfully to have his old Alabama brigade transferred to his division. The men of the 11th Alabama would never again fight under the direct command of General Wilcox.

Colonel Sanders wrote a letter home about the news of General Wilcox's promotion (Sanders's File). He states that the army was in good spirits at present, and the brigade in his opinion was nearly as strong now as it was before Gettysburg. Regarding General Wilcox he writes:

> Gen'l Wilcox has, at last, been made a Maj. Gen'l has been assigned to Penders old Division of this Corps. His promotion was gratifying to the brigade, as they believed he deserved it, and it recognizes somewhat the voice of the brigade, though we regret to lose him as a brigade commander.

Colonel Sanders goes on to suggest that Colonel Forney would probably become the next brigade commander; that is, if he ever became fit for field service. It was thought that he would lose the entire use of one arm, and the partial use of one foot. Colonel Royston of the 8th Alabama was the senior Colonel of the brigade, but popular opinion was not in favor of his advancement. In the mind of Colonel Sanders, Royston was not the best candidate for the brigade commander either. At present, Colonel Sanders himself was in charge of the brigade, and he believed that it would so remain until Colonel Forney was well enough to take command. As it turned out, Colonel Sanders would remain in command of the brigade until late in 1864.

Regimental Developments at Orange Court House

Even thought the big military news at Orange Court House concerned the promotion of Gen. Cadmus M. Wilcox, there were other developments within the regiment that deserve our attention. It seems that General Wilcox was desirous of the services of Walter E. Winn on his staff. He had been the Assistant Adjutant General since June of 1862. He penned a recommendation for Winn's promotion to Major on August 17, 1863 (CSR). On August 19, 1863, Secretary of War James Seddon reported that they would gladly recommend Captain Winn's promotion if he so desired it. However, on August 22, 1863, General Lee stated that in his opinion there was no vacancy for Winn to fill on Wilcox's staff. This appears to have been a major disappointment to Captain Winn, as we shall see in later developments in 1864.

Elections were taking place in Co. B during this time. Fleming Thompson mentions that both he and Robert Schoppert had been nominated for Jr. 2nd Lieutenant (Fleming W. Thompson Letters). Since Winfield Bird's promotion to 2nd Lieutenant back in April 27, 1863, the company had been without a Jr. 2nd Lieutenant. The final tally of votes came to thirteen in favor of Schoppert, and twelve voting for Thompson. Fleming felt that if Robuck, Hamilton, Morris, and John Hatter had been in camp the result might have been different. Yet for all that, Thompson felt that he had done better than he had expected to do in this election. Company B now had George Clark as Captain, Frank Mundy as 1st Lieutenant,[3] Winfield Bird 2nd Lieutenant, and Robert Schoppert as Jr. 2nd Lieutenant.

The other companies looked like this at Orange Court House: Co. A had John B. Rains as Captain, William B. Young as 1st Lieutenant, John H. Adams as 2nd Lieutenant, and Thomas Witherspoon as Jr. 2nd Lieutenant; Co. C had Benjamin Higginbotham as Captain, William H. Richardson as 1st Lieutenant, Richard Kennedy as 2nd Lieutenant, and James C.B. Harkness as Jr. 2nd Lieutenant; Co. D had John Prince as Captain, Frank Glover as 1st Lieutenant, Cornelius Watlington as 2nd Lieutenant, and John W. Cole Jr. 2nd Lieutenant;[4] Co. E had John James as Captain, no listed 1st Lieutenant, John Atchison is listed as 2nd Lieutenant as is Egbert Ashe, and even another reference listing Wooten O'Neal as 2nd Lieutenant;[5] Co. F had Joseph C. Caddelle as Captain, William J. Suttle as 1st Lieutenant, Zachariah Abney as 2nd Lieutenant, and Philip Vance as Jr. 2nd Lieutenant; Co. G had John B. Hughes as Captain, Henyard T. Williamson as 1st Lieutenant, James N. Hayes as 2nd Lieutenant, and Joseph R. Britt as Jr. 2nd Lieutenant; Co. H had Martin L. Stewart as Captain, Walter T. Palmer as 1st Lieutenant, and Reuben Thom as 2nd Lieutenant; Co. I had Lemuel Harris as Captain, Abel Walden as 1st Lieutenant, Rufus H. Shelton as 2nd Lieutenant, and William T. Davis as Jr. 2nd Lieutenant; finally, Co. K had James Brazleton as Captain, Edward Lucas as 1st Lieutenant, and Beverly L. Waddell as Jr. 2nd Lieutenant.[6] This is essentially how the regiment looked in the summer of 1863 until the spring of 1864.

It seems from the records we have that a certain amount of recruiting went on during this encampment. Elam P. Horton and John W. Tadlock enlisted in Co. K, while Enoch Sikes and Asa Anthony enlisted in Co. I (CSR). John W. Brady joined Co. A, while David W. Smelly, James W. Smelly, and John D. Hamilton enlisted in Co. F. On August 20 O.M. Lucas of Co. G, 5th Alabama Infantry, transferred to Co. K of the 11th Alabama, while Thomas Ferrell likewise transferred to the 5th Alabama.

Later on in the year, and into 1864, further recruiting efforts can be detected among the companies. On November 12, 1863, James Roberts enlisted in Co. D at Demopolis. On January 2, 1864, John A. Allen enlisted in Co. H, while Bryant Platt enlisted on January 12 in Co. F at Centreville. On February 16, 1864, Jesse Clanton enlisted in Co. I, while on March

Old Third Alabama Hospital in Richmond, Virginia, as it looks today. Here Basil Gillmore died.

12 E.V.F. Thornton enlisted in the same company. On March 1, 1864, Co. G added Andrew Burrage to its ranks, while the Marengo Rifles added Moses M.D. Moore to their rolls.

Deaths in the Regiment

The ranks continued to thin out during the long encampment at Orange Court House. Edwin Sherwood of Co. E died on July 28, 1863, at Ft. Delaware Prison (CSR). Robert R. Morgan of Co. A died on August 5, 1863, at General Hospital in Mount Jackson, Virginia, and is buried in Our Soldier's Cemetery. Solomon A. Tucker of Co. A died at Ft. Delaware Prison of dysentery on September 16, 1863. On October 1, 1863, William Lowe of Co. I died at home in Pickens County of wounds he received at Gettysburg (CSC). Strudwick Young of Co. D died at home on October 12, 1863 from wounds he received at Gaines' Mill. Basil Gillmore of Co. A died on October 19, 1863, of pneumonia at the Third Alabama Hospital in Richmond (CSR). Several soldiers died in November and December at Ft. Delaware, and were buried on the New Jersey shore opposite the camp. On November 3, 1863, John W. Horton of Co. K died of scurvy, Thomas Tucker of Co. A died on November 25, 1863, of smallpox, as did James Hankins of Co. A on December 13, 1863. John B.P. Poole of Co. G died on January 29, 1864, at Orange Court House. Tristram Thomas of Co. H died at Ft. Delaware of smallpox on January 29, 1864. Leslie Horn of Co. F succumbed to smallpox on February 15, 1864, while Willis Person of the Bibb company died back at Centreville the very next day. Thomas W. Shaw of Co. H died on March 1, 1864, of wounds he received at Gettysburg, and was buried on March 2 at Louden Park Cemetery in Baltimore, Maryland (Confederate Hill).

David A. Bennet of Co. G died at Salisbury, North Carolina, on March 13, 1864, while undergoing a court-martial.

Camp Life at Orange Court House

There were several personal notes that were made by the men during this time of encampment that we need to make mention of. Fleming Thompson of Co. B on August 14, 1863, tells the story of not having seen any fresh fruit in such a long time, and how he would love to see some now (Fleming W. Thompson Letters). Listen to his own words:

> I have not seen a ripe peach, apple, plum, watermellon nor nothing of the kind & I know they are just in their prime at hom. Some of our boys was over at Orange C.H. the other day when the train came in, and they told me that they saw a watermellon weighing six pounds sell for 15 dollars, this is the way we get what little we do get by paying ten prices for it.

He also mentions how useless the Confederate money was becoming at this point. He said he was going to send home fifty dollars, and he wanted it to be loaned out rather than to be kept. The reason for this was that Confederate money wasn't going to be worth five cents on the dollar when the war was over! Colonel Sanders also mentions the high price of many of the items that a soldier desperately needed (Sanders's File). He states that a soldier's boots now cost a hundred dollars a pair, while a hat ran for about seventy to eighty dollars.

Captain John James of Co. E wrote a letter that was preserved in a Mobile newspaper on November 13, 1863, which captures well the spirit of the soldier during this period of time. He speaks about the honor of the soldier, and the recognition he desires from those he is serving. His words deserve to be quoted:

> Honor is all the pay the soldier gets; and how emptily it lies, if his countrymen do not take it up and treasure it for him. How gratifying it is to the poor faint soldier, after battle, to read the public appreciation and honors given his conduct by his countrymen, and what a sweet consolation to him is the receipt of praise from the dear ones at home.... Now, what I wish you to notice is this, that on every battlefield in Virginia, the Alabamians and Mississippians have distinquished themselves. They have been the backbone, as it were, of Longstreet's corps. Over a thousand miles from home, which many of them have not seen since they left it nearly three years ago, fighting on the soil of another State, they have maintained the victorious reputation of this army, equally with Stonewall Jackson's veterans, without receiving any reward except the inward sense of having done their duty [*Mobile Advertiser & Register*, 13 November 1863].

We hear in the words of Captain James the heart of the soldier in 1863. They have sacrificed so much on behalf of their country, and all they desire is to know that their efforts are appreciated by their countrymen. He feels that the Alabama and Mississippi boys have been the heart and soul of Longstreet's Corps, and have duly gained this reputation in the Army of Northern Virginia.

A consideration of the encampment at Orange Court House would not be complete without an examination of the revival of religion which took place at this time. Many of the men write about it in their letters back home. Fleming Thompson mentions that they had preaching in the camp every day of the week, and prayer meeting at night (Fleming W. Thompson Letters). He noted that some twenty or thirty had joined in since it began, and in his opinion, he had never seen more of an interest in spiritual things in his life. Henry Cribb's letter of August 28, 1863, likewise mentions that a revival is sweeping the entire brigade:

> I had forgotten to tell you a bout our Meetings we have had a meeting going on in our brigade ever since we have been hear. a great many have professed Religion and joined the church it is

a genuine (illegible) thing.... To much we have had to much confidence in our own thinking that we could do any thing but it is a mistake. There is some things that we can't do with out the help of providence [Honnoll Family Papers 1861–1865].

It is evident that this revival had spread throughout the entire brigade. William T. Jackson was in Co. A, 8th Alabama Regiment, and he wrote home on August 23, 1863, in which he states, "We have plenty of good preaching & meeting.... I am sorry to tell you that I don't enjoy the meeting as I want to & want you to pray for me that I may get right & feel & serve God as I ought" (Wood and Jackson 2002, 45). Charles Wesley Foust was in Co. B, 10th Alabama Regiment, and in his letters home we find a detailed account of the revival meetings held during August and September of 1863:

> Well I suppose that you would like to know how our meeting terminated that had been going on so long in our camp it lasted 4 weeks with preaching day and night with the exception of 4 or 5 times and was attended by very large congregations of attentive men. I never saw a meeting in my life where there was more interest manifested by the attendants it seemed that ever one both saint and sinner felt the importance of the occasion the anxious seats were crowded all the while with enquiring souls and the results was that about 150 souls were converted to Christ and scores were added to the Church both Baptists and Methodists. The meeting was carried on by Baptist preachers mostly our Chaplain being a Baptist preacher but a mighty good man as his works prove.... I feel now that I am reinstated into God's favor and feel a determination to live more as becometh a follower of Christ. I feel a deeper interest in the religion of the Lord Jesus than I ever did before in all of my life. I love to talk about Jesus and about Heaven and love to read his blessed word more than I ever did before in my life [Underwood n.d.].

On September 10, 1863, one newspaper notes the establishment of the Young Men's Christian Association in the brigade composed of the 8th, 9th, 10th, 11th, and 14th Alabama Regiments (*Mobile Evening News*, 10 September 1863). The article describes the situation in this fashion:

> Feeling the great need of all moral influences to extend and keep alive genuine, heartfelt piety in the army, the members of this association would be thankful for all contributions of religious reading in the shape of tracts, newspapers, reviews, small volumnes & c. Contributions may be sent to individual members of the association, or to the Corresponding Secretary.

I think it can be said that the men were greatly stirred during this time of religious revival. They came to realize their own limitations, their dependence upon God, and their own sinfulness. It was a time of rededication to the values they had learned in their youth, and of corporate celebration in the religious meetings held during this encampment.

The Bristoe Station Campaign

On or about October 9, 1863, the 11th Alabama left its camp at Orange Court House. It was thought that it might be necessary to confront George Meade's army, which was now encamped north of Culpeper extending all the way to the Rapidan (Freeman Vol. 3, 239). The Confederate Army pursued Meade's retreating Federals all the way to Bristoe Station, where they arrived on October 14, 1863. Captain Clark recalls how the men, along with the remainder of the brigade, were held in reserve at the fight at Bristoe Station (Clark 1914, 43). He remembers the following:

> ...flanked Culpeper Court House about fifteen or twenty miles, finally reaching Warrenton, and then passed on to Bristoe Station. Here a heavy engagement was fought. Our brigade was held in reserve and did not come into contact with the enemy, but the accompaniment of the

enemy's shells was severe. After remaining at Bristoe Station two or three days, the army retired to Culpeper Court House again, Anderson's division being the rear guard.

In Major General R.H. Anderson's official report, he states that on October 14, 1863, when near Bristoe Station, he received orders from Lt. Gen. A.P. Hill of the Third Corps to move two of his brigades to the right of the road approaching the station (OR Series 1 Vol. 29/1, 428). In compliance with this request, Anderson send Posey's and Perry's brigades to intercept the enemy troops which had been moving along the railroad toward the station. When the brigades approached, and were not even within striking distance, the enemy double-quicked off into the forest near the railroad. The brigades continued forward toward the railroad until they found the enemy posted behind the railroad embankments and cuts, with a battery of artillery firmly in place so as to enfilade the road. Anderson directed the remainder of his brigades, which would have included the Alabama Brigade, to come up and form in line of battle. They remained in line of battle all that night, and in the morning the enemy was gone (OR Series 1 Vol. 29/1, 428).

The Alabama Brigade was not engaged in the fight at Bristoe Station, but members could still recall the artillery fire they were exposed to in this engagement. We already alluded to Captain Clark's words that the artillery fire at Bristoe was "severe" (Clark 1914, 43). Fleming Thompson states that although the brigade was not in the fight, it still had three or four men killed, and thirty or so wounded from artillery shells (Fleming W. Thompson Letters). He recalled that one man of the 11th was wounded at Bristoe, but he was not from Co. B. The man he alluded to was Joseph C. Whiteside of Co. C (CSR). He was a native North Carolinian, the son of John N. and Elenora Whiteside.[7] Joseph had enlisted at the outbreak of the war back in Clinton, Alabama, and would live to see the end at Appomattox Court House.

Clark recalls that after several days' stay at Bristoe Station the brigade retired to Culpeper Court House (Clark 1914, 43). This was probably the encampment that was near Brandy Station. One note states that they remained here until November 8 before retiring again to Orange Court House (11th Alabama). In an interesting letter from Brandy Station on October 24, 1863, Henry Cribbs states that this new encampment was about six miles from Culpeper Court House (Honnoll Family Papers 1861–1865). Some talk was circulating that they might leave here and go into Tennessee. This would prove to be just another false rumor that made the rounds among the men.

On the same day Henry Cribbs wrote his letter back home, Fleming Thompson did as well. What he was already concerned about was the soon to arrive winter of 1863–1864:

> Emily, I want you to help me out a little in the clothing line this winter if you can. I am out of shirts, socks, drawers. I would be glad if you could send me about 2 good cotton shirts. I don't want them white, any other color. 2 pair of drawers and 2 or 3 pr. of socks. If you can't send all, send me what you can of them. I have no clothes only what I have on, and they are very sorry [Fleming W. Thompson Letters].

He was also interested in getting some good food from back home in Alabama. He asks Emily to inform John Hatter, who was home recuperating from a wound at Gettysburg, that he must bring him something good to eat when he returns to the army. He was getting tired of the same old beef and flour they were drawing.

Winter Quarters at Orange Court House, 1863–1864

It was around November 9 that the men returned to their old encampment on the Rapidan,[8] and it wasn't long before the feeling set in that active operations were over until the spring of 1864. Dr. Sanders reflects this feeling when he writes about his own winter accommodations:

> ...we have gone to work and fixed up for the winter very comfortably and would be somewhat disappointed with an order to move. We have incurred the expense and trouble of a brick chimney to our tent, and to leave it would make it an unprofitable investment. The men have already rendered themselves much more comfortable than they were at any time last winter, and with a little assistance from the Government in the way of furnishings flys & blankets.... They build little huts with chimneys to them and cover them generally with the little shelter tents, with which they have supplied themselves from the battlefields [Sanders's File].

Dr. Sanders also mentions that President Jefferson Davis was at that very time visiting the army, and he would soon be on hand to review the Third Corps. This was the first time that President Davis had visited them since the battles around Richmond back in 1862.

THE MINE RUN CAMPAIGN

Just as the men, in the words of Dr. Sanders, were settling down for a long winter on the Rapidan, news was received of a new Federal threat. Cavalry scouts had spotted an enemy movement for the lower fords of the Rapidan, and the Confederate army was unsure of where the Federals might strike (Freeman Vol. 3, 269). Captain Clark recalls that Meade crossed the Rapidan about fifteen miles south of where they were camped (Clark 1914, 43).

In response to this development, the Third Corps left their encampment on the morning of November 27, 1863, and made their way towards Fredericksburg by the Plank Road (OR Series 1 Vol. 29/1, 895). They bivouacked about two miles past Verdiersville. Here Hill received information that the enemy was advancing down the Plank Road and was driving back the cavalry. At around 4:00 P.M., and several miles in advance of this, Hill found General Stuart disputing the enemy movement; in response to this, Hill ordered Heth's division into line, and Walker's brigade was deployed as skirmishers. In Hill's words:

> An order was received from the general commanding to send a division to the support of the Second Corps, on my left, and to establish communication between my own corps and the Second. Leaving directions for Anderson's division to be diverted for this purpose, I galloped over to the left to examine the ground. Anderson was soon put in communication with General Hays, commanding Early's right [OR Series 1 Vol. 29/1, 896].

Information was then received that the enemy was in the front, and one corps of the enemy on Hill's left and rear. Hill was also concerned that the ground he was now on was unfavorable to deal with the enemy threat. He therefore determined to occupy the west side of Mine Run, which was about one and one half miles from his present position. He issued the necessary orders, and by daybreak his line of battle was now formed. He posted Anderson's Division on the left, resting on the old turnpike, and Wilcox's division on the right, crossing the Plank Road and resting upon Catharpin Road. The men quickly threw up rifle pits in anticipation of the battle to come, and when the enemy troops displayed themselves on the opposite hills the Alabama boys were ready to receive them.

All remained in this state of readiness on November 28. Then, on November 29, it was discovered that the enemy was concentrating and extending themselves to Hill's right. In response to this development Hill extended two brigades of Wilcox's Division to the right. For the next couple of days there was skirmishing between the two armies (Clark 1914, 43–44). On daybreak of December 2, 1863, it was discovered that the enemy had left during the night. Hill's Corps was moved down the road in pursuit, but upon reaching Parker's Store it discovered that the rear guard had already recrossed the Rapidan. The men were then ordered back to their old camps on the Rapidan near Orange Court House.

The 11th Alabama had several men wounded and captured during this time of skirmishing near Mine Run. Curtis Roane of Co. D was wounded in the right knee, and Henry T. Williams of Co. I was wounded in the left arm on November 30, 1863 (11th Alabama; CSR). In addition, Richard Sullivan and Elbert Bolton of Co. I were both captured at Mine Run on November 27, 1863. The reason given in their records is for "straggling" (CSR). Both of these men were taken to the Old Capitol Prison on December 5, 1863, and eventually to Ft. Delaware on June 15, 1864, where they spent the remainder of the war.

Camp Conditions in Winter Quarters, 1863–1864

Fleming Thompson penned a letter dated December 24, 1863, in which he relates the conditions of this winter encampment:

> ...we have at this time, one bushell of corn meal, the hind leg and backbone of a sheep, 3 fine cabbage heads, ½ bushel of Irish potatoes, extra of our rations, I have also got 1 pound of butter 1 peck of dry beans & a gallon of peas dont you think we will live? Some of the boys say that I have more good luck than any fellow they ever saw [Fleming W. Thompson Letters].

He was living at the time in a Yankee wall tent with a fireplace. Fleming Thompson fared well then for the first part of the winter, but things appear to have taken a turn by early 1864. On February 29, 1864, Thompson states that rations were very short at this time, and he was not sure how long these would last. A month later, on March 29, 1864, he relates how difficult the harsh conditions of the winter had become for the men:

> ...for one to see what kind of weather we have had here during the last 2 weeks they would not once think that the cold weather was near over. About a week or ten days ago we had the largest snow that we have had here this winter, and I am not sure if it was not the largest that we have ever had in Va. since we came out. It averaged from 8 to 10 inches & on the low grounds, where it drifted was from 2½ to 3 ft. deep. It has all melted now, except on the Moutains they are perfectly white yet. It is raining here now, and the weather is very disagreeable [Fleming W. Thompson Letters].

Captain Clark recalls that this was a very harsh winter for the men from Alabama to endure (Clark 1914, 44). He notes:

> We had that winter a time of starvation, a day's rations being a quarter of a pound of bacon and a pint of meal, which was very hard on me as I had my servant to feed out of this slim amount of rations. We ate only one meal a day, which was about eleven o'clock, and in order to protect my servant, before beginning to eat, I would separate the food and turn his over to him for safekeeping.

This assessment of Captain Clark is confirmed by the testimony of Dr. Sanders in a January 31, 1864, letter (Sanders's File). He informs his father that rations now were: one quarter pound of bacon or salt beef, or one half pound of fresh beef, and one pound and an eighth of flour. Along with this, the men were getting rice and small quantities of molasses. Yet for all of this, he perceived that the men were still in excellent spirits. Each man was still determined to do his duty until the enemy was driven from Confederate soil, and Southern independence was acknowledged.

Basil M. Hughes finally rejoined his company sometime in January of 1864 (Strawbridge 1998). He remembered that the cold and dismal winter was made even more unbearable by the ragged clothes many had to wear. Many had shoes that were in terrible condition, and very little food was to be found for the men. He states that the horrors of this winter were in fact indescribable. It seems that this condition of things remained so until the opening of the spring campaign in May of 1864. On May 1, 1864, Fleming Thompson again reflects upon the plight of the army (Fleming W. Thompson Letters). He affirms that rations are still short, and they have not been paid in over four months. They couldn't buy tobacco or anything else to eat. He was down to his last two dollars.

Regimental Developments

One of the things that comes to light during this winter encampment is the desire on the part of Colonel Sanders for an appointment in the regular army. We first learn of these desires in a letter written to his father on December 6, 1863 (Sanders's File). He states that he was thinking of obtaining a commission in the regular army. He had already obtained letters of recommendation from a variety of sympathetic men, like David Clopton, F.S. Lyon, and others. He said that he expected to apply for the position of First Lieutenant. This appeared to him to be the best course of action to take, since he didn't know what else he could do at the close of the war. On January 24, 1864, he noted that he had traveled to Richmond in order to attend to the matter of an appointment in the regular army. He carried with him letters of recommendation from both Generals Wilcox and Anderson. He stated that no appointments were being made in the regular army at this time, but he was being recommended for a Captaincy. While he was in Richmond, Colonel Sanders had the opportunity of attending a reception held by President Jefferson Davis.

The letters mentioned by Colonel Sanders have been preserved in the Confederate Service Records. On December 31, 1863, General Wilcox wrote:

> It gives me pleasure to recommend Col J.C.C. Sanders of the 11th Ala Regt of Vol for appointment in the Confederate States Army. Col Sanders entered this war as a Captain in June 61; for more than two years he has served with me and I can consistently and with confidence recommend him as a gentlemen well adapted to the military profession. His moral character is good, active and attentive in the discharge of his duties, and as a disciplinarian [Sanders's File].

In General R.H. Anderson's letter of recommendation he states that Sanders was a gentlemen in all respects, and a very capable officer. He had risen to his present position through a strict discharge of his duties. It is certain from the observations made by his superiors that Col. John C.C. Sanders was held in the highest regard with respect to his moral character, as well as his abilities to command on the field.

We have noted previously the desire of both Walter E. Winn and newly promoted Gen. Cadmus M. Wilcox that Winn be promoted to Major on his staff. These men still desired to work together on the same staff as the year of 1863 was nearing an end. On December 27, 1863, Colonel J.H. King of the 9th Alabama Regiment commends Winn for being brave and untiring in the discharge of his duties (CSR). The next day General Wilcox writes that he would be gratified if Captain Winn would be promoted and assigned to his division. In spite of these strong recommendations on Winn's behalf, it doesn't appear that the appointment was ever acted upon.

On April 26, 1864, Governor Watts requests that Winn be assigned Inspector of Conscription in Alabama until a vacancy appears on the staff of General Wilcox. The Office of Conscription in Alabama had its hands full as early as October of 1863 (Supplement to the Official Records Series 95 Vol. 3, 281). Lieutenant Colonel Harrison C. Lockhart writes about the problem of desertion from the Confederate Army, and especially now in light of how the country needs every soldier. Those who will not return to their companies will be brought to justice. Although the need for leadership in this area was acute in Alabama, this request for appointment to Inspector of Conscription was denied by the President on June 9, 1864. For all of this effort, Captain Winn never realized his desire to be reunited with General Wilcox.

Reuben Thom of Co. H resigned his commission as 2nd Lieutenant on March 14, 1864. His letter of resignation has been preserved:

> I beg leave respectfully to tender my resignation as an officer in the Provisional Army of the Confederate States.
>
> I entered the services at the commencement of the war, and served in the ranks for nearly two years. I am now between forty-five and fifty years old, and for reasons based upon the enclosed certificate of disability, I hereby tender this my resignation [CSR].

Another officer, Maj. Richard J. Fletcher, was pursuing a different course of action following the amputation of his leg at Gettysburg. On April 22, 1864, he wrote from Staunton, Virginia, the following letter to Colonel John Withers:

> I lost my leg in the battle of Gettysburg & have not yet sufficiently recovered to take the field. In the meantime I desire to be assigned to some Post duty. The Post here has just been vacated by the resignation of Commandant. I should be glad to be assigned to duty here, & advice or assistance you may give me in the matter, will be duly appreciated. I shall be in Richmond [CSR].

Major Fletcher was not assigned to this post due to the fact that another officer had already been singled out for the duty. He eventually asked to be reassigned to the General commanding the reserve forces in Alabama in a letter dated September 30, 1864. He had by this time been retired to the Invalid Corps on August 24, 1864, but still felt he could be of some service back home in Alabama. There is no record as to whether Major Fletcher returned to Alabama; but if he did, it was not for long. We know that he wrote a letter to Dr. Sanders on January 24, 1869, from Louisa County, Virginia (Sanders's File). In this letter he states that he had been living in Prospect Hill, some three miles from Gordonsville, for the past two years.

Captain Benjamin Higginbotham of Co. C never sufficiently recovered from his wound at Gettysburg to resume command. In Captain Higginbotham's file we find several letters, the first of which was written April 5, 1864, from Officer's Hospital in Uniontown, Alabama. It was written to Thomas M. Jack, A.A. General, Demopolis, Alabama:

> I respectfully ask leave of absence for twenty days, 20, I reported under General Orders No. 41, having been disabled by a wound in the left arm which disables me for active field service. Application for light duty has been forwarded my commanding officers to appear before the Medical Board in compliance with Gen Order No. 34. Adj Gen Office Richmond, Va, which will take about twenty days to return at which time I will report at this place my leave is granted.
>
> Respectfully Submitted
> Benj. T. Higginbotham
> Your Obt. Servt
> Capt Co. C 11th Ala Regt
> Northern Army Va. [CSR].

Eventually, on August 12, 1864, Captain Higginbotham was retired from the service as Captain of Co. C. The 1st Lieutenant, William H. Richardson, no doubt served as commander of the company after Gettysburg. He was, however, never officially promoted to Captain as far as I can determine from the records.

On February 9, 1864, Lieut. Col. George E. Tayloe married Delia Willis (Witherspoon 1947, 497). Dr. Sanders wrote a letter on Tayloe's behalf requesting an extension of his furlough in light of his recent marriage:

> I am requested by Lt. Col. Geo. E. Tayloe to write you that he has forwarded from this place a application for an extension of furlough for fifteen days and as the paper will be sent to the War Office for the Secretary's action, he desires that you will call and get the application and sent it to him at Big Lick Depot, Roanoke Co., Va. So far as we have ascertained the application has been approved here and I trust there will be no difficulty in securing its approval in Richmond. Col. Tayloe was married last evening and expects to leave for his Father's tomorrow morning going by way of Charlottesville [CSR].

The letter referred to by Dr. Sanders was written by Lieutenant Colonel Tayloe on February 4, 1864, in which he states that his father needed him for various reasons to come home. He was grieving over the loss of two sons in Confederate service, the death of a daughter, and other necessary business he himself needed to urgently attend to.

Some Evaluations of the Spirit of the Army

On January 31, 1864, Colonel Sanders mentions how that recently the 11th Alabama became the first regiment in the brigade to reenlist (Sanders's File). Colonel Sanders then bares his heart about the state of the army at this time:

> All the Ala regts in this army sustain a high reputation for gallantry and devotion to the cause. I regret to learn that many of our men at home are becoming discouraged. This bad feeling at home has an injurious effect on the soldiers in the field and tends more to cause desertion than an hundred defeats. If our men will only stand firm during the next campaign, in my opinion the war will be over, let all who are not in the army and are able to join it. All absentees return and we will not only close the war this campaign but we will dictate our own terms of peace.

Fleming Thompson has his own thoughts about the army in a letter dated May 1, 1864 (Fleming W. Thompson Letters). In his opinion, the Army of Northern Virginia had to do most of the heavy fighting in the war. In his own mind he believed that unless things changed they would have to continue to do so. He hated seeing his noble comrades butchered up in battle after battle while those western troops did nothing!

It seems appropriate to end this discussion of the spirit of the army by mentioning Henry Cribbs' letter dated March 18, 1864 (Honnoll Family Papers 1861–1865). In this letter he picks up a previous discussion in which he had asked Miss Ann Honnoll to describe her sweetheart. Apparently she had indicated to Cribbs that her sweetheart was the one whom she was waiting to marry after the war was over. In their previous correspondence they had progressively been revealing their feelings for one another. Henry realizes that Ann regards him as her sweetheart, and his feelings for her are the same:

> Well now concerning the discriptioin of your *sweet heart*. I take it that it is my self that you was aluding to. I am proud to Ann that I am claimed & as such especialy by such a patiatic person as you Ann. I don't think that I would be any us to describe who my *sweet* heart is. I have told you in two or three letters who is was. I am still of the same notion yet I don't think that my notion will ever changed. I love you and don't car if you know it. you have completely won my affections and I am glad that they rest on such a worthy person. You are worthy of any persons love.... I will close and will imagin that I am with you and gaseling on that Beautiful form and that smiling countinance shining forth its sytums of love.

This letter is one warm note in an otherwise cold and dreary winter for the men. As we have noted at the beginning of this chapter, the period following Gettysburg, until the opening of the campaign in the Spring of 1864, was for the most part the lull before the final storm for the boys from Alabama. It afforded them a time to heal from their wounds incurred in Pennsylvania, and to get reorganized for the final year of the war. Even though they had suffered greatly in the winter of 1863–1864, their greatest tests of endurance still lay ahead of them in the trenches of Petersburg.

10

The Conflict Fiercely Intensifies: The Wilderness and Spotsylvania

In this chapter it is our aim to trace the 11th Alabama from its departure from winter quarters along the Rapidan to the two great battles of the Wilderness and Spotsylvania Court House. The men would now be entering into a new phase of the war. Now the battles would start coming more quickly, and as hard-hitting as they had ever experienced. The boys from Alabama participated in some of the fiercest struggles during this period, and lost some of their most capable soldiers as well.

The Battle of the Wilderness: May 6, 1864

While the men continued to stay in winter quarters along the Rapidan near Orange Court House in early May of 1864, the Federal army, now under the command of U.S. Grant, was preparing to move. General Lee on the evening of May 5, 1864, reported to the Secretary of War that the Federal army had indeed crossed the Rapidan on May 4, 1864, at Ely and Germanna Fords (OR Series 1 Vol. 36/1, 1028). In order to counter the Federal move, General Lee sent the Second Corps under General Ewell down the Turnpike, or the Old Stone Road, while General Hill's Third Corps was dispatched down the Plank Road. The First Corps moved toward the Wilderness by means of the Catharpin Road. It was here that the men bivouacked the night of May 5 (OR Series 1 Vol. 36/1, 1061).

At the time of the opening of this spring campaign the 11th Alabama was part of the brigade commanded by Brig. Gen. Abner Perrin, of Major General R.H. Anderson's Division, in General A.P. Hill's Third Corps (*ibid.*, 1025). As we noted above, the Third Corps was ordered to proceed down the Plank Road to counter the Federal advance; however, R.H. Anderson's Division did not pull out with the rest of the Corps that May 4 morning. Anderson's Division was left behind on the Rapidan Heights as the rear guard of the army (SHSP Vol. 14, 523). They had orders to guard the approaches to the Gordonsville loop of the Virginia Central Railroad, but once it was certain that the entire enemy had departed eastward, the division was to proceed in order to rejoin its corps (Freeman 1991, 370). Nothing of note took place on May 4, but on May 5 they could hear in the distance the rumble of artillery (Clark 1914, 46). The time had come to take up the line of march, and that is exactly what the men did sometime in the afternoon on May 5, 1864.

General Anderson led his men down the Plank Road just as his corps commander had done on the previous day. Captain Clark recalls that the regiment marched down the Plank Road toward the scene of battle until late on May 5, before bivouacking for the night in some timber along the side of the road. Just before daylight dawned on May 6, the men in Abner Perrin's Brigade were roused from their bedrolls in order to continue the march toward the Wilderness (Clark 1914, 47). Prior to reaching the front they encountered Longstreet's First Corps filing in ahead of them on the Plank Road. The men now had to wait while the First Corps passed on through. After this was accomplished, the men resumed their march down the Plank Road until they reached their destination perhaps around 8:00 A.M. (Longstreet 1992, 561).

Perrin's Brigade Forms on the Left of the Plank Road

It was estimated that about three miles below Parker's Store on the Plank Road was where the battle was raging prior to the time of the arrival of the Alabama Brigade (OR Series 1 Vol. 36/1, 1054–1055). The men from Heth and Wilcox's divisions were being beaten back by the Federal charges, and a perfect state of confusion reigned. Before General Longstreet could even get his lead divisions into position, with Kershaw on the right, and Field on the left of the Plank Road, men were retreating through their ranks on a run. The men of Abner Perrin's Brigade were coming up behind the lead divisions of the First Corps. Perrin filed his brigade to the left of the Plank Road into what one veteran recalled as an old field (Saunders 1969, 156). Here the men waited anxiously for their orders from General Longstreet.

One can only imagine what thoughts filled the minds of the men as they waited that morning. All around them they could see men breaking for the rear as well as the wounded being taken to the field hospital. Captain Clark recalled an incident involving two soldiers, one of whom had been wounded, making their way to the rear (Clark 1914, 47–48). His account is a very interesting one since it also involved his overhearing General Lee address these men:

> Just at this time two men came from the front to pass through our lines. One of them evidently was wounded pretty badly and the other unhurt. They were close to me, when General Lee, looking at them, stopped at once in his talk and said to the wounded man, "My friend, I trust you are not badly hurt." The man replied, "No, General," tipping his hat with his left hand. "My right arm is broken, but I hope to be well as soon as possible and take my place in the ranks again." The old General said, "Go back on the old plank road about a mile, and on the right side of the road you will see two tents and an ambulance. This is the quarters of my medical director, Dr. Lafayette Guild. Tell him I sent you there and I want him to dress your arm nicely." The man thanked him, and just then the old General fired up and said to the man who was not wounded, "Go back to the front." The man replied, "I am out of cartridges." The old General said, "That makes no difference, sir. A true soldier never leaves the field as long as he has his bayonet."

Captain Clark noted the Alabama boys began to chide this man for his retreat from the field. General Lee told the men to let him alone, that perhaps they could make a man of him yet. The unknown soldier did turn around and return to the front. How could he not do so, after having such an encounter with Gen. Robert E. Lee?

After Longstreet had gotten his lead divisions into position, General Lee, now fired up and determined to drive the Federals back, placed himself in position to lead the attack himself (Longstreet 1992, 560–561). No one in the Army of Northern Virginia would have consented to such a thing, and so General Lee and General Longstreet conferred together about the movements to be undertaken. Longstreet then ordered his skirmishing lines forward to be followed by infantry in line of battle. These efforts proved to be successful in checking the Federal advance, and progress was made in pushing the enemy backward toward their entrenched line. Soon after this, the men from Alabama under the command of General Perrin were ordered forward in support (Longstreet 1992, 563).

Captain Clark recalls that they had only gone forward about a quarter of a mile into the dense woods before they engaged the enemy (Clark 1914, 48). Here they exchanged Minié ball for Minié ball in a fierce struggle that lasted for about fifteen to twenty minutes. After this exchange with the enemy the men were ordered to rise up and charge. It was here that many men were lost in the fight:

> We moved forward and encountered numerous lines of the Federals that you could hardly see ten paces in front, but we continued for a mile in this dense growth and thicket, sometimes receiving fire in our rear, and were forced to turn about and fight to kill them out. This continued all day until about four o'clock in the afternoon, when we had evidently approached very close to the strongest line of the enemy. We could not see them, but groped our way, keeping in line as well as we could, and finally were ordered to lie down and await further orders [*ibid.*, 48–49].

Samuel W. Vance of the Tuscaloosa Rifles recalled the advance that day (*Confederate Veteran 1893–1912* Vol. 7, 492–493). He remembers that the regiment's advance took place over the littered dead from the previous day's battle. They moved forward to the crest of a little ridge in the thick woods of the Wilderness. It was here that they could hear the Federals giving orders for their advance. Confederate sharpshooters were sent forth in an effort to counter the Union move; however, they were soon driven back. As the Federals came forward two men in Co. G rose up to fire into their ranks: William Barry and Joseph Shuttlesworth. Both men were shot and killed. At this point a furious exchange with the enemy took place, followed by the charge mentioned by Captain Clark.

Intersection of Orange Plank and Brock Roads in the Wilderness. Confederates came charging from out of these woods.

The common thread in many of the accounts of the regiment's battle at the Wilderness was the inability of the men to see the enemy clearly. The Wilderness thicket made it difficult to see the enemy, almost until a man was literally on top of them. A man might have passed by the enemy in the bush, and find that he was being fired on in the rear! Saunders of the 9th Alabama summed up the battle conditions very well:

> These battles were fought in a jungle, where men could not see each other twenty yards off. Science had little to do with it, for officers were seen guiding their men by the compass. Death came unseen; regiments stumbled upon each other, and sent swift destruction into each other's ranks, guided by the rustling of the bushes. In this mournful and desolate thicket did the campaign of 1864 begin [Saunders 1969, 157].

After the men had reached their advanced position they were told to lie and await their orders. The men remained in this position perhaps no more than seventy-five yards from the enemy line, for approximately a half an hour (Clark 1914, 49). Sharpshooters' Minié balls were whizzing into the ranks of the waiting men with deadly precision. The order then came for the men to quietly fall back to the rear. Clark recalls that this was due to the wounding of General Longstreet, and the confusion this caused in pursuing the projected advance. The men successfully retraced their steps close to the spot where they had left that morning.

The Battle of the Wilderness: May 7, 1864

The next morning found the men of Perrin's Brigade once more in line of battle awaiting the possible attack of the Federals. Somewhere around 10:00 A.M. the enemy did launch an attack of a rather feeble nature. It was determined that the attack was designed to feel out the position and strength of the Confederate forces more than anything else. This demonstration was easily repulsed, and the men remained in their positions on the left of the Plank Road for the remainder of May 7. When darkness fell the men were moved about a mile to the right of their position across the Plank Road for the night.

On May 8, 1864, after it was discovered that the enemy had moved from their front in a flanking movement, the men were ordered to march towards Spotsylvania Court House. This brings to an end the first major engagement of the 11th Alabama in the spring campaign of 1864. It proved to be a costly one, as the casualty list would demonstrate. The following list comprises our best estimate at the number of casualties suffered by the regiment in these two days of fighting.[1] The following men were casualties from Co. A: William H. Bareford (killed) and James Spiva (killed). From the ranks of Co. B we find: James B. Fuller (severely wounded in the right side) and James S. Gibson (slightly wounded).[2] Company C lists only two casualties: Daniel M. Hooppaugh (killed) and Wiley J. Coleman (wounded in hand and arm). The Canebrake Legion lists: William S. Leighton (killed, shot in the abdomen), James J. Roberts (wounded), and Robert Elmore (hip, right thigh). William D. Hooks of Co. E was killed. James M. Waggoner (wounded in head), and Newton H. Smitherman (wounded), both belonged to Company F. Of all the companies of the 11th Alabama, Co. G suffered the most with some eight casualties in the Wilderness. Here are those listed as killed and wounded from the Tuscaloosa Rifles: James H. McMahon (severely wounded in the left hand resulting in the loss of two fingers), William H. Barry (killed),[3] Pleasant L. Hayes (wounded slightly in head), John A. Redd (wounded in the right shoulder), Joseph R. Shuttlesworth (killed; he was wounded in both thighs, right leg was amputated), Joseph D. Bryson (severely wounded in left arm, requiring amputation), John Hasty (wounded slightly in hand), and John Brent (killed). From the ranks of Co. H we include: Thomas W. Speed (wounded).[4] We find George J. Collins as the only casualty from the Fayette and Pickens Rifles (wounded). Finally, Co. K lists these men as casualties of the Wilderness: Williford H. Curb (wounded), William C. Muse (wounded in thigh), Oscar M. Lucas (wounded slightly in head),[5] and Benjamin F. Gray (wounded in thigh).[6] We have a total of at least twenty-six casualties from the ranks, including eight killed and eighteen wounded.

The Battle of Spotsylvania Court House: May 8–12, 1864

We have already noted that the men began the march to Spotsylvania on May 8, 1864, perhaps reaching near Shady Grove by nightfall (OR Series 1 Vol. 36/1, 1093). By early morning of May 9 Perrin's Alabama Brigade had reached their destination. As the men marched from the Wilderness battlefield they did so under a new commander. With the wounding of General Longstreet at the Wilderness, Richard H. Anderson was now placed in temporary command of the First Corps. Brigadier General William Mahone was now placed in command of R.H. Anderson's Division (*ibid.* Vol. 36/3, 802). In addition to this temporary change in command structure, the entire Third Corps was being led by General Jubal Early (Freeman 1991, 380). General A.P. Hill was too sick to continue in command.

Upon reaching the field at Spotsylvania early on May 9, Perrin's Brigade was placed on the right of the Confederate line (*Confederate Veteran 1893–1912* Vol. 17, 381). The First Corps then anchored the left of the Confederate line on the Po River, the Second Corps the center, while

The Confederate Apex at Spotsylvania.

the Third Corps commanded the right, crossing the Fredericksburg Road (BLCW Vol. 4, 128). The most distinguishing part of the entire Confederate line was of course the bulging Salient near the center of the defensive line. The Salient was almost three quarters of a mile long, and nearly 1,200 yards wide at its peak (Cannan 1997, 66). The reason for the incorporation of this into the Confederate line was the high ground which it encompassed at the apex of the Salient. If the Salient weren't in possession of the Confederates, it would provide the Federals the opportunity to command a height upon which artillery might be placed. It had to be held.

Upon reaching their position on the right of the Confederate line, Perrin's men joined the rest of the corps in fortifying its position against the anticipated Federal attack. Trees were cut, abatis placed out in front, and protective mounds were built up to provide cover from the enemy's fire (Cannan 1997, 67). In a diary of the First Corps that is recorded in the Official Records, it mentions that the men stayed in line all day on May 9, and that they spent their time digging trenches in anticipation of an enemy attack (OR Series 1 Vol. 36/1, 1056).

The 11th Alabama Is Moved to the Confederate Left

Perrin's Brigade stayed in position on the right throughout the entire day of May 9. By the end of the day it was determined that an attack might be forthcoming on the Confederate left (*Confederate Veteran 1893–1912* Vol. 17, 381). In response to this, General Lee ordered General Early to dispatch one of his divisions to the left of Gen. Charles W. Field's Division of the First Corps (OR Series 1 Vol. 36/1, 1056). The division General Early sent to the left was that of Gen. William Mahone (Cannan 1997, 74).

The men moved throughout the night before arriving east of the Block House Bridge at daybreak on May 10. The men faced the Po River to their front trailing off to their left, while the Block House Bridge and Shady Grove Road were to their right. In General Lee's report he mentions how a large body of the enemy had moved to the Confederate left on the evening of May 9, and had taken possession of the road midway between Shady Grove Church and the Court House (OR Series 1 Vol. 36/2, 982). After their arrival on the extreme left, the men began digging in for the fight to come on the high ground overlooking the bridge.

It was General Hancock's desire to try to turn the Confederate left. To effect this end, Brig. Gen. Francis C. Barlow was sent across the Po River in the direction of the Block House Bridge early on the morning of May 10 (BLCW Vol. 4, 128). The battle which ensued appears to have taken place prior to 2:00 P.M. (OR Series 1 Vol. 36/1, 370). It was about this time that the First Brigade of Barlow's Division began to make its way back to the Po where they had initially crossed at the beginning of the day.

The Sixty-First New York under the command of Maj. George W. Scott of Mile's First Brigade, Barlow's Division, was sent out in front to find a suitable crossing place. Major Scott's report reveals something about both the battle, and the nature of the position occupied by Perrin's Alabamians:

> By order of Colonel Miles the regiment skirmished down the south bank of the Po River to Glady Run. A portion of the regiment sent across to the north side to reconnoiter the enemy's position. Found his line of battle in breast-works. Were withdrawn by direction of General Barlow, with slight loss. Heavy musketry in our rear. ... under heavy musketry and artillery fire all the afternoon, but not directly engaged. Recrossed to north bank of Po River about 5 P.M. under cover of our artillery [OR Series 1 Vol. 36/1, 379].

When the Federal troops began to make their appearance near the Block House Bridge, the Confederates launched a vigorous attack to repulse them. In this attack the Confederate troops, including the 11th Alabama, crossed over the Po River to meet the advancing Union troops (*Confederate Veteran 1893–1912* Vol. 17, 381). The approaching enemy was attacked in their immediate front, and they swept their lines back. In General Lee's report it is stated that one gun of the Federals was taken in their hasty retreat, as well as several prisoners (OR Series 1 Vol. 36/2, 982). Thus, in this engagement at Spotsylvania Court House on May 10, the Alabama boys proved themselves brave, as is evidenced by the commendation given them by General Lee. This light engagement on May 10 would prove to be a harbinger of more desperate fighting to come on May 12, 1864.

The 11th Alabama's Fierce Engagement at Spotsylvania Court House on May 12, 1864

May 11, 1864, began with the men of Perrin's Brigade still resting on the Confederate left. Captain Clark recalls that they skirmished on and off all day long (*Confederate Veteran 1893–1912* Vol. 17, 381). It was no doubt during one of these skirmishes on May 11 that 1st Lieutenant William H. Richardson of Co. C was killed (CSR). His muster roll lists him as being killed in a skirmish on May 11. Lieutenant Richardson was shot through the head. His body servant, who went with Lieutenant Richardson to the war, brought his body back home for burial in Greene County.[7]

Early on the morning of May 12, 1864, the men of Perrin's Brigade heard the roar of battle emerge to their right across the river (*Confederate Veteran 1893–1912* Vol. 17, 381). Captain Clark recalls that it was not long after the battle began that the brigade was ordered back toward the right of the Confederate line. The men passed over the Po River by way of the Block House Bridge on the Shady Grove Church Road (OR Series 1 Vol. 36/1, 1091). They continued with the march all the way to the Brock Road, then turned north as they made their way towards the Harrison House.

It was perhaps while the men were traveling up the Brock Road that they began to catch a glimpse of the disastrous results of the Federal breakthrough at the Salient. Captain Clark recalls the scene to be "appalling" (*Confederate Veteran 1893–1912* Vol. 17, 382). The field was covered with fugitives, artillery was rushing toward the rear, and it seemed as if catastrophe was imminent if not already a reality for the army.

The 11th Alabama Moves Toward the Salient

General Perrin received orders from General Gordon to move forward across the McCoull fields into the fight (Cannan 2002, 106). It is difficult to determine the exact path the men took on their way toward the captured works; however, the men most likely traveled in the direction to the right of Ramseur's Brigade of North Carolinians.[8] It seems that early in the forward movement of the brigade Brigadier General Abner Perrin was shot off his horse.[9] The fierceness of the conflict at this point is attested by the fact that seven balls struck the body of General Perrin (Cannan 2002, 106).[10] In a report to the Secretary of War, General Lee mentions the death of the "Brave General Perrin" (OR Series 1 Vol. 36/1, 1030).

In a report recorded in one newspaper we discover a more vivid account given of General Perrin's death:

> Perrin's brigade of Anderson's Division, sent up to reinforce Battle, formed behind some light works in the rear. Ordered to charge into the salient, its chief, as he rode at the head of its left wing received a Minnie bullet in the thigh. The femoral artery cut, he had hardly time to say,

"Carry me back, boys," when the poor fellow fellow had bled to death [*Montgomery Weekly Advertiser*, 15 June 1864].

With the death of General Perrin, Col. John Sanders took command of the brigade. Since Ramseur's right was bring exposed to a terrible fire from the works to the left of the Salient, the need existed for the gap to be filled and the enemy driven from the works they had captured (BLCW Vol. 4, 133). Colonel Sanders had the formidable task of leading his Alabamians into this hailstorm of crossfire at the Salient. The 11th Alabama was thrust into the heart of the "Bloody Angle" at Spotsylvania Court House. According to one account of the charge, two of the regiments of the brigade were being led to the right by Colonel Sanders (*Montgomery Weekly Advertiser*, 15 June 1864). These two regiments were successful in making a lodgement in the defenses on the left of General Gordon. Three other regiments of the brigade bounded forward to the left into the breastworks to the right of Harris's Mississippians and McGowan's South Carolinians.

Captain Clark writes of his recollections of that time when the boys were ordered into the thickest of the fight:

> ...it was soon ascertained that Gen. Edward Johnson's division line had been assaulted and broken and practically captured and destroyed. The brigade and others were formed into line promptly, and at once moved forward to the attack. Advancing with a rush, the enemy were soon encountered and the rattle of musketry began. The lines of the enemy were broken, and the chase continued to Johnson's works [*Confederate Veteran 1893–1912* Vol. 17, 382].

Dr. Sanders recalls in his Richmond lecture in 1916 that under a baptism of fire the men had to charge across open ground to recapture a part of the line that had been lost (Sanders's File). The Alabama Brigade eventually battled their way to the Salient. It didn't take the boys long to see that their position at Johnson's old line was a precarious one. They found themselves under fire from different directions as they sought to hold onto the bloody real estate that they had so bravely recovered.

Apparently while at the Salient, Captain Winn tried to communicate with Colonel Sanders (*Montgomery Weekly Advertiser*, 15 June 1864). What happened next is vividly recounted in this newspaper description:

> Captain Wynne, the Adjutant General of Perrin's brigade, attempted to communicate with the Col. commanding, but, venturing recklessly with that view across the immediate rear of the salient — where nothing human could apparently survive — returned ... after having run the gauntlet of the enemy's skirmishers, with a painful wound in his arm.

Captain Clark recalls the feelings of the men at this point of the battle:

> Upon reaching Johnson's works we found ourselves in a serious condition. Those works had been constructed without much regard to the essentials of military engineering or the proper protection of those standing behind them, and that portion occupied by us was subject to a direct cross fire from right and left. True, there were traverses and cross sections, but they afforded little or no protection, and we soon ascertained that we were in the middle of a bad fix. The fire of the enemy never ceased during the entire day, and I could not undertake to say how many assaults were made upon us by the enemy. The cannon's roar was continuous, and many of the brave boys with us were killed shot in the back of their heads [*Confederate Veteran 1893–1912* Vol. 17, 382].

The graphic accounts of the struggle at the recaptured works are found in many places. Hand-to-hand fighting, bayoneted rifles thrown over the parapet of the Salient, musket fire through the cracks of the works, and of course the deadly crossfire that was peculiar to the Salient's construction (Freeman 1991, 388): these were the kinds of horrific conditions of battle that the men of Alabama were subjected to on that unforgettable May 12, 1864. Colonel Sanders threw out some of the men of the brigade as sharpshooters (*Montgomery Weekly Advertiser*, 15 June 1864). They apparently were somewhat successful in silencing some of the deadly guns that were casting shells into the ranks.

The nightmare would continue for what probably seemed like an eternity, but no man shirked his duty. Several times when ammunition had given out, men were sent to the rear for fresh supplies only to meet their deaths (*Confederate Veteran 1893–1912* Vol. 17, 382). For Captain Clark, this may have been the most depressing point in the entire war. The once mighty 11th Regiment of Alabama Volunteers was now reduced to a small command huddled together, tenaciously resisting repeated attacks from the Federals across the way. With the coming of nightfall some of the men dropped with exhaustion in the water-filled pits of the Salient. Here the men stayed until early in the morning of May 13, when the order was given to fall back to the new line that had been prepared some quarter of a mile in the rear. Upon reaching their new line many of the men fell to the ground in complete physical exhaustion.

THE TERRIBLE COST OF SPOTSYLVANIA COURT HOUSE

The cost for the entire Army of Northern Virginia was high at Spotsylvania. Freeman makes the observation that the struggle at Gettysburg had greatly weakened the command, but now with the battles of the Wilderness and Spotsylvania it had shattered the army to a degree that no one fully realized at the time (Freeman 1991, 389). The following men were casualties from the ranks of the 11th Alabama at Spotsylvania. From Co. B: William Thetford (wounded severely in the arm), Corp. William P. Bird (wounded severely in the head), and Alexander M. McIntosh (wounded severely in the finger). The men from Co. C who are listed as casualties are: Lt. William H. Richardson (wounded mortally in the head), Francis Tarr (wounded), David Montgomery (wounded in the left breast severely), David Grizzle (severely in the face), and Thomas Winn (wounded slightly in the shoulder). Canebrake Legion casualties are: John Schirm (killed) and William McCauley (wounded severely in the arm). Company E had no casualties listed, and only Thomas F. Roper is found from Co. F (killed). Company H lists: James Hodo (wounded severely in the hand), Corp. William Davis (slightly in the head), William J. Shaw (wounded slightly in the hand), Calvin W. Free (slightly in the head), and both George Craig and Andrew J. Gannon were captured. The casualties from Co. I included: William T. Summers (wounded dangerously in the shoulders), Samuel H. Horton (mortally wounded in the thigh and hand), and Jesse Threat (severely through the face). Finally, from the ranks of Co. K the following men were killed or wounded: James Horn (killed), Joe Thompson (wounded severely in the back), Oscar M. Lucas (slightly in the head), and John Marlow (flesh wound in the thigh).

Thus we have a total of twenty four casualties at Spotsylvania. Of the twenty-four casualties, four were killed, and at least seven that we know of were wounded in the head or face. If we take together the battles of the Wilderness and Spotsylvania, we reach a total of twelve killed, thirty-six wounded, and two captured, bringing the sum for both battles to fifty casualties. It was now a time of mourning according to Captain Clark (*Confederate Veteran 1893–1912* Vol. 17, 382). The men had lost their commanding General, Company C had lost its commander, and every company in the regiment had men killed or wounded in these two desperate battles. What the men didn't know at this point as they sought to catch their breath, was that their current reprieve was to be very short-lived. Another life and death struggle was waiting for them at a place called Hanover Junction.

11
The Battles to the Trenches of Petersburg

In this chapter our goal is to follow the steps of the 11th Alabama from the days following the battles in the Wilderness to their entrenchments around the city of Petersburg. The battles would now become exceedingly accelerated in nature. Some of the engagements during this period were literally just days apart, while others were only a few weeks apart. Each battle brought the Union Army closer to its objective: Richmond.

The Engagement at Hanover Junction: May 24, 1864

The first battle the boys had to face following the affair at Spotsylvania Court House was at Hanover Junction. By May 21, 1864, it was becoming apparent to General Lee that the Federal forces had begun a flanking movement eastward from Spotsylvania (OR Series 1 Vol. 36/3, 814–815). Reports he had received confirmed that the enemy was on the move toward Richmond by way of Milford. In light of this information, General Lee gave instructions to his corps commanders to sweep their fronts in an effort to determine the disposition of the enemy. If they were satisfied that the enemy was indeed gone, preparations were to be made for a movement south. The question that General Lee had to answer next was this: Where do I go from here? General Lee had to make sure to get between Grant's forces and Richmond. Not knowing exactly how much of a jump the Federals had on him, Lee had to be sure not to cut his redeployment too close. It seemed that the North Anna River near Hanover Junction would be the safest place to position his army in front of the invading Federals (Freeman Vol. 3, 496).

Placing his army at Hanover Junction had its good and bad points. On the positive side, the deep banks on the south side of the river would provide an excellent vantage point to repulse Grant's forces. It would also allow them easy movement in the event of an enemy shift eastward by way of the Mattapony River. On the negative side, Hanover Junction was only about twenty-three miles north of Richmond. The enemy would be gaining ground on their march toward the Confederate capitol. On May 22, 1864, General Lee sent a letter to President Davis from Dickinson's Mill on the Telegraph Road informing him of his intentions of moving to Hanover Junction (Dowdey 1961, 746). In this letter he states his ambivalence over the move to Hanover Junction, how he would rather have contested the enemy inch by inch, yet his concern that the enemy might get between him and Richmond outweighed this desire. Richmond must be protected even at the cost of placing his army only twenty-three miles in front of it. By 9:30 A.M. General Lee had arrived at Hanover Junction at the head of the Second Corps. The First Corps would soon be arriving, but the Third Corps, now under the command of a restored A.P. Hill, had not been heard from since the previous evening. The Third Corps was moving on the right of the army.

THE POSITION OF THE ARMY AT HANOVER JUNCTION

General Lee had a very strong line at the North Anna (*Mobile Register & Advertiser*, 1 June 1864). In a letter to his wife from Hanover Junction on May 23, 1864, General Lee affirms the benefits of this line in several ways (Dowdey 1961, 748). They were nearer to their supplies, and they had the benefit of the railroad lines as well. The Second Corps formed the right of the Confederate line, which extended from the Telegraph Road eastward past Cedar Farm Bridge (Official Military Altas 1983, Plate 81 no. 7). The First Corps occupied the center, and A.P. Hill's Third Corps extended on the left to Jericho Mills (*ibid.*, Plate 55 no. 4).

On May 23, 1864, the Union Army began appearing on the north side of the North Anna River (Freeman 1991, 395). The Federals began to cross three miles from Ox's Ford at Jericho Mills at about 3:00 P.M. The old commander of the Alabama Brigade, Cadmus M. Wilcox, led the repulse against the Federal crossing (OR Series 1 Vol. 36/3, 825). The Federal advance was halted here, but the 11th Alabama was not engaged in this battle.

General Lee now formed his lines at the North Anna into the shape of an inverted V, the purpose of which was to bait the Federal Army into a trap. With the apex of the V at Ox's

North Anna Battlefield breastworks as they appear today. These works are in the approximate location of the 11th Alabama at North Anna.

Ford on the high ground, General Lee hoped to lure the Federals across the North Anna where he would be able to bring both flanks to bear to "close the trap." On May 24 the Federals did take the bait, and crossed over the North Anna; however, there was a severe problem: General Lee came down with a debilitating intestinal sickness (Freeman 1991, 397). This did not allow the commanding general to coordinate the attack in the way he had envisioned it to take place. It seems that an opportunity was lost here.

Nevertheless, the Alabama Brigade, now under the command of Col. John C.C. Sanders, did find itself clashing with the enemy on this day of lost opportunity. In a telegram sent by General Lee to the Secretary of War James A. Seddon, mention is made of the engagement in which the 11th was involved:

> The enemy has been making feeble attacks upon our lines today. Probably with a view of ascertaining our position. They were easily repulsed. Gen'l Mahone drove three regiments across the river, capturing a stand of colors & some prisoners, among them one aide-de-camp of Gen'l [James H.] Ledlie [OR Series 1 Vol. 36/3, 827].

We have one very brief account of this battle (*The Selma Morning Reporter*, 7 June 1864). Captain Knox of Co. D, 8th Alabama Regiment, relates to the readers the role played by both the 8th and 11th Alabama Regiments in the battle at Hanover Junction:

> On the evening of the 24th, the 8th and 11th Alabama regiments charged a brigade of Yankees, who were strongly posted in a thick wood, routed them completely, captured about one hundred and fifty prisoners, a quantity of arms and a stand of colors. One of my company alone captured nine Yankees.

Captain Clark only states that at this place the regiment was engaged in what he called "heavy fighting" (Cark 1914, 54).

The casualty list confirms that some heavy fighting did take place at the North Anna. The following men were wounded during this successful charge on May 24, 1864: Joseph Wooten of Co. B was wounded in the hand, James Hitt of Co. C was mortally wounded in the thigh (he died June 9, 1864), Henry C. Cabe of Co. D was wounded, Wright Wall of Co. E was wounded severely in the left arm, Color Corp. Elias M. Thomas of Co. F was wounded severely in the back and left side, and James P. Shaw of Co. H was wounded severely in the leg. The 11th had a total of six casualties at Hanover Junction, with one being mortally wounded.

The Battle at Atlee's Station: June 1, 1864

On May 27, 1864, the Union army moved south again. In a notice on May 27, 1864, General Lee wished for General Anderson to determine whether the enemy was in his front; and if not, to prepare to move to the south side of the South Anna River (Dowdey 1961, 751). By 6:45 A.M. General Lee had sent a telegram to Secretary of War Seddon that the Federals had retired to the North Anna the previous night, but cavalry and infantry had crossed at Hanovertown (Dowdey 1961, 752). Indeed, the Federal army had recrossed the North Anna and were marching down its northern bank (Freeman 1991, 397–399). The Federals crossed at Hanovertown on the Pamunkey River. Grant was now within fifteen miles of Richmond.

Ewell's Corps was quickly dispatched with Anderson to follow, and A.P. Hill's Corps was to make up the rear of the movement. Lee was not as yet sure of Grant's next movement, and unfortunately as May 28 dawned, no new revelation was forthcoming about the exact route

Grant would take in his quest for Richmond. He might strike directly westward toward Atlee's Station, or he might turn south and make his way toward Mechanicsville. By the end of May 28 General Lee had his troops stationed, with Ewell taking up the right along the Shady Grove Road, Anderson in the center, and A.P. Hill making up the extreme left.

THE POSITION OF THE 11TH ALABAMA AT ATLEE'S STATION

We lack a great deal of information regarding the days from May 28, 1864, until the battle on June 1, 1864. There just is not much out there to tell us about the position and involvement of the 11th Alabama in this fight. For example, Captain Clark only recalls that they were on the left of the battle line, and that they were not actively engaged in this battle (Clark 1914, 55). The Alabamians as part of A.P. Hill's Corps were on the extreme left of the Confederate line that June 1. They were stationed in rifle pits, with artillery to their rear (*Mobile Advertiser & Register*, 17 June 1864). The left of Hill's Corps was said to be resting on the Chickahominy swamp west of Atlee's Station (Freeman 1991, 402).

It seems that Captain Clark's recollection that the 11th Alabama was not actively engaged at Atlee's Station is to some degree inaccurate. The indications are that the regiment was engaged to some extent, as is evidenced by the casualties that were sustained in this fight. We know that after Anderson's Corps attacked at dawn on June 1, 1864, it met with bitter failure (Freeman 1991, 403). General Lee reports officially that General Anderson attacked the enemy in their front, and drove them from their entrenchments (Dowdey 1961, 760); nevertheless, General Anderson's advance was quickly checked by the Federal forces (Freeman Vol. 3, 506). From the information at our disposal it seems that Hill's Corps began their attack sometime in the afternoon of June 1. Hill was facing the formidable 2nd Corps of the Union army under General Hancock. General Lee in a report to the Secretary of War affirms that Generals Breckinridge and Mahone drove the enemy from their fronts while taking about 150 prisoners (Dowdey 1961, 760). In General Burnside's report of this action, he states that they repulsed the Confederates and took their own prisoners (OR Series 1 Vol. 36/3, 498). He states that the prisoners taken showed that A.P. Hill was in their front in entrenched positions. From this scant information it would seem that the 11th Alabama was engaged with Hancock's men of the 2nd Corps.

The casualties that resulted from the battle at Atlee's Station total seven in all. Company B lost Arthur M. Perry (killed). Two men were wounded from Co. C: Samuel M. Hill (severely wounded in the right leg) and James Vaughn. Daniel Coleman of Co. E, William Harrison Brown of Co. F, Jasper W. Wooten of Co. H, and Henry C. Cribbs of Co. I round out the wounded soldiers.

The Battle of Turkey Ridge: June 3, 1864

On Thursday, June 2, 1864, General Lee learned that General Hancock had been moved from the Union right to the Union left (Furgurson 2000, 124–125). It was in response to these developments that A.P. Hill was ordered to send two of his three divisions southward immediately. Hill ordered Wilcox and Mahone's Divisions to remove themselves to the Confederate right. Upon their arrival on the right, Wilcox placed his division on the extreme right flank closest to the Chickahominy, while General Mahone's division was placed in reserve behind him. The Alabama Brigade, under the command of Col. John Sanders, left their entrenchments on the Confederate left around noon on June 2, 1864 (*Mobile Advertiser & Register*, 17 June 1864). A member of the 8th Alabama Regiment, also under Sanders's command, recalls that they didn't reach their position on the right until around sundown (*Mobile Advertiser & Register*, 17 June 1864). Once they arrived they formed into line of battle. The men had no idea that they had just removed to a place that would be a very hot bed of fighting the following day. Forming the first line of defense from left to right were Hoke, Breckinridge, and Wilcox, while Mahone and Finegan formed the second line of defense behind Breckinridge and Wilcox.

The boys in blue across the way were divisions of Hancock's Corps. On the extreme Union left was Gen. Francis Barlow, and to his right, Gen. John Gibbon. The Union attack began at around 4:30 A.M. on June 3, 1864. In General Lee's report on June 3, 1864, he speaks of the battle in these terms:

> About 4:30 A.M. to-day the enemy made an attack upon the right of our line. In front of General Hoke's and part of General Breckinridge's line he was repulsed without difficulty. He succeeded in penetrating a salient on General Breckinridge's line and captured a portion of the battalion there posted. General Finegan's brigade, of Mahone's division, and the Maryland Battalion, of Breckinridge's command, immediately drove the enemy out with severe loss [OR Series 1 Vol. 36/1, 1032].

In this report, as in all the other battle reports on both sides, no mention is made of the Alabama Brigade being involved in stopping the break in the line of General Breckinridge. In light of the casualties experienced by members of the 11th, it would seem reasonable to assume that they had some part to play in this effort to reinforce the Confederate front line, but not to the extent of that displayed by Finegan's Floridians. One member of the Alabama Brigade also stated that after the battle concluded they were moved into position on the front line in the earthworks (*Mobile Advertiser & Register*, 17 June 1864). As this member of the 8th Alabama was writing his letter, bullets from Yankee sharpshooters were whizzing over his head at a rate of twenty a minute! Anyone who raised his head up from the earthworks would most certainly be picked off.

The casualties of the 11th Alabama at Turkey Ridge were as follows: Lucius W. Crawford of Co. A (mortally wounded, died June 9 or 11, 1864, shot in the shoulder and lung). Erastus A. Chambers and Evander C. Ellis of Co. C were wounded, while Co. D had William W. Ellington (wounded) and George Michael (killed on picket). Co. E lost Captain John James (killed), and Co. F lost Alexander P. Hill (killed). Co. H had two casualties: Calvin M. Makamson (severely wounded in the jaw) and James Phillips (killed). Another two casualties were recorded in Co. I with James Falk (mortally wounded in the head, died June 14, 1864) and John W. Shelton (wounded). Finally, Co. K had a single casualty in William W. Brazelton (wounded). Twelve casualties are recorded for the battle at Turkey Ridge, with half of these casualties resulting in death. The Yancey Rifles were especially hit hard with the loss of their Captain, John James. James had been Captain of Co. E since the promotion of Richard Fletcher to Major way back in September of 1862. Thus brings the end of the regiment's involvement in the Battle of Cold Harbor. They were engaged in two separate battles at Cold Harbor: Atlee's Station and Turkey Ridge. They suffered nineteen casualties at this place including seven deaths.

The Battle of Wilcox Farm: June 22, 1864

On June 13, 1864,[1] it was discovered that the Union troops opposing General Lee's army had once again moved to the left in a flanking movement (Dowdey 1961, 777). On this very

11— The Battles to the Trenches of Petersburg

Garthright House. This served as a hospital for both Union and Confederate soldiers after the battle of Turkey Ridge.

day A.P. Hill's Corps was put in motion, and before the day had ended they had reached the old Frayser's Farm battlefield (Robertson Jr. 1987, 282). By daylight of June 14 the corps was on the march once again. By the time of bivouac on June 15, the 11th Alabama was resting in a front that had its right over the Willis Church Road, and its left covering the White Oak Swamp Bridge. This was in the area known as Riddell's Shop, where Long Bridge and the Charles City Roads intersect (Dowdey 1961, 782). Here the men would remain until June 18, 1864.

On June 17 General Lee sent a telegram to General Hill informing him of Grant's crossing of the James River, and the threat to General Beauregard at Petersburg (Dowdey 1961, 782). He then ordered General Hill to move his command at 3:00 A.M. on the morrow for Chaffin's Bluff. He was then to take the Petersburg Turnpike until receiving further orders (*ibid.*, 1961, 790). General Lee was using Hill's Corps as a shield for Richmond against any possible attack from the north. After General Hill reached Chaffin's Bluff he paused for about two hours (Robertson Jr. 1987, 283). After this brief pause, the Alabama boys crossed the pontoon bridge and began the long march down the dusty Petersburg Pike toward Grant's army. Upon reaching Petersburg the Alabamians held a position that was both south and west of the city (Sanders's File). They were stationed in works a quarter of a mile at a right angle to the Jerusalem Plank Road (Clark 1914, 55). Here they remained until the battle of Wilcox Farm. On the eve of the battle two soldiers from Co. B were taken prisoners while they were out on a foraging run (Fleming W. Thompson Letters). William McCracken and Robert R. McCulley were both captured on June 21, 1864, and sat out the remainder of the war (CSR). Thompson says that when a search was made for them, all that was found were their cartridge boxes. Later, after capturing some Yankees, they were told that they had taken some Alabama soldiers prisoner at a house in the direction where both McCracken and McCulley had been.

The 11th Alabama at the Battle of Wilcox Farm

General Grant desired to sever the railroad which led southward to Weldon, North Carolina. To that end, he sent both the Second and Sixth Corps southwest beyond the Confederate flank (McPherson 1994, 184). The Second Corps was under the command of Gen. David B. Birney, while the Sixth was led by Horatio Wright (Robertson Jr. 1987, 285). It was hoped that they would not only be successful in getting to the railroad, but also in turning the right of General Lee's flank. It was in response to this Federal movement on June 22, 1864, that forces under the command of Gen. William Mahone were sent to block this Union threat. The Confederate brigades involved included newly brevetted Brig. Gen. John C.C. Sanders's Alabamians, D.A. Weisiger's Brigade, and Brig. Gen. Ambrose R. Wright's Brigade.

As the two Union Corps moved out toward the woods west of the Jerusalem Plank Road, the Confederate forces under General Mahone prepared to intercept them. General Mahone personally led these three brigades through a ravine which shielded their movements from the Federals (Robertson Jr. 1987, 286). This ravine not only provided a shield to the Union forces, but it also allowed the Confederates to come within yards of General Birney's left flank. The two Union corps had become separated in this forward movement through dense woods. The Sixth Corps under General Horatio Wright was on the left of the Second Corps under General Birney. The Second Corps was to conform its movements with that of the Sixth Corps, but Birney's men found themselves in advance of the Sixth Corps in an exposed position (OR Series 1 Vol. 40/2, 325). In this advanced position the Second Corps proceeded from right to left in this fashion: General Gibbon's Second Division, General Mott's Third Division, and finally, General Barlow's First Division (*ibid.*, 326).

With the Union left flank "in the air," General Mahone saw the opportunity he was looking for in launching an attack. Mahone placed Sanders on the right, Wright in the center, and Weisiger on the left (*Mobile Advertiser & Register*, 19 July 1864). General Sanders recalls that they advanced through the woods until reaching near to the enemy's lines (Sanders's File). They then had to cross over an open field. They were now in position to attack the unsuspecting Federal troops.

It was now late in the afternoon, perhaps as late as 5:00 P.M. (Robertson Jr. 1987, 286). The Confederates slammed into the left flank of General Barlow's First Division. Captain Patrick S. Tinen was commander of the Sixty-Ninth Pennsylvania Regiment, which occupied the extreme left of Barlow's Division (OR Series 1 Vol. 40/1, 385). He writes that his men behaved as well as could have been expected on this occasion. They showed respectable signs of resistance, but it was not until the Confederates had succeeded in getting to their left and rear that retreat was necessary. He laid part of the blame on the Third Division's failure to manifest an acceptable show of resistance, which would have aided them in trying to stiffen their own ability to stand and fight.

Barlow's Second, Third, and Fourth Brigades were the ones in the exposed position at the time of the Confederate attack (OR Series 1 Vol. 40/1, 329). The attack was so severe by Mahone's men that the Union commanders did not even give orders for the changing of fronts to meet the onslaught (*ibid.*, 388). General Mott placed blame on the failure of the First and Second Divisions giving way, which thereby placed his Third Division in an exposed

Wilcox Farm. General Mahone attacked to the left of this road, now spotted with houses and commercial development.

position to enemy attack at both his rear and flank. General Gibbon's report stated that after the enemy attack on Barlow and Mott's Divisions had successfully taken place, troops on his left then gave way without much firing (*ibid.*, 366). The Confederates captured McKnight's Battery, and then turned the guns on the retreating Federals.

As one can tell from these battle reports, the Confederates offered a surprise flank attack that had the effect of rolling up the entire left flank of the Union position. It began with Barlow's men, proceeded to Mott's troops, and ended with Gibbon's left. One writer notes:

> Mahone's troops drove the routed II Corps to within three hundred yards of the Plank Road before stopping to regroup.... Mahone shattered two Federal divisions, inflicted 3,000 casualties, seized four guns and eight regimental flags, all with minimum losses [Robertson Jr. 1987, 287].

THE CASUALTIES OF THE 11TH ALABAMA AT WILCOX FARM

The outstanding victory did not come without a price tag for the members of the 11th Alabama. The following men are confirmed to have been killed or wounded at Wilcox Farm: Paul Shaw from Co. A (killed). From Co. C, Nathaniel S. Norwood (mortally wounded, died June 23, 1864)[2] and James R. Stafford (wounded). Company D lost the brave Walter Winn (mortally wounded in the arm and thigh, he died July 12, 1864). Company E list only Henry C. Atchison as wounded. Company F casualties included Wesley E. Latham (killed), General Marion Powell (wounded in left side), Daniel E. Lightsey (mortally wounded in the right knee, he died July 11, 1864), and Henry Davis (mortally wounded in left arm). From the ranks of

Co. G we find Charles Farrington (severely wounded in left arm and leg, arm requiring amputation) and William Ashworth (wounded). From Co. H, James H. Allen (wounded), Joseph N. Bell (wounded), Abner Knight (severely wounded), John W. Yateman (wounded), Thomas J. Hatcher (killed), Henry Hill (wounded), James P. Ferguson (wounded), and Benjamin M. Gammill (died). Company I have listed Benjamin F. Smith (severely wounded), and John W. Shelton (wounded). Finally, Co. K casualties included John B. Wallace (killed), John W. Tadlock (wounded), David C. Lovelady (killed), Williford H. Curb (wounded), D.C. Wallace (severely wounded, right leg amputated), and James J. Cook (wounded in the leg). In the battle of Wilcox Farm we find a total of ten killed and seventeen wounded. This high casualty figure shows just how important a part the regiment played in this fierce engagement southwest of Petersburg. Company H suffered the highest rate of casualties in this battle. The total number of casualties from Co. H number eight, and from that number two were killed. Captain Clark reflected back at the cost of this engagement:

> Capt. Walter E. Winn, the spendid adjutant-general of the brigade, was seriously wounded in the knee, and died a few days afterward in Petersburg. Some of our best soldiers met their death in the assalt on the enemy, but we were quite successful, and the forces were withdrawn after a short engagement [Clark 1914, 55].

This battle resulted in the loss of a very important member of the regiment: Walter E. Winn. One newspaper pays tribute to Captain Winn in a very favorable fashion:

> Capt. Walter E. Winn, of Demopolis, and A.A. General of Wilcox's old brigade, died a few days ago from the effects of wounds received in the battle near Ream's Station. He joined the army at the beginning of the war, and has participated in all the battles in Virginia, and on all occasions born himself like one of the knights of the olden time, bravely and chevalrously, and in the hour of victory fell mortallly wounded. In private and public he was a gentleman, "than which" says Sir. Phillip Sydney, "no nobler name can be given a man" [*Mobile Evening News*, 2 August 1864].

Skirmish Near Ream's Station: June 23, 1864

On June 23, 1864, General A.P. Hill decided to allow Mahone to probe out the Federal left (Robertson Jr. 1987, 287). The Union left was held by Maj. Gen. Horatio G. Wright's Sixth Corps. We can piece together this skirmish by an examination of the Union correspondence during the course of the day. In a dispatch around 7:30 A.M. delivered to Lieutenant General Grant from George Meade, an evaluation of the present position of the Union Second and Sixth Corps was stated (OR Series 1 Vol. 40/2, 331–332). At daylight both the Sixth and the Second Corps were advanced forward to a position close to the enemy on the Jerusalem Plank Road. General Wright's Sixth Corps moved forward, attempting at the same time not to lose contact with the Second Corps on his right. The woods were so terribly dense that it made the going difficult (OR Series 1 Vol. 40/2, 349). By 10:15 A.M., it was General Wright's observation that his own right was in advance of General Barlow's left. By this time a detachment from General Wright had gone ahead about one and a half miles to his left, and taken possession of the Weldon Railroad. In this dispatch Wright desired to know whether they should attempt to destroy the rail at that point or not. He was very concerned that he might lose contact with the Second Corps, since he believed it would take a sizable force to destroy the track effectively.

Wright was instructed to continue to move forward in line of battle, while at the same time deploying Bryan's Cavalry to destroy the railroad. General Barlow's skirmishers would be instructed to advance along with Wright's line of battle (OR Series 1 Vol. 40/2, 351). General Wright had sent a group of some ninety sharpshooters under the command of Captain Beattie of the Third Vermont to the Weldon Railroad in order to commence its destruction (*ibid.* Vol. 40/1, 501–502). In order to protect the work of the railroad's destruction, a group of some two hundred men from the Eleventh Vermont were deployed in a skirmish line from the right of the Fourth Vermont to the railroad itself.

Around 12:45 P.M. the signal officer reported a column of Confederate infantry about a mile long moving from their works along the Weldon Railroad (OR Vol. 40/2, 351–52). We know that this force was under the command of General Mahone, and included the 11th Alabama Infantry. General Mahone led this attack, which proceeded to strike the party at work destroying the railroad (OR Series 1 Vol. 40/1, 502). It appears that Perry's Florida Brigade took a leading role in this attack, since General Lee credits them with taking most of the prisoners in the skirmish (*ibid.* Vol. 40/2, 685). General Hill's brief report stated that Mahone had not accomplished too much, taking about one hundred prisoners from the Sixth Corps (*ibid.* Vol. 51/2, 1027). The undergrowth was so thick, and the weather so hot, that the thing was not pressed even though the Union troops retreated before them. In a later report to Colonel W.H. Taylor, General Hill notes that Perry's Florida boys took some 600 prisoners, including about twenty-eight officers (OR Series 1 Vol. 51/2, 1028). He commends Mahone's men, who had now gone without sleep for some two nights.

Brigadier General Lewis A. Grant, commanding the Second Brigade in the Second Division of the Sixth Corps, gives some additional details about the skirmish (*ibid.* Vol. 40/1, 502). He states that indeed they gradually fell back after being attacked in what they considered to be a significant force of Confederates. Major C.K. Fleming, Eleventh Vermont, was in command of this force that came under attack. They tried to strengthen their position initially by the construction of breastworks when it was thought that the attack would come from their front; however, the Confederates came at them from the left flank. He writes:

> The enemy bore still farther to the left and attacked the right of Major Walker's battalion. Two regiments of the First Brigade were hurried forward to strengthen the line in that direction.... I went to General Wright, commanding the corps, and expressed to him my fears. He went with me to observe the situation. He attention was called to the position of the Fourth Vermont and Major Fleming's command, and to the fact that if the line should be broken at the point then threatened the enemy would come quite into their rear [OR Vol. 40/1, 502].

The boys under Mahone's command did break through as feared by Fleming, and as a result occupied a position to the rear of the Fourth Vermont. When the Union forces sought to rejoin the main body, they found their path blocked in every direction. It was this that led to the large number of men captured by the Confederates.

The men of the 11th Alabama played a significant part in this skirmish. We have record of the following men who were casualties in this battle: William P. Loyd of Co. B (wounded in ankle), and William D. Allen of Co. H. Company K suffered the most casualties in this skirmish with: James B. Cook (killed), William P. Walton (severely wounded in the leg, amputated), and Capt. James L. Brazelton (killed).

Skirmish with Kautz and Wilson's Raiders: June 29, 1864

After the skirmish at Ream's Station on June 23, 1864, the siege of Petersburg began in earnest (Robertson Jr. 1987, 287). It now seemed that every hill along the line became an emplacement for an artillery battery. Earthworks were being continuously dug by the men of both armies. In the meantime the railroads were still the objects of Union cavalry attacks. General Meade gave instructions to Gen. James H. Wilson on June 20 to conduct an expedition against the South Side and Danville Railroads (OR Series 1 Vol. 40/1, 620–622). Brigadier General August Kautz's Division reported to General Wilson the next day for his orders. They began the raid on June 22 with a force of about 5,500 cavalry, and twelve guns.

The Union cavalry inflicted damage at a variety of points on the South Side Railroad. Depots were burned, water tanks destroyed, cars were captured, and most of the track of the South Side was destroyed from north of Burkeville, and all of the Danville from the Junction to Roanoke bridge. Now that Kautz's assignment was completed, the time had come to make his way back to the army. After meeting a much stronger force at the Stony Creek Depot on June 28, a new march was undertaken in the direction of Ream's Station in an attempt to unite with the Union left (OR Series 1 Vol. 40/1, 623).

The 11th Alabama Marches to Ream's Station

On June 28, 1864, Confederate Maj. Gen. Wade Hampton notified the commanding General that in light of what he was facing at Stony Creek Depot, infantry and cavalry should be sent to Ream's Station (OR Series 1 Vol. 40/1, 808). In was in response to this that General Mahone was dispatched along with his Alabama Brigade to the vicinity of Ream's Station. Captain George Clark recalls being given the order that evening to prepare to move (Clark 1914, 56). It was understood that the purpose of the movement was to head off the Wilson and Kautz raiders. They left their Petersburg entrenchments and began to march south down the Weldon Railroad. It was a march that consumed most of the night for the men, since they didn't reach the vicinity of Ream's Station until daylight of June 29.

After arriving on the morning of June 29, the men of Mahone's Division rested quietly along the side of the road. Meanwhile General Wilson arrived on the scene around 8:00 A.M., and began to reconnoiter the Confederates' line (OR Series 1 Vol. 40/1, 623). He soon discovered a heavy body of infantry in his front blocking his crossing of the railroad, and added to this were the reports of his scouts that Confederate cavalry were moving around their left flank. The cavalry that was moving to the Federal left was that of Maj. Gen. Fitz Lee (*ibid*. Vol. 51/2, 1028). He did successfully turn the Federal left, and in the process took wagons, ambulances, caissons, and prisoners beyond his ability to maintain.

It appears that Fitz Lee's cavalry began the Confederate attack, and the men of Mahone's Division had to wait to hear of their developments before making their next move (Clark 1914, 56). In the meantime, General Wilson came to the conclusion that there was no way they could break through the Confederate forces opposing him. He determined to withdraw by the Boydton Road to the Double Bridges on the Nottoway (OR Series 1 Vol. 40/1, 623). Wilson quickly ordered General Kautz, along with Colonels McIntosh and Chapman, to withdraw their commands as soon as possible.

While the Union forces were making the necessary adjustments for their withdrawal, the Confederates began to strike at their left. The Confederate infantry was able to get around the left of the Second Ohio Cavalry (OR Series 1 Vol. 40/1, 637). Captain Clark gives some of the details of the movement of the 11th Alabama at the time of this attack:

> After a time I was ordered into line in command of one hundred skirmishers. We went forward about a mile when I ascertained that the enemy was across the little stream and was awaiting attack. I reported back to General Mahone the condition of affairs and was ordered to

> hold my position there with the skirmishers until further orders.... After a time I received orders to go forward and then move to the left of the attacking line and go in with them. This I did, and the enemy was soon dispersed. My part of the line had gone out into the open field, and the enemy's cavalry started a charge, seemingly about a brigade of them. General Mahone was near me and I called his attention to it. He at once ordered a Pegram battery, which came rapidly and it began firing over our line as we lay down in front. A few rounds from the artillery soon put an end to the charge and soon scattered the enemy's forces [Clark 1914, 56].

The enemy that Captain Clark may have initially met that day was the Third Vermont (OR Series 1 Vol. 40/1, 503). They were deployed as skirmishers and were said to have met the enemy within a half a mile of Ream's Station. According to one report, the Third Vermont drove the Confederate skirmishers from the field.

General Lee's report squares with the accounts entirely. He stated that Fitz Lee's cavalry turned their left flank, while General Mahone attacked them in the front at Ream's Station (Dowdey 1961, 810–811). Kautz reported as well that they were confronted with Alabama troops in a flank attack (OR Series 1 Vol. 40/1, 730). In the report of Col. Samuel D. Spear of the Eleventh Pennsylvania Cavalry, the brigade of Gen. John C.C. Sanders is actually mentioned by name:

> Just as the First District of Columbia got into position (they had dismounted to advance as skirmishers) the Alabama Brigade (rebel), Colonel Sanders commanding, charged upon my skirmish line, when the mounted portion of the Eleventh (Pennslyvania) and First District of Columbia, dismounted, charged them, driving them back under cover of woods. In the charge of the Eleventh captured a large number of prisoners belonging to several different Alabama regiments [OR Series 1 Vol. 40/1, 740].

It may well have been that both William E. McCracken and Robert R. McCulley of Co. B were captured at this time (Fleming W. Thompson Letters). We also know that Adjutant Ruffin Y. Ashe of Co. D was killed in this skirmish with Wilson and Kautz's raiders (CSR). This skirmish in which the 11th Alabama was involved proved to be a Confederate victory, yet it didn't entirely stop the Union cavalry from getting away. Though the enemy was completely routed at Ream's Station, they did successfully withdraw by way of the Double Bridges to Jarratt's Station on the Weldon Railroad (OR Series 1 Vol. 40/1, 624).

The Battle of the Crater: July 30, 1864

The Alabama Brigade was stationed at the time of the Battle of the Crater a short distance west of the right angle in the Confederate defensive works near the Plank Road (Clark 1914, 57). A deserter from Mahone's Division on July 23, 1864, pointed out that Hill's Corp occupied their old position west of the Jerusalem Plank Road going west to the Weldon Railroad (OR Series 1 Vol. 40/3, 426). The point of their encampment was known as Wilcox's Farm (SHSP Vol. 33, 359).[3] Captain Clark was serving at the time as temporary Assistant Adjutant General on the staff of General Sanders. General Sanders had made his headquarters at a very small house near the brigade's defensive position. It was actually while the brigade staff was at their headquarters that the noise from the explosion of the mine was heard.

The men from the 11th were fully settling into life in the trenches at Petersburg. One soldier from the 60th Alabama relates life in the trenches of Petersburg in July of 1864 in this fashion:

> Our troops are in the best spirits, notwithstanding their long continued confinement in the trenches, unremitting vigilance which they are called upon to exercise. The lines are distant from each other, at some places 250, and at other places not more than 80 yards. Two men from each company at a time are required to keep the firing up, each man firing once in five minutes [*Mobile Advertiser & Register*, 3 August 1864].

In addition to this, earth-shaking artillery fire at regular intervals was being discharged around them. The men had made for themselves bomb-proof shelters for protection (*Mobile Advertiser & Register*, 21 August 1864). The soldier would dig a hole, cover it with railroad ties, and then throw dirt about five feet deep over the top. It made what the writer in the *Advertiser* called the appearance of a "prairie dog village."

At this point of the war in July of 1864 the men were still in fairly good spirits. In a letter from General Sanders on July 25, 1864, he makes mention of the condition of the regiment at the time. He states that the men were amazed at how relatively tranquil things could be when the armies were so close to one another (Sanders's File). Rations at this point were tolerable. They were able to enjoy a cup of coffee in the morning, corn meal, bacon, small quantities of peas, sugar, and rice. It was also fairly common for "pie peddling" to go on. When a soldier passed through the city his eyes would see in almost every window plates of pies. The townsfolk were courteous to the soldiers as well.

Communication was an acute problem for the soldiers in July of 1864 (Dr. Sanders's Papers). Dr. Sanders lamented the fact that due to communication breakdowns no letters or dispatches had gotten through in weeks. He also writes of the position of the enemy:

> Grant keeps his army massed behind a very short line with his flanks strongly protected and fortified. From this position he continues to throw shells into the city at all hours of the day and night. The nearest point of his line to Petersburg is about two miles I am told. He has mounted heavy guns which have an easy range of three miles. We hardly anticipate an assault after so much delay and entire confidence exists as to the final result.

THE 11TH ALABAMA ON THE MORNING OF JULY 30, 1864

At around 3:00 A.M. General Sanders was awakened from his headquarters with an order from Division Headquarters (Clark 1914, 58). The men were to occupy the trenches of their defensive positions. At around 3:30 A.M. the order was received by the regiment, and the men immediately took up their positions in the trenches with their guns and accouterments (Fleming W. Thompson Letters). Here the men remained entrenched until a little before 5:00 A.M., when their watch was interrupted by the sound of a tremendous explosion to their left.

After the initial explosion was heard a heavy barrage of artillery fire began. Upon hearing the explosion, General Sanders and staff immediately mounted their horses and rode to the front (Clark 1914, 58). The artillery bombardment continued to be heard for several hours; the word gradually leaked out that the Yankees had blown up a part of the Confederate line of defense (Fleming W. Thompson Letters). The men were instructed to be ready to leave at a moment's notice. Orders to leave came to the Alabamians around 11:00 A.M. (Parker n.d., 71). General Sanders received the orders from an officer on General Mahone's staff. One soldier recalled the urgent message from General Mahone, "'Suh,' he exclaimed to General Saunders, 'General Mahone advises you to withdraw all your men from the works except the skirmishers.'"

The 11th Alabama immediately moved out from the defensive positions west of the

Old Blandford Church Cemetery on the Jerusalem Plank Road.

Jerusalem Plank Road. It was a rather circuitous route that had to be taken in order to arrive at the site of the explosion. It was perhaps a distance of only about a mile and a half to the Crater, yet it may have actually been a distance of two and half due to the roundabout nature of the course that they were required to take (SHSP Vol. 25, 79). A member of Mahone's Brigade recalls vividly the line taken by the men after leaving their trenches (SHSP Vol. 18, 5–6). After withdrawing into a cornfield behind their entrenchments, the men moved to the left until they reached the Ragland House, where they were halted. Here the men removed all unnecessary accouterments in preparation for the battle to come.

After leaving the Ragland House, the men would have been marched beside an edge of the hills that ran along Lieutenant Run to what was called New Road, or Hickory Street. On this road they proceeded to within a few yards of the bridge over this run, then turned northward down the ravine on the east to a place called Hannon's old ice pond. Here they filed eastward up another ravine which ran along a military footpath to the Jerusalem Plank Road. This location was near the old Blandford Cemetery (Parker n.d., 72). At the Jerusalem Plank Road they would have entered into a covered way which ran across the road southeastward to a another ravine. This ravine was in the rear of the Confederate works that was at that point occupied by the Yankees. Thompson recalls that as they moved toward the Crater they soon encountered prisoners (Fleming W. Thompson Letters). Their excitement continued to grow as they learned that the Yankees still held a part of the Confederate lines, and that they would soon be expected to engage the enemy.

It was around 11:00 A.M. when the Alabama Brigade reached their position in the ravine. It was some two to three hundred yards from that portion of the Confederate lines held now by the Union forces (Sanders's File). For the next two and a half hours the boys were

Ravine area near the Crater.

subjected to an intense heat from exposure to the hot July sun. One member of the 9th Alabama stated that there were four cases of sunstroke in his regiment alone (Saunders 1969, 161).

The 11th Alabama Charges the Crater

Before the men had ever arrived at the ravine in front of Elliot's Salient that early afternoon of July 30, 1864, their comrades from Mahone's Brigade had already had some hot work to deal with. The Virginia Brigade led by Colonel D.A. Weisiger, and the Georgia Brigade under the command of A.R. Wright, had already been summoned soon after the explosion of the Crater. The Virginia Brigade had been successful in dislodging the Union troops to the left of the Crater, while the Georgia troops had been unable to drive the enemy from the right (Clark 1914, 58). The Crater was still filled with both black and white Union soldiers. The Ninth Corps of the United States Army had filled the Crater and the fortifications surrounding the chasm (OR Series 1 Vol. 40/1, 546). New Hampshire, Vermont, Maine, Massachusetts, Maryland, New York, and Michigan boys were among those who had filed into the vacated breastworks of the Confederates.

Upon arriving in the ravine with his brigade, General Sanders was apprised of the situation by General Mahone (SHSP Vol. 33, 361). Featherston gives us his take on the orders given to General Sanders that early afternoon:

> He informed us that the brigades of Virginians and Georgians had successfully charged and taken the works on the left of the fort, but that the fort was still in possession of the enemy, as

was also a part of the works on the right of it, and that we of the Alabama brigade were expected to storm and capture the fort, as we were the last of the reserves. He directed us to move up the ravine as far as we could walk unseen by the enemy, and then to get down and crawl still further up until we were immediately in front of the fort, then to order the men to lie down on the ground until our artillery in our rear could draw the fire of the enemy's artillery, which was posted on a ridge beyond their main line and covering the fort.

When this was accomplished our artillery would cease firing, and then we should rise up and move forward in a stooping posture at "trail arms," with bayonets fixed, and should not yell or fire a gun until we drew the fire of the infantry in the fort, and the enemy's main lines, and then we should charge at a "double quick," so as to get under the walls of the fort before the enemy could fire their part of some fifty pieces of artillery....

Captain Clark's words confirm Featherston's as to the substance of the discussion that took place between Generals Mahone and Sanders. Here are Captain Clark's recollections of the orders for battle that day:

The attack was now set for two o'clock upon the firing of two signal guns from the rear. Upon the firing of the signal guns, every man must be ready to go foward, slowly at first, then at the double quick as soon as the hill was reached. The objective was to capture the rifle pits on the right, as well as the crator. In order to effect this end, the brigade would need to right oblique after starting forth, and no man was to fire until he reached the works. Arms were to be carried at the right shoulder shift [Clark 1914, 59].

At around 2:00 P.M. the signal guns indeed fired, and the men rose up at the right shoulder shift with the knowledge that General Lee would be watching their every movement. Slowly they moved forward at first until the crest of the hill was reached, and it was then that the enemy could get its first unobstructed view of the brigade (Clark 1914, 59). Now the grand charge of the day was made by the men of General Sanders's Brigade. All who witnessed it could only express the magnificent sight that it was to behold:

About this time General Mahone, having ordered up Sander's Alabama brigade, sent it forward to recapture the rest of the works. Led by their gallant Brigadier, they moved forward in splendid style, making one of the grandest charges of the war, and recapturing every vestige of our lost ground and our lost guns, and capturing 35 commissioned officers, including Brig. Gen. Bartlette, commanding first division 9th corps, 324 white and 150 negroe privates, and two stands of colors. The enemy made but slight resistance to this charge, whilest our men swept everything before them [*Mobile Daily Tribune*, 12 August 1864].

The only problem with the statement of the *Tribune* that I see is the emphasis upon the enemy offering the "slight resistance." Another writer, in retrospect, also offers a similar suggestion about the lack of difficulty the Alabamians encountered (*Confederate Veteran 1893–1912* Vol. 3, 12–14). Colonel George T. Rogers of Mahone's old brigade described the work of Sanders's men as one "without loss, comparatively. It was a handsome walkover for them" (*ibid.* 14). I hardly think what the brigade faced could be labeled a "walkover." What they faced when they came over the top of that crest was nothing less than a murderous fire. We need to let the men who recall what happened tell it in their own words.

FIERCE FIGHTING AT THE CRATER

As you might expect, as soon as the men reached the crest of the hill blocking them from the enemy, they began a dash for the works at the double-quick. At first the enemy's fire overshot them, as Clark recalls (Clark 1914, 60). The closer they came to the enemy's works the more deadly the fire became. Large gaps in the line of battle were made as the enemy found

Area where Mahone's men charged into the Crater from the ravine.

its target. Featherston called it a dash into "the mouth of hell" (SHSP Vol. 33, 363). If this dash into a rainstorm of lead were not bad enough, the worst, it seems, awaited them once they reached the Crater.

Once the men reached their objective it soon became a melee of hand-to-hand fighting. General Sanders led this charge to the captured Confederate works. General Sanders's brother would speak of his brother's leadership in this battle in an address delivered many years later:

> One of the most brilliant charges he led was at the battle of the Crater, it having been the final charge made to recover the ground lost by the terrific explosion. A member of the Brigade, who participated in the battle, wrote a lengthy account therof to an Ala paper. After describing very fully the charge, he uses the following language: "The highest eulogy is due the intrepid Sanders for the fearless, daring manner in which he mounted the works, and pushed forward, exhorting his command onward to victory. When within ten or fifteen feet of the enemy's guns, death being the certain fate of almost every one who showed himself at that point, he stood and watched the progress of the battle, and marked with coolness the changes of position by the enemy, being able thereby to throw his command to those points where they could fight to the best advantage [Dr. Sanders's Papers].

For the next fifteen to twenty minutes it became a desperate affair. General Sanders's own account is a fitting place to begin to understand what took place at this point of the battle:

> When we got to the works the men were fighting hand to hand with the Yankees, very soon however all of the enemy in the works numbering about five hundred surrendered to us. Among them one Brigr Genl and one hundred and forty negroes. We captured their (three) stands of colors. This is the first time we have ever come in contact with Negroes, they fight much better than I expected but they were driven on by the Yankees and many of them were

Inside the Crater near where the 11th Alabama fought.

shot down by the latter. The bottom of the mine was filled with dead and wounded Yankees and negroes piled indiscriminately together, one hundred and thirty-three were buried in the bottom of the chasm [Sanders's File].

Lieutenant Colonel William H. Stewart of Weisiger's Virginia Brigade noted that the Alabamians tumbled clubs, clods of dirt, muskets, and cannon balls over the works onto the heads of the enemy (SHSP Vol. 25, 83). Clark remembers when the men poured over into the works held by the Unionists that many of the men were brained by guns and run through with bayonets. General Sanders had a duel with a black soldier in which both of them proved to be bad marksmen (Clark 1914, 60)! One soldier of the 9th Alabama wrote a letter to his wife in which he described this terrible clash:

> The fort was literally covered with Yankees and bristled with bayonets as the quills of the "fretful porcupine." ... The enemy have shouted: "No quarters!" We then gave them what they justly deserved. There we were on one side of the walls of the fort and the Yankees on the other. The fight was the bloodiest of the war considering the numbers engaged. We fought with muskets, with bayonets, with rocks, and even with clods of dirt [SHSP Vol. 33, 371].

After this most brutal type of warfare had finally taken its toll, the Union soldiers asked for quarter (Fleming W. Thompson Letters). The Battle of the Crater was now over. What remains is to take account of the casualties suffered by regiment.

The Casualties of the 11th Alabama at the Crater

The number of killed and wounded among the ranks was significant, as you would expect from a conflict as bloody as this was. Beginning with Co. A, we have the following casualties[4]:

Wm. H.H. Boozer (killed), Henry Brame (wounded), John J. Carter (killed), Thomas H. Johnson (killed), James T. McDonald (killed), and Joseph J. Williams (wounded). Company B had Matthew P. Hamilton severely wounded in the leg (Fleming W. Thompson Letters). From the ranks of Co. C the following were casualties: Thomas W. Winn (wounded), Robert L. Waller (severely wounded), John W. Carnes (severely wounded in right arm by shell, arm amputated), and James F. Gandy (mortally wounded, died at Clinton on October 15, 1864). The Canebrake Legion lost the following men: Calvin Noble (wounded), Lt. John W. Cole (killed), and James W. Thompson (killed). Albert J. Johnson from Co. E was killed, and the only casualty from his company. The Bibb company lost: P. Simpson Wright (wounded), Capt. Joseph C. Caddelle (wounded in the left shoulder), and Philip M. Vance (wounded in left thigh). The men from Co. G that were listed as casualties included: David Shamblin (wounded), James McGee (wounded), Peter Thomson (wounded), James M. Kent (mortally wounded, died August 10, 1864), William H. Leopard (killed), and Henyard T. Williamson (killed). Company I lists only Capt. Lemuel Harris (killed). Finally, Co. K records the following casualty: William Lovelady (killed).

If we add up the total of casualties of the 11th Alabama at the Battle of the Crater we arrive at the following: twenty-six casualties, thirteen wounded, and thirteen killed or mortally wounded. This means that of the total number of casualties, half of them ended in the death of the soldier. This is an extremely high death ratio, and attests to the horrific nature of the engagement at the Crater. In a letter written by 1st Lieutenant Abel A. Walden of Co. I on August 12, 1864, it contains information on the death of Captain Harris (Harris 1861–1864). It states that Captain Harris was struck in the head with a ball, but he did not die for several hours afterward. Harris had been in command for over two years of Company I. His leadership would be sadly missed.

It seems appropriate to conclude this discussion of the Battle of the Crater with mention of the valor demonstrated by a member of Co. G. James N. Keeton, a private in the Tuscaloosa Rifles, made the Confederate Roll of Honor for his part played in the Crater battle (OR Series 1 Vol. 40/1, 754). It was Keeton who was responsible for capturing the Guidon (Stars and Stripes). He is the only member of the regiment listed who was involved in the capturing of a stand of colors at the Crater. The 11th had been instrumental in sealing off a tremendous breach in the Confederate line that fateful day of July 30, 1864. Had they not been successful, it may very well have led to a severe compromising of the Confederate defensive position.

The Battle of White's Tavern: August 16, 1864

The next major development that would engage the 11th Alabama had its beginning in a major troop movement by General Grant on August 13 ,1864 (*Richmond Enquirer*, 31 August 1864). Grant moved both the Second and Tenth Corps from City Point to the area known as Deep Bottom north of the James River. The next day they attacked surprised Confederate pickets near Four Mile Run with the result that the line in front of Law's and Bratton's Brigades gave way.

The feeling among some was that this was simply a diversionary tactic on Grant's part, for his real objective still lay with the Union left near the Weldon Railroad (Robertson Jr. 1987, 296). General Lee telegrammed General Charles W. Field on August 14 with the news that he was sending both cavalry and infantry assistance (Dowdey 1961, 835–838). The Confederate commander would send two brigades of infantry to Field's aid, although he clearly affirms his belief that this may in fact just be a feint. One of those brigades which left their Petersburg defenses by rail somewhere between 7:30 and 9:30 P.M. included Sanders's Alabama Brigade.[5]

THE 11TH ALABAMA IN THE BATTLE OF WHITE'S TAVERN

Sanders took a position near Deep Bottom on a ridge that extended some three hundred yards before making connection with Wright's Georgia Brigade. This Georgia brigade was being commanded by General Victor J.B. Girardey (Clark 1914, 62). General Sanders was placed in command of the Confederate left wing consisting of General Lane's North Carolina Brigade, Wright's Georgia Brigade, and Sanders's own Alabama Brigade (Sanders's File). These brigades composed the extreme left of the Confederate position at Deep Bottom, and appear to have been stationed in exactly this order.

Around 1:00 P.M. the Union forces attacked in strength against Wright's Brigade to the left of the Darbytown Road (*Richmond Enquirer*, 31 August 1864). When the attack commenced, the Confederate brigades were all in one rank in an attempt to keep from being flanked by the Union troops (Sanders's File). In the heated attack against Girardey's boys, the Georgia line was forced to give way, which in turn led to the confused scattering of the North Carolina brigade (*Richmond Enquirer*, 31 August 1864). The line had been breached and Union troops were now on the flank and rear of the Alabamians.

At this point of the battle things looked extremely bleak. The Alabama Brigade of necessity did fall back (Clark 1914, 62); however, they did not give way, but in stubborn fashion held their ground until reinforcements could be brought to their aid. In this critical moment many of the members of the 11th Alabama were taken prisoner. It was inevitable since they now had the enemy on their flank and in their rear. Aaron Curb was a private in Co. K at this time. He recalls being overrun by the Federal forces with vividness. He and one of his buddies were lying behind an embankment. They were both firing away at the enemy before they discovered that the rest of the company had fallen back (Curb Papers). About this time some of the Yankee soldiers jumped up and yelled, "Hurrah, Hurrah!" Monroe and his buddy began shooting away at them. Before long, however, they heard from behind them the command to surrender. They were now prisoners of war, and were eventually taken to Point Lookout, Maryland, on the Chesapeake Bay.

It is without a doubt true to affirm that Sanders's Alabama Brigade helped to save the day at Deep Bottom. Multiple testimonies state that they held their ground until ample manpower could be brought to bear on the invading Federals. Listen to the words of the *Richmond Enquirer*:

> The giving way of Wright's Brigade caused Lane's and McGowan's to change front, and in doing so the former was very much scattered. General Sanders, who was on the right, held his position, though a brisk fire was kept up on his front and flank. The enemy, taking advantage of the breach and confusion, had occupied our breastworks in force and was pressing our men far back to the rear [*Richmond Enquirer*, 31August 1864].

General Sanders played a leading role in this part of the battle. He rallied the men by word and by example, and in the process exposed himself to the enemy fire in the most fearless manner (Sanders's File). Erlander M. Richardson of Sanders's old Co. C recalled many years later the role General Sanders played at this crucial moment of the battle. His account is found in the *Eutaw Whig* on May 24, 1893:

How vividly it will call to mind of every member of the 11th Alabama regiment, who can see him now as he rode in front of us at Deep-bottom and said, "Here is my brave old regiment. Boys you have fought yankees and you can do it again." All was in confusion; our line broken and with this regiment the foe was held in check, with Sanders in front offering words of cheer, until the 11th Ala regiment would have staid there until the last man was killed. It was Sanders who, when reinforcements came, led the charge, restored the broken line and all was well again.

Dr. William H. Sanders relates some of the perilous moments that his brother experienced during this part of the battle. It shows how fearless a leader General Sanders was:

A furious assault was made by the enemy and Lane's & Wrights Brigades driven back — ours holding its position. John exerted himself in driving back the enemy and reestablishing the line in its original position. He remarked to me the next day that so far as he was concerned it was the severest battle he had passed through. He was exposed to a more concentrated fire than ever before and for a much longer time. He also spoke of several very narrow escapes he made during the day. A shell passed in few inches of his side and struck his horse on the ear. At another time he rode up to Lane's Brig, and as he returned he found the enemy's skirmishers in possession of the road and got very near before he discovered them. The pines were so thick on each side that it was impossible to ride through them. He looked round and very fortunately there was a little path going to the right. As he turned his horse four shots were fired at him with very close range but without effect [Sanders's File].

The Causalities of the 11th Alabama at White's Tavern

Due to the nature of this battle there were many soldiers that were taken as prisoners of war. Company B was especially hit hard by this engagement. William P. Robuck of Co. B states that the enemy literally took what was left of the entire company (Fleming W. Thompson Letters)! In fact, in the historical memoranda for Co. B it confirms that due to the smallness of numbers after this battle Co. B was temporarily consolidated with Co. K (11th Alabama). It states that only four men remained from the company. We can confirm that the following men from Co. B were captured at Deep Bottom: John W. Skates, William F. Morris, Albert L. Moore, Moody H. May, James S. Gibson, Lt. Winfield S. Bird, William H. Moore, John S. McCulley, and Fleming W. Thompson (CSR). There is no record of anyone from Co. B being wounded or killed. It appears as if they were simply overwhelmed before they could react.

Company C lists two causalities: Elmore A. Steele (captured) and Little Berry Pippen was wounded. The Washington County company had these men captured: Charles H. Griffin, William R. Deshazo, Joseph M. Heard, and Wooten O'Neal. Company F list these causalities: Lt. William J. Suttle (killed), David E. Lightsey (severely wounded in thigh), and Martin N. Lightsey (killed). The Tuscaloosa Rifles had many men captured: William S. Hayes, John T. Burchfield, Andrew J. Burrage, Joseph E. McMath, James N. Keeton, Capt. John B. Hughes, and Robert A. Watson. Two causalities are found from the ranks of Co. H: William J. Kerr was wounded in the left elbow, while James E. Williams was captured. Company I lists Ephraim Long as captured, along with Joseph A. Bolton. Finally, Co. K was hit hard, as the following list demonstrates: John T. Church, William A. Austin, Beverly L. Waddell, Robert B. Griffin, John W. Guthrie, Daniel L. Stewart, and Aaron M. Curb were captured. William W. Brazelton was wounded. The total casualties among the men were: two men killed, four wounded, and thirty-one captured. Company B was the hardest hit, since it lost nine men in addition to its ability to stand alone in the ranks.

The Battle of Davis Farm: August 21, 1864

The boys remained at Deep Bottom until around August 18 or 19, according to Captain Clark (Clark 1914, 63). At this time they were ordered to report back to their old position at Petersburg. Upon their arrival at Petersburg the afternoon of August 20, they could hear that a heavy engagement was in progress on the right. They knew that the Federals were attempting to move their left flank further around the Confederate right.

The Federals had now become strongly entrenched on the Weldon Railroad. It was thought that perhaps they could be dislodged by a concentrated effort. General Mahone ordered Sanders to move his brigade out in an attempt to protect the Weldon Railroad (Hoole 1985, 10). Early on the morning of August 21, 1864, the men were formed up to move (Clark 1914, 63). Captain Clark recalls that it was about 2:00 A.M. when this formation took place. The men then began the march to the right in order to intercept the enemy's movements. The desired position was reached at daybreak, and the men were then formed into their line of battle. Not long after moving forward they encountered enemy skirmishers. The skirmishers were easily captured, and the men continued their movement. Dr. Sanders recalled that there were two heavy skirmish lines out front of the main entrenched body of Federals (Dr. Sanders's Papers). Whether there were two or simply one doesn't matter, because in any event the skirmishers were driven back or captured in the forward movement. This initial movement appears to have been made in a dense thicket. There was a growing confidence among the men after successfully overwhelming the Federal pickets. Perhaps the worst of the battle was over. These feelings of confidence were soon to be shattered by Federal muskets.

What the Alabamians didn't know was that across the open field they had entered into

Davis Farm. Looking out from Vaugh Road toward the open field Sanders's men covered.

from the thicket lay heavily entrenched Union forces. Across this perhaps mile-wide open field, Union artillery batteries began barking shot and shell at the gray soldiers. The Alabama boys did not turn tail and run. They bravely moved forward in the midst of the barrage of artillery fire to within a hundred yards of the enemy's fortifications (Clark 1914, 63). Men were dropping left and right among the ranks of the 11th. Lieutenant Able A. Walden of Co. I fell severely wounded in the leg, while William F. Lane from the Fayette company fell dead nearby (CSR). William Griffin of the Bibb company was shot severely in the left foot. Later the surgeons had to amputate his left leg in order to save his life.

Philip M. Vance of Co. F vividly recalled this brave charge, and also some very personal experiences that took place that day:

> After passing through this timbered land, we came to a cleared field, and found the Federals concealed behind a row of fence rails, with which they made breastworks. Coming to open ground, the Federals fired a volley of musketry into our line, which caused it to waver, the soldiers jumping behind trees. General Sanders, at this moment, dashed to the front on his beautiful black war horse and ordered me to take my company and go forward and charge them. Giving the order to my men, they rushed forward, yelling and firing as they advanced. The Federals broke back from their hiding into a thick huckleberry swamp in their rear. The bushes were so thick and full of smoke from the firing of the guns that a man could scarcely be seen ten steps distant. I continued to advance, and, becoming separated from my company, crowded through the dense brush. I suddenly came upon a company of Federals lying in an old ditch; and as I was alone, I felt that my time had come. I decided in a flash to use a bold bluff, so I leaped down into the ditch in front of the captain and, waving my sword over his head, ordered him to surrender. He did so, handing me his sword, which I have yet. I then ordered the Federal soldiers, forty, fifty, or more, to lay down their guns, which they did, to my delight. Then I ordered them to the rear. As they commenced to file out of the ditch, seeing no other Johnnies in sight, several stooped to pick up their guns; but just at this moment, my comrades began to emerge from the bushes, to my great joy. They at once took charge of Hancock's boys in blue [11th Alabama].

Vance goes on to describe that he took a Federal captain's canteen and shook it. Since it seemed full, he took a swallow only to find it filled with good apple brandy. After taking a drink he then invited the Federal captain to drink also, to which he responded, "Johnny, you are d___ cheeky," but went ahead and took a drink anyway.

The Death of General John C.C. Sanders

General John Sanders was leading the charge of the brigade over the open field when he was struck by a Minié ball. The ball's entry resulted in the severing of his femoral artery. Captain Clark is our best source of information about the death of General Sanders. Let us listen to his description of the event:

> Just at the break of day we reached our position and forming lines, began to move forward. We soon ran upon enemy skirmishers, but captured them and emerged upon an open field fully a half a mile wide and encountered a storm of cannonading as we pressed forward boldly. When we reached within a hundred yards of the enemy's fortifications, General John C. Saundes, commander of the brigade and upon those staff I was serving as assistant adjutant general, pressed forward with me at his side, when I heard a bullet hit the General. As I was quite close to him I saw him reel, and grasping him around the waist I helped him up and asked him if I should go on, but he said, "No, stay with me," and immediately lapsed into unconsciousness. I got two men who were passing to assist me and we carried him out of the fire to a branch, but in a few moments he was dead [Clark 1914, 63].

General Sanders's brother, Dr. William Sanders, was not able to be present at this battle. In a letter to his parents he sadly reflects back on the death of his brother, and perhaps what might have been if he had been present:

> Its a hard reflection for me that he should have bled to death, and although I know the almost impossibility of saving life when so large an artery is cut so high up as was the case, still I cannot escape the bitter thought that if I could have been there I might at least have prolonged his life [Sanders's File].

Captain Clark was helpless to prevent the General's death. In his recollection he lived only a few minutes after being laid down by a tree about a hundred yards to the rear of the fighting. He desired to keep the news from the men, but once the men realized that their leader had been killed they lost the heart to fight any longer. William Robuck of Co. B expresses the feelings no doubt of the entire regiment at the loss of General Sanders:

> ...we had our general killed dead on the field general John C.C. Sanders was killed day before yesterday, he has been with us ever since we have been in the army he came ought a capten in clinton company & from that he was purmoted colonel & then general pore fellow he was kild day before yesteday we all morne his loss vary mutch. I don't think we ever can git another sutch a general [Fleming W. Thompson Letters].

Newspapers spoke of the death of General Sanders. He was noted for his skill, promise, and bravery. The *Mobile Advertiser & Register* on September 1, 1864, mentions General Sanders's death, "Brig Gen. Sanders of Alabama, who was struck in the thigh by a minie ball and the femoral artery severed, while attempting to storm the enemy's breastworks. He bled to death in a few minutes. General Sanders was a very young and very promising officer." Another newspaper had these words of praise for General Sanders:

> The 8th, 9th, 10th, 11th, and 14th Alabama Regiments, composing General Saunder's brigade, were engaged, but did not lose many men. General Saunders was killed by a minnie ball that cut the femoral artery. He was a native of Greene county, a graduate of the University of Alabama, was only 24 years of age, and was a gallant and skillful officer [*Mobile Evening News*, 5 September 1864].

The young man from Greene County, Alabama, was dead. He had exuberantly led a company from Clinton, Alabama, to Lynchburg, Virginia. His obvious leadership skills had led to his promotion to Colonel of the entire regiment. Finally, the highest levels of command in the Army of Northern Virginia had taken note of this disciplined Colonel, and so recommended his promotion to Brigadier General. He had led his men through some of the heaviest fighting that the Army of Northern Virginia ever had to experience. General Sanders was truly irreplaceable at this point of the Southern conflict.

General Sanders's body was taken to the Petersburg home of Mr. Bernard Todd (Dr. Sanders's Papers). The next day his body was removed to Richmond, where it was placed in a vault in the Hollywood Cemetery. The inscription over his grave read: "To the memory of Brig General J.C.C. Sanders of Alabama. Who was killed near Petersburg Va. Augt 21st 1864. 'Forget not the Dead, who die for us.'"

The Casualties of the 11th Alabama at Davis Farm

From the ranks of Co. D we have these casualties: John W. Jones (wounded) and Jesse L. Burton (wounded in the left hand, lost middle finger). Jacob B. Hardy of Co. E was captured at Davis Farm. James M. Waggoner and James W. Smelly were both wounded from Co.

F. We previously noted that William Griffin from the Bibb Company was severely wounded in the left foot. A head wound was received by Joseph R. Britt of Co. G. The Pickens County Guards list the following causalities: William A. Davis (wounded), Benjamin F. Ferguson (wounded), and James B. Hodo (captured). Company I had these casualties: William M. Mathis (right leg amputated), William F. Lane (killed), Lt. Abel Walden (severely wounded in the leg), and Henry L. Rodgers (mortally wounded, died September 15, 1864). The total number of casualties at Davis Farm were: three killed or mortally wounded, two captured, and ten wounded.

The Battle of Ream's Station: August 25, 1864

The regiment remained in what Captain Clark called a little depression under constant fire the remainder of August 24, 1864 (Clark 1914, 63–64). After dark they withdrew to Petersburg and here they remained until the order came to march to Ream's Station on August 25. Colonel J. Horace King of the 9th Alabama was placed in charge of the brigade at this time. This movement was A.P. Hill's attempt to once more dislodge the Federals from their hold on the Weldon Railroad (Long 1971, 558).

We have very little information about the action played by the regiment in this battle. We know that they reached Ream's Station around 5:00 P.M., and that the fighting had already commenced. Captain Clark notes:

Ream's Station. Looking out towards the woods from old Stage Road in the direction of the Depot Road, where the fighting most likely took place.

> We had not been assigned our position in the lines, but were standing on the side of the road about one-fourth of a mile from the fighting waiting orders. Colonel King of the 9th Alabama was commanding officer, and not being accustomed to battle on a horse, he insisted on my getting down. We were discussing the matter when finally I threw my right leg over the horse, but just as my foot reached the ground, a heavy piece of shell came down on my instep giving me severe pain. I had to go back to the field hospital on my horse, but by the time I reached there, which was one-half mile, the foot has so swollen that my boot had to be ripped off. This put an end to my war experience for a time [Clark 1914, 64].

Hancock's Second Corps was the objective of this operation (Freeman 1991, 435). Hancock's men had constructed rather inferior works at Ream's Station. Here they were in a position of weakness as well, since they were entirely separated from Warren's Fifth Corps. In the initial assault against this Union position the Confederates were unsuccessful (Robertson Jr. 1987, 300). A massive bombardment by Pegram's Artillery in the late afternoon preceded a second attack. This bombardment slackened by 5:40 P.M., at which time Lane, Cooke, and MacRae swept forward in a successful charge of the Federal position.

In General Lee's report of the battle no mention is made of the participation of the Alabama Brigade (Dowdey 1961, 845). He mentions only Cooke and MacRae's North Carolinian Brigades, and Lane's North Carolinian Brigade. The 11th Alabama must have been engaged, however, in the last charge of the day against the Federal position at Ream's Station. The official reports give the following casualties: John T. Hamiter, Co. H (wounded); John A. Gordy, Co. E (wounded in left shoulder & collarbone); William T. Davis, Co. I (wounded in right thigh); Erastus A. Chambers, Co. C (wounded in left leg); Chesterfield W. Quinn, Co. F (wounded); James E. Lee, Co. H (killed); and Francis M. Doss, Co. C (wounded in right thigh). This means that the 11th suffered seven casualties at Ream's Station.

The pace of the war after the battle at Ream's Station changed for the regiment. Battles would no longer be coming fast and furious. There were indeed several battles yet to be fought by the proud men from Alabama; nevertheless, the character of the fighting was different. Just how different the war became will now occupy our attention in the pages to follow.

12

The Desperate Struggle for Petersburg Is Lost

In this chapter we will follow the 11th Alabama Infantry from the final days in the Petersburg trenches until the laying down of arms at Appomattox Court House. There were additional battles and skirmishes awaiting the regiment in 1864 and into 1865, but they would no longer be led by the young Brigadier General from Greene County, Alabama. John Sanders was gone. The battle facing the regiment now took on a desperate character. It became a literal struggle for survival.

Events Following the Battle of Ream's Station

There were some necessary adjustments within the regiment and brigade which required some attention following the Battle of Ream's Station on August 25, 1864. It appears that Col. John H. King of the 9th Alabama was placed in temporary command of the brigade following the death of General Sanders (CSR). Lieutenant Colonel George Tayloe was still in command of the regiment, but before the year would finish he would be promoted to the rank of Colonel. In fact, in a letter dated September 11, 1864, Colonel King recommends to General Cooper that Lieutenant Colonel Tayloe be promoted to Colonel to fill the vacancy caused by the death of General Sanders. Colonel Tayloe's appointment did come on October 31, 1864, and it was to date from August 21, 1864. Colonel Tayloe would finally be placed in command of Sorrel's Brigade by February 27, 1865. Lieutenant Colonel Tayloe made the recommendation that 1st Lt. Cornelius Watlington of his old Co. D be appointed Regimental Adjutant on September 25, 1864 (CSR). The previous adjutant, Ruffin Y. Ashe, had died back on June 29, 1864. Lieutenant Watlington was eventually confirmed in this position on either November 3, or 5, 1864.

What can be said about the command structure of the companies within the regiment at this point? Company A still had John B. Rains as their Captain. He had taken over command following the death of Thomas H. Holcombe on June 30, 1862. Captain Rains would remain the Captain until the surrender. In addition to Captain Rains, William B. Young was still 1st Lieutenant and John H. Adams was still in command at 2nd Lieutenant. Thomas M. Witherspoon was also Jr. 2nd Lieutenant, and was in addition appointed an aide to Colonel King. Company A had one of the more stable command structures of the regiment for the entire war.

What about the Greene County Grays? We noted in the previous chapter that following the Battle of White's Tavern on August 16, 1864, Co. B was temporarily consolidated with Co. K. It seems that this temporary consolidation became a permanent one. In the *Historical Memoranda* of Co. B dated at the end of 1864, it mentions the consolidation with Co. K (11th Alabama). No mention is made that this state of affairs had in any way been changed. When Captain Clark returned to his company in January of 1865 he had no command to return to (Clark 1914, 64). The only other officer of Co. B was 2nd Lt. Robert P. Schoppert, who was detailed in command of the brigade Pioneer Corps. The battle of White's Tavern effectively ended the independent existence of Co. B for the remainder of the war.

What about the other Greene County, Alabama, company? This company still had Capt. Benjamin T. Higginbotham in command until his official retirement on August 12, 1864 (CSR). Colonel George Tayloe believed that of the two lieutenants of Co. C, James C.B. Harkness and Richard M. Kennedy, 2nd Lieutenant Harkness would make the better Captain. He penned this letter of recommendation to Colonel W.H. Taylor, Chief of Staff of the Army of Northern Virginia on October 12, 1864:

> Under the act of Congress approved Feb 1864 I respectfully recommend 2nd Lt. J.C.B. Harkness Co. C for Captancy of said company.... Lt. Harkness displayed signal gallantry on the 30th July when my brigade attacked and drove the enemy from the position that they had gained on our lines. When the enemy had been driven from the first ditch and our men hesitated in attacking them in the second, Lieut Harkness with the colors jumped over and by his courage urged on others. He is the more competent of the two Liets of his company and I respectfully urge his promotion.

This recommendation was officially approved on March 2, 1865, and was to date from February 9, 1865. An interesting twist to the appointment of Lieutenant Harkness is a paper written by Lt. Richard M. Kennedy (Dr. Sanders's Papers). Lieutenant Kennedy notes that at the time of *his* appointment as Captain, Lieutenant Harkness was absent without leave in another command, and never was Captain of the company.[1] Kennedy goes on to state that after a court of inquiry, Gen. William H. Forney was going to recommend Lieutenant Kennedy for promotion to Captain based upon his gallant conduct in the battle of April 7, 1865. Obviously this did not eventuate due to the surrender two days later. In any event, one note states that Richard M. Kennedy surrendered at Appomattox as 1st Lieutenant of Co. C (CSR).

The Canebrake Legion from Marengo County, Alabama, still had Capt. John H. Prince in command. He would remain in this position through the remainder of the war. We have already noted that 1st Lt. Cornelius Watlington would be promoted to Adjutant of the regiment in November of 1864. When this promotion took place, it left a hole that was filled by Hillard J. Askew. One note places his promotion to 2nd Lieutenant on November 23, 1864, while the official muster rolls give February 19, 1865, as the date of his official promotion. It may have been that he was brevetted 2nd Lieutenant in November pending his official appointment in 1865.

The Washington County company lost its Captain, John James, on June 4, 1864. No other Captain was ever officially elected for Co. E for the remainder of the war. According to one source, Augustus Fletcher Hooks was recommended as Captain prior to the surrender, but his commission never reached him (*Washington County News* n.d.). The only other known officer of this regiment that can be ascertained is Benjamin F. Porter (CSR). He was promoted to 1st Sergeant in February of 1863. I could find no other record of a commissioned officer in this company. James N. Hayes of Co. G appears to have been in command of Co. E in January of 1865. I found his name in a petition signed asking for the promotion of Colonel Forney to Brigadier General. He may have temporarily been assigned to command the company as 2nd Lieutenant.

From left to right: Jacob Mayberry, Phil Vance, Evelyn Abney (niece of Zach Abney), and Captain Zach Abney (courtesy A.H. Brewer).

A look at Co. F reveals the following details of command structure. Joseph C. Caddelle was Captain of the Bibb County company. He had been wounded at the Crater back on July 30, 1864. He would return to his company on October 15, 1864, and lead his men in the Battle of Burgess Mill. Unfortunately, he returned only to be killed less than two weeks later. Upon his death, 1st Lieutenant Zachariah Abney would be promoted to Captain. Abney had assumed the 1st Lieutenant position following the death of 1st Lt. William J. Suttle on August 16, 1864. With Abney's move up in the ranks, Philip M. Vance then took the 2nd Lieutenant position. Following Burgess Mill, 2nd Lieutenant Vance would be promoted to 1st Lieutenant. He would remain at this rank for the remainder of the war.

The Tuscaloosa Rifles' Captain was John B. Hughes; however, Captain Hughes had been captured at White's Tavern on August 16, 1864, and would remain absent from his command for the remainder of the conflict. Henyard T. Williamson was the 1st Lieutenant of Co. G, but was killed at the Crater back on July 30, 1864. James N. Hayes is listed as 2nd Lieutenant of Co. G, a position he held until the surrender. There is no record that he was promoted to 1st Lieutenant. Joseph R. Britt is also listed as 2nd Lieutenant. He was wounded at Davis Farm, and it appears from the muster rolls that he remained absent due to his wound for the duration.

The Pickens County company had Martin L. Stewart as its Captain for the remainder of the war. Walter T. Palmer was 1st Lieutenant of Co. H, a rank he would hold until his death at the Battle of Hatcher's Run on February 6, 1865. Company I lost its Captain, Lemuel Harris, at the Crater battle on July 30, 1864. With the death of Captain Harris the highest-ranking officer in the company was Abel A. Walden as 1st Lieutenant. Unfortunately, Lieutenant

Walden had been severely wounded at Davis Farm back on August 21, 1864, and as far as we can tell was never able to rejoin his command. William T. Davis became the next ranking officer as Jr. 2nd Lieutenant, and he was promoted to 2nd Lieutenant on November 23, 1864. Nevertheless, Lieutenant Davis had been badly wounded at Ream's Station on August 25, 1864, and was not able to rejoin his command due to the severity of the wound. Francis A. Brotherton was eventually promoted on November 23, 1864, to Jr. 2nd Lieutenant. He went on a leave of indulgence from which he was absent by January 14, 1865. He may have gone home to marry and never returned to his command.[2]

Captain Edward Lucas would remain the commander of Co. K for the remainder of the war. The only other officer that we can say with certainty that existed was Beverly L. Waddell. He was promoted to at least Jr. 2nd Lieutenant; however, he was taken prisoner at White's Tavern and sat out the remainder of the war.

THE DANGERS OF LIFE IN THE TRENCHES OF PETERSBURG

Life in the Petersburg trenches was a perilous daily existence for the men. One unidentified soldier's report of life during these days was recorded on September 2, 1864, in a Mobile newspaper:

> Life in the trenches is very monotonous and weary; day after day and night after night passes slowly by without variablness, or shadow of change. We are becoming tired of the long confinement, tired of eating cold bread and bacon, tired of the continual popping of rifles from the picket line, and the almost incessant howling and bursting of shell — and most of us would gladly welcome a march, with its change of scene, excitement and wild bivouacs, camps and blazing log fires [*Mobile Advertiser & Register*, 13 September 1864].

Men would be systematically picked off by enemy sharpshooters either in the trenches, or while out on picket duty. The following men of the regiment were either wounded or killed during this period: Samuel A. Black of Co. I (wounded on September 11), Thomas J. Johnson of Co. B (killed on picket September 13), Alfred B. Cox of Co. H (wounded in trenches September 14), Milton A. Hamilton of Co. B (wounded severely on picket September 14), Asa Vaughan of Co. D (wounded on picket September 15, died October 31), Edward Blunt of Co. D (killed on picket September 16), John A. Hayes of Co. A (wounded on picket September 23, died October 1 or 2), Nathaniel Walker of Co. A (wounded severely in leg September 12), Merrit J. Morgan of Co. A (severely wounded in leg September 19), David Brown of Co. F (wounded in left hand September 25), William Odum of Co. E (killed on picket October 1), William F. Kirkland of Co. I (wounded on picket October 11), Albert Brown of Co. A (killed on picket October 28), Nathan Y. Hankins of Co. D (killed on picket October 31), James W. Oliver of Co. I (wounded on picket November 2), and Michael M. Linebarger of Co. H (wounded while visiting Gracie's Brigade near Petersburg November 9). This gives us a total of some fifteen casualties in the regiment from September through November 1864. Half of these casualties resulted in death, with Co. A sustaining the highest number of casualties at four. Company D had only three casualties, but all of them were mortal (CSR).

The Battle of Burgess Mill: October 27, 1864

The battle which took place on October 27, 1864, was the result of the Federal objective of extending their lines to the South Side Railroad (OR Series 1 Vol. 42/3, 404–405). This operation would involve three Federal Corps: the Fifth, Second, and Ninth. General Hancock's Second Corps would take the Vaughan Road to Hatcher's Run according to the battle plan. Hancock crossed at Armstrong's Mill and proceeded in the direction of Burgess' Tavern. General Hancock crossed the run around 7:30 A.M., after what he called a "brief firing" (OR Series 1 Vol. 42/3, 378–380). By 12:30 General Hancock reported that he had reached the Burgess House on Boydton Plank Road. He was now only six miles from the railroad, and two miles to the bridge where Boydton crossed the run.

In the meantime, General Lee had been informed from General Hill that the Federals had crossed Hatcher's Run at Armstrong's Mill (OR Series 1 Vol. 42/3, 1177). In order to meet this threat General Mahone and General Hampton's cavalry were dispatched. By 4:14 P.M., General Hancock was informed that Confederate troops had amassed in his front to dispute his crossing of the bridge at Burgess Mill (*ibid.*, 380). General Hancock formed his men in line of battle over the Boydton Plank Road; however, Hancock's right flank was not protected from a possible assault. Hancock was in advance of the Fifth Corps whose division on the left was commanded by Brig. Gen. Samuel W. Crawford. It was this weakness which gave General Mahone his opportunity.

It was around 5:00 P.M. when General Hancock made his attempt to carry the bridge over Hatcher's Run and from there on to the South Side Railroad (*ibid.*, 405–406). According to the report of Gen. George G. Meade, Hancock's men were attacked on the right, left, and rear. The attack on the rear was carried out by Hampton's men, while the attack in the front was carried out by three brigades under General Mahone (OR Series 1 Vol. 42/1, 853). General Lee gives this report of the battle:

> General Hill reports that the attack of General Heth upon the enemy on the Boydton Plan road, mentioned in my dispatch last evening, was made by three brigades under General Mahone in front, and General Hampton in the rear. Mahone captured 400 prisoners, 3 stand of colors, and 6 pieces of artillery. The latter could not be brought off, the enemy having possession of the bridge. In the attack subsequently made by the enemy General Mahone broke three lines of battle, and during the night the enemy retired from the Boydton road, leaving his wounded and more than 250 dead on the field [OR Series 1 Vol. 42/1, 853–854].[3]

In an extract from the *Philadelphia Inquirer* we read of General Mahone's attack on the Second Corps. It illustrates how the Confederates brought it to Hancock on every side:

> At this time General Hancock had reached and had his line of battle formed across the Boydton plank road. At this moment, however, Mahone struck him heavily on his right flank, and he found himself at the same time immediately in front of a strong line of rebel works, heavily defended. The rebel cavalry simultaneously swept around his left and a column of them charged down the telegraph road, which ran parallel with his line of battle, and come into the Boydton plank road in his rear. Under circumstances like these even the splended skill of Hancock and soldierly ability of Mott and Gibbon could avail but little. The corps was forced back, and for an hour and a half the contest was desperate and the safety of the corps for a moment or two was doubtful [OR Series 1 Vol. 42/3, 485].

The Casualties of the 11th Alabama at Burgess Mill

The casualties suffered by the 11th Alabama of Mahone's Division attest to the fierceness of this battle, and to the personal involvement of the regiment in the fighting. We find a total of fourteen casualties in the ranks at Burgess Mill. This is a breakdown of the men who were killed, wounded, or captured on October 27, 1864. Among the men killed was John R. Springfield of Co. D. According to one account of Springfield's death, he was reported to have

Burgess Mill. Mahone executed a flank attack against Hancock near here off Dabney Mill Road.

died in the arms of his half-uncle, Cornelius Watlington (Rembert, 2001). In addition to Springfield's death, John B. Jolly of Co. A and Capt. Joseph C. Caddelle of Co. F were killed. The list of wounded men included: Sterling Clanton of Co. I, Francis M. Norris of Co. A, Henry L. Bruce of Co. A, John A. Stewart of Co. C, John C. Adams of Co. H, James T. McFarland of Co. A, Robert E. Allen of Co. A, Benjamin F. Porter of Co. E, William H.H. Sanders of Co. C, and William J. Shaw of Co. H (CSR). Leslie Rain of Co. E was captured in the battle.

The Battle of Burgess Mill had at least temporarily stopped the Federals from further encroachment on the Confederate lines. It was a significant battle. With the defeat at Burgess Mill the most ambitious attempt at outflanking the Richmond-Petersburg line by the Federals in 1864 ended in a defeat (Freeman 1991, 441). The 11th Alabama played an important role in this last major battle of the year in securing their lines for another day. The next major engagement for the regiment would not take place until February of 1865.

Events Between Burgess Mill and the End of 1864

There were many significant developments from the time of the battle at Burgess Mill until the end of 1864. One of the first things of note to occur following the Battle of Burgess Mill was an aggressive assault by General Mahone against the Union picket lines on October 30, 1864. General Lee mentions this in a very brief note dated October 31, 1864, in which he commends Mahone for his effort. In this report General Lee indicates that Mahone swept the

Federal picket line for half a mile, capturing some 230 officers and men without himself sustaining a single loss (OR Series 1 Vol. 42/1, 854). In the *Historical Memoranda* of Co. H, it is noted that the men assisted General Mahone in capturing a picket line without themselves sustaining a single loss (11th Alabama).

During this period following Burgess Mill and the end of 1864, the number of men in the ranks continued to drop to alarming levels. We have already noted how Co. B had been consolidated with Co. K due to its meager numbers; yet, Co. B was not the only company in the regiment that was experiencing hard times. On November 4, 1864, Col. George Tayloe states that Co. I had only thirty-seven men (CSR). This total included both enlisted men and officers, as well as those absent and present for duty. By the end of the year Co. I still had about forty men total, but many of these were totally disabled and unfit for field service. Lieutenant Brotherton writes in the *Historical Memoranda* of Co. I at the end of 1864, "Those who are yet with the company are by no means willing to give up the struggle until the enemy shall have recognized us a Separate Nation" (11th Alabama). In his same letter of November 4, 1864, Colonel Tayloe requests that the office of 2nd Lieutenant be filled in Co. I. The company at present had only two officers, both of whom were believed to be permanently disabled. Colonel Tayloe is referring to Able Walden, 1st Lieutenant, wounded at Davis Farm on August 21, 1864, and 3rd Lieutenant William T. Davis, wounded at Ream's Station on August 25, 1864. Both of these officers were disabled for the remainder of the war. This resulted in the promotion of Francis A. Brotherton to 3rd Lieutenant on November 23, 1864, and he remained the ranking officer for the Fayette and Pickens Rifles.

On November 7, 1864, Colonel Tayloe again penned a letter stating his concerns about the situation of his old company (CSR). There were only twenty-three men present in the ranks, and only one officer present with the company. The sole officer was Capt. John Prince. Colonel Tayloe wished that a 1st Lieutenant might be appointed for Co. D. I have found no record that a 1st Lieutenant was ever appointed for this company after this request was made. It does appear, however, that Hillard Askew was appointed 2nd Lieutenant of Co. D on November 23, 1864.

A new brigade commander arrived for General Sanders's Brigade in November of 1864.[4] Colonel William Henry Forney was born in North Carolina on November 9, 1823 (William Henry Forney Papers). He came to Alabama with his family in 1835, and graduated at the State University in 1844. He read law with his brother, D.P. Forney in Jacksonville, and went to the Mexican War in Coffey's First Alabama Volunteers. After the Mexican War, Forney was elected by the Legislature to be a Trustee at the University of Alabama. Colonel Forney began his career in the War between the States as the Captain of Co. G, 10th Alabama Infantry, and rose to Colonel of the same before coming to Sanders's old brigade in November of 1864.

Colonel Forney was still a colonel as the year came to a close. The officers of the brigade were concerned that he receive his appointment as Brigadier General. We have a letter dated January 18, 1865, in which a petition is found from the old Sanders's Brigade. This petition asks that Colonel Forney be appointed to the rank of Brigadier General. It is signed by the following officers from the 11th Alabama: George E. Tayloe, commander of the 11th Alabama; Cornelius Watlington, Adjutant of the 11th Alabama; John H. Prince, Captain of the Sharpshooters Battalion; John B. Rains and John H. Adams of Co. A, Philip M. Vance of Co. F, Hillard J. Askew of Co. D, James C.B. Harkness of Co. C, Martin Stewart of Co. H, John B. Hughes of Co. G, J.N. Hayes commanding Co. E (this appears to be James N. Hayes, a 2nd Lt. in Co. G), and Edward R. Lucas of Co. K (CSR). Colonel Forney would not receive his promotion until February 13, 1865.

Experiences in the Winter of 1865 to Hatcher's Run

We want to look a few of the experiences of the regiment leading up to the Battle of Hatcher's Run on February 6, 1865. The first thing to note is that furloughs and leaves of indulgence were being granted at the beginning of the year 1865. Dr. Sanders on January 25, 1865, mentions that furloughs were being granted for soldiers who had captured colors (Sanders's File). In one Alabama newspaper it mentions that Maj. John G. Pierce was passing through Greensboro on February 8, 1865, on a short furlough (*Alabama Beacon* [Greensboro], 17 February 1865). He was heading home, perhaps to Eutaw, Alabama, and is described as the Brigade Quartermaster. Pierce, a lawyer by profession, had been elected the Regimental Quartermaster way back on July 8, 1861. Now he was still functioning in this capacity—but on the brigade level. John may not have returned to the brigade since his name doesn't appear on the lists of paroles for Forney's Brigade.

We have evidence of many others who were granted furloughs. John Parham of Co. B, and William Sanders of Co. C, were both home on furlough in the month of February of 1865 (*Whig & Observer* [Eutaw], 9 February 1865). On January 25, 1865, Capt. Edward Lucas of Co. K took a leave of indulgence. Since his name doesn't appear on the list of those paroled at Appomattox, we may assume that he never returned to his command. On January 26, 1865, Thomas M. Witherspoon, 2nd Lieutenant of Co. A, was on leave of indulgence. Lieutenant Witherspoon did return from this forty-day leave to his command. Other men we know who took leaves of indulgence included: Cornelius Watlington (February 2, 1865), Charles H. Bulloch (February 3, 1865), James C.B. Harkness (February 3, 1865), Robert P. Schoppert (February 18, 1865), and Hillard Askew (February 20, 1865). It was no doubt due to the apparent hopelessness of their situation in 1865 that some of the men who took leaves of indulgence chose not to return to their companies. Dr. Sanders mentions the difficulties facing the soldiers at this time. He states that the supplies were short, and much of the meat was bad upon its arrival to the men (Sanders's File). The men had grown weary of these conditions. They had been asked to submit to such intolerable circumstances for so long that the majority of the desertions should probably be understood in this light.

When Captain Clark was finally able to rejoin his men on January 15, 1865, he found that he had no command (Clark 1914, 64–65). He recalls that there were just two privates left in the company. Captain Clark was now interested in obtaining another appointment, and convinced General Forney to grant him a leave to Richmond. Upon Clark's arrival at Richmond in the last days of March, 1865, he discovered that he had not received a desired appointment to Judge Advocate in the military courts of Wheeler's Corps. He then lingered about Richmond all that day, and what he found was very appalling, to say the least. The Provost Guard was arresting everyone they found wandering around the streets. Hotels were charging from between $300.00 to $400.00 a day, theatre tickets cost $150.00, and drinks in the barrooms ranged around $25.00 apiece!

Richard M. Kennedy of Co. C wrote a letter from Greensboro, North Carolina, on February 3, 1865, to his home in Alabama (Kennedy Papers). Lieutenant Kennedy had been wounded on October 22, 1864. He had eventually been sent back to Alabama on furlough. On January 9, 1865, he had been admitted to Way Hospital in Meridian, Mississippi, but was now just about at the end of his return trip back to the regiment. He describes for us the difficulty of traveling during those days in early 1865. He had left home on January 23, and as of February 3, he was still not in Petersburg. The cars were packed everywhere, especially with members of the Army of the Tennessee. On every car they had a fire making them all a black mess in appearance. Listen to his own words:

> The cars have not run one night since I left home. What a sad commentary is this on the situation of our country! Four years ago we could go to NY City in five days, now we are 12 or 15 days in going less than half the distance. I look at every subject in as cheerful yet practical way, and I am convinced that our country is on the verge of ruin [Kennedy Papers].

Kennedy mentions that there was talk of consolidating the army. If this proved to be true, he would tender his resignation as soon as he reached camp in order to go into another branch of the service nearer to home. Lieutenant Kennedy finally arrived back in camp on February 4, 1865. He wrote a letter to Colonel W.H. Taylor, Chief of Staff of the Army of Northern Virginia, in which he stated the reasons for his prolonged absence. He had actually started out on January 4, 1865, but upon reaching Montgomery he was refused transportation beyond that point on account of the break in the railroad in east Alabama. He went back home and started out again on January 23, but the many breaks in the road in Georgia made it impossible for him to return to camp any sooner than what he did.

Finally It should also be noted that the 13th Alabama Infantry was added to the brigade under Colonel Forney in January of 1865. Now Forney's Brigade consisted of the 8th, 9th, 10th, 11th, 13th, and 14th Alabama Regiments.

The Battle of Hatcher's Run: February 6, 1865

The next major conflict in which the 11th Alabama was engaged was known as Hatcher's Run. It all began on February 5, 1865, with the movement of Gregg's Cavalry and the Second and Fifth Corps (OR Series 1 Vol. 46/1, 253–257). It was the Fifth Corps under the leadership of Maj. Gen. Gouverneur K. Warren that the men had to encounter that cold day in February.

Warren began moving toward Hatcher's Run on February 5 around 7:00 A.M. They crossed near Rowanty Creek at W. Perkins at about 10:00 A.M., and encountered only light resistance. After crossing they made their way toward the Vaughan Road in the direction of Dinwiddie Court House. By later afternoon they had reached the Vaughan Road, and learned that Gregg's Cavalry had gone on to Dinwiddie Court House. About 9:00 P.M. Warren received orders to join General Humphreys at the Vaughan Road crossing of Hatcher's Run. They marched during the night in order to reach their objective. The next day at 12:15 P.M., Warren received orders to make a reconnaissance south and west of Hatcher's Run to ascertain the lines of the Confederates. General Crawford, commander of the Fourth Division, received orders to move out on the Vaughan Road to the point where it turns off toward Dabney's Mill. He was then to feel out the enemy, and to determine where exactly the fixed Confederate lines existed. General Ayres, commander of the First Division, was to follow Crawford and take with him General Winthrop's Brigade. Gregg's Cavalry was directed to watch the left of the infantry column. General Griffin, commander of the Second Division, remained posted in reserve at the place where the road divided.

General Crawford had not gone very far down the road before he encountered Confederate General John Gordon's men of the Second Corps. Colonel William R. Peck's battle report contains some information about this clash that would eventually involve Mahone's Division (OR Series 1 Vol. 46/1, 391–392). He was commanding the Louisiana Brigade in the Corps, and was ordered to the assistance of General John Pegram. When Peck arrived with his command in the early afternoon of February 6, the Confederates were formed up in the woods. The Union soldiers were in an open field opposite the woods near a sawdust pile. Twice the enemy was driven back from the sawdust pile, but the Confederates were eventually forced back themselves. The fight continued and was quite fierce. General Crawford's men were taking a severe fire, and General Ayres was sent to support with two of his brigades (*ibid.*, 255). General Warren was forced to send back for reinforcements from General Griffin's Division; however, it would prove to be too late to save the Union effort. General Mahone's boys, including the men of the 11th Alabama, were on their way.

Colonel Peck recalls that his command was getting to a critical point in the battle (OR Series 1 Vol. 46/1, 292). They were running short of ammunition, and many of the troops on his right had fallen back, leaving a great gap between the connecting brigades. It was then that Mahone showed up. General Gordon also makes mention of how Mahone's Division arrived and was placed in a position to fill a gap between General Evan's and Pegram's lines. At this point, the entire line was able to advance and drove the enemy in great confusion (OR Series 1 Vol. 46/1, 390).

General William H. Forney led the Alabamians that day at Hatcher's Run. He writes of the battle:

> ...on the evening of the 6th my Brigade became engaged and three others of the Division. We moved over some troops which had been fighting the enemy the greater part of the day, the enemy sometimes victorious & then our troops triumphant.... My Brigade behaved just as well as I could wished and I am certain if we had more such men in camp in this Division we could whip the enemy. We drove them back easily and did it handsomely nothing easier. I feel proud of the Alabamians and we rejoiced. I can say they have lost none of their fervant spirit [William Henry Forney Papers].

Lieutenant Kennedy wrote that on February 5, 1865, they had been ordered to be ready to move out, and he was placed in command of his company (Kennedy Papers). He recalls that when they arrived at the battle on February 6, they could see the Stars and Stripes marching triumphantly over a section of the battlefield. They were immediately ordered to attack, and he then describes his feelings as they charged over the open field toward the enemy:

> I unsheathed my sword and moved forward on a battle field with no little [illegible] and with almost a feeling of security for I felt that the prayer of at least one perfect being were perhaps at that moment ascending to the God of battles on my behalf, and if I fell it seemed to be, to be all right, as it was His holy will, for nothing comes by chance. Often amid the storm of bullets and the shriek of shells, did I think of the possibilities of never meeting you again on earth, but the thought did not alarm me, as I believe firmly that I would again meet those.... We attacked the enemy with so much vigor, that although he was flushed with momentary victory, he could not withstand the onset, we pursued until darkness, put an end to the horrible scene.

Thus was brought to an end the Battle of Hatcher's Run. The reports are indeed a tribute to the lingering fighting spirit of the men of the 11th. They were few in number, fighting on empty stomachs, poorly equipped, and yet they fought tenaciously.

There were at least six casualties suffered by the regiment in this fierce battle at Hatcher's Run (CSR). Robert L. Lyon of Co. C was killed, as was Walter T. Palmer of Co. H. Aurelius Dumas of Co. I was wounded in the right thigh and left hand. James M. Quinney of Co. D, Francis M. Doss of Co. C, and John W. Yateman of Co. H were all wounded. Yateman was wounded so severely in the right arm that amputation was necessary on February 7.

Some Closing Scenes of the War

We can learn some things about the mood of the regiment from letters written by Richard M. Kennedy. A couple of days after Hatcher's Run, on February 10, 1865, Kennedy wrote a letter home. He notes just how horrible the weather was. This certainly did not help with the attitude of the men. Then on February 11 he was ordered to take a detail of men out to the front to destroy a temporary field works. He states that the enemy opened fire on them with some artillery, resulting in one man having his leg shot off (Kennedy Papers). Kennedy goes on to speak about what he calls the "intense feeling of insubordination" among the men of the army. He believes that these feelings are not just restricted to the men of the regiment, but also pervasive throughout the entire army. It was very understandable from his point of view, for sometimes it was three or four days before they got anything to eat other than corn meal. In a letter written on February 27, 1865, some of the darkest feelings he had came to the surface. He states that it is the darkest hour of the existence for the army. Any light of hope is obscured by a gloom of despair. The feeling was very widespread that if something was not done very soon the prosperity of the cause was in grave doubt. Desertions were becoming extremely common every night. Men would go over to the enemy, or just return to their homes.

In a letter dated February 13, 1865, John P. Hatter of Co. B wrote from the Alabama Soldier's Home in Richmond, Virginia (Fleming W. Thompson Letters). He appears to have been detailed following his wounding at Gettysburg. In this letter we discover Hatter's intense longing for an end to the war:

> I am for peace.... I have become so discouraged at war speakers, I never intend to hear another one speak without my mind changes.... I do often wish when I am sitting in the Churches, unacquainted with any person, that I was at home, where I could attend the Churches in my old County where I can see all the acquaintence of my youthfullness. I sometimes think that war will end soon, then again I think it will last along time.

Aaron Curb of Co. K had been taken to Point Lookout, Maryland, after the Battle of White's Tavern on August 16, 1864. During this winter of 1864–65 he recalled that due to the freezing temperatures that winter, the water had frozen over in the bay (Aaron Monroe Curb Papers). Somebody was able to obtain a few pairs of skates, and some of the Southern boys tried their best to use them! One fellow he recalled kept getting further and further out, until at last he just took off like a shot. The guards began shooting at him, but the man was never seen again. As the war began to wind down, Curb recalls that some of the sicker of the men were released. This release, it seems, took place in March of 1865. Aaron recalls that after a buddy of his was released, he grabbed a blanket and ran to the guard and said, "My buddy went off without his blanket and will never make it without it, can I take the blanket to him?" The guard waved Curb on, and Curb never looked back, he walked most of the way from Point Lookout, Maryland, to his home back in Perry County, Alabama. By the time Aaron reached his home, the surrender had taken place.

On March 14, 1865, many soldiers at Point Lookout were released in order to be exchanged (CSR). The following men we know for certain were released on this day: M. Daniel L. Stewart of Co. K, Joseph E. McMath of Co. G, William F. Morris of Co. B, Robert R. McCulley of Co. B, John S. McCulley of Co. B, Ephraim Long of Co. I, William S. Hayes of Co. G, John W. Guthrie of Co. K, William A. Austin of Co. K, Robert B. Griffin of Co. K,[5] John W. Skates, Albert L. Moore, Fleming W. Thompson, and William E. McCracken of Co.

B, James N. Keeton, Robert A. Watson, and John T. Burchfield of Co. G. Lt. Frank M. Mundy of Co. B was transferred to Point Lookout from Johnson's Island, Ohio, prison camp.

THE PROMOTION OF CAPT. JOHN H. PRINCE

There is a letter in Captain Prince's file dated February 11, 1865, in which Gen. William H. Forney requests that Captain Prince be appointed Assistant Adjutant General of the brigade (CSR). The letter reads:

> General,
> I have the honor to request that Captain John H Prince Co. D 11th Ala. Regt be apppointed A.A. Genl of this brigade vice Walter E Winn who died July 12, 1864 from wounds received in battle. No one since the death of Captain Winn has been asigned to the brigade. Capt Prince entered the service June 11, 1861 as 1st Lieut. Has made an excellent officer — behaved gallantly upon the field and I am satisfied will make an efficient staff officer and at all time will discharge his duties honestly and faithfully. His place in the line can be filled by competent officers and his assignment to this position asked will not conflict with the good of the service.

It appears that a Captain Balfour of Mississippi was given the appointment in place of Captain Prince; however, Captain Balfour had not reported for duty by March 13, 1865. This turn of circumstances once again led General Forney to write a request on behalf of Captain Prince. On March 13, 1865, General Forney urgently requested that Captain Prince, who was very desirous of the appointment, be given the position. He added that Captain Prince had developed a "horror" for walking, and was very desirous of trying a horse for a change! It doesn't appear from the records that are available to us that Captain Prince was ever promoted to this position in the brigade. What does appear in the records are indications of his being placed in command of a battalion of sharpshooters. His muster rolls contain the note that when he surrendered at Appomattox, he surrendered a horse and other equipment as commander of a battalion of sharpshooters.

When did this change of Captain Prince's assignment take place? We do know that on January 18, 1865, when the list of commanders of the brigade requested Colonel Forney's appointment as General, that Captain Prince is listed as commanding a battalion of sharpshooters (CSR). Yet there is nothing in Captain Prince's file that makes mention of this independent command. Paul H. Lewis is listed as the Adjutant of the battalion of sharpshooters. Paul H. Lewis was a 2nd Lieutenant in Co. C, 10th Alabama Infantry Regiment. We have not been able to determine any of the other men who served in this special unit.

The Battle of Farmville: April 7, 1865

The final conflict that the 11th Alabama would find themselves engaged in would be known as the Battle of Farmville. There were several important developments which led up to this culminating battle that must be considered. The trenches around Petersburg had been the home away from home for the boys from Alabama since the summer of 1864. On April 2, 1865, the soldiers of the Army of Northern Virginia began pulling out of their entrenchments. On this very day the long-time commander of the Third Corps, A.P. Hill, was killed. The Third Corps was then assigned to the command of General James Longstreet (Longstreet 1992, 608). The immediate objective for the army was to reach Amelia Court House, and the reception there of the necessary supplies to sustain the army. General Mahone's command was under orders in the evacuation to march to Chesterfield Court House in order to cover the army on the north side of the Appomattox River. Captain Clark recalls that the men moved out very slowly before crossing the railroad at Chester (Clark 1914, 66). By April 3 Mahone's command would have made it to the area of Chesterfield Court House.

The Alabamians then proceeded in their march toward the crossing of the Appomattox River at Goode's Bridge (OR Series 1 Vol. 46/3, 1384). The men reached Goode's Bridge on the afternoon of April 4. General Lee noted their arrival in a dispatch to General Ewell, and also their role in preserving the bridge:

> I am very much gratified by your letter of today to learn there is such a favorable prospect of your crossing at Mattoax Bridge. I hope your anticipations may be realized, and that you may be safely over by this time. Notify General Mahone of your crossing, who is preserving the bridge at Goode's Ferry only until he shall hear you do not require it. He has orders to destroy the bridge as soon as he hears you do not need it.

The men crossed Goode's Bridge on April 4, and continued their march to Amelia Court House. The arrival at Amelia Court House brought disappointment to all the men of Mahone's Division. The eagerly expected supplies at Amelia were not there. Captain Clark remembers that no supplies were ever distributed to the men of the 11th Alabama (Clark 1914, 66). The greater part of the day had to be spent in foraging the nearby farms (Longstreet, 1992, 609).

On April 5, 1865, the march continued toward the new objective of Burkeville (Longstreet 1992, 610). It was hoped that supplies could be obtained here, and that the army could then proceed in order to join forces with General Johnston's army in North Carolina. The route to be followed ran alongside the Richmond and Danville Railroad. Apparently Mahone's

Goode's Bridge, where the retreating troops crossed the Appomattox River.

Division wrongly marched down the Paineville Road rather than staying closely beside the railroad, and as a result had to do some countermarching (OR Series 1 Vol. 46/3, 1385). We read of this confusion in an official note from W.H. Tayloe:

> The general commanding directs me to say that the troops (Mahone and Pickett's) took the wrong road from the first. They were pursuing the Painevill road and deviating every step from the railroad. They are now retracing their steps, and will turn in and march parallel with the railroad toward Jetersville. He gives you this information that you may avoid a similar mistake.

The men arrived at Jetersville on April 5 and found an unexpected Union force facing them. It was the decision of General Lee that the enemy's position was too strong for an aggressive Confederate offensive (Longstreet 1992, 610). Since the way to Burkeville was now blocked, the next countermove involved traveling further westward towards Farmville. Supplies traveling down the Southside Railroad could be obtained at Farmville. With his army resupplied there the march southward could continue. It was to be, however, a grueling twenty-three mile march from Jetersville to Farmville. They had to stay ahead of the enemy, and this would require an all-night march towards Farmville. Longstreet led his command over Flatcreek on this desperate march.

At Sailor's Creek the road forks: one way goes to Farmville by way of Rice's Station, the other crosses the Appomattox by way of High Bridge. General Mahone's Division was sent to cross the Appomattox River by way of the High Bridge crossing, and rejoin the rest of the command at Farmville (Longstreet 1992, 611). The Federals were in hot pursuit of the men of Mahone's Division, and this sets the stage for the Battle of Farmville.

The Alabamians Fight Near Farmville

Mahone's Division crossed the Appomattox at High Bridge. Lieutenant Vance of Co. F recalls the events at this time:

> When we reached the Appomattox River, we crossed over on pontoon bridges, and then we were marched up the river, following a road by the side of a canal toward Farmville. Just before that village night overtook us, and we had to cross High Bridge. We marched across four deep, bracing ourselves against each other, for if we had made a misstep, we should have been hurled to death below, for a part of the distance we were above the tree tops. But by the protection and guidance of the Supreme Being we got across safely about the dawn of day, and were marched out beyond the bridge a short distance and halted to rest [11th Alabama].

Early on the morning of April 7 Federal cavalry approached, and Union artillery soon opened up on the men. Lieutenant Vance notes that it was here that Co. F suffered its final casualty: David Smelly. Smelly was killed by a fragment of Union artillery. There were three Union batteries employed at this time: Tenth Massachusetts Battery M, First New Hampshire Artillery, and First Rhode Island Artillery (OR Series 1 Vol. 46/1, 793). After this skirmish the men marched to within three and a half miles of Farmville. Here they stopped at a place called Cumberland Church (Longstreet 1992, 617). Mahone deployed his men for battle at this location. Here the Confederates were successful in driving off an attack to their front, and in the process took many Federal prisoners.

In the report of Maj. Gen. Andrew A. Humphreys, commander of the Second Corps, he readily acknowledges how well entrenched Mahone's men were at Cumberland Church (OR Series 1 Vol. 46/1, 674). He writes these words about what they encountered when they clashed with the Confederates that day:

Cumberland Presbyterian Church. Mahone's men were entrenched on the high ground around this place.

Seeing our approach the enemy opened their artillery upon us with some effect. Our skirmishers advanced at once and drove in those of the enemy and developed their position. The troops and artillery were quickly formed for attack, but the enemy's position was too strong and too well intrenched to admit of a front attack, and an effort was made to take it in flank, but their flanks were found to extend beyond ours.

So both frontal and flanking maneuvers were attempted by the Federal forces that day, but both were unsuccessful in their efforts. Men from Michigan, New York, New Hampshire, and Pennsylvania were involved in these attacks (*ibid.*, 715). The last battle in which the 11th Alabama Infantry was engaged turned out to be a decisive Confederate victory.

Most of the casualties suffered by the regiment at Farmville involved men being captured. There were at least seventeen men captured in the ranks at Farmville. The following soldiers were taken: William J. Wilson, Frederick James, John W. Johnson, Richard Barton, Fulton M. Lee, Arthur W. Avery, and Martin V. Barnes, all of Co. F (CSR). Since we have the report of Lieutenant Vance that David Smelly was killed near High Bridge, it may have been that some of these men were taken prisoner at High Bridge rather than at Cumberland Church. Other men taken prisoner included: John R. Wood, William C. Muse, and Larkin Bagwell of Co. K; Thomas B. Jolly and George C. Post of Co. A; Elias E. Phillips and John D. Curry of Co. E; Thomas H. Clark of Co. G, John H. Floyd of Co. H, and George W. Williams of Co. C.

There were other men who were wounded in this battle. We have already noted the only soldier in the regiment known to have been killed at Farmville: David Smelley. Jacob D. Mayberry of Co. F was wounded, as was Needham Ward of Co. E. Ward suffered the amputation of his left leg as a result of his wounding. Two other members of the regiment were also wounded as well as being taken captive: William J. Wilson of Co. F lost his left leg, and Richard Barton of Co. F lost his leg as well. We have come up with a total of twenty casualties for the 11th at Farmville: seventeen men taken prisoner or wounded, and three men wounded.

The 11th Alabama at Appomattox Court House: April 9, 1865

The Army of Northern Virginia continued its march now towards Appomattox Station some twenty-five miles west of Farmville. Lynchburg appears to have become the new objective for the army. General Mahone began his movement around 10:00 P.M. on April 7 (OR Series 1 Vol. 46/3, 1389). The head of the column of General Lee's army reached Appomattox Court House on the evening of April 8 (OR Series 1 Vol. 46/1, 1266). There is no further record that the men of Mahone's Division had to fight another engagement. They just continued the march westward in the direction of Appomattox. By April 9, 1865, it had become apparent to General Lee that he had no other course than to surrender.

The List of Men Paroled in the 11th Alabama at Appomattox

We have very good documentation of the names and numbers of men who were surrendered at Appomattox. First we will look at the officers surrendered, and then we will note the enlisted men of the regiment. The Captains surrendered included: Martin L. Stewart of Co.

The rise upon which General Chamberlain stood for the official surrender of the Confederate troops.

H, John B. Hughes of Co. G, John H. Prince of Co. D, and Zach Abney of Co. F (SHSP Vol. 15, 314). Lieutenants of the regiment were: James N. Hayes of Co. G, Hillard Askew of Co. D, William B. Young of Co. A,. Richard M. Kennedy of Co. C, Philip M. Vance of Co. F, and John H. Adams of Co. A. Other officers included: Sgt. Maj. William Brazelton of Co. K, Cornelius Watlington the Adjutant of the regiment from Co. A, Surgeon William H. Sanders, and Assistant Surgeon William D. Witherspoon. One hospital steward is listed: William H. Stephenson of Co. A, and a musician, F.W. Erdman.[6]

The following list comes from the individual companies of the regiment. Company A lists the following men: Sgt. Robert E. Allen, Sgt. Joseph Williams, Corp. William McIntosh, Corp. Benjamin Ogletree, Corp. William Worthington, William Griffith, Moses M.D. Moore, William C. Morgan, Benjamin McClinton, William Tice, Thomas Pearl, Daniel Ogletree, John R. Varner, Henry B. Tucker, John W. Brady, Henry Brame, John Blackwell, John Blakeney, John C. Reves, Alexander Wayne, John W. Boozer, James Wilkinson, William Rogers, and William C. Ross. From the ranks of Co. B we find: Sgt. John Cullin, Musician Frank Henderson,[7] Corp. Pharis Bevill, Corp. Alexander McIntosh, Corp. James P. Lee, Corp. Milton Hamilton, Corp. Robert Hamlet, Corp. William Robuck, Corp. William L. Hunter, Corp. Joseph Eubanks, Charles Galloway, James R. Evans, William Loyd, James Fuller, and Meady Williford. The Confederate Guards list these men surrendered: Orderly Sgt. Albert Baldwin, Sgt. Erlander M. Richardson, Corp. James O. Duncan, Corp. Alexander Hitt, Corp. Francis Doss, David M. Montgomery, James Wilson, J.A. Gandy,[8] John H. Mahaffy, Thomas Smith, James Stafford, Joseph Whiteside, Andrew Hooppaugh, Josiah Jones, Francis C. Wilson, Charles Sanders, Beverly Pierce, and Francis Tarr. The Cakebrake Legion had the following men paroled: Sgt. John W. Deans, Corp. Dewitt C. Carter, Corp. Andrew W. Barr, William Frisby, Thomas J. Foster, Robert Springle, James Stewart, Henry Cabe, Thomas Anderson, George Jones, Clairborn Wright, Charles F. Kirker, Thomas Cathey, Robert Elmore, and Carroll Williamson. Company E lists: A. Fletcher Hooks, George Allen,[9] Wright Wall, William R. Deshazo,[10] and James Stoker. The Bibb County company lists: Sgt. Jesse Brown, Sgt. Perry Edwards, Corp. James W. Smelly, Corp. Asa Stanley, Corp. John Digby, Ervin Stacy, Elias Thomas, John H. Smelley, David Brown, David Lightsey, Brantley Garner, Elbert Arnold, David L. Cochrane, John C. Henry, Thomas Rayfield, William M. Childress, and William W. Watkins. From the Tuscaloosa Rifles we find: Sgt. Stephen Barber, Corp. James McGee, William Cole, Edward Kizziar, Peter K. Thomson, Randolph Thomson, John P. Green, George Pierson, David Cox, Pleasant Hayes, James L. Lacy, John Hasty, Raleigh Gaddy, Leva Gallant, and John A. Redd. Company H has this list of men: Sgt. Joseph Bell, Sgt. Isaac M. Noland, Sgt. David Duncan, Sgt. Henry O. Love, Corp. Benjamin F. Ferguson, Washington McGraw, Joel Hamiter, Daniel F. Johnson, John W. Turnipseed, James H. Allen, Elisha D. Johnson, Abner Knight, Henry Hill, Benjamin Marler, John C. Adams, Franklin L. Smith, Thomas A. Wier, George Hall, Simeon Brannon, Charles Wilson, Joseph E. Everett, James Shaw, Elisha Duncan, Jason Wilson (Quartermaster Sergeant), Alexander Dunlap, John T. Hamiter, Elijah J. Foster, James S. Hemphill, James W. Henry, William Speed, Andrew J. Story, Benjamin F. Bell, and Leroy Speed. Company I has these men paroled at Appomattox: Corp. Allen H. Propst, Corp. Calvin Kirkland, Samuel Black, James Oliver, William Cranford, Francis Gregg, Enoch Sikes, Jesse Threat, Simon P. Traweek, George W. Walden, Sterling D. Clanton, Henry Cribbs, Wiley H. Nall, Asa Anthony, John W. Shelton, and David Lowe. Finally, the Independent Volunteers list these men paroled: Corp. William Hopkins, Corp. Frank M. Ezell, William B. Massingale, James Bounds, Williford Curb, John W. Tadlock, John McCormick, Thomas Ballard, John A. Gray, Malcomb Tadlock, Little S.B.J. Ratliff, Benjamin Sanders, Oscar M.

Lucas, William Hay, Elam P. Horton, Archibald Hunsucker, Benjamin F. Gray, and L. Williams.[11]

If we count the number of Captains, four, the number of commissioned officers, ten, along with non-commissioned officers, musicians, and privates, 178, we come to a total of 192 men surrendered at Appomattox. Of this total, here is a breakdown of the individual companies: Co. A: 27; Co. B: 15; Co. C: 20; Co. D: 17; Co. E: 5; Co. F: 19; Co. G: 19; Co. H: 35; Co. I: 16; and Co. K: 19. The largest company surrendered at Appomattox was the Pickens County Guards with thirty-five in the ranks. Conversely, the smallest company by far was the Washington County company with only five. Many other men from these companies simply went home before the surrender at Appomattox. This included many of those who had been released from the Point Lookout camp in Maryland. There may have been other men present, but these are the only men that we have been able to verify at Appomattox.

Some Closing Thoughts on the 11th Alabama

The 11th Regiment of Alabama volunteers traveled to Lynchburg, Virginia, at the beginning of the summer of 1861 with about 1000 men. It surrendered four years later at Appomattox Court House, Virginia, with less than 200. The largest company in the regiment in 1861 was Co. H with around 116 men. It was still the largest company four years later with thirty-five! Likewise, the smallest company of the regiment in 1861 was Co. E with around eighty-three, and it surrendered four years later with the smallest number of men at five.

The boys had been led to Virginia by the proud Col. Sydenham Moore, only to lose him in the first battle at Seven Pines. The regiment ended the war without actually having an official Colonel appointed. They had watched a young Captain from Greene County, Alabama, John C.C. Sanders, rise from that post all the way to Brigadier General before losing his life at Davis Farm, Virginia. Not a single company had the same Captain in 1865 that it had in 1861.

The 11th Alabama was one of the hardest-fighting regiments in the Army of Northern Virginia. It was part of the Wilcox-Sanders's Alabama Brigade. This brigade proved its mettle on many a hard-fought battlefield

Battle flag of the 11th Regiment of Alabama Volunteers (Alabama Department of Archives and History, Montgomery).

in Virginia. They participated in some of the most heated conflicts fought during the War between the States. They fought in the battles at Gaines Mill, Sharpsburg, Fredericksburg, Gettysburg, the Wilderness, and the Crater, just to name a few. They have left a legacy behind of what a typical Confederate infantry regiment would have been like. They left their wives, children, siblings, jobs, and homes for their country: the Confederate States of America. Most of these men were not fighting in defense of some abstract political ideology which most of them couldn't have articulated to begin with, let alone a particular institution provided for within the Confederate Constitution. What they fought for we have discovered through the reading of the many letters, diaries, and personal notes left behind by the soldiers of the regiment. These were brave men, patriotic men, and soldiers of a new country that had been given birth less than a year before their picked up their first musket. The men of the 11th Alabama should not be forgotten. It is right that all men who have fought in defense of their country be remembered. As long as this writer lives, their lives, faces, and accomplishments will be proudly displayed. It is in honor of the boys from Tuscaloosa, Washington, Marengo, Greene, Perry, Pickens, Fayette, and Bibb Counties that this work has been written. We are indeed grateful for your dedication and sacrifice for Southern honor and independence.

13

The Final Roll-Call of the 11th Alabama Infantry

In this final chapter we want to look briefly at the postwar years of the men of the regiment. It has been my interest not simply to look at the men from 1861 to 1865, but to try to find out what happened to them after they returned to Alabama. For some of the soldiers there is a great deal that has been preserved, while for others little to nothing exists of their lives following the war. I wish to thank many of the ancestors of the men of the regiment for providing so much helpful personal information that made this chapter a possibility.[1]

The Field Officers

Following Colonel Sydenham Moore's mortal wounding at the battle of Seven Pines he was laid to rest in the Hollywood Cemetery in Richmond (*Register of the Confederate Dead* 1869, 73). He was buried in Section H, Number 143. His body was removed to Alabama in February of 1863 in order to be buried in the Greensboro Cemetery. One Alabama newspaper made note of the event:

> The remains of the late Colonel Syd. Moore reached here from Virginia last Monday morning, and after funeral services in the Episcopal Church, were interred in the Greensboro Cemetery. The very great procession which followed his corpse to its final resting place, evidenced the great respect and esteem in which he was held by our community [*Alabama Beacon* [Greensboro], 27 February 1863].

On August 6, 1862, the widow of Lieutenant Colonel Stephen F. Hale wrote a letter regarding the money due her in connection with her husband's death. Mary Hale names Surgeon William C. Ashe as her attorney in this matter:

> Know all men, by these presents that I Mary E. Hale, widow and Executer of the last Will & Testament of the late Stephen F. Hale, do nominate constitute and appoint, and by these presents have nominated constituted and appointed Dr. Wm. C. Ashe my true & lawful Agent & Attorney for men and in my name to ask demand and recover all and any sums of money whatever which may be due, accured or coming to the said Stephen F. Hale as the late Lieut Col commanding the 11th Alabama Regiment in the military service of the Confederate States [11th Alabama].

In view of his distinguished career and service to the state of Alabama, in 1866 the Alabama Legislature named Hale County in his honor (Garrett 1872, 665).

Major Isham W. Garrott left the 11th Alabama very early in the history of the regiment,

Grave of Colonel Sydenham Moore.

as we have noted. He helped to raise the 20th Alabama Regiment, and commanded this regiment until he was mortally wounded in the Battle of Vicksburg (Owen 1921 Vol. 3, 640). He was buried on June 17, 1863, in the Vicksburg Cemetery (SHSP Vol. 35, 54). Major Archibald Gracie rose to the rank of Brigadier General in the Army of Northern Virginia. He commanded his own brigade in Longstreet's Corps before being killed on December 2, 1864, around Petersburg, Virginia (SHSP Vol. 30, 67). He is buried in the Woodlawn Cemetery in New York City.

The Officers and Enlisted Men of Company A

Charles J. Adams: is probably the C.T. Adams listed as buried in Oakwood Cemetery on April 27th, 1862. He is buried in Grave 31, Row I, Division A (Oakwood Cemetery Register).

John H. Adams: may have eventually moved to Montague County, Texas (NARA Texas 1880 T9–1320, 407a). His wife is listed as Jane.

Robert E. Allen: is listed as marrying a Matty Evans on April 22, 1867, in Marengo County, Alabama (Wood 2004).

Henry L. Bruce: died on August 4, 1870, and is buried in the Old Linden Cemetery in Linden, Alabama.

Arthur W. Corley: is buried in the Oakwood Cemetery in Richmond, Virginia. He was interred there on March 28, 1862, and was placed in Grave 48, Row F, Division A (Oakwood Cemetery Register).

Anderson S. Crawford: is buried in the Oakwood Cemetery in Richmond, Virginia. He was interred there on June 13, 1862, and was placed in Grave 52, Row M, Division B (Oakwood Cemetery Register).

George W. Doss: is buried in the Oakwood Cemetery in Richmond, Virginia. He was interred there on July 12, 1862, and was placed in Grave 63, Row N, Division C (Oakwood Cemetery Register).

William R. Forniss: died on January 15, 1898, and is buried in the McNeil Cemetery in Marengo County, Alabama (Wood 2002).

Joseph A. Gamble: is said to be buried at Sardis Church in Tallapoosa County, Alabama (Stroud, 2001). This is some ten miles south of Dadeville.

Benjamin Franklin Glass: was the son of Jonathan Glass, and the grandson of William Glass (Mike Glass, 2000). According to Mike Glass, Benjamin's grandfather was a spy in the War of 1812, while his great-grandfather helped to build Fort Glass in Clarke County, Alabama. He was living in Octagon, Alabama, according to the 1907 census of Confederate soldiers living in Alabama (CSC).

James Hankins: died on December 13, 1863, at Ft. Delaware prison camp of smallpox (CSR). He was buried on the Jersey shore opposite the prison camp in Finn's Cemetery.

Needham B. Hogan: was a contributor to the *Confederate Veteran* after the war. Not long after the war he removed to Christian County, Missouri, and then for some twenty years to Springfield, Missouri, were he died (Hogan, 2000). He was known as a wonderful conversationalist as well as an excellent newspaper writer.

William Jolly: applied for an artificial limb from Marengo County, Alabama, on June 3, 1867, No. 92 (CSC).

Wiley Paul Jones: was discharged in 1862 due to the possible contracting of consumption (Jones, 2000). The army sent out recruiting parties toward the end of the war. One of these parties came to Wiley's farm looking for him. He held a gun on them and refused to go, saying he had already lost two brothers, and the war was nearly over. He married Sarah Rebecca Moring, with whom he had four children: William Henry Jones, Rebecca D. Jones, Richard A. Jones, and J. Clairbon Jones. He is listed as living in Wayne, Alabama, on the 1907 census of Confederate veterans in Alabama (Harris n.d.). Wiley died on April 12, 1927, and is buried in Shiloh Cemetery.

Benjamin McClinton: is said to be buried in the cemetery at First Baptist Church in Leroy, Alabama (Leach, 2000).

James Thomas McFarland: was living in Linden, Alabama, per the 1907 census of Confederate veterans (Harris n.d.).

Jesse Berryman Mobley: was the son of Allen Mobley and Allie O'Neal (Carl Mobley, 2000). Jesse was born April 16, 1839, and died on December 27, 1867. He is buried in Dixon's Mill in Marengo County, Alabama, in the O'Neal Family Cemetery.

Young Marshall Moody: left the 11th Alabama in the spring of 1862 in order to help Archibald Gracie raise the 43rd Alabama Infantry (CSR). He eventually rose to the rank of Brigadier General. After the war Moody moved to Mobile where he became a successful businessman. He later removed to New Orleans where he contracted yellow fever and died on September 18, 1866 (*Montgomery Daily Advertiser*, 25 September 1866). General Moody was interred in the Greenwood Cemetery in New Orleans.

Moses Davis Moore: married Olivia Ray on October 31, 1867, in Wilcox County, Alabama (Marstaller, 2000). They had the following children: Elizabeth and John Moses. Moses died sometime between 1871 and 1880 in Marengo County, Alabama.

Alfred Johnson Morgan: was the son of Merrit Morgan and Sarah Breckenridge (Bragg Vol. 3, n.d.). He was born November 2, 1839, in the Geneva area of Marengo County, Alabama. He was married on January 19, 1865, to Emily Melissa Mathers. They had the following twelve children: Celesta Morgan on October 14, 1865; a son born and died July 29, 1868; Emma Mae Morgan on October 23, 1869; Julia S. Morgan on January 2, 1872; Robert Edward Lee Morgan on November 17, 1873; George Baxter Morgan on January 22, 1876; Cornelius Mentor Morgan on January 20, 1878; Sallie Bertha Morgan on January 10, 1880; Mary Eva Morgan on August 30, 1882; Ammie Evandice Morgan on August 6, 1885; Alfred Kirskey Morgan in March 1889; and Leon Bowers Morgan on January 4, 1890.

Merrit J. Morgan: was born June 17, 1842 (Graham, 2000). He married Sarah Ann Breckenridge. He died on April 1, 1891, and is buried in Geneva Presbyterian Cemetery in Marengo County, Alabama.

Robert Russell Morgan: was buried in Our Soldier's Cemetery in Mt. Jackson, Virginia. The date of his death is given as August 5, 1863.

William Carr Morgan: married Eliza Ann Dilsworth (Graham, 2000). They had the following children: Lizzie Lee, February 7, 1869; Alice Eliza, March 6, 1872; Carrie Mae, August 26, 1877; Leona Blanche, September 14, 1879; and Birdie Z., December 29, 1890. William was a strong Presbyterian, and died on March 10, 1925. He is buried in the Geneva Presbyterian Church Cemetery. William kept a diary of the war for the first few months of the war. Part of his diary was published in a Mobile newspaper (*The Mobile Press Register*, 13 May 1934).

Lemuel Napier: appears living in Gallion, Alabama, in Hale County on the 1907 census of Confederate soldiers (CSC).

Moses Nichols: was buried in the Oakwood Cemetery in Richmond, Virginia, on June 17, 1862 (Oakwood Cemetery Register).

Francis Marion Norris: died on October 21, 1934, and is buried in the Shiloh Baptist Cemetery in Shiloh, Alabama.

Frederick E. Solley: was said to be living at Luther Store on the 1907 census of Confederate veterans (Harris n.d.). He is buried in the Campground Cemetery in Marengo County, Alabama (Wood, 2002).

Henry B. Tucker: may be the son of William H. Tucker and Mary Glass (Walker, 1993, 240). This would make him Henry Baker Tucker, born March 29, 1840, and who married Mattie Bradley on February 3, 1869. They had one son, James W. Tucker, who was born in 1870. Mattie was said to have stepped on a rattlesnake and died. According to one story, Henry killed a man in a dispute, and fled to Texas for his life. He appears in Gonzales County, Texas, on December 20, 1877, when he married a Sarah Ann Miller. He purchased some 469 acres of property in the same county in 1881. In 1885 he also suffered a rattlesnake bite that resulted in a serious handicap for him. Sometime after 1887 he moved to Coos County, Oregon, with his wife. He died of senile debility at this place.

John Rufus Varner: was living in Thomaston, Alabama, in 1921, when he applied for Confederate Pension #15807 (CSC).

Nathaniel R. Walker: was the son of Nathaniel Rogers Walker and Martha Ann Rogers (Almond, 2001). Nathaniel was born on September 19, 1826. He married Susan Ann Nichols on September 19, 1849, and together they had ten children: Susan Rebecca, August 3, 1850; Amanda Jane, March 7, 1852; William Nathaniel, February 26, 1854; Allen Jones, January 13, 1856; Jackson Rogers, May 15, 1858; James Brooks, January 24, 1860; Eli Thomas, November 24, 1862; infant male, July 1865; George Malone, September 29, 1868; and an infant male, September 8, 1870. Nathaniel died on October 1, 1899, and he and his wife Susan are buried in Payne's Chapel UMC.

Thomas M. Witherspoon: came from one of the oldest families to settle in Marengo County, Alabama (Bragg Vol. 4, n.d.). His parents were James M. Witherspoon, a distinguished physician in Marengo County, and Mary Dick. Thomas M. Witherspoon lived for many years at Myrtlewood. The Witherspoons owned plantations along Beaver Creek near Myrtlewood.

The Officers and Enlisted Men of Company B

Calvin Brett: applied for an artificial limb from Sumter County, Alabama, on August 27, 1867, No. 171 (CSC).

Samuel B. Browne: was the son of Phreaudius P. and Cornelia (Ewing) Browne (Owen 1921 Vol. 3, 238). He was admitted to the bar in 1867, and served as a tax assessor from 1865 to 1868 in Greene County, Alabama. He later moved to Mobile, and in 1904 was made the Judge of the 13th Judicial Court. He was reelected to this same position in 1910. He was known as a lawyer of great ability, sound judgment, and an earnest desire to uphold the integrity of the legal profession (*Washington County News* n.d., 28–29).

George W. Clark: was born on July 18, 1841, in Eutaw, Alabama (Owen 1921 Vol. 3, 333). He was the son of James Blair and Mary (Erwin) Clark. After the war Captain Clark studied law under his father, and was admitted to the bar in 1866. Not long after this, Captain Clark moved to Texas in January of 1867, where he eventually settled down in Waco. He was Attorney General of Texas from 1874 to 1876, and Judge of the Court of Appeals in 1879. In 1892 he was candidate before the Democratic primaries for the nomination as governor of Texas, but was defeated at the convention. He wrote the book, *A Glance Backward: Or Some Events in the Past History of My Life*. It was a major source for the writing of this work.

Captain George W. Clark.

Anderson Crenshaw: was the son of Willis Crenshaw (Crenshaw, 2001). Willis Crenshaw was the brother of Judge Anderson Crenshaw for whom Crenshaw County, Alabama, was named. The Department of Archives and History in Montgomery holds a partial diary that was thought to be that of Captain George Field; however, upon closer examination of this diary I have concluded that it was in fact the diary of Corp. Anderson Crenshaw.

Stephens Croom: had a distinguished career in Confederate service. He left the 11th Alabama to become the Adjutant General to John H. Forney (Owen 1921 Vol. 3, 430). He rose to the rank of Major, and was eventually assigned to General Loring's staff. Later he was again assigned to General Forney's staff in the Trans-Mississippi Department, where he remained until the end of the war. After the war he moved to Mobile, where he practiced law the remainder of his life. Croom left behind an extensive written record of his life in Confederate service. This collection is found in the University of South Alabama Archives in Mobile, Alabama: Velma and Stephens G. Croom Collection.

George Field: resigned as Major of the 11th Alabama in the fall of 1862. What became of Major Field is somewhat of a mystery. We are told that he died unmarried (Brownell 1878, 20). In addition to this, Owen states that he died in Eutaw, Alabama, in 1866 (Owen 1921 Vol. 3, 575). This is all the information I could find on Major Field following his resignation from the regiment.

Anderson H. Greenwood: died on August 3, 1862, and was brought back to Alabama to be buried in the Mesopotamia Cemetery in Eutaw, Alabama.

Nathan K. Greenwood: died August 8 or 10, 1861, and was brought back to Eutaw, Alabama, for burial in the Mesopotamia Cemetery.

Matthew P. Hamilton: was the son of Peter H. Hamilton and Mary A. Hamilton (Calvit, 2000).

Matthew was born February 16, 1840, and married Martha A. Phillips from Greene County, Alabama. The couple had ten children together. Matthew walked with a limp due to his wounding he received during the war. He died on July 3, 1913, in Bowie County, Texas.

John P. Hatter: was born December 10, 1841, and married Elizabeth Jane Barnett in 1867 (Anderson, 2002). John died on October 26, 1905, and is buried along with his wife in Dunn's Creek Cemetery in Tuscaloosa, Alabama. He had the following children: Joseph William, May 29, 1870; Mary Jane, August 12, 1872; and John Pickney Jr., July 18, 1875.

Francis J. Inge: was the son of Dr. Richard and Rebecca Eaton Inge (Owen 1921 Vol. 3, 878). He was born on April 18, 1832, and died in Mobile on January 8, 1891.

James D. Kimbrough: was the son of Marmaduke and Elizabeth Alston Douthitt Kimbrough (*Heritage of Greene County, Alabama* 2001, 147). James was one of eight children born to this couple. He married Martha E. Patton, and was a tax collector for Greene County, Alabama, after the war.

William P. Loyd: died in Mobile, Alabama ca. 1900 (CSC). His wife, Margaret L. Loyd, filed for a pension on March 4, 1919.

Moody Huff May Jr.: was the son of Moody Huff May Sr., born in 1793 in Pendleton District, South Carolina (*The Heritage of Greene County, Alabama* 2001, 161). On December 21, 1868, Moody Huff May Jr. married Mary Ann White, and together they had three daughters: Della in 1871, Lizzie Ann in 1874, and Lula Pearl. Before he left for the war he had built a log cabin on his property in Knoxville, Alabama. The cabin had one room with a detached kitchen.

Frank H. Mundy: never saw any further action in the war following his capture at Gettysburg. He returned to Eutaw, Alabama, following the surrender. Under Reconstruction rule, Frank found himself at odds with the authorities on one occasion (*The Heritage of Greene County, Alabama* 2001, 171). In 1868 a carpetbagger owed some money to one of Lieutenant Mundy's friends. Frank and six of his friends got a railroad rail, put the carpetbagger on it, and rode him around the courthouse square. There was no intent to hurt the man, and in fact he suffered no injury whatsoever; however, Frank and the six others were court-martialed in Selma, Alabama, and sentenced to several years in prison. They were sent to Dry Tortugas, Florida, which is a small island near Key West. Alabama was readmitted to the Union in 1868, and the entire group of men were pardoned. Frank married Mary Elizabeth Jarvis Ustick on November 12, 1874, and they had three children together: Frank Perrin Mundy, Mattie Browning Mundy, and Thomas Gustave Mundy. Frank served as Deputy Tax Collector of Greene County, and later as Tax Collector. He was known to be the life of the social party, as well as a passionate sportsman. He died in August of 1896, and is buried in the Eutaw Cemetery.

Stephen F. Nunnalee: farmed near Springfield, Alabama, until 1877 (Butler 1998, 14). He then purchased the Tuscaloosa Gazette, which he published along with his sons James and Luman. In 1887 he successfully applied for a Mexican War pension. He died on March 18, 1907, and is presumed buried in Tuscaloosa, Alabama.

John W. Phares: applied for a pension after the war from Sumter County, Alabama (CSC).

Arthur Berry Phillips: married and was the father of three children: Fannie Artelia, Walter, and Pete (Phillips, 2004).

Robert P. Schoppert: was the son of Phillip Schoppert. The Phillip Schoppert House appears on the National Register of Historic Homes. The address is 230 Prairie St., Eutaw, Alabama. Robert applied for pension #13107 from Greene County, Alabama (CSC). He died February 13, 1913, and is buried in the Mesopotamia Cemetery in Eutaw, Alabama.

John Wesley Skates: was born May 9, 1841, in Russell County, Alabama (McCown, 2002). John was a Mason and lamplighter in Tuscaloosa. He married Martha E.J. Abernathy on December 14, 1865. John died on April 23, 1887, with cancer that had spread over his face. He is buried in Greenwood Cemetery, Tuscaloosa, Alabama.

William Fletcher Thetford: was born in 1840 in Greene County, Alabama (*The Heritage of Greene County, Alabama* 2001, 212). He was a physician in Boligee. He married first Cora Arena Johnston, and after her death, Zannie B. Knox. He had three children: William F. Jr., Kennon, and Samuel Lewis.

The Officers and Enlisted Men of Company C

James Breathwait: is buried in the Ebenezer Presbyterian Church Cemetery in Clinton, Alabama. The date of his death is given as May 4, 1866.

James Samuel Brown: is given a Mobile, Alabama, address in 1907 (CSC).

Charles H. Bulloch: is called a true soldier and good citizen in one issue of the *Confederate Veteran 1893–1912* (Vol. 7, 175). He died of pneumonia on February 13, 1899.

John Wesley Skates. (courtesy Leonard J. McCown).

James Fell Cameron: was the son of William Love Cameron and Suzanne Dupre Clay (*The Heritage of Greene County, Alabama* 2001, 86). Suzanne professed Christ as Savior and joined the Ebenezer Presbyterian Church in Clinton, Alabama. James Fell Cameron was their first-born son. The date of his birth is given as November 4, 1840.

James Fleming Cross: died on March 5, 1917, and is buried in the Mesopotamia Cemetery in Eutaw, Alabama.

James Oscar Duncan: ran away from home at sixteen to join the army (*The Heritage of Greene County, Alabama* 2001, 110). He was the son of James D. Duncan and Elizabeth E. Duncan. He was born in Pleasant Ridge, Alabama. On December 2, 1871, James married Juliet Jolly, and together they had four children. They lived in Mt. Hebron, Alabama.

Newton Jasper Eatman: lost his leg at the Battle of Salem Church. He made application for an artificial limb Number 183 from Greene County, Alabama, on September 23, 1867 (CSC).

Phelan Eatman: appears in Birmingham, Alabama, on the 1907 census for Confederate veterans (CSC).

Calvin W. Fason: is buried in the Union Chapel Cemetery in Pickens County, Alabama. The cemetery is located some five miles south of Carrollton.

James C.B. Harkness: became a renowned sheriff in Texas for many years (*The Heritage of Greene County, Alabama* 2001, 130).

William O. Harrison: was born July 1, 1842 (Harrison, 2001). He was married on October 27, 1870, to A.M. Harrison, and moved to Leon County, Texas. He died on September 23, 1898, in Parker County, Texas.

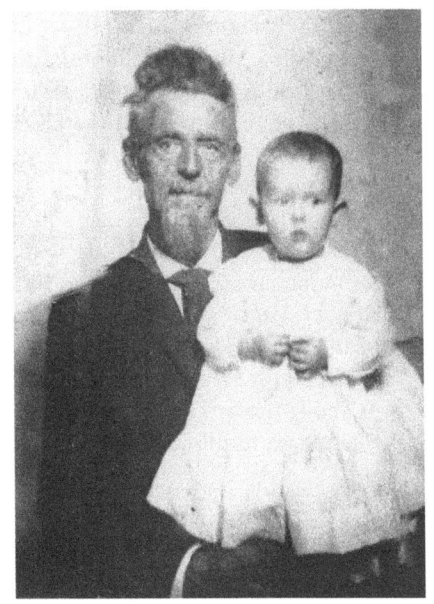

Phelan Eatman (courtesy Luisa and Michael Amann).

Matthew A. Jolly: was the son of Peter and Hannah Jolly (*The Heritage of Greene County, Alabama* 2001, 144). He married Sarah Neely in 1868.

Richard M. Kennedy: wrote a letter to his future wife, Mattie Hughes, on June 26, 1865, about their wedding (Kennedy Papers). He hoped that Mattie's brother would consent to be one of the attendants. A little over a year later Richard wrote another letter to his wife. The letter is dated June 29, 1866, and he mentions that this is the very anniversary of their wedding. Richard and Mattie had eight children together. Richard died in Greene County, Alabama, on January 29, 1879.

John H. Mahaffy: died in 1881 and is buried in the Beulah Baptist Cemetery (*The Heritage of Greene County, Alabama* 2001, 41).

David Milton Montgomery: died on February 2, 1899, and is buried in the Presbyterian Church Cemetery in Pleasant Ridge, Alabama (*The Heritage of Greene County, Alabama* 2001, 47). His wife, Jennie B. Montgomery, made an application as a widow of a deceased soldier from Pickens County, Alabama, on July 19, 1915.

Erlander M. Richardson: was the son of John Addison Richardson and Sallie Neal Coleman (Farrington, 2002). Erlander was born October 14, 1840, in Greene County, Alabama, and died on March 27, 1900. The *Eutaw Mirror* carried a piece written by Erlander M. Richardson on May 24, 1893. In this article he makes the suggestion that General John C.C. Sanders's body be brought back to Greene County, Alabama, from Virginia (Sanders's File).

John C.C. Sanders: was buried after his death in the Hollywood Cemetery in Richmond, Virginia. He was, however, brought back to his native state on April 8, 1918, and buried in the Greenwood Cemetery in Montgomery, Alabama.

William H. Sanders: was born on July 9, 1838, in Tuscaloosa, Alabama (Owen 1921 Vol. 4, 1499). He died on January 2, 1918, in Montgomery, Alabama. Dr. Sanders is buried next to his brother in the Greenwood Cemetery in Montgomery, Alabama. After the war he returned to his home in Clinton, Alabama (Sanders's File). He practiced medicine here until deciding to study medicine abroad in Europe. He left for Europe in 1873, and studied in Berlin, Munich, Vienna, Strasburg, and Paris. When he returned from abroad he relocated to Mobile, Alabama, in 1877. He was the Professor of Diseases of the Eyes, Nose, and Throat at the University of Alabama Medical School in Mobile for many years. He served as the president of the State Medical Association from 1890 to 1891. He eventually became the State Health Officer in the state of Alabama, and therefore removed from Mobile to Montgomery. Any man who had served in the Confederate cause, or his widow, could be assured of receiving treatment from Dr. Sanders.

William H.H. Sanders: is mentioned in an issue of the *Confederate Veteran 1893–1912* (Vol. 23, 184). He struck up a friendship with a Berdan sharpshooter. He died in Cooksville, Mississippi, on January 6, 1915, and was returned to Greene County, Alabama, for his burial.

James I. Vaughn: married Amanda Rachel Pendergrass in Greene County, Alabama, on June 18, 1873 (*The Heritage of Greene County, Alabama* 2001, 123). In 1880 he left Greene County with his family in a covered wagon for Mississippi. They were going to join Amanda's sister, Ida Pendergrass. They found the water of the Tombigbee River too high to cross at Columbus, and as a result had to wait for months before they were able to finally get over.

The Officers and Enlisted Men of Company D

Andrew William Barr: was the son of Robert T. Barr and Martha "Patsy" Ross (*The Heritage of Marengo County, Alabama* 2000, 125). Andrew married Americus Landrum on May 31, 1859. He died on April 13, 1913, and is buried in the Nanafalia Baptist Church Cemetery.

Henry Shubal Bartlett: was born June 13, 1841, in Petersburg, Virginia (Owen 1921 Vol. 3, 108). After the war Bartlett returned to Dayton, Alabama, where he had studied law under Judge William C. Clark. He remained in Dayton until 1875 when he began teaching in Tuskegee in 1876. In 1885 Bartlett both organized and served as principal of a high school in Montgomery. In 1886 he was elected superintendent of the public school system of Montgomery, Alabama.

Ralph Barton: was still living in Forkland, Alabama, according to the 1907 census of Confederate soldiers taken that year (CSC).

William Henry Compton: married Mary A. Lewis in 1865 (Walker 1993, 50). He was married again in 1899 to a lady named Laura Simmons. He had two sons prior to his death in 1917: H.C. "Hal" Compton, and Edgar Compton. Hal was a minister who lived in Alpine, Texas, in 1917, while Edgar died at a young age.

Waverly William Duggar: was a young attorney at Prairieville, St. Andrews Parish, when the war broke out in 1861 (Witherspoon 1947, 515). After the war he opened a law office in Demopolis.

Robert Elmore: applied for a pension in Washington County, Alabama (*Washington County Alabama Pension Records Civil War Veterans* n.d.). He was living in Frankville, Alabama, and is listed as being fifty-five years of age.

John W. Jones: married Florence W. Taylor in Marengo County, Alabama, on February 13, 1878 (*Marengo County Marriages*). He died on May 13, 1894, and is buried in Jefferson Cemetery in Marengo County, Alabama.

Samuel S. Lomax: was born February 29, 1840, and died in 1884 in Portland, Oregon (Lomax, 2000).

Payton B. Mason: died on May 1, 1872, and is buried in the Old Spring Hill Cemetery in Marengo County, Alabama.

Jordan W. Oakley: was born May 6, 1838, in Jefferson, Alabama, in Marengo County (Oakley, 2001). He was wounded in both the knee and head during the war, and bore these scars to his death. He died October 10, 1871, and is buried in the Jefferson Cemetery.

Robert Allen Patterson: was born March 25, 1837, the eldest son of Ira Patterson (Johnson, 2000). He never married, and died in California on February 14, 1907.

William Crosland Pegues: was born in Alabama on September 3, 1838 (Pegues, 2000). He was educated at the University of Alabama, and married Quitera Decima Hartley on May 1, 1861. Together they had one son, Christopher James Pegues, who was born February 27, 1863. Quitera died on September 11, 1864, and is buried in Old Spring Hill Cemetery in Marengo County, Alabama. William moved with his son to Texas, where he married Julia R. Montgomery. They had six children: Jennie Decima, Ruby Mae, Lila, Mary Zula, Wille Grey, and William Clyde. William died on January 12, 1899, and is buried at Zion Cemetery, Grimes County, Iola, Texas.

Charles Augustus Poellnitz: is found living in Greensboro, Alabama, on the 1907 census of Confederate soldiers living in Alabama (CSC).

James Alexander Poellnitz: was born the son of Julius Edwin Poellnitz and Mary Rembert on March 4, 1840 (Bragg Vol. 3, n.d.). He returned home after being discharged in 1861. He died February 3, 1865, and is buried in Rembert Hill Cemetery in Marengo County, Alabama.

John Haywood Prince: was born on October 7, 1825, in Chatham County, North Carolina (Gresham, 2001). He married Arabella Chloe Anne Elizabeth Boddie on May 16, 1849, and together they had ten children: Julia Elizabeth, John Edmund, Sydney Alexander, Oliver Haywood, Robert Joseph, Richard Knott, Emma Boddie, Belle Eleanor, Mary Brown, and Jennie Moore. John Prince returned to Marengo County completely broke after the war. He found his plantation run down after four years of neglect. His real estate was valued in 1860 at $34,000, but the same acreage in 1870 had fallen to a value of $7,900.00. By October of 1866, Captain Prince sold his home in Dayton to relocate to some of his lands in Macon, Alabama. Captain Prince was not able to recover from his financial losses after the war, and as a result he filed for bankruptcy in Mobile in February of 1868. John appears as a delegate on August 6, 1870, in a convention of Democrats which met in Demopolis. He appeared active in the Democratic cause in several subsequent meetings held in the county as well. On January 14, 1897, Capt. John Prince passed away. A local newspaper ran the following article:

> The announcement of the sudden death of Capt. Jno. Prince, at his home near Gallion, yesterday morning was a great shock to his many friends in this place. We learn that the immediate cause of his death was paralysis of the heart. Capt. Prince was about seventy years old. He served during the war as Captain in the gallant 11th Alabama, and was known as a soldier of force and ability. He was Lt. Commander of Camp Gracie, Confederate Veterans, and many is the member who will miss and mourn the loss of their warm hearted and gallant comrade [*Demopolis Express*, 14 January 1897].

Simon Hancock Rawls: was born November 4, 1836, and married Keturah Roxanna Diana Elizabeth Nowell. He had six children: James Thomas, Simion Seth, Connie, Della, Charles Spurgeon, and Georgia (Rawls, 2001). He moved to Waller County, Texas, in 1872, then Harris County, and finally Montgomery County. He is buried in Oakwood Cemetery in Huntsville, Texas. He wore a beard to hide the scars and disfiguration that were the result of the shot he received in the jaw at Gaines' Mill (Copeland, 2001).

Curtis R. Roane: wrote a letter to his brother Spencer Roane in Plaquemine, Louisiana, on June 19, 1866 (Luke, 2001).[2] The letter was found by a local family in an old wooden desk drawer floating in Bayou Teche after the flood of 1927. In the letter he speaks of renting out his old place in Spring Hill, Alabama. He stated that he had rented out his old plantation he owned before the war, and that he had a decent prospect for a cotton crop that year. He asks how things were going for his brother, and whether it might be to his advantage to move to Louisiana. Perhaps together they could help one another, but only if the prospects are at least as good, if not better than what he already had in Alabama. He also asked about the prospect of finding a wife in Louisiana!

Richard M. Robertson: had a claim for a pension made by his wife, Ella F. Robertson, from Dallas County, Alabama, on August 10, 1910. It is pension #30951 (CSC).

John Edmunds Ruffin: died on January 15, 1880, and is buried in the St. Michaels Cemetery in Marengo County, Alabama. His wife, Roberta Ruffin, is also buried there.

James H. Stewart: was the son of Dubose and Hannah Holliday Stewart (Owen 1921 Vol. 4, 1624). After the war he studied law in Marengo County, and was successfully admitted to the bar in 1866. He moved to Uniontown to form the firm of Christian, Lovelace, and Stewart (Owen 1921 Vol. 4, 1624). He later moved to Marion, Alabama, to practice law, and in 1880 was elected Probate Judge of Perry County, Alabama. In 1901 Stewart was a member of the Constitutional Convention. Stewart died on January 23, 1912.

George Edward Tayloe: returned to Marengo County following the surrender at Appomattox (Witherspoon 1947, 497). He had married Delia Willis during the war, and now took her back with him to Elmwood Plantation. They were to remain in Alabama for only one year before returning to Delia's old home in Virginia. According to letters written by his wife to Thomas Owen, Colonel Tayloe spent the remainder of his life as a farmer. Colonel Tayloe had the following children: George Willis, Mary L., John K., William Randolph, James Sterling, Edward, Catherine, Rosa Fielding, and Lomax P. (11th Alabama). Colonel Tayloe died on March 9, 1879, at only forty-one years of age in Orange County, Virginia.

Needham Ward: applied for an artificial limb No. 37 on February 12, 1879. He was living at an address in Magnolia, Alabama, in 1907 (CSC). He died on May 4, 1920, and is buried in the Magnolia Cemetery in Marengo County, Alabama.

Cornelius Watlington: lived to the ripe old age of eighty-eight (Butler, 2001). He was born on August 7, 1841, and died on June 15, 1930. He wrote a number of letters about his experience in Confederate service. On September 9, 1929, Cornelius wrote a letter to his niece in which he summarized his experiences in the 11th Alabama. In another letter written in 1910 he speaks of his experience after the surrender:

> ...on the evening of April 11, I got a yankee horse and "rig" and with six of my comrades started on the morning of April 12 for our homes. The first one fell out at Talladega [Alabama], the last one at Marion, Alabama. I reached Dayton in the afternoon of May 8, 1865 with nothing but health and a good name which I have tried to protect to this day [Butler, 2001].

Cornelius goes on to share how he secured a good job after his return to Dayton, and by 1866 had begun to farm on a small scale. Not long after he returned, his father died, leaving his mother and four children to be cared for. They all lived together until January of 1874 in the old home place. After this Cornelius moved to the Mississippi Delta, where he began a working relationship with Colonel Ed Richardson.

The Officers and Enlisted Men of Company E

Henry Clay Atchison: married Mary Lavena Mosley on January 28, 1868, in Washington County, Alabama (*The History of Washington County, Alabama* 1982 Vol. 2, 4). They had the following children: Joseph, Daniel M., Fannie, Woodie, Glovie, Leona, Harry, and Hattie. Henry died in 1939.

Cato W. Bethea: was last heard of in South Carolina, according to one source (11th Alabama).

John D. Curry: was last heard of in Summerdale, Texas, according to one source (11th Alabama).

Richard J. Fletcher: may never have returned to Alabama after the war. He wrote a letter to Dr. William H. Sanders on January 24, 1869, from Prospect Hill, Louisa County, Virginia (Sanders's File). This is where he was living, and he does a little reminiscing about their days together in the 11th Alabama. He still has very strong convictions regarding the Southern cause, and writes that he hopes one day they may yet gain their freedom. He also informs Dr. Sanders that he has learned very well how to walk on his artificial leg. Major Fletcher died on June 18, 1906, and is buried in the Thornrose Cemetery at Staunton, Virginia.

John A. Gordy: There is a picture of John in a history volume (*The History of Washington County, Alabama* 1982 Vol. 1, 80).

Joseph R. Green: is said to have been a politician who died in Clark County, Mississippi, in 1912 (*Washington County Alabama*, GenWeb).

Augustus Fletcher Hooks: was born on August 16, 1846, in Sumter County, Alabama (CSC). He appears in an article written in the *Washington News* (Washington County Public Library). He was one of the most prominent businessmen of Washington County. He made his home in McIntosh, Alabama, with his wife, Ella E. Posey. After the war Hooks engaged in timber, mercantile, naval stores, and agricultural pursuits. He owned three river plantations, a large mercantile business, and a cotton gin in McIntosh. He was also a partner in a large tobacco business in Mobile, and for many years served as the postmaster of McIntosh. He was a member of the Methodist Church, and Commander of Camp John James U.C.V. He was said to have walked all the way home from Virginia to Alabama.

Daniel James: was born in November of 1836 (Hines, 2003). He married Hesperia Laventine Whitlock, with whom he had the following children: Margaret in 1865, John G. in 1868, Daniel in 1872, and Mary in 1880. Daniel was a judge in Washington County, Alabama, from 1858 to 1868.

Elias Phillips: was born in 1837 in Choctaw County, Alabama (Phillips, 2003). He died on August 7, 1918, in Jones County, Mississippi. He was buried in the Crosby Cemetery.

Benjamin F. Porter: was the son of John C. Porter of North Carolina (*Washington County Historical Society Fall Newsletter*). After being captured in the battle at Sharpsburg, Benjamin was given a Bible by a lady from Baltimore. He kept the Bible with him throughout the remainder of the war, and his grandson was said to be in possession of this Bible in Leroy, Alabama. Not long after the surrender Porter married Mary Eliza Shinn, and established his home on St. Stephens Road near Leroy, Alabama. In 1880 Porter was elected Probate Judge of Washington County, Alabama, and served for some eighteen years. It was said of Judge Porter that he never campaigned for office, but he would only announce his candidacy and leave the voting to the people. He had the following children: Frank W., Mary, Sank, Mattie, Thomas Lee, Jimmy Woodfin, and Davis. He died in 1917, and was buried in the Pine Grove Methodist Cemetery.

James S. Stoker: is said to have died on September 22, 1875 (*Washington County Alabama Pension Records Civil War Veterans*). His wife, E.S. Stoker, applied for a pension on August 8, 1899.

Wright Wall: may be Wright Wall III, who was born in 1828 (Cuthriell, 2003). After the war he married Rhoda Ann, and together they had the following children: Melvin in 1867, Monsfield in 1869, Joel in 1871, and Annis in 1874. He appears to have died in Butler County, Alabama.

Pleasant Lee Worsham: was sheriff in Washington County, Alabama, in 1870 (Worsham, 2001). He was in Lamar County, Texas, by 1880. On June 26, 1899, he applied for a pension in Henderson County, Texas. He died on February 7, 1901, in Ellis County, Texas.

The Officers and Enlisted Men of Company F

Zachariah Abney: was born September 10, 1835, in Bibb County, Alabama (Brewer,1999). He and his identical twin brother, Samuel, were the ninth and tenth children of Thomas H. Abney and Mary Anne Gausden. After the war Zachariah returned to Randolph, Alabama, to practice law (Abrams 1981, 91). Later he removed to Prattville, Alabama, where he both farmed and practiced law. On March 31, 1867, Zach married Alexandria Victoria Doster. Captain Abney served as Register in Chancery in Autauga County from 1883 until his death in 1911. It is said that many Prattville attorneys can trace their careers in the legal field back to reading law under Zachariah Abney. Zach is buried in the Doster Family Cemetery in Prattville, Alabama.

Henry W. Avery: appears on a slip of the Confederate Soldiers Home dated January 17, 1916. It is addressed to the Commandant, Mountain Creek, Alabama, from the Adjutant General's office (CSR). He was said to have died of arteriosclerosis at Bryce Hospital on August 15, 1916 (Williamson, 2004). He was the twin brother of Arthur Avery.

Richard Barton: applied for an artificial limb from Perry County, Alabama, on July 19, 1867 (CSC). A family tradition states he is buried near Hamburg, Alabama (Barton, 2003).

David L. Brown: may be the David L. Brown who is buried in the Brown Graveyard some five and a half miles north of Centreville off Highway 25 (McCord 1979, 244).

William Wesley Brown: was born August 31, 1842 (*Heritage of Bibb County, Alabama* 1998, 77–78). He married Martha Sanford on November 21, 1869, in Bibb County, Alabama. He applied for a pension on May 17, 1921, and later moved to Ethel, in Attala County, Mississippi. He married a second time and had five children: Lillie, Alice, Amos, Sallie, and Margaret. He died on March 15, 1932, and is buried in Kosickco Cemetery in Attala County.

James Lafayette Davidson: moved to Mobile after the war to enter the grocery business

(*Heritage of Bibb County Alabama* 1998, 104). This business was named Cribbs, Davidson & Co. Wholesale Grocers (*Mobile Daily Advertiser* & *Register*, 12 January 1867). After a year in this grocery venture, Davidson returned to Centreville to join in a mercantile business with Robert McIlvain. He married Susan A. Powell in 1867, and together they had seven children: Margaret, Annie, Fannie, Ella, Dora, James, and Ida. He became politically active when he served as chairman of the Democratic Party Committee, and then later was elected Postmaster of Centreville in 1882. James L. Davidson is buried in the Centreville Memorial Cemetery on Mill Street in Centreville.

Samuel Wilson Davidson: is buried in the Centreville Memorial Cemetery. He died on June 25, 1896.

John Harrison Digby: was the son of Wiley James Digby. He was born in Alabama in 1840, and married Martha A. Meggs on August 5, 1866, in Perry County, Alabama (Barnett, 2004). John had a son, John Thomas Digby, with Martha. Later John married Amanda Caroline Mashburn in 1874. John had the following children with Amanda Mashburn: Wiley Lanson, John G., James Russell, William Harrison, David Franklin, Henry Allen, George Calvin, and Milford Howard. According to Milford Howard Digby, John Harrison's wound was so large that a rag could be run through the wound to clean it! Whether this refers to John's wound at Gaines' Mill or Gettysburg, he does not say. John died September 8, 1913, in Etowah County, Alabama. It appears that John was buried at Golden Springs Church Cemetery at Hoke's Bluff, Alabama.

John H. Digby and wife Amanda (courtesy Martha Barnett).

Perry Edwards: was born near Maplesville, Alabama, on October 8, 1839 (Owen 1921 Vol. 3, 532). He was a school teacher in both Mississippi and Alabama after the war for some fifteen years. He then served as the Justice of the Peace in Washington County, Alabama, for thirty-five years. He was elected to the House of Representatives from Washington County, Alabama, in 1907. He lived in Escatawpa, Alabama.

John B. Fondron: is buried in the Sandy Chapel Cemetery some three miles east of Centreville, Alabama, on Highway 82.

John Simpson Gardner: was born August 20, 1840, in Bibb County, Alabama, to Jackson and Margaret Gardner (Owen 1921 Vol. 3, 635). He served as Sheriff of Bibb County for some three years, and later as clerk of the Circuit Court from 1867 to 1870. In 1880 Garner was elected Probate Judge of Bibb County. He died on May 10, 1920.

Fletcher J. Goss: was born September 22, 1831 (Frances, 2004). He married Frances Ray with whom he had the following children: Maud B., Carolina L., Indiola, Joseph Ray, Samuel Edwin, Helen G., Florence Rosa Rubel, Henry Laurens, and James Halstead. Goss died on March 9, 1905, in Fannin, Texas, and is buried in Telephone, Texas. He is listed as a physician and Justice of the Peace.

William Griffin: applied for an artificial limb from Bibb County, Alabama, on June 30, 1875 (CSR).

John Carroll Henry: was the son of Hugh Henry and Didimiah Cates (*Heritage of Bibb County, Alabama* 1998, 140). John was born around 1834, and married Sarah Margaret Suttle on October 29, 1868. They had three children: Hugh, a girl who died in infancy, and Julius Goodwin. John moved around 1875 to Coldwater, Alabama. He married Sarah Ponder on December 23, 1889, in Calhoun County, Alabama. They had the following children: John W. and Mary D. Henry. John died on March 19, 1905, and is buried in Winn's Chapel Congregational Methodist Church Cemetery on the outskirts of Anniston. The church no longer exists, and the exact location of his grave is unknown.

Patrick Clay Henry: was born January 18, 1843 (Henry, 2004). He married Margaret Shropshire, and they had one son together named Wirt Shropshire Henry. When Wirt was young Patrick simply disappeared from the family.

Marion Hogan: was the son of Archibald Hogan and Jane Caffee (*Heritage of Bibb County, Alabama* 1998, 146). He was born December 15, 1843. The Hogan home is in the Tannehill State Park. Marion died on August 19, 1888, and is buried in Caffee Cemetery near Woodstock.

Richard Hogan: was the brother of Marion Hogan. He died on April 21, 1905, and is buried along with his brother in the Caffee Cemetery (McCord 1979, 249).

Absalom H. James: made pension application from Perry County, Alabama, (CSC). He died January 31, 1914, and is buried in the Mt. Olive Church Cemetery (McCord 1979, 434).

Adam F. James: states in his pension application from Bibb County, Alabama, on August 20, 1901, that he was unable to make a living due to his wounding at Seven Pines (CSC). He is listed as fifty-six years of age, and living in Eoline, Alabama.

Jacob D. Mayberry: was living in Centreville in 1907, and died in 1921 (McCord 1979, 271). He is buried in the Centreville Memorial Cemetery on Mill Road.

James M. McCraw: was born October 29, 1840, in Alabama (McCraw, 2004). He married Amaritta Alzira Stanley in Bibb County, and together they had the following children: Betty Bertha, Laura Ann, Letha Orianna, Mabry Adams, and Inez Mae. On his application for a pension on July 11, 1913, he states he was unable to make a living on account of his age. He was living at a Centreville address and owned 180 acres. He died on January 7, 1917, and is buried in Mt. Gilead Church Cemetery at Abercrumbie.

Thaddeus M. Phillips: was said to be living in Hamburg, Alabama, in 1907 (Harris n.d.). He was born October 15, 1839.

Chesterfield W. Quinn (courtesy Ken May).

Chesterfield W. Quinn: was born on January 18, 1839, in Alabama (Simmons, 2003). Quinn married Olive Perilee Waggoner, and together they had the following children: Robert Chester, Lula M. Grace, Oliver Judson, Halsey, Velmer Lee, Warren Lee, Martha V., Dovie, Sarah F., Thomas Walter, Phillip M., William Peyton, Pearl, and Maggie Bell (May, 2004). Chester was elected the Justice of the Peace in Tuscaloosa County, Alabama, in 1877. He was part of the committee that served for the election of Hancock in 1880. Chester's father, Oliver Quinn, served in the Alabama House of Representatives, and was also the Sheriff of Bibb County. Chester died March 31, 1894, and was buried in Mt. Carmel Cemetery in West Blocton, Alabama.

John H. Smelley: was born November 5, 1840 (Butler, 2004). He married Martha Jane Smitherman on January 3, 1866, in Bibb County, Alabama. They had twelve children together: James David, William Jackson, E. Lula, R. Walters, March C., Jason E., Wilson, George Bluford, Henry

Clarence, M. Columbus, Montera, and Pearl. Around 1869 he moved to Liberty Hill, Louisiana, where he bought 1000 acres of property. He became a very successful farmer in both cotton and peanuts. He also operated a cotton gin, grist mill, sawmill, syrup mill, and blacksmith shop. He used to love to sit on his front porch and tell stories of the war.

David W. Smelly: was born around 1846 to Simpson Smelly and Caroline Terry (Butler, 2004).

James W. Smelly: was born January 2, 1844 (Butler, 2004). He moved to Bienville Parish, Louisiana, in 1869. He married Margaret C. Hall and Frances R. Ricks. He had many children before his death on November 15, 1899.

Thomas J. Smitherman: was born February 28, 1837, in Centreville,

Newton Rasberry on the left and William Rasberry; both served in Co. F (courtesy Mitcheline Shaddix).

Alabama, the son of Joseph and Sarah Latham (Owen 1921 Vol. 4, 1599). He went to Lebanon Law School in Tennessee, where he graduated in 1860. He served as Probate Judge after the death of Judge J. Gardner in 1867. He married Mary E. Howard on June 20, 1861. Thomas died on August 26, 1896, and is buried in the Centreville Memorial Cemetery (McCord 1979, 267).

James Newton Suttle: died on October 10, 1886, and is buried in the Sandy Chapel Cemetery near Centreville.

Elias M. Thomas: died in 1908 in the insane hospital from epilepsy (Brown, 2004). Family stories have it that he still had a bullet in his neck from the war. It was thought that this is what triggered his "fits."

The Officers and Enlisted Men of Company G

William H. Barry: is buried in the Oakwood Cemetery in Montgomery, Alabama.

Henry H. Bennet: had a wife named Nancy, who applied for pension #32584 from Fayette County, Alabama (CSC).

George W. Brewer: applied for an artificial limb from Tuscaloosa County, Alabama, on May 20, 1867 (CSC).

Joseph D. Bryson: married Sarah J. Higginbotham and moved to Bell, Texas, (Pettit, 2000). They had at least two children: a daughter, F.A.V. Bryson, in 1877, and a son, G.W. Bryson, in 1879.

John Thomas Burchfield: married Martha Gallant on March 2, 1860, in Tuscaloosa County (Chappius, 2000). Together they had the following children: Octavia Louise, Sallie M., Nancy Mary Jane, Elizabeth, Alma Margaret, Ella Doveyelier, Daniel A., Felix Marion, and Estrella. He died on June 24, 1914, and is buried at Pleasant Grove Cemetery in Tuscaloosa County.

John Thomas Burchfield and family (courtesy Lynn Comiskey).

Charles L. Farrington (courtesy Jan Roberts).

William M. Cole: moved to Archer, Louisiana, in 1869 (11th Alabama). He wrote a letter to Thomas M. Owen that is dated July 9, 1908.

Frank Englebert: made a pension application on August 29, 1891 (CSC). He states he was eighty-six years of age, owned no land of any kind, and was unable to make a living.

Charles L. Farrington: returned to Alabama after the war and went to school (Roberts, 2000). He joined the Methodist Conference in 1868, and served in Alabama until 1870. He traveled all the way to Texas on horseback before he finally settled in Huntsville. He married Elizabeth Oliphint on February 21, 1872. Charles died on May 4, 1923, in Huntsville, and is buried in the Oakwood Cemetery.

Thomas M. Finley: applied for a pension from Tuscaloosa County on July 28, 1883 (CSC).

Leva Gallant: married Louisa Ann Yeager in 1870 (Gallant, 2000). Together they had six children. Soon after the birth of James Crow Gallant, Louisa died. At the time of Louisa's death the Gallants were living in Mississippi. Leva moved his family to Houston County, Texas, where he married Annie Jefferson in 1898. Together they had three children before Leva died in 1920. He is buried in Corinth Cemetery, Houston County, Texas.

Marion Gallant: died on August 15, 1871, and is buried in the Old Hepzibah Cemetery in Tuscaloosa County, Alabama (Hester, 2000).

Thomas W. Hamner: is buried in the Whitley–Whitson–Strong Family Cemetery in Fayette, Alabama. His wife, Elizabeth, filed for a pension from Fayette, Alabama (#32663) (CSC).

Benjamin F. Hasty: may be the B.F. Hasty buried on March 30, 1928, in the Bethel Methodist Cemetery at Dixon Mills in Marengo County.

Pleasant L. Hayes: is buried in Hurricane Cemetery in Brookwood, Alabama (Mitchell, 2000).

Thomas Benton Howell: had an address in Scott Station, Perry County, Alabama, in 1921 (CSC).

Jesse Hughes: wrote a letter in 1905 in which he states

that his brother John Bell Hughes was living in Jasper, Alabama, and Basil Manly Hughes was living near Luling, Caldwell County, Texas (Strawbridge, 1998).

Allen Johnson: made application for a pension on June 12, 1899, from Blocton, Alabama (CSC). He states that both old age, and his leg wound from the war, now prevented him from making a living.

James McGee: died on February 3, 1910, in the Soldiers' Home for Confederate soldiers at Mountain Creek, Alabama.

James McMahon: applied for a pension from Tuscaloosa County on August 16, 1883 (CSC).

John Clay Powell: never mustered into Co. G, 11th Alabama, but rather into Co. H, 24th Alabama Infantry (Powell, 2000). He died on February 2, 1907, and is buried in Jennings Chapel Cemetery in Northport, Alabama.

Jesse Shackelford: is said to be buried at Green Pond in the First Presbyterian Church Cemetery (Stone, 1999).

David Daniel Shamblin: married Sue Hendon on September 16, 1869, in Hale County, Alabama (Shamblin, 2000). They had no children together. He was said to have operated a sawmill near Red Bay, Alabama, in Franklin County. Here he died on December 26, 1904, and is said to have been buried along the side of a creek in Red Bay. Unfortunately no marker exists to mark the spot of his burial.

Robert A. Watson: married Martha Jorge Gallion sometime between 1870 and 1875 (Whisenant, 2001). They had thirteen children together: Jonathan, Amos, Joseph, Charlie, Della, Bazzel, Benjamin, Alice, Finis, Edward, Dock, James, and Leroy. Robert lived most of his life in Cullman County, Alabama, and there he died on April 5, 1905. He is buried in Jones Chapel Baptist Church Cemetery.

Basil M. Hughes of Co. G in 1877 (courtesy Herschel Kelley).

David Shamblin (courtesy Harold Shamblin).

The Officers and Enlisted Men of Company H

Joseph P. Acker: returned from the war and married Annie Rebecca Whitaker Jennings (Brock, 2000). He moved to Texas around 1875, and died on November 27, 1891. He is buried in Providence Cemetery in Cherokee County, Texas.

John C. Adams: appears on November 25, 1889, in Carrollton, Alabama, at the Pickens Chapter of the United Confederate Veterans (*The Heritage of Pickens County, Alabama* 1999, 13).

Joseph P. Acker and wife Annie (courtesy Kerry Acker).

He is buried in Crossroads Cemetery west of Carrollton (*PIckens County Alabama Cemetery Records* 1984, 94).

William Dolphus Allen: appears on November 25, 1889, in Carrollton, Alabama, at the Pickens Chapter of the United Confederate Veterans (*The Heritage of Pickens County, Alabama* 1999, 13). The purpose of this meeting was to raise money for the disabled veterans in the county (Clanahan 1964, 143). There is an article on William in the *Confederate Veteran* in which we find that in the fall of 1865 William engaged in farming near Reelfoot Lake, Tennessee (*Confederate Veteran 1893–1912* Vol. 23, 323). After two years he returned to Alabama, where he lived until his death on November 14, 1914. He was a member of the Missionary Baptist Church from the age of thirteen years, and truly lived the life of a Christian. He married Miss Fannie Sims of Pickens County, and together they had two children. T.R. Spell mentions a Confederate reunion that was held in Reform, Alabama, on August 17, 1910, in which William D. Allen was present (Spell, n.d.).

Benjamin Franklin Bell: resided at Sharpe in Pickens County, Alabama, where he was known as a very industrious man (Clark, 2004). He worked a medium-sized plantation complete with its own cotton gin, grist mill, sawmill, and carpenter shop. He raised four children of his own along with three grandchildren. He was also known as a man of few words and no foolishness. All the Bells were strong Presbyterians, and attended the church across the road from their home. In 1914 Benjamin's wife, Valerie, traveled to Paragould, Arkansas, for health reasons to live with their son. In 1918 Benjamin auctioned his land and holdings and traveled to Clay County, Mississippi. Here he lived for the next year with his son-in-law Web Griffith, and granddaughter Paula Griffith, whom he had helped to raise. The next year Benjamin traveled to Arkansas to rejoin his family. He died on November 20, 1922 (Junker 1990, 173).

Joseph Newton Bell: died in June of 1910 near Forest Church, and is buried in Bethsaida Cemetery (Junker 1990, 173).

Frank Black: married Amelia Melton on December 16, 1868, in Fayette County, Alabama. They had at least four children: Sallie, Robert L., Samuel W., and Lula (Benjamin, 2004).

David Burgess: died at the home of his nephew, Mr. Josh Abrams, in Columbus, Mississippi. He was then buried in Mineral Springs Cemetery at McShan, Alabama (Junker 1990, 188).

Thomas Carson: married Bellzora Nichols (Junker 1990, 239). He appeared on November 25, 1889, at Carrollton for the first meeting of the United Confederate Veterans. Thomas died on July 20, 1912, and is buried in the Carrollton Cemetery.

Reuben Chapman Jr.: has an article written about him in Owen's work (Owen 1921 Vol. 3, 317–318). After the war Chapman moved to Livingston, Alabama, where he continued in the practice of law. He served as Mayor of Livingston from March of 1887 to March of 1892. He was also a member of the House of Representatives of Alabama in the session of 1900–1901. The nephew of the thirteenth Governor of Alabama died on April 30, 1902, and is buried in Myrtlewood Cemetery in Livingston, Alabama.

Benjamin Franklin Bell around 1918 in Clay County, Mississippi (courtesy Bill Clark).

Alfred B. Cox: married Martha Fitzgerald after the war, and resided in the Memphis community in Pickens County (Jean, 2004). He died in 1910, and is buried in the Pickensville Lower Cemetery near Pickensville, Alabama (*Pickens County Alabama Cemetery Records* 1984, 104).

Elisha Duncan: appeared on August 17, 1910, in Reform, Alabama, for a Confederate reunion (Spell, n.d.). He died on October 28, 1924, and is buried in Hebron Cemetery west of Carrollton (*Pickens County Alabama Cemetery Records* 1984, 140).

John Francis Duncan: applied for an artificial limb on February 13, 1879 (CSC). He appeared at the United Confederate Veterans' meeting in Carrollton on November 25, 1889. His address in 1921 is listed as McShan, Alabama.

Joseph E. Everett: is buried in Carrollton Cemetery (*Pickens County Alabama Cemetery Records* 1984, 187).

Benjamin F. Ferguson: was present at the United Confederate Veterans' meeting on November 25, 1889. He also attended a Confederate reunion held at Reform on August 17, 1910 (Spell n.d.). He died on January 4, 1916, and is buried in Spring Hill Cemetery six miles northeast of Pickensville (*Pickens County Alabama Cemetery Records* 1984, 270). He was survived by wife Lizzie, and eight children: Walter, Edward, Albert, Homer, Green, Mrs. Florence Goree, Miss Pin Ferguson, and Miss Pearl Ferguson (Junker 1990, 195).

Elijah J. Foster: is found in Hunt, Texas, on the 1880 census (NARA Texas 1880, 544b). His wife is Fannie S., and children: Nannie L., Sallie S. and Grace G.

Calvin Wesley Free: appears on the 1880 census in Speed Mills, Pickens County, Alabama (NARA

Alabama 1880, 632c). His wife was Melvina Free, with children: Willia, Effie, Mary, Alice, and Fanney. Calvin appears in Carrollton at the first meeting of the United Confederate Veterans on November 25, 1889. According to one source, Calvin died in Meridian, Mississippi, of heart failure (Junker 1990, 150). He died July 20, 1908, and is buried in Salem Church Cemetery south of Gordo off Highway 86 (*Pickens County Alabama Cemetery Records* 1984, 225).

Jacob J. Funderburk: died on January 25, 1908, and is buried in Mineral Springs Cemetery in Pickens County (Junker 1990, 165).

Benjamin M. Gammill's: wife was Mattie J. Gammill, and she applied for a pension on July 6, 1889, from Pickens County, Alabama (CSC).

Walter M. Gilkey: was born June 15, 1841, the son of William M. Gilkey and Mary Ann Savannah (Williams, 2005). He married Laura Pierce Stewart, and had two daughters: Emm Mine, and Alda V.

Joel James Hamiter: never married. He died in Texas on March 29, 1882, and was buried at Naruna, in Burnet County, Texas (Hamiter 1993, 30).

John Tyler Hamiter: married Margaret Ann McCafferty on November 7, 1865 (Hamiter 1993, 31–32). They had seven children together: Lela, Frances Eva, William Frederick, Annie Maude, John Tyler Jr., and Mattie. He was present at Carrollton on November 25, 1889, for the United Confederate Veterans' meeting. He was made sheriff on August 6, 1892, and lived his latter days with Tyler Jr. in what was known as the Lipsey–Hamiter House some four miles southeast of Carrollton. He married Julie Edwina Trantham on April 10, 1895. Throughout his life John was known to be quite outspoken on many subjects. John died November 7, 1926, and is buried in Union Chapel Cemetery five miles south of Carrollton. John's photo is found in John Cecil Hamiter Jr.'s book (Hamiter 1993).

John P. Hatcher: was buried at Woodlawn on March 6, 1864. This is located at the old Elmira Prison Camp (CSR). He is buried in grave #1981.

James Hemphill: died either on May 21, 1936, or March 23, 1935 (Betty, 2004). He is buried in Enon Cemetery in Ackerman, located in Choctaw County, Mississippi.

James B. Hodo: attended a Confederate reunion held at Reform on August 17, 1910 (Spell n.d.). James died on November 15, 1916, and is buried in Fellowship Church Cemetery off old Highway 82 between Reform and Gordo (*Pickens County Alabama Cemetery Records* 1984, p. 83).

Joseph Marshall Land: is found on the 1880 census in Springhill, Pickens County, Alabama (NARA Alabama 1880, 591a). His wife is listed as E.G. Land, and children: L.A. Land, Mary E. Land, and Joe H. Land. He died in 1904, and is buried in Crossroads Cemetery west of Carrollton (*Pickens County Alabama Cemetery Records* 1984, 96).

Michael Linebarger: attended a Confederate reunion at Reform, Alabama, on August 17, 1910 (Spell n.d.). Michael died on November 27, 1917, in Reform, Alabama (*Pickens County Alabama Cemetery Records* 1984, p. 196). He is buried in the Shady Grove Methodist Cemetery on Highway 17, some three miles north of Reform.

Henry O. Love: died on March 24, 1924, in Maben, Mississippi, in Oktibbeha County. He was buried in the Double Springs Methodist Cemetery.

Calvin Makamson: is found in Monroe, Mississippi, on the 1880 census (NARA Mississippi 1880, 192b). His wife is listed as M.A.L. Makamson, and children: W.J. (son), G.E. (son), Hortense (daughter), Minnie Lee, and J.T. (son).

Benjamin Marler: owned a newspaper and saloon in Carrollton before the war (Marler, 2004). He came back after the war and was broke. He and his family had to live for a time on parched corn. He attended the United Confederate Veterans' meeting in Carrollton on November 25, 1889, and died the following year on March 4, 1890 (*Pickens County Alabama Cemetery Records* 1984, 141). He is buried in the Hebron Cemetery west of Carrollton.

Washington L. McGraw: died on December 11, 1866, in Pickens County (Wilson, 2001).

Milus J. Moorehead: is found on the 1880 census in Yorkville (NARA Alabama 1880, 566c). His wife is listed as Mary, and children: Nancy and Mattie. He was present at the first United Confederate Veterans' meeting in Carrollton on November 25, 1889. He died in 1907 in Millport, Alabama, and is buried in the Odd Fellows Cemetery (Junker 1990, 158).

Isaac M. Nolan: married three times in his lifetime (Junker 1990, 204). First, Nolan married Miss Bryant, then Frannie McDowell, and finally Mollie Roberson. He was present at the first United Confederate Veterans' meeting in Carrollton on November 25, 1889. He died on March 31, 1917, and is buried in the Carrollton Cemetery (*Pickens County Alabama Cemetery Records* 1984, 191).

James Lawson Randall: was said to have moved to Denton, Texas, after 1885 (Teresa, 2004).

John H. Richardson: is probably the John H. Richardson listed as dying on August 26, 1904, in Baldwin, Mississippi (Junker 1990, 149).

James P. Shaw: was unable to attend the November 25, 1889, meeting of veterans in Carrollton, but he did send his affirmation of support.

Thomas W. Shaw: is buried in the Loudon Park Cemetery in Baltimore, Maryland (*Confederate Hill*). Thomas is buried in that section known as "Confederate Hill," C-84, and he is listed as buried on March 3, 1864.

John T. Shepherd: married Marietta Castles at her home on November 29, 1865 (Dare, 2004). Together they had the following children: Andrew Earlie, Lula, Hiram E., Martha F., and Susan Lenorah. John died on May 23, 1884, and is buried in Windham Cemetery one and one half miles off Highway 17 on Lake Hallalla Road (*Pickens County Alabama Cemetery Records* 1984, 286).

Franklin L. Smith: was present at Carrollton on November 25, 1889, for the Confederate Veterans' meeting.

Leroy Hammond Speed: married Marianne Caroline on March 6, 1866 (Junker 1990, 199). He was unable to attend the veterans' meeting in Carrollton on November 25, 1889, but sent his support. He died on February 5, 1913, and was buried in Bethany Cemetery in Aliceville off Lewiston Road (*Pickens County Alabama Cemetery Records* 1984, 133).

William Alexander Speed: was able to attend the veterans' meeting in Carrollton on November 25, 1889. He died the next year on January 3, 1890, and was buried in Pickensville Lower Cemetery near Pickensville (*Pickens County Alabama Cemetery Records* 1984, 107).

Andrew J. Story: received this tribute: "Comrade A.J. Story died at his home, surrounded by his loved ones. During the war the Southland had no braver soldier than A.J. Story" (*Confederate Veteran 1893*–1912 Vol. 11, 230). Andrew married on January 7, 1867, Ellen Keturah Wilson (Williams, 2005). They had six children: Georga Mayes Story, Benjamin Ferdinand Story, Leila Story, Susan A. Story, Willett Wilson Story, and a child that died in infancy. He died on March 23, 1903, and was buried in Friendship Cemetery in Columbus, Mississippi.

Pleasant A. Sutton: is found on the 1880 census for New Hope, Chickasaw, Mississippi (NARA Mississippi 1880 T9-0643, 241a). His wife is Mary, and children listed are: Maggie L., George S., Emma J. and Jesse E.

James Andrew Turnipseed: married Mary B. Lipsey on August 23, 1865 (Junker 1990, 167).

John Wesley Turnipseed: died September 7, 1899 (*Pickens County Alabama Cemetery Records* 1984, 184). He is buried in the Oak Grove Franconia Cemetery near Aliceville, Alabama.

John A. Wilkins: may be the John A. Wilkins who died December 6, 1899, and is buried in Arbor Springs Church Cemetery in Reform, Alabama (*Pickens County Alabama Cemetery Records* 1984, 249). He appears on the 1880 census in Pickens County (NARA Alabama 1880, 550c). His wife was Eliza, and children Robert, Tanin B., and John. A Confederate pension was applied for on May 7, 1895 (CSC).

Charles S. Wilson: appears in Carrollton on November 25, 1889, for the veterans' meeting. He is perhaps the Charles S. Wilson who died on June 10, 1894, and is buried in the Carrollton Cemetery (*Pickens County Alabama Cemetery Records* 1984, 195).

John Richard Woods: married Grace Ann Brownlee (*Pickens County Alabama Cemetery Records* 1984, 286). He died on February 19, 1874, and is buried in the Woods Family Cemetery near McShan, Alabama.

John W. Yateman: died in December of 1907 (Junker 1990, 157). He was one of Millport's leading citizens. He was laid to rest in Payne's Chapel Cemetery.

The Officers and Enlisted Men of Company I

Prince William Aldridge: was born on April 16, 1832, in Walker County, Alabama (McKinney, 2004). After the war he married Patsy Robertson on November 5, 1868. He died on January 25, 1916, at Crews Depot. He may be buried at Mt. Hebron Methodist Church Cemetery in Lamar County.

Asa G. Anthony: appears on the 1880 census in Chickasaw, Mississippi (NARA Mississippi 1880 T9–06434, 326 d). His wife is listed as D.J., and children: W.S. (son), A.O. (son), M.A. (daughter), C.B. (daughter), and Pink (daughter). He died in 1915, and is buried at Beavoir Confederate Cemetery in Biloxi, Mississippi.

Elbert F. Bolton: married L. Catherine McCool on March 4, 1866 (David, 2004). Together they had the following children: Ida Lee, Charles Manley, Permelia Jane "Ginnie," Emily Isobel "Bell," Marion Elbert, Thomas Marshall, and George Washington. He lived for many years in Mississippi before moving to Lamar County, Texas. He died May 6, 1907, in Lamar County, Texas, and is buried in the center of McDonald Cemetery in Lamar.

Francis A. Brotherton: is found on the 1880 census for Fayette County (NARA Alabama 1880 T9–0013, 520a). His wife is listed as Mary, and children are: Ethel, John A., Clyde B., Irma A. and Adda. He still appears in Fayette County on the 1907 census of Confederate soldiers living in Alabama.

John B. Burris: returned to Fayette following the war (Cruiksharnk, 1920). He married Miss Elizabeth Robertson, and together they had three children: Robert Claude, Charles E., and Leila E. Burris. He struggled financially in the years following the war, and then in 1877 he opened a general store in Columbus, Mississippi (Cruiksharnk 1920, 125). This business did very well, and then in 1887 he came to Birmingham and started another business at Woodlawn. He died on September 14, 1914.

David Sterling Clanton: was the son of David C. Clanton (Arnold, 2004). He was born in December of 1840 in Pickens County, Alabama, and died in 1926.

John B. Burris (courtesy Frank Burris).

Jesse C. Clanton: was the son of David C. Clanton and was born around 1847 in Pickens County, Alabama (Arnold, 2004). He died in 1900, and was buried in Mt. Tabor Cemetery at Palmetto, Alabama.

Moses J. Coleman: is found on the 1880 census for Pickensville in Pickens County, Alabama (NARA Alabama 1880 T9–0028, 544b). His wife is listed as Sarah, and children: William, Eliza, Jane, Donna, James, Pearl, and Joseph K.

George J. Collins: is found on the 1880 census in Fayette County, Alabama (NARA Alabama 1880 T9–0013, 527c). He is listed as a physician, with wife Nancy, and children: Alonz, Alice, Eller, Arlando, Roca, and Leander.

Henry Clay Cribbs: was living in Bedford, Lamar County, Alabama in 1907 (CSC). His wife, Nancy, made a pension application in Lamar County.

James A. Darr: is found on the 1880 census for Lamar County, Alabama (NARA Alabama 1880 T9–0017, 657 d). His wife was Hattie, and children: Robert E., G. Joseph, Ruffus L., Anna, James M., and Nancy E..

Aurelius Whitfield Dumas: married Margaret Ellwood King on January 27, 1869 (Allen, 2004). He died in Heber Springs, Arkansas, on February 24, 1913 (*Confederate Veteran 1893–1912* Vol. 21, 300). He was the Adjutant of Stonewall Jackson Camp U.C.V.

Calvin R. Kirkland: is mentioned in the *Confederate Veteran 1893–1912* (Vol. 37, 305). He died at his home in Senatobia, Mississippi, and was laid to rest in Bethesda Cemetery. He married Miss Emily Thornton, and together they had two children. The *Veteran* gives a glowing account of the life he lived:

> He contributed much to the upholding of law, and especially in those trying times of reconstruction his section did not have a braver defender. He was a true son of the South, and lived a life enriched by splendid emotions, one rich in the love of family and friends; and though he had outlived most of those with whom he took part in those fighting days of old, he lived again in memory those stirring scenes, and his comrades were a vivid part of those memories. To the last he was faithful to the principles for which the South had fought.

William F. Kirkland: has an obituary in the *Fayette Banner* (*Fayette Banner*, n.d.). It reads:

> William F. Kirkland, Co. I, 11th Alabama Regiment, who died at his home near Bankston, November 3, 1907.... He was a good and brave soldier in the true sense. He never flickered in battle, nor shirked a duty in camps; was ever found at his post of duty and always willing to bear his part without murmuring.

Ephraim Long: is found on the 1880 census for Lamar County, Alabama (NARA Alabama 1880 T9–0017, 652d). His wife was Lucinda, and children: William, Francis, Lorenza D., T. Jefferson, Julia, Liberty, Margaret, Tildon, Gorda, and Tener.

Henry M. McCollum: is found on the 1880 census in Fayette County (NARA Alabama 1880 T9–0013, 435a). His wife is Lucy, and children are: Josievine, Elizabeth, Tack, and Neuman.

John W. Miles: appears in an article in the *Confederate Veteran 1893–1912* (Vol. 26, 218). It states John was born July 4, 1841, in Georgia, and died on March 16, 1918. He died in the home of his brother near Bartow, Florida.

John A. Mixon: may be the John Mixon listed in the 1880 census record in Lamar County, Alabama (NARA Alabama 1880 T9–0017, 578a). His wife is listed as Minerva, and children: Richard, Benjamin, John, and Carrie.

Wiley H. Nall: was said to have met his end on September 22, 1865 (Poe, 2004). Wiley's father heard an unusual noise in their front yard on this evening and went out to investigate. He grabbed a hatchet on his way out, and soon confronted three men who were standing in his yard. These men demanded all his money, he responded by attacking the men with his hatchet. In the skirmish Wiley's father was shot and killed. In the meantime Wiley was awakened by the shot, ran out into the yard where he too was then shot and killed. He is buried in the Nall Cemetery at Newtonville, Alabama.

Philip May Newton: was still living in Fayette County as of 1880 (NARA Alabama 1880 T9–0013, 459a).

James W. Oliver: may be the man mentioned in the 1880 census record in Somerville, Morgan County, Alabama (NARA Alabama 1880 T9–0013, 459a). Listed are wife, Ann, and children: Sarah J., Ann, and Mattie C. In his muster roll is also found a Service Reference Slip from the Adjutant General to the Board of Commissioners of the State of Texas for James W. Oliver. This slip is dated May 14, 1915.

Ezekiel R. Powell: was dead by the 1880 census in Fayette County (NARA Alabama 1880 T9–0013, 453d). His wife Jane is listed, as well as children Zenomia, Eliza, Fannie, Jane, and Reuben.

Allen Hamby Propst: married Frances Brent on September 5, 1865 (Kasten, 2001). They had one child before her death. He then married Martha Russell, with whom he had five more children. Allen died in Columbus, Mississippi, on December 31, 1896.

John W. Shelton: was born around 1834 in North Carolina. In 1860 he was a merchant according to one source (Callahan, 1969, 25). According to Teresa Bransby, John Wesley Shelton was born in Lincoln County, North Carolina, and married Sarah Alcanza Randall (Bransby, 2003). Shelton died on April 14, 1920, in Groesbeck, Limestone County, Texas. He was buried in Lampkin Cemetery in Lamar County, Texas.

Rufus H. Shelton: married Alice Roseman after the war, and moved to Memphis, Tennessee. Together they had one daughter named Alice (Kasten, 2001).

Enoch Sikes: married Mary Francis Lindsey, and together they had eight children: Ginnie, Oscar, Ella, Harvey, Elbert, Arthur, Mauda, and Lillian Sykes (Baumgardner, 2004). Enoch died on December 24, 1923, in Strickler, Arkansas.

Reuben J. Stewart: died in 1917, and was buried in the Hopewell Primitive Baptist Church Cemetery in Fayette, Alabama.

William T. Summers: had a wife listed as M. Summers (CSC). She applied for a pension from Lamar County, Alabama.

Preston Wren Thornton: married Matilda Elzada Marshall, with whom he had twelve children: Nancy E., Thomas J., Mary E., William Lee, Lottie E., James Murray, Lucinda B., Edward Levi, Glen Everett, Eunice May, infant that died, and Susan Florence (*Heritage of Fayette County, Alabama* 1999, 434–435). He moved to Navarro County, Texas, and then to Abilene around 1908. He died on April 13, 1916, and is buried in the Old Abilene Cemetery.

Richard Hampton Wait: was in Walker County, Alabama, in 1907 (CSC).

Abel A. Walden: served as sheriff in Fayette County from 1874–1877 (Fayette County Historical Society 1971, 92). He died in his brother's home in Waco, Texas, on June 21, 1909.

William Wilson: was the son of Burr Wilson who was the Probate Judge in Fayette County from 1868 to 1874.

Alexander F. Yearby: returned to Fayette after the

Abel A. Walden (*150 Yesteryears*).

war, but then moved to Mississippi (*Heritage of Fayette County Alabama* 1999, 489). Here he married Mary Beard and had two sons: Arthur Frank and Thomas Adley. After his death Mary moved with the children to the home of her brother in Van Buren, Arkansas.

The Officers and Enlisted Men of Company K

Thomas B. Ballard: is found on the Confederate monument in Marion Cemetery for those boys who did not return home from Virginia.

William Leander Brown: died on July 23, 1882, and is buried in Fairview Cemetery in West Perry, Alabama (England, n.d.).

John T. Church: married Martha Ann Rogers on December 29, 1870, and applied for a grant to homestead 140 acres adjoining the Rogers' farm (*Heritage of Perry County Alabama* 1999, 75). He eventually became a wine maker, and hauled wine by covered wagon to Montgomery. He also raised cotton. He had six girls and three boys before his death on April 23, 1912. He is buried in the Church Family Cemetery in Perry County, Alabama.

William Wilson (*150 Yesteryears*).

John Thomas Church and wife Martha Ann (courtesy Jeff Stanifer).

David Willis Colburn: married Frances Baer, and together they had the following children: George W., Sarah Elizabeth, Nancy, Rachel, John Thomas, Joseph Francis (Colburn, 1999). Frances died in 1882, and David then married Frances Lavonia Moore on April 14, 1886. The couple had the following children: Susie, Judson E., Howard, Maritte, and Ida Belle. David W. Colburn died on October 5, 1912, in Chattanooga, Tennessee.

Henry Clay Cook: returned to Alabama and continued his education. In 1874 he moved to Texas and became an educator and teacher. He also served as a county clerk and judge. Finally, he served as an editor of a newspaper (Cooke, 1998).

Aaron M. Curb: married Fannie Christenberry on October 19, 1865 (Bazzell, 1999). They moved to Texas in 1873, to Chickasaw Indian Territory in 1883, and finally to Green County, Oklahoma, in 1900. Together they had the following children: Margaret Lena, Mary Viola, Ella Josephine, Daniel Napoleon, Edward Andrew, Etta Martha, Charles McLeod, William Abner, Pickney Walter, Irene, Beata, Oscar Monroe, and Emma Geneva. Aaron died on January 29, 1932, in Oklahoma. His death was noted in the *Galveston Daily News*, on February 14, 1932:

> The death of A.M. Curb at his Oklahoma farm home last January 29 brought to an end the colorful and varied career of a man who had been both a confederate soldier and one of the pioneers who developed the Southwest.... It was at the age of 30 that Curb, together with his wife and son, started for Texas in a prairie schooner drawn by oxen. Going along routes where there were no highways or bridges, and where rivers were either forded or crossed by ferries when large, the family had many interesting adventures, which Mr. Curb would often relate. After three months of such travel the family reached Belton, Tex., where Mr. Curb had his first experience as a pioneer farmer. After ten years he went to Oklahoma with his family, going to what is now Love County. In 1900, pushing further west, Mr. Curb went to what is now Harmon County with his family, and there lived until his death [Aaron Monroe Curb Papers].

Jonathan Wiley Guthrie (courtesy Ed Guthrie).

Napoleon B. Curb: died on August 13, 1870, and is buried in Mt. Zion Cemetery in Perry County, Alabama.

James H. George: may be the Dr. James Hosea George buried in the Old Linden Cemetery in Linden, Alabama. He died November 11, 1901. George was a Mason.

John A. Gray: died on December 14, 1913, and is buried in the Medline Cemetery in Medline, Alabama.

Lysander J. Gray: grew a long beard to cover up a shattered jaw he suffered at Frayser's Farm (Arinder, 2001). He moved to Texas after the war, where he owned a small hotel, livery stable, and cattle ranch. He died on March 4, 1916, in Deport, Texas.

Robert B. Griffin: was released from Point Lookout Prison Camp on March 14, 1865, in very bad physical condition. He was able to make it back home to Perry County before his death on April 12, 1865. He is buried in the Mt. Zion Cemetery in Perry County.

Jonathan Wiley Guthrie: married Zoe Smith, and together they had three children: Zowie, Allen, and James Marion (Guthrie, 1999). He died in

1916, and is buried in Tucker Missionary Cemetery in Philadelphia, Neshoba County, Mississippi.

William J. Hay: is probably the William J. Hay who married a lady by the name of Alabama (*Heritage of Perry County, Alabama* 1999, 114). Together they had the following children: Lanora, Emma, Mattie, John D., J.P., and Milton. They were living as late as 1907 in Pinetucky Beat in Perry County, Alabama.

William D. Hopkins: married Rebecca A. Saunders on March 12, 1866 (*Heritage of Perry County, Alabama* 1999, 119).

Thomas B. Howell: died on June 18, 1927, and is buried in Marion Cemetery in Marion, Alabama (England n.d., 52).

Archibald Monroe Hunsucker: married Martha Jane Arnold on February 28, 1866 (Hopkins and Hunsucker, 2000). Together they had the following children: Idella Clara, Malachi, Estella, Hezikiah Columbus, Rebecca, Monroe Harrison, Robert Edward, Martha, Effie, Ebenezer, and Grover Cleveland. Mrs. Adrianne lists an excerpt from the *Brookhaven Leader* April 1, 1903, Vol. 21, Number 14: "It was a real pleasure to see Rev. O.M. Lucas and A.M. Hunsucker, two old war Comrades, embrace each other at Sunday meeting. They had not met since their regiment at the 11th Alabama, stacked arms at Appomattox." Both Archie and Martha died just a month apart in 1918. They are both buried in the Bogue Chitto Cemetery, Lincoln County, Mississippi.

Robert P. Lockhart: had a Selma, Alabama, address in 1907 (CSC).

Bryant L. McInnis: is listed as living in Sumter County, Alabama, on the 1907 veterans' census (CSC). His mailing address is listed as York, Alabama.

Walter C.Y. Parker: has his name listed on the Confederate monument in Marion Cemetery of those unreturned dead (England n.d., 7).

Isham W. Pound's: wife, Lucinda, applied for a pension from Chilton County, Alabama (CSC).

Little Seabern B.J. Ratliff: was living in Maplesville, Alabama, in 1907; however, in 1920 he made application to Mountain Creek, Alabama, to the Confederate Soldiers' Home (CSC).

Benjamin F. Sanders: married Mary E. Lovelady (*Heritage of Perry County, Alabama* 1999, 178).

Jesse B. Shivers: returned to Alabama after his war-ending wound to be admitted to the bar in 1863 (Owen 1921 Vol. 4, 1549). He was also the mayor of Marion where he lived for the next four years. From 1876 to 1886 he was the Superintendent of Education of Perry County, Alabama. Jesse died on September 25, 1914, and is buried in the Marion Cemetery at Marion, Alabama.

James H. Tadlock: moved to Texas after the war (Schwab, 1999).

Malcomb D.C. Tadlock: married Selina Gray on November 8, 1865 (Arinder, 2001). After having several children they removed to Scott County, Mississippi. Malcomb died on March 24, 1908, and is buried in Sims Hill Cemetery near Morton, Mississippi.

Henry Talbird: was in poor health following the end

Malcomb D.C. Tadlock (courtesy William P. Arinder).

of the war, and accepted a country pastorate in Carlowville, Dallas County, Alabama (Owen 1921 Vol. 4, 1641). He stayed here for two and a half years before resigning due to continued health problems. Six months after his resignation he took a church in Henderson, Kentucky, where he remained for the next three years. Finally, on April 11, 1872, he accepted the pastorate of First Baptist Church, Lexington, Missouri. He remained many years in this position, and was eventually elected a trustee of William Jewell College. He later served as president of its board of education.

John B. Underwood: died on July 13, 1874, and is buried in Fairview Presbyterian Cemetery in West Perry, Alabama.

Ruffus Beatrice Wallace: died on November 26, 1923, and is buried in Marion Cemetery in Marion, Alabama (England, 42).

William P. Walton: applied for a pension from Jefferson County Alabama (CSC).

Aaron Warren: married Mary Elizabeth Terry on January 16, 1862 (*Heritage of Perry County Alabama* 1999, 197–98). They had the following children: Sarah J., Mosely, Mary, General Marion, William, John Franklin, Linard, and Isaac. Aaron died on February 9, 1890, and is buried in a single grave near Bethlehem, Alabama.

Chapter Notes

Chapter 1

1. Hale is mentioned as presenting a communication from a John B. Read on February 16, 1861, on the subject of projectiles (*J.C.C.S.A.*, Vol. 1, 56). Hale laid before Congress a communication regarding a flag for the Confederate States on February 22, 1861, as well as February 26 (ibid., 73, 86). These are only a sample of the things Hale was involved in during his brief stay in the Confederate Congress.

2. The Linden Hotel was located on Cahaba Street in what is now referred to as old Linden. Two buildings remain on Cahaba Street which date from that time: the old courthouse, and the old jail (Folders I & II: *Towns in Marengo County*, in the Marengo County Public Library).

3. Other towns in Marengo which produced recruits for the Rifles were Uniontown, Sweetwater, Clay Hill, Dixon's Mill, Spring Hill, and Dayton.

4. A sizable number of men were recruited for Co. A after this initial group left for Virginia. James Devoy was enlisted on July 10, while the following men's enlistments date from July 30, 1861: John W. Boozer, William H.H. Boozer, James M. Brady, Ebenezer Breckenridge, Arthur W. Corley, Nathan Daniel, William R. Ethridge, Joseph A. Gamble, James M. Gillmore, Benjamin F. Glass, John F.M. Heard, Lucius Huckabee, Edmund D. Landrum, William A. McLaughlin, Merrit J. Morgan, Hugh L. Rogers, William C. Ross, James S. Singleton, Joseph L. Singleton, James Spiva, Jesse H. Varner, Thomas H. Wade, William H. Wade, John S. Waller, James J. Wilkinson, and William Worthington (*Compiled Service Records of Confederate Soldiers who Served in Organizations from the State of Alabama*, hereafter CSR)

5. This list contains most of the men who enlisted on February 16, 1861, and who subsequently enlisted for the war on May 27: Charles H. Bulloch (enlisted in Co. C), Robert Newton Crawford, Anderson Crenshaw, John Collins, James M. Gordon (enlisted in Co. C), Anderson H. Greenwood, Nathan K. Greenwood, Wm. B. Harkness Jr. (enlisted in Co. C), J.W. Hill (he didn't enlist May 27), Benjamin T. Higginbotham (enlisted in Co. C), Francis Inge, John Hughes (didn't enlist May 27), Richard M. Kennedy (enlisted in Co. C), C.L. Knox (enlisted in Co. C), Richard McCulley, Frank Mundy, John Murphy (enlisted in Co. C), Martin Norris, Erlander M. Richardson (enlisted in Co. C), and John C.J. Ridgeway (CSR).

6. One finds the company name spelled both as the "Greys" and the "Grays."

7. Additional towns providing recruits included Holly Square, Gainesville, New Prospect, Orion, Pleasant Ridge, and Clinton.

8. Matthew Pinkney's father, Peter Hollis Hamilton Jr., interestingly served under Sydenham Moore in the war with Mexico in the 1st Regular Alabama Volunteers (Norris, n.d.).

9. Additional towns which provided soldiers were Pleasant Ridge, Hopewell, Eutaw, and Mantua.

10. Robert Haynes Gordon was the son of Samuel Otterson Gordon, a wealthy man, who was proprietor in 1856 of the Eutaw House, or Gordon Hotel (*The Heritage of Green County, Alabama* 2001, 119).

11. John W. Witherspoon, "Chronicles of the Canebrake," *Alabama Historical Quarterly* 9 (1947): 475–613.

12. John enlisted as a corporal in Co. H, First Regiment of Alabama Volunteers, during the Mexican War, and was promoted to Second Lieutenant before the war's end (Gresham 2000). He was a large landowner in Dayton, Alabama, and became the Chairman of the Dayton Female Academy

13. Other cities providing men for the Legion were Nanafalia, Forkland, Jefferson, Mt. Sterling, Bladon Springs, Spring Hill, Uniontown, and Linden.

14. Both "Yancy" and "Yancey" are attested in spelling.

15. John Gordy enlisted in Co. E on September 23, and James E. Warthen transferred from Co. D in the fall of 1861 (*Alabama Confederate Service Cards*, hereafter CSC).

16. Other towns providing men for the Rifles included Mobile, Citronelle, Clayton, Pollard, Stockton, and Eufaula in Barbour County.

17. Jericho, Scottsville, Benson, and Six Mile also provided recruits for the Greys.

18. In a brief work called *The Hughes Family History*, both J.B. and B.H. Hughes were said to have joined May 9, 1861 (Strawbridge 1998).

19. Other towns which provided recruits were Moore's Bridge, Montevallo, Mars, Adison, Six Mile, and Scottsville.

20. A list of the men and officers of the Calhoun Guards is found in the work by Barefield, which includes some ninety men (Barefield 1984, 63). The above mentioned men are only a few those who eventually joined to form the new company.

21. Other towns providing recruits for Co. H were Antioch, Bridgeville, Raleigh, McShan, and Pleasant Grove.

22. The following towns also contributed soldiers: Crossville, Newtonville, Millport, Crawfordsville, Hill, Dublin, Carrollton, Asbury, Moore's Bridge, Pilgrim's Rest, and Tuscaloosa.

Chapter 2

1. The University provided public notice of the availability of the cadets to assist in the training of military companies being formed. In a May 1, 1861, notice, it is stated that any company destitute of officers competent to drill them may make application to Dr. L.C. Garland, the Superintendent (*The Independent Monitor* [Tuscaloosa], 1 May 1861). See also the excellent article on the University Cadet Corps (Murfee 1943, 55–58).
2. We verified 116 men in our research. By the time they reached Virginia they would number at least this many.
3. See Miller 1945, 37–59.
4. One writer notes that it was a plantation toward Uniontown that the company encamped upon (Witherspoon 1947, 496).
5. Witherspoon states that it was ordered by Miss Mary F. Lewis, who was later to become the wife of Lt. Gen. W.J. Hardee. The flag had a portrait of a young woman upon it.
6. Velma and Stephens G. Croom Collection is located at the archives of the University of South Alabama. It contains a fine collection of letters written by Stephens G. Croom. Hereafter, we will refer to this as the Croom Collection.
7. The men may have left the very next morning for Montgomery. McClelen notes that his company boarded a steamer late on June 21 (McClelen 1995, 7).
8. Whitfield was eventually discharged in July of 1861 (CSR).
9. It should be noted that in the historical memoranda of the company it states that they remained at Mobile for a day. Of course, it may mean most of the day and not a day and night (11th Alabama)
10. The time it took for the company to reach Montgomery by steamer appears to be accurate. The steamer, *Kimball*, would take its passengers from Mobile to Montgomery in twenty-two hours (*The Mobile Register and Advertiser*, 10 October 1861).
11. I will be employing the volume number of the 1996 CD–ROM version of the OR.
12. It should be noted that Brewer calculates 972 men for the original muster, while another regimental history gives the figure of 981 (11th Alabama), and another source gives 960 men (*Mobile Press Register*, 23 April 1863).
13. The following men never mustered into Confederate service as part of the 11th Alabama: E.A. Heidt, James B. Sellick, O. Shevernell, John C. Powell, James Thames, A.D. White, Richard Bailey, and William Burgey. Burgey was absent without leave and had not reported.
14. John C. Risinger, William W. Morrow, Martin V. Barnes, and Richard Brown of Co. F, and Thomas J. Ogletree of Co. A.
15. James D.L. Fant, John A. Moore, James L. Randall of Co. H, Thomas B. Howell, James H. Raiford of Co. K, John A. Mixon of Co. I, and Joseph Hall of Co. E.
16. It should be noted that this diary is listed in the Alabama Archives as the diary of Capt. George Field; however, it became apparent to me that the internal evidence demonstrated that it was not Captain Field's diary at all, but the diary of Corp. Anderson Crenshaw.
17. Harris mentions that the orders to march to Richmond arrived on the evening of July 3, and they were put on warning to be ready to march at a moment's notice (Harris 1861–1864).
18. Companies A, B, C, F, and K left on the evening of July 4, and probably Co. I as well.
19. Captain James McMath notes that the arrival time was 5:00 A.M. (James McMath Diary), while Morgan simply states that they arrived the morning of July 5 (*The Mobile Press Register*, 13 May 1934). Croom likewise notes the Greys' arrival on July 5 (Croom Collection).
20. George Field also received some twenty-five guns that had been reworked by J.D. Brown on July 12 (CSR).

Chapter 3

1. Co. H also affirms they arrived at Winchester on July 14 (11th Alabama).
2. This is found in the compiled service records for military units of the Confederate States held in the National Archives and Records Administration Microfilm M861, hereafter labeled as CRMU.
3. Both the McMath Diary and the history of Co. G affirm July 13 as the date of their departure from Richmond.
4. This issue of the *Register* contains part of a diary kept by William C. Morgan of Co. A.
5. Johnson gives a figure of 1,700 (*Battles and Leaders of the Civil War* Vol. 1, 244, hereafter known as BLCW), while E.K. Smith estimates between 1,400–1,800 (Edmund Kirby Smith Papers).
6. Many pension applications are attested in the Confederate Service Cards held at the Alabama Department of Archives and History, hereafter known as CSC.
7. Smith is buried at the Stonewall Cemetery in Winchester (Kurtz and Ritter n.d., 2).
8. Dr. William H. Sanders describes how Walter Gordon of Co. C was taken sick on the march from Winchester to Piedmont (Dr. Sanders's Papers).
9. *The Southern Historical Society Papers* Vol. 9, 130 hereafter known as SHSP (this information comes from the 1998 Guild Press CD–ROM).
10. Gabriel L. Hill of Co. B is said to have been sick at Piedmont (CSR). He was eventually discharged on January 24, 1862.

Chapter 4

1. McMath and Crenshaw both state that it was 11:00 A.M. when they arrived, while most of the sources simply state that it was Monday morning
2. The Sydenham Moore Papers are held at the

Alabama Department of Archives and History in Montgomery, Alabama, Box 166.

3. The reporter in this article states that by July 31, 1861, all of the dead had been buried, although for many it was in rather shallow graves *(Daily Richmond Enquirer,* 31 July 1861).

4. The Cadmus M. Wilcox Papers are contained at the Library of Congress Manuscript Division in Washington D.C.

5. There is not uniformity as to the exact date for this encampment at Bristoe Station. Company A memoranda give August 9 as the date, while Co. K gives August 11 as the time of departure from the Lewis House (11th Alabama).

6. *Richmond Daily Dispatch,* 14 August 1861.
7. *Richmond Daily Dispatch,* 17 August 1861.
8. *Richmond Daily Dispatch,* 28 August 1861.

9. It should be noted that only about 700 men made this trek to Centreville. Some 300 or so were too sick to make the journey *(The Pickens Republican* [Carrollton], 3 October 1861).

10. Wilcox recalls the location to be about a mile beyond Centreville (Cadmus M. Wilcox Papers).

11. It should be noted that October 17, 1861, is also given as the date for his promotion.

12. Crenshaw is probably speaking of 1st Lieutenant A. Newton Steele of Co. G.

13. Crenshaw also notes later in December of 1861 that his uncle Phil Schoppert arrived in camp bearing some sixteen boxes of uniforms (Crenshaw 1861–1862).

14. Crenshaw mentions that James Edmiston, Thomas J. Johnston, and Richard J. McCulley of Co. B were sent on to Richmond (Crenshaw 1861–1862). Although it is impossible to be sure of the exact numbers, the muster rolls attest to the following men being sent to Richmond on October 24: Jesse Varner, Samuel Varner, Wm. H. Wade, Alexander M. Waller, and Lemuel Napier of Co. A; Thomas Childers, Rufus Harris, Daniel Hooppaugh, Robert McClain, and Elmore Steele of Co. C; Francis Adcock, James Burrage, Charles Farrington, James Keeton, and John Morrow of Co. G; Thomas Ballard, Isaac Cottles, Jacob Funderburk, Robert Miller, John Sanders, David Smith, Wm Speed, Davidson Stoker, and John Woods of Co. H (CSR).

15. This skirmish took place on December 4, 1861 (Long 1971, 146).

16. Harris also mentions that Abel A. Walden was elected 2nd Lieutenant without specifying his opponent, and that A.W. Dumas was elected Corporal in his stead (Harris 1861–1864).

17. This date is based on several pieces of information. First, in a letter dated January 3, 1861, Dr. Sanders noted that Colonel Moore had returned home on furlough for health reasons (Dr. Sanders's Papers). In addition, the *Alabama Beacon* on January 17 states that Colonel Moore had reached home on Friday, January 10 (11th Alabama). It would have taken about a week for Colonel Moore to get from Manassas to his home in Greene County.

18. This date suggests itself based on two pieces of information. J.C.C. Sanders states on February 3, 1862, that in a day or two Captain Field was leaving on a sixty-day furlough. Finally, Colonel Moore wrote a letter to his wife from Montgomery on February 10, 1862, on his return visit. This means that they probably left around the 4th or 5th of February for home. In the Co. B muster roll, it states that Lieutenant Clark left on February 3, 1862.

19. The known recruiters for the 11th Alabama were: John B. Rains, Thomas M. Witherspoon, and Paul G. Shaw of Co. A; William M. Bratton, George Clark, and Meady M. Williford of Co. B; James Cross, Carlos L. Knox, and Albert Baldwin of Co. C; John Prince and William Pegues of Co. D; Richard Fletcher and George Allen of Co. E; James Davidson and James Suttle of Co. F; James McMath and Solomon Ward of Co. G; James H. Moorehead and Reuben Thom of Co. H; Abel A. Walden and James C. Terry of Co. I; and Bryant McInnis and Edward R. Lucas of Co. K (CSR).

20. John C. Reves was transferred to Co. A on March 24, 1862, from Co. K of the 9th Georgia (CSR).

21. Around April 30, 1862, Clairborn and Franklin Wright, as well as George Jones, enlisted at the Peninsula (11th Alabama). Thomas Foster enlisted April 4, 1862.

22. This number is confirmed by Captain Fletcher's requisition for eight pairs of pants and coats at Richmond on April 2, 1862 (CSR).

23. There is a Sergeant W.E. Saxon listed in the muster rolls for Co. E. The first mention of him is on August 1, 1862, but no service record remains.

24. McMath states in his diary that he recruited twenty-five men.

25. Jesse Humphries enlisted January 25, 1862, while Malcomb Tadlock enlisted March 1, 1862 (CSR).

Chapter 5

1. Two soldiers were admitted to the General Hospital of Orange Court House: Samuel E. Hooks of Co. E, and William J. McCain of Co. G (CSR). This hospital was open from July 22, 1861, until April 23, 1862 (Weaver, *Confederate Military Hospitals*). Hooks returned to duty on April 18, 1862, but McCain was eventually transferred to Chimborazo, where he died on June 23, 1862 (CSR). McCain is buried in Oakwood Cemetery, Grave 101, Row O, Division B.

2. The 11th lost the following men from the time of their departure from Manassas to their breaking of camp at Orange Court House: George W. Law of Co. D on March 11, John R. Griffin of Co. K on March 20, William F. Herman of Co. K on March 21, and Marion Warren of Co. K on March 22 (CSR).

3. There is evidence that the regiment reached King's Mill on March 28, 1862 (11th Alabama).

4. Captain Robertson had been appointed A.C.S. in July of 1861. On May 1, 1862, he was appointed Major A.C.S. to take rank from April 29, 1862 (CSR).

5. During this brief stay at Lebanon Church the following soldiers died: James D. Chism of Co. F on March 28, Arthur Corley of Co. A on March 29, Corporal Jesse Robinson of Co. C on April 1, and Thomas C. Jordan of Co. C on April 3 (CSR).

6. Company B was most likely the company detached for this service. I base this conclusion upon several pieces of evidence. Clark mentions that his company was taken very early on to a place he calls Green's Farm (probably Lee's Farm) where they continually did picket service (Clark 1914, 17–8). We know that Lee's Farm was the place

where the company from the 9th Alabama was detached under Gracie's command (OR Series 1, Vol. 10/1, 594). In addition, he states that *at least his company* was taken there, which gives the impression that the rest of the regiment was not necessarily present. According to General Wilcox this detachment under Gracie continued until after the battle of Williamsburg (Cadmus M. Wilcox Papers). Gracie's Battalion, in Kershaw's Brigade, formed part of the rear guard in the withdrawal from Yorktown (CSR). In addition, Croom plainly states that Co. B was made a part of a skirmish party under Gracie's command (Croom Collection). This detachment took place the second day after their arrival.

7. Colonel Moore mentions that on April 22 a slight skirmish took place between the men of the regiment and the Yankees, but it resulted only in a few wounded on either side (Sydenham Moore Papers).

8. The day the 11th reached New Kent Court House, Maj. Archibald Gracie was relieved as Major of the regiment. He proceeded to Mobile and, along with Capt. Y.M. Moody, raised the 43rd Alabama Regiment (CSR). On the day before the battle of Seven Pines, Thomas H. Holcomb was appointed the new Captain of Co. A in place of Young M. Moody. Captain Field of Co. B became the new Major. He was appointed on May 13, 1862, but he was to rank from May 7, 1862 (11th Alabama).

9. Upon leaving the Peninsula, the Wilcox Brigade was placed in Longstreet's Division (Freeman 1970, 168).

10. M.S. Jolly was relieved on May 20, 1862 (CSR).

11. I found a letter penned by General Wilcox in the file of J.H. King of the 9th Alabama in which the reason for Colonel Hale's assignment is made clear. After the battle of Williamsburg, Colonel Samuel Henry of the 9th Alabama was sentenced to suspension for six months. General Wilcox did not regard him as competent for his position as Colonel (CSR).

12. McMath recalls this move to have been taken on May 25 (McMath Diary).

13. The reasons for Longstreet's decision would take us too far from our primary purpose here. See Longstreet's own account (Longstreet 1992, 87–92).

14. It appears from the casualty lists that Companies A, D, and F were the detached units.

15. Colonel Moore is reported to have been shot twice in the battle: the leg wound, and another shot that grazed his spine (Owen 1921 Vol. 3, 1236).

16. It is interesting that in this article by General Wilcox he affirms that there were four companies detached rather than three.

17. Dr. Sanders noted that the men were able to secure much camp equipage: tents, utensils, blankets, overcoats, medical supplies, and barrels of food. They had, in Dr. Sanders' words, an abundance of everything (Sanders's File).

18. Apparently there was some misunderstanding about this order to withdraw (Longstreet, 1992, 108). According to General Longstreet, he only wished for General Wilcox to withdraw to the defensive entrenchments around Seven Pines, not to withdraw from the engagement.

19. A family story exists which states that Jordan Oakley watched his brother Thomas fall wounded. Jordan propped him against a tree, but when he returned he found his brother dead from a loss of blood (Oakley 2001).

20. This soldier may be the same as Marshall Norred on Hogan's list of casualties.

21. N.B. Hogan lists Parker as wounded at Seven Pines (*Confederate Veteran 1893–1912* Vol. 10, 169).

22. This was also called Greaner's Factory Hospital, a former tobacco factory, located on the east side of 22nd Street between Main and Franklin Streets (Waitt 1979, 15). It opened in the spring of 1861.

23. The muster rolls consistently give July 19, 1862, as the date of Hale's death, while the legal forms filed by his widow consistently give July 18, 1862, as the date.

24. The following information is taken from CSR, 11th Alabama, and *Alabama Beacon* [Greensboro], 18 July 1862. My total is 176.

25. Compare this list with *Mobile Advertiser and Register*, 9 July 1862.

26. Murphy lost his arm after twenty-two days of suffering (Sanders's File). He died from these wounds on August 4, 1862.

27. It should be noted that in several accounts mention is made of two charges on the Randol Battery (*Confederate Veteran 1893–1912* Vol. 1, 333–334; Vol. 2, 87). According to some veterans of the 11th, after initially taking the battery they were forced back, then reinforced, and then took the battery a second time.

28. Some talk was made that the 11th was trying to deceive the enemy by waving the captured Union flag (*Confederate Veteran 1893–1912* Vol. 2, 87). The flag was taken by the 11th in their first charge of the battery, but it was retaken later by the Yankees (*Confederate Veteran 1893–1912* Vol. 1, 333–334).

29. A different story is offered by Randol in his report when he states that the Fourth Pennsylvania acted badly, and retired after receiving only one volley from the enemy (OR Series 1 Vol. 11/2, 256).

30. One note in the regimental history also gives the figure of 182 killed and wounded (11th Alabama).

31. General Wilcox also states that forty-nine were killed at Frayser's Farm, including five captains. He also mentions that eleven men were taken prisoner, and that these men escaped and returned the next day (Cadmus M. Wilcox Papers).

32. In a letter written by George Clark on June 21, 1910, he states that Captain Bratton was a "brave soldier and most elegant gentleman in every respect and died gallantly at the head of his company at the battle aforesaid" (11th Alabama).

33. Robert Upchurch is listed as wounded in the Confederate Service Records, while Dr. Sanders listed him as killed. Perhaps he was mortally wounded at Frayser's Farm.

34. One note states that Gordon died from his wounds, but no date is given for his death. In addition, Dr. Sanders states only that Gordon was severely wounded. In a letter by C.P. Sanders dated July 21, 1862, Gordon was still alive, but his wounds severe (Sanders's File). In a later letter by Dr. Sanders he mentions that Gordon died from his wounds.

35. A family tradition states that William Jesse Keeton's brother, James, found his brother's body on the battlefield (Scarpinato, 1999). Thanks to Wanda for the photo.

36. Parker was said to have received seven wounds at Frayser's Farm (*The Alabama Beacon* [Greensboro], 26 June 1863). It looked as if he would die at first, but he

showed some signs of improvement and was moved to his uncle's home in Warrenton, North Carolina. He lingered on for some five or six months before dying on May 25, 1863.

Chapter 6

1. The date of April 29, 1863, is also given for his official commissioning (CSR).
2. Oakwood Cemetery Register.
3. Many other members of the 11th, including Col. Sydenham Moore, were buried at Hollywood Cemetery following the departure from the Darbytown Road encampment (Register of the Confederate Dead 1869, 13–115).
4. It should be noted that the Official Records give August 13, 1862, as the date for Longstreet's Wing to depart for Gordonsville (OR Series 1 Vol. 16, 552).
5. General Wilcox's account is consistently one day later than that given by General Longstreet. This continues from Kelly's Ford until they reach White Plains.
6. According to General Wilcox's memory, they had only been in their position about a half an hour (Cadmus M. Wilcox Papers).
7. Another note gives the same figure of twenty-five wounded and killed at Second Manassas (11th Alabama).
8. Sources for these include: 11th Alabama, CSR, and Sanders's File.
9. It was at General Longstreet's insistence that Anderson's Division as well as Wilcox's three brigades be attached to McLaws' command (Longstreet 1992, 202–205). In light of his assignment at Harper's Ferry, Longstreet was not satisfied with the strength of McLaws' command. It was for this reason that these changes were made.
10. Not only General Wilcox, but Maj. George Field left his command on September 11. It was on this date that Field tendered his resignation as Major, stating that he felt unfit for the duties of that position (CSR).
11. General Cobb states that the Wilcox Brigade reached him during the night after the battle (OR Series 1 Vol. 27, 870). Also, William B. Franklin's article states that Wilcox's Brigade arrived too late to take part in the engagement (BLCW Vol. 2, 595).
12. The battle line was about one and a half miles below Crampton's Gap, and it extended across the entire valley (OR Series 1 Vol. 27, 856). The Federal commander, Wm. B. Franklin, regarded it suicidal to attack the Confederate forces in this position (BLCW Vol. 2, 596).
13. His Confederate service card states he deserted to the enemy, while his muster roll states he was captured and took the oath of allegiance on September 27, 1862.
14. John was officially discharged on July 26, 1864, when he was elected 2nd Lieutenant of Co. B, 8th Alabama Cavalry.
15. Our sources included: CSR; 11th Alabama Infantry; *Confederate Veteran 1983–1912* Vol. 26, 218; Vol. 4, 51; and Confederate Service Cards.

Chapter 7

1. In a report of Major General Franz Sigel of the United States Army on October 9, he confirms that Longstreet was camped six miles out of Winchester on the Martinsburg Road (OR Series 1 Vol. 19/2, 27).
2. Carlos Knox died on October 27, 1862 (CSR).
3. Dr. Sanders recalls that the regiment arrived at Culpeper on November 2, 1862 (Dr. Sanders's Papers).
4. Both Hurst and Wilcox give November 23, 1862, as the date of arrival at Fredericksburg (Hurst 1863, 62; Cadmus M. Wilcox Papers).
5. Henry C. Cook had his right hand shattered by Federal shell (Cooke 1998).
6. In the Official Records it gives a casualty list of eight, with three killed and five wounded (OR Series 1 Vol. 21, 559).
7. General Wilcox also notes that the men slept under arms in line of battle with strong pickets out in front (Cadmus M. Wilcox Papers).
8. One newspaper notes that the brigade was exposed to the enemy's shells at Fredericksburg, although they were not engaged during the fighting (*Mobile Advertiser and Register*, 25 December 1862).
9. In his official report General Wilcox lists that 3 Federal prisoners were taken, while in another he states that eighteen prisoners were taken (Cadmus M. Wilcox Papers). Parker's narrative confirms that three prisoners were taken (Parker n.d., 50).
10. Martin is buried in the Fredericksburg Confederate Cemetery (*Fredericksburg/ Spotsylvania Civil War Cemeteries*).
11. Lemuel Kelly is buried in the Fredericksburg Confederate Cemetery (*Fredericksburg/Spotsylvania Civil War Cemeteries*).
12. McMath is buried in the Fredericksburg Confederate Cemetery (*Fredericksburg/ Spotsylvania Civil War Cemeteries*).

Chapter 9

1. In one note in the regimental files of Co. C, it mentions that a skirmish with the enemy took place on July 8 at Saint James College (11th Alabama).
2. Dr. Sanders states that the men crossed the Potomac on July 14, and encountered very little problem from the Federal forces who had made appearances several times prior (Sanders's File).
3. It will be remembered that Lieutenant Mundy was now a prisoner of war, and he would remain so for the duration of the conflict.
4. Cole was elected Jr. 2nd Lieutenant on June 9, 1863 (CSR).
5. There is a confusion of data in Co. E making it difficult to sort through who was who, especially with regard to 2nd Lieutenant. Wooten O'Neal is also listed as 2nd Sergeant in February of 1863, and only one note lists him as 2nd Lieutenant (CSR).
6. Waddell was elected Jr. 2nd Lieutenant on September 1, 1863 (CSR).
7. National Archives Microfilm Publication Number 432, 290a.
8. 11th Alabama.

Chapter 10

1. This list takes into consideration, as in our previous casualty lists, information from the Confederate Service Records as well as official reports contained in the 11th Alabama Infantry records in the Department of Archives and History in Montgomery, Alabama.
2. Gibson is listed as absent sick in his service record, but he is listed as slightly wounded in the arm at the Wilderness (*Selma Morning Reporter*, 17 June 1864).
3. William H. Barry is buried in the Oakwood Cemetery in Montgomery, Alabama.
4. He died July 8, 1864, and is probably buried in Oakwood Cemetery in Richmond, Virginia in Division G, Row C, #58, even though it is listed as G.W. Speed (Oakwood Cemetery Register).
5. We don't know which battle he was wounded in for sure. We only know it was before May 25th, 1864. In any event, it didn't keep him from continuing to fight.
6. Gray may also have been wounded in any of the battles before May 25th, 1864.
7. Hugh Horton shared this family tradition. Lieutenant Richardson was his great-great uncle.
8. Note the reference by General Harris of a private approaching him from the 10th Alabama directing him to Ramseur's right (OR Series 1 Vol. 36/1, 1091).
9. A note in Dr. Sanders's Papers asserts that General Perrin was killed early in the action, and was succeeded by Col. John C.C. Sanders, who led the brigade's continued assault on the Salient.
10. It should be noted, however, that in one note it states that General Perrin was not shot dead until just prior to reaching the works at the Salient (BLCW Vol. 4, 133).

Chapter 11

1. The day before, June 12, Henry C. White of Co. B died at Howard's Grove with typhoid fever (*Mobile Advertiser & Register*, 29 July 1864).
2. Dr. Sanders notes that Norwood was shot through the pelvis and abdomen (Dr. Sanders's Papers).
3. One member of Mahone's Brigade states that Wilcox Farm could perhaps be reached by a prolongation of Adam's Street (SHSP Vol. 18, 4).
4. Unless otherwise indicated, the information on casualties for the 11th comes from their muster rolls (CSR).
5. Major W.H. Taylor's telegram to General Field stated that the two infantry brigades left by train at 7:30 P.M. and 9:30 P.M. (Dowdey 1961, 837–838).

Chapter 12

1. It does state that Lieutenant Harkness was on a leave of indulgence dated February 3, 1865, and was still absent at least through the end of the month (CSR). There is no record in his file to definitely state if and when he may have returned to the company.
2. According to Erica Mungle Cooper on Rootsweb, May 19, 2004, Francis Brotherton married Mary Amelia Brent on February 19, 1865.
3. A brief account of the battle is also found in: *Mobile Advertiser and Register*, Nov. 8, 1864.
4. The earliest reference in Colonel Forney's muster roll of his being in command of the brigade is November 30, 1864 (CSR).
5. Robert B. Griffin was one of my ancestors. He made it home to Perry County Alabama a sick man. He didn't live long following his release from Point Lookout, Maryland. He died April 12, 1865, and was buried in Mt. Zion Cemetery in Perry County, Alabama.
6. I am not sure who this is. He is not listed on any muster roll for the 11th Alabama.
7. He is found on the muster rolls as paroled with Co. B, and his place of residence is given as Federal, South Carolina.
8. I am not sure who this is. James F. Gandy of Co. C died back in Clinton, Alabama, from wounds received at the Crater on October 15, 1864 (CSR).
9. George Allen appears in a Washington County newspaper as surrendered, but does not appear in either CSR, or Southern Historical Society Papers (*Washington County News*).
10. It should be noted that Deshazo's name doesn't appear in the CSR, nor on the Southern Historical Societies list, but it is found in a Washington County newspaper. In this light, I am including Deshazo's name with these qualifications.
11. I don't know who this soldier is, but he appears both in the CSR, and on the list given in the Southern Historical Society Papers.

Chapter 13

1. I make no claim to the complete accuracy of the information received from ancestors of those who served in the 11th Alabama.
2. The original letter is in the archives at Grevemberg House Museum, Franklin, Louisiana.

Bibliography

Books

Abrams, Ulysses Huey. *A History of Early Bibb County, Alabama, 1820–1870.* N.p.: Mattie Sandford Johnson, 1981.

Alabama Confederate Service Cards. Alabama Department of Archives and History, Montgomery.

Alabama Governor (1857–1861: A.B. Moore). Military Correspondence, 1860–1861 in SG6435. Alabama Department of Archives and History, Montgomery.

Alabama Records. Vol. 94. Compiled by Kathleen Paul Jones and Pauline Jones Gandrud, 1972.

Amann, William Frayne, ed. *Personnel of the Civil War.* 2 vols. New York: Thomas Yoselott, 1961.

Barefield, Marilyn Davis, and Carr Byron Barefield. *Pickens County, Alabama 1841–1861.* Montgomery, Alabama: Southern Historical Press, 1984.

Barney, William. *The Secessionist Impulse: Alabama and Mississippi in 1860.* Princeton: Princeton University Press, 1974.

Barton, Michael, ed. "The End of Oden's War: A Confederate Captain's Diary." *Alabama Historical Quarterly* 42 (1981): 73–98.

Black, Robert C. *The Railroads of the Confederacy.* With a new foreword by Gary W. Gallagher. Chapel Hill: The University of North Carolina Press, 1998.

Bragg, Luther. *Marengo County Families.* Vols. 1–4. Demopolis: Demopolis Public Library, n.d.

Brewer, Willis. *Alabama: Her History, Resources, War Record and Public Men.* Spartanburg, SC: Reprint Co., 1975. Original edition, Montgomery: Barrett and Brown, 1872.

Bridges, Edwin C. "Juliet Opic Hopkins & Alabama's Civil War Hospitals in Richmond, Virginia." *The Alabama Review* 53 (April 2000): 83–111.

Brownell, Harriet A. *Genealogy of the Fields of Providence, Rhode Island.* Providence: J.A. & R.A. Reid Printers, 1878.

Burrell, Charles Edward. *Prince Edward County, Virginia, From its Formation in 1753, to the Present.* Farmville: Southside Virginia Historical Press, 1997. Original Edition, Richmond: Williams Printing, 1922.

Butler, Steven R., ed. *The Eutaw Rangers in the War with Mexico: The Mexican Journal & Letters of Capt. Sydenham Moore and the Mexican War Journal of Pvt. Stephen F. Nunnalee, Company D, First Regiment of Alabama Volunteers.* Richardson: The Descendants of Mexican War Veterans, 1998.

Callahan, Marguerite Tarwater. "People and Events, 1860." In the *Sesquicentennial Broadcaster,* September 1969.

Cannan, John. *Bloody Angle: Hancock's Assault on the Mule Shoe Salient, May 12, 1864.* Cambridge: Da Capo Press, 2002.

_____. *The Spotsylvania Campaign: May 7–21, 1864.* Conshohocken, PA: Combined Books, 1997.

Clanahan, James F. *The History of Pickens County, Alabama: 1840–1920.* Carrollton: Clanahan Publications, 1964.

Clark, George. *A Glance Backward: Or Some Events in the Past History of My Life.* Houston: Press of Rein & Sons, 1914.

Compiled Records Showing Service of Military Units in Confederate Organizations. National Archives Microfilm Publications Microcopy No. M861. Roll 2, Alabama First Through Eleventh Infantry. The National Archives and Records Service, General Services Administration, Washington, 1971.

Compiled Service Records of Confederate Soldiers who Served in Organizations from the State of Alabama. National Archives Microfilm Publications Microcopy No. 311. Rolls 201–208, Eleventh Infantry. The National Archives and Records Service, General Services Administration, Washington, 1960.

Confederate Veteran, 1893–1912. Oakman: H-Bar Enterprises.

Cooke, H.C. A brief biography written by H.C. Cooke. I received this on September 28, 1998, from his great grandson, Mr. Jack Brundrett.

Crenshaw, Anderson. An unpublished 1861–1862 diary held in the Alabama Department of Archives and History, Montgomery, Alabama.

Cruikshank, George. *A History of Birmingham & its Environs.* Chicago: Lewis Publishing, 1920.

Curb, Aaron Monroe Papers. Collection in the hand of Carole A. Bazzell, Birmingham, Michigan.

Current, Richard N. *Encyclopedia of the Confederacy*. Upper Saddle River, NJ: Prentice Hall, 1995.
Davidson, Henry Damon. *Inching Along: An Autobiographical Story of the Life and Work of Henry Damon Davidson*. Nashville: National Publication, 1944.
Davis, Charles S. *The Cotton Kingdom in Alabama*. Montgomery: Alabama State Department of Archives and History, Montgomery, Alabama, 1939.
Davis, William C., and Julie Hoffman, eds. *The Confederate General*. 6 volumes. The National Historical Society, 1990–91.
Delauter, Roger U. *Winchester in the Civil War*. Lynchburg: H.E. Howard, 1992.
Denman, Clarence P. *Secessionist Movement in Alabama*. Montgomery: Alabama Department of Archives and History, 1933.
Dill, J.S. *Lest We Forget: Baptist Preachers of Yesterday that I Knew*. Nashville: Broadman Press, 1938.
Dowdey, Clifford, and Louis H. Manarin, eds. *The Wartime Papers of Robert E. Lee*. Boston: Da Capo, 1961.
DuBose, Joel C., ed. *Notable Men of Alabama: Personal and Genealogical with Portraits*. Vol. 1. Atlanta: Southern Historical Association, 1904.
Duncan, R.S. *A History of the Baptists in Missouri*. St. Louis: Scammell & Company Publishers, 1882.
11th Alabama Infantry Regimental Files. A catalog of documents containing muster rolls, regimental histories, company histories, field staff, and correspondence in Box RH 9. Alabama Department of Archives and History, Montgomery.
Ellison, Rhoda Coleman. *Bibb County, Alabama: the First Hundred Years, 1818–1918*. Tuscaloosa: University of Alabama Press, 1984.
England, Flora. *Cemetery Inscriptions for Perry County, Alabama*. N.p.: F.D. England, 1955.
Evans, Clement A., ed. *Confederate Military History Extended Edition*. Vol. 8, *Alabama*, by Joseph Wheeler. Wilmington: Broadfoot Publishing, 1987.
Fayette County Historical Society. *150 Yesteryears*. Vol. 2. January 1971.
Fleming, Walter L. *Civil War and Reconstruction in Alabama*. New York: Peter Smith, 1949. Original edition, New York: Columbia University Press, 1905.
Forney, William Henry. *William Henry Forney Papers 1865–1894*. Southern Historical Collection, The University of North Carolina.
Fox, William F. 1889. *Regimental Losses in the American Civil War 1861–1865: A Treatise on the Extent and Nature of the Mortuary Losses in the Union Regimentals, With Full and Exhaustive Statistics Compiled from the Official Records on File in the State Military Bureaus and at Washington*. Albany: Albany Publishing.
Freeman, Douglas S. *Lee: An Abridgment in One Volume*. Foreword by James M. McPherson. New York: Simon & Shuster, 1991.
_____. *Lee's Lieutenants: A Study in Command*. Vol. 1: *Manassas to Malvern Hill*. New York: Scribner Classics, 1970.
_____. *Lee's Lieutenants: A Study in Command*. Vol. 2: *Cedar Mountain to Chancellorsville*. New York: Touchstone Books, 1971.
_____. *Lee's Lieutenants: A Study in Command*. Vol. 3: *Gettysburg to Appomattox*. New York: Touchstone Books, 1972.
Furguson, Ernest B. *Not War But Murder: Cold Harbor 1864*. New York: Vintage Civil War Library, 2000.
Gallagher, Gary W. *Fighting for the Confederacy: The Personal Recollections of General Edward Porter Alexander*. Chapel Hill: The University of North Carolina Press, 1989.
Garrett, William. *Reminiscences of Public Men in Alabama for Thirty Years*. Atlanta: Plantation Publishing, 1872.
Glass, Mary Morgan. *A Goodly Heritage: Memories of Greene County*. Eutaw: Greene County Historical Society, 1977.
Greene County Alabama Records. Columbus: Blewett Company, 1980.
Gregory, G. Howard. *38th Virginia Infantry*. The Virginia Regimental Histories Series. Lynchburg: H.E. Howard, 1988.
Gresham, William B., Jr. *Southern Breezes: The Migration of a Southern Family*. N.p.: self–published, 2000.
Hamiter, John Cecil, Sr. *John Tyler Hamiter Sr. August 26, 1841–November 7, 1926. Some Ancestors, Siblings and Descendants*. Birmingham: Ebsco Media, 1993.
Harris, W. Stuart. *CSA Veterans Living in Perry County, Alabama, in 1907*. N.d. Held in the Probate Judge's Office, Perry County Courthouse, Marion, Alabama.
Hendrix, Beasey S. *Tuskaloosa's Own: A Short History and Muster Roll of Confederate Units from Tuskaloosa County, Alabama*. Tuscaloosa: Colonial Press, 1988.
Herbert, Hilary A. "Colonel Hilary A. Herbert's 'History of the Eighth Alabama Volunteer Regiment, C.S.A.'" *Alabama Historical Quarterly* 39 (1977): 5–111.
The Heritage of Bibb County, Alabama. Clanton: Heritage Publishing, & The Bibb County Heritage Book Committee, 1998.
The Heritage of Fayette County, Alabama. Clanton: Heritage Publishing, & The Fayette County Heritage Book Committee, 1999.
The Heritage of Greene County, Alabama. Clanton: Heritage Publishing Consultants, & The Greene County Historical Society, 2001.
The Heritage of Marengo, County Alabama. Clanton:

Heritage Publishing Consultants, & The Marengo County Heritage Book Committee, 2000.
The Heritage of Perry County, Alabama. Clanton: Heritage Publishing Consultants, & The Perry County Heritage Book Committee, 1999.
The Heritage of Pickens County Alabama. Clanton: Heritage Publishing Consultants, & The Pickens County Heritage Book Committee, 1999.
The History of Washington County, Alabama. Vols. 1 & 2. Washington County Historical Society, 1982.
Hodgson, Joseph. *The Cradle of the Confederacy.* Mobile: Register Publishing Company, 1876.
Honnoll Family Papers, 1861–1865. A collection of letters held in the Special Collections Department, Robert W. Woodruff Library, Emory University, Atlanta, Georgia.
Hoole, William Stanley, ed. *History of the Eighth Regiment of Alabama Volunteers (Infantry).* Confederate Regimental Series No. 10. Tuscaloosa: Confederate Publishing, 1985.
Howard, Milo B., Jr., ed. "A.B. Moore Correspondence Relating to Secession." *Alabama Historical Quarterly* 23 (1961): 1–27.
Hurst, Marshall B. *History of the Fourteenth Regiment Alabama Vols. With a List of the Names of Every Man that Ever Belonged to the Regiment.* Richmond, 1863.
Johnson, Robert U. *Battles and Leaders of the Civil War.* Vols. 1–4. Edison, NJ: Castle Books, 1985.
Johnston, General Joseph E. *Narrative of Military Operations During the Civil War.* Introduction by Frank E. Vandiver. Indiana University Press, 1959. Original edition, New York: D. Appleton, 1874.
Jones, James P., and William Warren Rogers, ed. "Montgomery as the Confederate Capital: View of a New Nation." *Alabama Historical Quarterly* 26 (1964): 1ff.
Jordan, Weymouth T. *Antebellum Alabama: Town and Country.* Tuscaloosa: University of Alabama Press, 1957.
Journal of the Congress of the Confederate States of America, 1861–1865. Vol. 1. Washington: Government Printing Office, 1904.
Junker, Betty. *Deaths, Marriages, & Confederate Soldiers, Pickens County, Alabama 1841–1931.* 1990.
Kennedy, Richard. *Richard McKinne Kennedy Papers.* Southern Historical Collection, University of North Carolina at Chapel Hill.
Kurtz, Lucy Fitzhugh, and Benny Ritter. *A Roster of Confederate Soldiers Buried in Stonewall Cemetery Winchester, Virginia.* N.d. Held in the archives of Handley Regional Library Winchester, Virginia.
Lay, Mrs. Orville. *Alabama Portraits Prior to 1870.* N.p.: Historical Society of the Colonial Dames of America in the State of Alabama, 1969.
Long, E.B., with Barbara Long. *The Civil War Day by Day: An Almanac, 1861–1865.* New York: Da Capo, 1971.
Longstreet, James. *From Manassas to Appomattox.* With an Introduction by Jeffry D. Wert. New York: Da Capo, 1992.
McClelen, Bailey George. *I Saw the Elephant: The Civil War Experiences of Bailey George McClelen, Company D, 10th Alabama Infantry Regiment.* Shippensburg, PA: Burd Street Press, 1995.
McCord, Howard F. *Cemeteries of Bibb County, Alabama, 1817–1974.* N.p.: Howard F. McCord, 1979.
McGuire, Judith W. *Diary of a Southern Refugee During the War.* New York: Arno Press, 1972.
McMath, James. An unpublished 1861–1862 diary held at the Department of Archives and History. Montgomery, Alabama.
McMillan, Malcolm C. *The Alabama Confederate Reader.* Tuscaloosa: The University of Alabama Press, 1963.
_____. *The Alabama Confederate Reader.* With an Introduction by C. Peter Ripley. Tuscaloosa: University of Alabama Press, 1992.
McPherson, James M. *The Atlas of the Civil War.* New York: Macmillan, 1994.
_____. *Battle Cry of Freedom. The Civil War Era.* New York: Ballantine Books, 1988.
Miller, Grace Lewis. "The Mobile and Ohio Railroad in Ante Bellum Times." *Alabama Historical Quarterly* 7 (1945): 37–59
Moore, Sydenham. A special collection of letters he penned from 1861 to 1862. They are held in Box 166 in the Alabama Department of Archives and History in Montgomery, Alabama.
Morris, George S., and Susan L. Foutz. *Lynchburg in the Civil War: The City, the People, the Battle.* 2nd ed. The Virginia Civil War Battles and Leaders Series. Lynchburg: H.E. Howard, 1984.
Murfee, James T. "University Cadet Corps." *Alabama Historical Quarterly* 5 (1943): 55–58.
Names of the Citizens of Mobile; A Business Directory. Vol. 5. Mobile: Henry Farrow & Company Publishers, n.d.
Napier, John H. III. "Montgomery During the Civil War." *The Alabama Review* 41 (April 1988): 103–131.
Oakwood Cemetery Register. 11th Alabama Infantry Regiment. Held at the Museum of the Confederacy in Richmond, Virginia.
The Official Military Atlas of the Civil War. Introduction by Richard Sommers. New Jersey: Gramercy Books, 1983.
Owen, Thomas M. *History of Alabama and Dictionary of Alabama Biography.* 4 vols. Chicago: S.J. Clarke Publishing, 1921.
Parker, Price. *From Alabama to Appomattox: History of the Fighting 9th Alabama, Its Soldiers and Its Generals.* Athens: Athens News Courier, 1969.
Patterson, Edmund DeWitt. *Yankee Rebel: The Civil War Journal of Edmund DeWitt Patterson.* Edited by

John G. Barrett. Biographical essay by Edmund Brooks Patterson. Chapel Hill: University of North Carolina Press, 1966.

Patton, Walter Scott, J. Glenn Little, and Luther Hill. *General Nathan Bryan Whitfield and Gaineswood*. The Alabama Historical Commission, 1972.

Pfanz, Harry W. *Gettysburg: The Second Day*. Chapel Hill: University of North Carolina Press, 1987.

Pickens County Alabama Cemetery Records. Pickens County Genealogical Society, Gordo, Alabama, 1984.

Population Schedules of the Seventh Census of the United States 1850. National Archives Microfilm Publications Microcopy No. 432. Alabama. Rolls 2, 5, 6, 10, 11, 12, 13, and 16. The National Archives and Records Service, General Services Administration, Washington, 1964

Population Schedules of the Eighth Census of the United States 1860. National Archives Microfilm Publications Microcopy No. 653. Alabama. Rolls 2, 9, 10, 15, 20, 25, and 26. The National Archives and Records Service, General Services Administration, Washington, 1967.

Population Schedules of the Tenth Census of the United States 1880. National Archives Microfilm Publications Microcopy No. T9. Texas. T9–1312. The National Archives and Records Service, General Services Administration, Washington.

Population Schedules of the Tenth Census of the United States 1880. National Archives Microfilm Publications Microcopy No. T-734. Alabama. T9–0028; T9–0013; T9–0017. The National Archives and Records Service, General Services Administration, Washington.

Population Schedules of the Tenth Census of the United States 1880. National Archives Microfilm Publications Microcopy No. T-757. Mississippi. T9–0658; T9–0643. The National Archives and Records Service, General Services Administration, Washington.

Register of the Confederate Dead Interred in Hollywood Cemetery, Richmond, Virginia. Richmond: Gary, Clemmitt & Jones Printers, 1869. Held in the Museum of the Confederacy, Richmond, Virginia.

Robertson, James I., Jr. *General A.P. Hill: The Story of a Confederate Warrior*. New York: Vintage Civil War Library, 1987.

Sanders, John C.C. Clapp Papers. W.S. Hoole Special Collections Library at the University of Alabama, Tuscaloosa.

Sanders, Dr. William H. *Dr. William H. Sanders Papers*. Alabama Department of Archives and History, Montgomery.

Saunders, James Edmonds. *Early Settlers of Alabama*. Baltimore: Genealogical Publishing, 1969.

_____, ed. "Sketch of Wilcox's Brigade. By Gen. Cadmus Marcellus Wilcox." *Publications of the Alabama Historical Society* 3: 133–141.

Sifakis, Stewart. *Compendium of the Confederate Armies: Alabama*. New York: Facts on File, 1992.

Smith, Edmund Kirby. *Edmund Kirby-Smith Papers, 1776–1906*. University of North Carolina at Chapel Hill Library

The Southern Historical Society Papers in 52 Volumes. Indianapolis: Guild Press of Indiana, 1998

Spell, T.R. *Pages from History and the Men from Pickens County Who Wore the Gray*, n.d. Held in the Hoole Special Collections at the University of Alabama. Gordo: Herbert L. Greer.

Supplement to the Official Records of the Union and Confederate Armies. 51 vols. Wilmington, DE: Broadfoot Publishing, 1994–1997.

Talbird, Henry. A Biography on the Life of Henry Talbird, n.d. Held at the Partee Center for Baptist Historical Studies at William Jewell College, Liberty, Missouri.

Thompson, Fleming W. *Fleming W. Thompson Letters*. The Center for American History at the University of Texas at Austin.

Towns in Marengo County Alabama. Folders I & II. Held in the Marengo County Library.

Velma and Stephens G. Croom Collection. Held in the University of South Alabama Archives, Mobile, Alabama.

Waitt, Robert W., Jr. *Confederate Military Hospitals in Richmond*. Richmond Independence Bicentennial Commission Reprint. Richmond: Eastern National, 1979.

Walker, Mary Tucker. *Marengo County, Alabama: Some Early Families*. Wolfe City, TX: Henington Publishing, 1993.

The War of the Rebellion: A Compilation of the Official Records of the Union and Confederate Armies. Series I, Vols. 1–2. Washington: Government Printing Office, 1880.

The War of the Rebellion: A Compilation of the Official Records of the Union and Confederate Armies. Series I, Vols. 51–53. Washington: Government Printing Office, 1898.

The War of the Rebellion: A Compilation of the Official Records of the Union and Confederate Armies. Series IV, Vol. 1. Washington: Government Printing Office, 1900.

The War of the Rebellion: A Compilation of the Official Records of the Union and Confederate Armies. The Civil War CD–ROM. Indianapolis: Guild Press of Indiana, 1996.

Washington County Alabama Pension Records Civil War Veterans. n.d. Held in the Washington County Public Library in Chatom, Alabama.

Washington County Historical Society Fall Newsletter. Vol. 2, 1981. Held in the Washington County Public Library in Chatom, Alabama.

Washington County Historical Society Summer Quarterly. Vol. 12, 1992.

Washington County Historical Society Summer and Fall Quarterly. Vol. 13, 1993.

Washington County News. n.d. Held in the Washington County Public Library in Chatom, Alabama.

Wilcox, Cadmus M. Papers. A large collection of military correspondence cataloging his activities while in the Army of Northern Virginia. Held in the Library of Congress Manuscript Division in Washington, D.C.

Williford, Joseph G. Letter. 1862. Held at the US Army Military History Institute Carlisle Barracks, Carlisle, Pennsylvania.

Wilson, Gary, ed. "The Diary of John S. Tucker: Confederate Soldiers from Alabama." *Alabama Historical Quarterly* 43 (1981): 5–33.

Withers, John. "One Year of the War: Civil War Diary of John Withers, Assistant–Adjutant–General of the Confederate Army." *Alabama Historical Quarterly* 29 (1967): 133–184.

Witherspoon, John W. "Chronicles of the Canebrake." *Alabama Historical Quarterly* 9 (Winter 1947): 475–613.

Wood, Wayne, and Mary Virginia Jackson, eds. *Kiss Sweet Little Lillah for Me: Civil War Letters of William Thomas Jackson, Company A, Eighth Alabama Infantry Regiment*. Birmingham: Ebsco Media, 2000.

Letters

Arinder, William P. A letter received on March 15, 2001.
Bazzell, Carole A. A letter received on January 12, 1999.
Ethridge, Carl. A letter received in June of 2000.
Gresham, William B. A letter received on January 18, 2001.
Harrison, Thomas. A letter received on June 21, 2001.
Kasten, Lawrence. A letter received on March 5, 2001.
Kelly, Herschel. A letter received on April 14, 2000.
Luke, Margie. A letter received on January 8, 2001.
McCown, Leonard J. A letter received on November 30, 2002.
Shaddix, Mitcheline. A letter received on February 3, 2004.
Shamblin, Harold. A letter received on December 5, 2000.
Standifer, Jeff. A letter received on April 30, 1999.
Strawbridge, Robert. *The Hughes Family History*.
Wilkerson, Carol Yates. A letter received on December 19, 1999.
Wilson, Baz. A letter received on March 9, 2001.

Newspapers

Alabama Beacon. 1860: 28 September; 30 November; 1861: 22 February; 12, 19, 26 April; 10, 24 May; 7, 21 June; 5 July. 30 August; 20 September; 11 October; 1862: 17 January; 13 June; 4, 18, 20 July; 1863: 27 February; 26 June; 1865: 17 February.
Alabama Whig. 1861: 14 February.
Clark County Democrat. 1861: 2 May; 27 June; 4 July.
Daily Richmond Inquirer. 1861: 1, 31 July; 4, 8, 10 October.
Demopolis Express. 1897: 14 January.
Eutaw Whig. 1893: 24 May.
Independent Monitor. 1859: 26 November; 10 December; 1860: 7 January; 1861: 1 February; 5 April; 1, 10, 31 May.
Linden Jeffersonian. 1859: 17 May; 1860: 6 June.
Mobile Advertiser and Register. 1861: 21 June; 14, 20 July; 10 October; 1862: 10 June; 9 July; 25 December; 1863: 23 April; November 13; 1864: 1, 17 June; 29 July; 3, 21 August; 1, 13 September; 8 November.
Mobile Daily Advertiser & Register. 1867: 12 January.
Mobile Daily Tribune. 1864: 12 August.
Mobile Evening News. 1863: 10 September; 1864: 2 August; 5 September.
Mobile Press Register. 1863: 23 April; 1934: 13 May; 18 June.
Montgomery Daily Advertiser. 1866: 25 September.
Montgomery Weekly Advertiser. 1862: 3 December; 1864: 15 June; 19 July.
Pickens Republican. 1861: 25 April; 30 May; 3 October.
Richmond Daily Dispatch. 1861: 14, 17, 28 August; 15 November; 6 December.
Richmond Daily Whig. 1861: 1 November.
Richmond Enquirer. 1864: 31 August.
Richmond Examiner. 1861: 7 September.
Selma Morning Reporter. 1864: 7, 17 June.
West Alabamian. 1860: 8 February; 21 March; 18 July; 22 August; 26 September; 28 November; 12 December; 1861: 6, 22 February; 27 March; 15 May; 5 June; 23, 28 August.
Whig & Observer. 1865: 9 February.

Descendants' Emails

(*In three instances, last names were omitted by request*)

Allen, Carol. February 22, 2004.
Almond, Phyliss. January 19, 2001.
Amann, Luisa and Michael. November 10, 2002.
Anderson, Novella. October 28, 2002.
Arnold, Wallace. July 7, 2004.
Barnett, Martha. January 21, 2004.
Barton, Joe. November 20, 2003.
Baumgardner, Jim. May 3, 2004.
Bazzell, Carol A. January 8, 1999.
Benjamin, A.J. January 9, 2004.
Betty. January 22, 2004.
Brewer, Abney H. December 1, 2001.
Brock, Peggy. April 4, 2000.
Brown, Linda. November 3, 2004.

Butler, Margie. January 6, 2004.
Butler, Marsha. April 6, 2001.
Calvit, Benny. February 9, 2000.
Chappius, Buffie. February 24, 2000.
Clark, Bill. January 12, 2004.
Colburn, Archie. 1999.
Comiskey, Lynn. September 1999.
Copeland, Helen. February 28, 2001.
Crenshaw, Annie. January 13, 2001.
Cuthriell, Jeanette. November 10, 2003.
David. February 16, 2004.
Farrington, Arthur A. November 21, 2002.
Frances, Mary. February 7, 2004.
Gallant, LaNelle. May 17, 2000.
Glass, Mike. July 5, 2000.
Goy, Kathryn. January 28, 1999.
Graham, Cheryl. August 16, 2000.
Guthrie, Ed. August 22, 1999.
Henry, Judy. January 10, 2004.
Hines, Kathryn Harris. October 12, 2003.
Hogan, Charles. July 21, 2000.
Hopkins, Adrianne, and Patsy Hunsucker. March 7, 2000.
Horton, Hugh. February 17, 2000.
Jean, Mary. February 8, 2004.
Jones, Billy. July 2000.
Leach, Doris McClinton. July 31, 2000.
Lomax, John B. December 26, 2000.
Marler, Shan. February 4, 2004.
Marstaller, Katherine. July 16, 2000.
May, Ken. January 1, 2004.
McCraw, Carol J. January 31, 2004.
McKinney, Veneta. October 8, 2004.
Mitchell, Harvey. April 16, 2000.
Mobley, Carl. July 11, 2000.
Oakley, Stanthia. February 25, 2001.
Orlando, Michelle Moreland. December 27, 2002.
Owens, Scott. February of 2001.
Patterson, Donna J. December 30, 2001.
Pegues, Euwyn. December 28, 2000.
Pettit, Jacquelyn O. March 1, 2000.
Phillips, Marla. October 28, 2003; April 5, 2004; and July 22, 2004.
Powell, Ron. September 9, 2000.
Rawls, Bobby. January 2, 2001.
Rembert, Franklin C. January 1, 2001.
Roberts, Jan. March 31, 2000.
Scarpinato, Wanda. February 16, 1999.
Schwab, Mary. May 24, 1999.
Simmons, Temple Q. December 16, 2003.
Snyder, Jonathan. April 9, 2000.
Stone, Jon. December 3, 1999.
Stroud, Glen. April 7, 2001.
Teresa. June 1, 2004.
Thomson, Jeff. February 19, 1999.
Weiss, M.J. February 26, 2006.
Whisenant, Theresa. February 8, 2001.
Williams, Charlotte. 2005. January 5, 2005.
Williamson, Eva Avery. October 30, 2004.
Worsham, Raleigh. February 9, 2001.

Internet Sources

Allison, Jan. 2004. *Families in the Deep South*. Rootsweb.
Bransby, Teresa. 2003. Information on John W. Shelton family. Rootsweb.
Camp Letterman History: July 1863. Preservation Project. Internet.
Confederate Hill. An Historic Background of Confederate Hill with a Roster of those Interred there. Internet.
Cooper, Erica Mungle. 2004. *L & L's Family Tree*. Rootsweb.
Fayette Banner. n.d. Fayette County Alabama GenForum message #196.
Fredericksburg/Spotsylvania Civil War Cemeteries. Soldiers from Alabama. Genealogy.com.
Harris, Lemuel. 1861–1864. A Collection of Letters in the hands of Monya Havekost. Musgrove Letters on the Marion County Alabama GenWeb Project.
Hester, Greg & Chare. 2000. *Old Hepzibah Cemetery*. Alabama GenWeb.
Johnson, Kathy DeFord. n.d. *User Home Page Outline Descendant Tree: Johnson Homepage*. FamilyTreeMaker.
Johnson's Island Prison 1862–1865. Article on Johnson's Island Prison found on the Internet. www.fred.net/stevent/JOHNSONS_ISLAND
Marengo County Marriages. Alabama GenWeb.
Mungo, Mary Clyde Reid. 2001. *User Home Page Outline Descendant Tree: Descendants of George Reid*. FamilyTreeMaker.
Norris, Jesse L. *Descendants of Thomas Hamilton*. FamilyTreeMaker.
Poe, William. 2004. Information on Wiley Nall on Rootsweb, February 26, 2004.
Snyder, Jonathan. 2000. *User Home Page Outline Descendant Tree: Descendants of Joseph McMath*. FamilyTreeMaker.
Underwood, Georgiana P. ed. *The Charles Wesley Foust Letters*. Internet.
Washington County Alabama. Alabama GenWeb Project.
Weaver, Jeff. *Virginia's Confederate Military Hospitals*. The Virginia Civil War Home Page on the Internet.
Wood, Carol. 2002. *Cemeteries*. Marengo County Alabama. Alabama GenWeb.
_____. 2004. *Marriage Records Marengo County Alabama*. Alabama GenWeb.

Index

Abercrumbie 242
Abernathy, Martha E.J. 234
Abilene 252
Abney, Evelyn 212
Abney, Samuel 240
Abney, Thomas H. 240
Abney, Zachariah 23, 116, 133, 144, 164, 212, 226, 240
Abrams, Josh 247
Accotink Creek 76
Acker, Joseph P. 30, 122, 245
Acker, Samuel M. 30, 158
Ackerman 248
Adams, Charles J. 9, 95, 230
Adams, Elisha B. 9
Adams, Jackson 27
Adams, James H. 15–16, 133
Adams, James H.E. 9, 100
Adams, John C. 30, 215, 226, 245
Adams, John H. 9, 115, 126, 143, 164, 210, 216, 226, 230
Adams, Thomas J. 9, 89
Adams, W.L. 28
Adams, William M. 26, 106
Adcock, Francis M. 26, 259
Adcock, Joseph 26, 113
Adison 257
Ainsworth, Levin 22, 84
Alabama and Mississippi Railroad 39
Alabama and Tennessee Railroad 38, 44
Alabama Hospital 130
Alabama Soldier's Home 220
Aldridge, Prince W. 32, 157, 250
Alexander, Abney W. 23, 112, 126
Alexander, E. Porter 52, 93
Aliceville 249
Allen, George 22, 226, 259, 262
Allen, Green M. 26, 116
Allen, James F. 14, 105
Allen, James H. 30, 192, 226
Allen, John A. 164
Allen, Josiah A. 29–30
Allen, Richard 157
Allen, Robert E. 9, 215, 226, 230
Allen, William D. 193, 246
Allman, John S. 87
Alpine 237
Alvis, Elijah T. 20, 84
Amelia Court House 221–222
Anders, Ezekiel M. 26
Anderson, Richard H. 123, 125, 130, 136, 168, 171, 175, 179, 186–187

Anderson, Thomas C. 20, 144, 226
Anderson, Warren A. 20, 106
Annandale 76, 82
Anniston 242
Anthony, A.O. 250
Anthony, Asa 164, 226, 250
Anthony, C.B. 250
Anthony, D.J. 250
Anthony, James W. 32, 144
Anthony, M.A. 250
Anthony, Pink 250
Anthony, W.S. 250
Antioch 257
Antioch Church 119
Appomattox Court House 225–227
Arbor Springs Church Cemetery 249
Archer 244
Archibald, Robert N. 15, 105
Arinder, William P. 255
Armstrong's Mill 214
Arnold, Elbert 23, 2263
Arnold, Martha Jane 255
Asbury 258
Ashe, Egbert B. 22, 133, 158, 164
Ashe, Ruffin Y. 20, 50, 115, 195, 210
Ashe, William C. 20, 50, 70, 72, 82, 85, 94, 101, 229
Ashworth, Marion B. 144
Ashworth, William T. 26, 106, 192
Askew, Hillard J.I. 20, 157, 211, 216–217, 226
Askew, Thomas W. 20, 106
Atchison, Daniel M. 239
Atchison, Fannie 239
Atchison, Glovie 239
Atchison, Harry 239
Atchison, Hattie 239
Atchison, Henry C. 22, 191, 239
Atchison, Henry L. 22, 144
Atchison, John W. 22, 116, 133, 164
Atchison, Joseph 239
Atchison, Leona 239
Atchison, Woodie 239
Atlanta 41–42
Atlanta and West Point Railroad 41
Atlee's Farm 108, 115, 118
Atlee's Station, Battle 186–187
Austin, John 88, 106
Austin, William A. 34, 204, 220
Avery, Arthur W. 23, 224, 240
Avery, Henry W. 23, 106, 240
Avery, Thomas N. 14, 105, 158

Baer, Frances 254
Bagwell, Larkin 87, 224
Bailey, Franklin L. 20
Bailey, Richard 34, 258
Baines, John B. 16, 62, 105
Baker, John W. 22, 85, 89
Baker, Newell 34, 70
Baldwin 249
Baldwin, Albert 16, 226, 259
Ballard, David A. 30, 106, 158
Ballard, Thomas B. 34, 107, 226, 253
Ballard, Thomas J. 30, 158, 160, 259
Baltimore 159, 249
Banks, Kindred P. 14, 112
Bank's Ford 136–137, 143
Bankston 251
Barber, Richard J. 26, 89
Barber, Stephen D. 26, 106, 157, 226
Barclay, Fanny 23
Bareford, William H. 178
Barge, John J. 34, 74
Barhamsville 95
Barksdale, William 143
Barlow, Francis C. 180, 188, 190–192
Barnes, Martin V. 23, 144, 224, 258
Barnes, McKindie 22
Barnett, Allen 88
Barnett, Elizabeth Jane 234
Barnett's Ford 162
Barr, Andrew W. 20, 100, 157, 226, 236
Barr, Robert T. 236
Barry, William H. 26, 177–178, 243, 262
Bartlett, Shubal Henry 20, 84, 237
Barton, Ralph A. 20, 100, 237
Barton, Richard 23, 224–225, 240
Bartow 251
Baskin, Isabella Reid 25
Baskin, Moses H. 16, 62, 105, 131–132
Bassett, Thomas E. 22
Bayou Teche 238
Beard, Mary 253
Beasley, Barzella 9, 157, 160
Beauregard, Pierre Gustave Toutant 59, 65, 78, 189
Beavoir Confederate Cemetery 250
Bedford 251
Bell 243
Bell, Benjamin F. 29–30, 226, 246–247

Index

Bell, John F. 32, 113
Bell, Joseph N. 29–30, 113, 192, 226, 246
Bell, Stephen E. 31–32, 66, 71, 79, 85, 113, 116
Bell, Thomas J. 87
Bell, Valerie 246
Belton 254
Benjamin, J.P. 11
Bennet, David A. 26, 166
Bennet, Henry H. 26, 243
Bennet, Nancy 243
Bennett, Adam F. 29–30, 74
Benson 257
Berdan, Hiram 151
Berlin 236
Berryville 148
Bethany Cemetery 249
Bethea, Cato 22, 112, 239
Bethel Methodist Cemetery 244
Bethesda Cemetery 251
Bethlehem 256
Bethsaida Cemetery 246
Beulah Baptist Cemetery 236
Bevill, Pharis 14, 226
Bibb, William H. 15–16, 112
Bibb Greys 23–24, 37, 41, 43–44, 100, 114, 226–227, 260
Biesecker's Woods 151
Biloxi 250
Bird, William P. 14, 84, 183
Bird, Winfield S. 14, 110, 112, 128, 133, 164, 204
Birmingham 235, 250
Birney, David B. 190
Black, Frank H. 30, 106, 247
Black, Lula 247
Black, Robert L. 247
Black, Sallie 247
Black, Samuel A. 32, 60, 106, 213, 226
Black, Samuel W. 247
Black Horse Tavern 150
Blackburn's Pond 75
Blackwell, John T. 9, 112, 226
Bladon Springs 21, 257
Blakeney, John 226
Blandford Church Cemetery 197
Block House Bridge 180
Blocton 245
Blunt, Edward D. 20, 213
Blunt, James Walter 19–20, 100
Bocock, W.R. 39
Boddie, Arabella Chloe Anne Elizabeth 237
Bogue Chitto Cemetery 255
Boligee 14, 235
Bolton, Charles Manley 250
Bolton, Elbert F. 32, 170, 250
Bolton, Emily Isobel 250
Bolton, George Washington 250
Bolton, Ida Lee 250
Bolton, Joseph A. 32, 204
Bolton, Marion Elbert 250
Bolton, Marshall C. 32, 81
Bolton, Permelia Jane 250
Bolton, Thomas Marshall 250
Booker's Tobacco Warehouse 51
Boonsborough 148

Boothe, J.A. 28
Boozer, John 67, 140, 226, 257
Boozer, William H.H. 67, 126, 140, 202, 257
Bostick, Andrew J. 30, 144, 146, 157
Bostick, Joshua D. 87, 112
Bounds, James 126, 226
Bowie County 234
Bowling, William R. 23
Boydton Plank Road 194, 214
Braddock Road 76
Bradley, James 20
Bradley, Mattie 232
Brady, James 67, 257
Brady, John W. 164, 226
Brame, Henry, Jr. 9, 100, 157, 202, 226
Brandy Station 119, 162, 168
Brannon, Simeon 226
Bransby, Teresa 252
Brantley, Robert J. 22, 84
Brassfield, James D. 14, 70
Braswell, Elias 9, 158
Bratton, William M. 13–14, 112, 259–260
Brazell, Green Washington 23, 69, 72
Brazelton, James L. 34, 116, 134, 145, 164, 193
Brazelton, William W. 34, 101, 188, 204, 226
Breathwait, James 15–16, 105, 235
Breckenridge, Ebenezer 67, 72, 257
Breckenridge, Jefferson 9
Breckenridge, John C. 187–188
Breckenridge, Sarah 231–232
Brent, Frances 252
Brent, John H. 26, 178
Breton, L.A. 19
Brett, Calvin 14, 112, 233
Brewer, George W. 26, 100, 243
Brewer, John G. 34
Brewer, Willis 4–5
Brice, Patrick 34, 113, 158
Bridgeville 6, 257
Bristoe Station 69–73, 167–168, 259
Bristol 41–42
Britt, Joseph R. 26, 106, 133, 144, 164, 208, 212
Broad Run 70
Brock Road 177, 181
Bronson, John 89
Brooks, William M. 7, 133
Brooksville 38, 45
Brookwood 244
Brotherton, Ada 250
Brotherton, Clyde B. 250
Brotherton, Ethel 250
Brotherton, Francis A. 32, 106, 144, 213, 216, 250, 262
Brotherton, Irma A. 250
Brotherton, John A. 250
Brotherton, Mary 250
Brown, Albert 9, 213
Brown, Alice 240
Brown, Amos 240
Brown, David 23, 122, 213, 226
Brown, David L. 23, 89, 240
Brown, James S. 87, 235

Brown, Jesse 226
Brown, Joseph E. 7
Brown, Lillie 240
Brown, Margaret 240
Brown, Richard 87
Brown, Richard M. 23, 106, 157, 258
Brown, Sallie 240
Brown, Samuel G. 26, 157
Brown, Searcy P. 26, 113
Brown, William H. 87, 100, 187
Brown, William L. 34, 253
Brown, William W. 23, 126, 157, 240
Brown Graveyard 240
Browne, Cornelia 233
Browne, Phreaudius P. 233
Browne, Samuel B. 87, 112, 233
Brownlee, Grace Ann 250
Brownlow, William G. 43
Brownsville Gap 123–124
Bruce, Henry L. 9, 60, 62, 157, 215, 230
Brunson/Bronson, John 22
Bryant, Henry 20
Bryant, William 87
Bryant, William T. 30, 106
Bryce Hospital 240
Bryson, F.A.V. 243
Bryson, G.W. 243
Bryson, George W. 26, 113, 158
Bryson, Joseph D. 26, 113, 178, 243
Bulloch, Charles H. 15–16, 144, 157, 217, 235, 257
Bulloch, James R. 9
Bunker Hill 58, 127, 162
Burchfield, Alma Margaret 243
Burchfield, Daniel A. 243
Burchfield, Elizabeth 243
Burchfield, Ella Doveyelier 243
Burchfield, Estrella 243
Burchfield, Felix Marion 243
Burchfield, John T. 87, 158, 204, 221, 243–244
Burchfield, Nancy Mary Jane 243
Burchfield, Octavia Louise 243
Burchfield, Sallie M. 243
Burgess, David 29–30, 84, 247
Burgess Mill, Battle 212–215
Burgess Tavern 214
Burgey, William 19–20, 258
Burk, Thomas 34
Burke's Station 82
Burkeville 52, 194, 222–223
Burkittsville 123
Burns, James G. 26
Burnside, Ambrose E. 187
Burrage, Andrew 165, 204
Burrage, James R. 26, 113, 259
Burris, Charles E. 250
Burris, Frank 250
Burris, John B. 32, 139, 146, 250
Burris, Leila E. 250
Burris, Robert Claude 250
Burton, Albert C. 26, 113, 139, 146
Burton, Jesse L. 20, 106, 207
Burwell Morgan Mill 60–61
Bush, Boaz W. 9, 71

Cabe, Henry C. 20, 106, 186, 226
Caddelle, Benjamin F. 23, 72

Index

Caddelle, Joseph C. 23, 116, 133, 164, 202, 212, 215
Cade, John C. 87
Caffee, Jane 242
Caffee Cemetery 242
Cahaba 46
Cahaba Marion and Greensboro Railroad 46
Calhoun Guards 29–30, 257
Cameron, James F. 16, 62, 112, 157, 235
Cameron, William Love 235
Camp Clay 52
Camp Letterman General Hospital 160
Campbell, Constantine J. 26, 72, 113, 144, 157
Campbell, Green H. 26, 72
Campbell, R.M. 18
Campbell, Robert 23, 106
Campground Cemetery 232
Canebrake Legion 17–20, 36, 39–41, 43, 54, 100, 114, 211, 226–227, 260
Carlowville 256
Carnes, John W. 15–16, 112, 202
Carpenter, William B. 16, 74
Carrington, Washington L. 22
Carroll, John, Jr. 87, 106
Carroll, John, Sr. 87
Carroll, Robert C. 26, 72, 113
Carroll, Robert S. 26
Carrollton 6, 27, 29–30, 235, 245–249, 258
Carrollton Cemetery 247, 249
Carrollton Guards 27–30
Carson, James 30, 89
Carson, Milton J. 23, 100
Carson, Thomas G. 30, 247
Carter, Dewitt C.C. 19–20, 112, 226
Carter, John J. 9, 112, 202
Carter, Samuel D. 9, 112
Carter, Townsend D. 34
Casey, Peter 34, 107
Casey's Redoubts 98
Cashtown 149
Castles, Marietta 249
Cates, Didimiah 242
Catharpin Road 169, 175
Cathey, John W. 19–20
Cathey, Thomas K. 87, 106, 138, 146, 226
Caulfield, Henry P. 14, 71, 105
Caulfield, William J. 87
Cedar Farm Bridge 185
Cemetery Ridge 153–154
Centreville, Alabama 23, 37–38, 43–43, 45, 133, 240–243, 259
Centreville Camp 74–77
Centreville Memorial Cemetery 133, 241–243
Centreville, Virginia 74, 78, 80, 90
Chaffin's Bluff 189
Chamberlain, Lawrence 225
Chambers, David B. 30
Chambers, Erastus A. 16, 122, 188, 209
Chambersburg 148–149
Chambersburg Pike 149
Champion, Henry 87

Chancellorsville 136–137, 143, 145, 147
Chantilly 122
Chapman, Benjamin J. 19–20, 89
Chapman, Mary Lucinda 30
Chapman, Oliver D. 87, 157
Chapman, Reuben 30
Chapman, Reuben, Jr. 27–28, 30, 54, 101, 116, 247
Chapman, Samuel 30
Charles City Road 96–97, 107
Chattanooga 41, 254
Cherokee and Indian War 4
Chester Gap 128
Chesterfield County 7
Chesterfield Court House 222
Chickahominy River 95, 101–102, 108
Childers, Thomas S.C. 16, 105, 144, 259
Childers, William H. 16
Childress, James T. 26
Childress, William M. 23, 100, 226
Chimborazo Hospital 80, 147, 259
Chinn House 121
Chipman, William M. 16, 75
Chism, James D. 23, 94, 259
Christenberry, Fannie 254
Christian, H. 19
Christian County 231
Church, John T. 87, 204, 253
Church Family Cemetery 253
Citronelle 257
City Point 91, 202
Clanton, David C. 250–251
Clanton, Jesse 164, 250
Clanton, Sterling D. 32, 113, 215, 226, 250
Clark, Bill 247
Clark, George W. 13–14, 35–36, 42, 48, 64, 68, 70, 76, 85–86, 94–95, 97–98, 102–105, 115, 131–132, 135–136, 138, 140, 142–143, 150, 152–156, 158, 161–162, 164, 167–170, 176–178, 181–183, 186–187, 192, 194–195, 199, 201, 205–208, 211, 217, 222, 233, 259–260
Clark, James Blair 233
Clark, Joseph P. 14, 50, 105
Clark, Mary 233
Clark, Thomas H. 26, 72, 139, 146, 157–158, 224
Clark, Virgil J. 26, 84
Clark, William C. 237
Clay, C.C. 79
Clay, H.L. 49
Clay, Suzanne Dupre 235
Clay Hill 257
Clayton 257
Cleland, James H. 9, 60, 62
Clements, John 22, 81
Clinton 15, 16, 38, 73, 79, 168, 207, 235–236, 257, 262
Clio 9
Clippard, James C. 32
Clopton, David 171
Cloverdale 17
Coats, John R. 9, 105, 126
Cobb, Howell 124, 261

Cochran, John W. 34, 122, 158
Cochrane, David L. 226
Coffeeville 21
Coffey's First Alabama Volunteers 216
Cohen, Lonzo B. 27, 30, 101, 113
Cohen, T.J. 28
Colburn, David W. 34, 139, 146, 254
Colburn, George W. 254
Colburn, Howard 254
Colburn, Ida Belle 254
Colburn, John Thomas 254
Colburn, Joseph Francis 254
Colburn, Judson E. 254
Colburn, Maritte 254
Colburn, Nancy 254
Colburn, Rachel 254
Colburn, Sarah Elizabeth 254
Colburn, Susie 254
Cold Harbor 188
Coldwater 242
Cole, John W. 19–20, 164, 202, 261
Cole, William M. 26, 113, 144, 158, 226, 244
Coleman, Daniel Walter 22, 187
Coleman, Donna 251
Coleman, Eliza 251
Coleman, James 251
Coleman, Jane 251
Coleman, Joseph K. 251
Coleman, Moses J. 32, 251
Coleman, Pearl 251
Coleman, Sallie Neal 236
Coleman, Sarah 251
Coleman, Wiley J. 16, 178
Coleman, William 251
Collet, M.W. 141
Collins, Alice 251
Collins, Alonz 251
Collins, Arlando 251
Collins, Eller 251
Collins, George J. 32, 144, 179, 251
Collins, John D. 19–20
Collins, John R. 14, 75, 257
Collins, Josiah, Jr. 15–16, 105
Collins, Leander 251
Collins, Nancy 251
Collins, P. 19
Collins, Roca 251
Colston, R.E. 97
Columbia 7
Columbus 38, 45, 236, 247, 249–250, 252
Colvin, Thomas B. 16, 89
Comiskey, Lynn 244
Compton, Edgar 237
Compton, H.C. 237
Compton, Joseph L. 19–20, 100
Compton, William H. 20, 100, 237
Confederate Congress 86
Confederate Guards 14–16, 38, 41–42, 49, 71, 73, 114, 211, 226–227
Confederate Soldiers Home 240, 245, 255
Connor, Henry 20
Cook, Henry Clay 34, 125, 131, 254, 261
Cook, Jacob J. 113, 158
Cook, James B. 34, 107, 193

Cook, James J. 107, 192
Cook, M.F. 27
Cooksville 236
Cooper, Charles 87, 112, 144, 157
Coos County 232
Cope, William L. 87, 96
Copp, John 87, 95
Corinth Cemetery 244
Corley, Arthur 67, 95, 230, 257, 259
Corley, Daniel N. 23, 106, 144, 147
Corley, David M. 23, 89
Cottles, Isaac L. 30, 84, 259
Couch, William E. 34
Cox, Alfred B. 30, 213, 247
Cox, David C. 26, 226
Cox, William S. 26, 84
Craig, George 30, 106, 183
Crampton's Gap 124, 261
Cranford, William J. 32, 226
Crater, Battle 195–202
Crawford, Anderson S. 87, 100, 230
Crawford, George J. 9, 112
Crawford, Lucius W. 9, 188
Crawford, Robert N. 14, 156–157, 257
Crawford, Samuel W. 214
Crawfordsville 258
Crenshaw, Anderson 14, 51–52, 55, 61, 63–64–66, 68, 70–71, 73–76, 79, 81, 83–84, 86, 95, 233, 257–258
Crews, Elias 158
Crews, James M. 34, 72
Crews Depot 250
Cribbs, Daniel J. 32, 113, 135, 157, 160
Cribbs, Henry C. 32, 113, 166, 168, 173, 187, 226, 251
Cribbs, Nancy 251
Crittendon County 5
Croom, Stephens 14, 52, 58, 60, 66, 79, 83, 88, 91, 233, 258, 260
Crosby Cemetery 240
Cross, James F. 15–16, 116, 126, 128, 235, 259
Crossroads Cemetery 246, 248
Crossville 258
Crowell, John 27
Cub Run Camp 77–81
Cullin, John 14, 121, 138, 226
Culpeper Court House 69–70, 91, 128, 130, 147–148, 162, 168, 261
Cumberland Church 223–224
Cumming, Alfred 124–125
Curb, Aaron M. 34, 71, 145, 203–204, 220, 254
Curb, Beata 254
Curb, Charles McLeod 254
Curb, Daniel Napoleon 254
Curb, Edward Andrew 254
Curb, Ella Josephine 254
Curb, Emma Geneva 254
Curb, Etta Martha 254
Curb, Irene 254
Curb, Margaret Lena 254
Curb, Mary Viola 254
Curb, Napoleon B. 34, 100, 254
Curb, Oscar Monroe 254
Curb, Pickney Walter 254

Curb, William Abner 254
Curb, Williford 158, 179, 192, 226
Cureton, David A. 34, 145
Curry, John D. 22, 224, 239
Curry, John M. 28
Curry, R.H. 27, 29

Dabney Mill Road 215
Dabney's Mill 218
Dallas Hall 46
Dalton 42, 48
Daniel, Jesse W. 9, 75
Daniel, Nathan 67, 257
Danville Railroad 194
Darbytown Road 108, 115, 117, 203
Darr, Anna 251
Darr, G. Joseph 251
Darr, Hattie 251
Darr, James A. 32, 144, 251
Darr, James M. 25
Darr, Nancy E. 251
Darr, Robert E. 251
Darr, Ruffus L. 251
Davidson, Annie 241
Davidson, Dora 241
Davidson, Ella 241
Davidson, Fannie 241
Davidson, Frances Stringfellow 23
Davidson, Ida 241
Davidson, James 241
Davidson, James L. 23, 54, 94, 101, 240, 259
Davidson, Margaret 241
Davidson, Samuel W. 23
Davidson, Samuel W., Jr. 23, 241
Davis, Calvin 22, 72
Davis, Henry 23, 100, 157, 191
Davis, James M. 31, 106, 117, 143–144
Davis, Jefferson 3, 6, 48, 71, 78, 102, 118–119, 169, 171
Davis, John M. 23, 100
Davis, Robert P. 29, 31, 117
Davis, William A. 29, 31, 106, 139, 157, 183, 208
Davis, William H. 28
Davis, William T. 32, 85, 133, 164, 209, 213, 216
Davis Farm, Battle 205–208, 213
Dayton 20, 40, 237–239, 257
Dayton Female Academy 257
Deale, Edward B. 14, 72
Deans, John W. 19–20, 106, 226
Decker's House 136
Deep Bottom 202–205
Delaware, Ft. 146–147, 159, 165, 170, 231
Demopolis 17, 20, 36, 39, 172, 237–238
Denton 249
Deport 254
Depot Road 208
Derby, Andrew J. 14, 71, 89
Deshazo, James M. 22, 89
Deshazo, William R. 22, 204, 226, 262
Devoy, James 60, 62, 84, 257
Dew, Duncan, Jr. 12
Dew, Duncan, Sr. 12

Dexter, Charles P. 12
DeYampert, T.J.L. 19
Diascund Bridge 95
Dick, Mary 232
Dickens, Francis A. Sr. 76
Dickinson's Mill 184
Didlake, George A. 34, 126
Digby, David Franklin 241
Digby, George Calvin 241
Digby, Henry Allen 241
Digby, James Russell 241
Digby, John G. 241
Digby, John H. 23, 106, 157, 226, 241
Digby, John Thomas 241
Digby, Milford Howard 241
Digby, Wiley James 241
Digby, Wiley Lanson 241
Digby, William Harrison 241
Dilsworth, Eliza Ann 232
Dinwiddie Court House 218
Dixon's Mill 231, 244, 257
Dodds, John 87, 106
Dodson, J. 15
Dollins, Andrew 22, 89
Donnelly, Thomas 34
Donovan, Matthew 152
Doss, Francis M. 15, 17, 209, 219, 226
Doss, George W. 9, 112, 117, 231
Doss, Joel A. 87, 144
Doss, John M. 87, 112
Dossett, James E. 19–20, 106
Doster, Alexandria Victoria 240
Doster Family Cemetery 240
Doub, Peter F. 14
Double Bridges 195
Double Springs Methodist Cemetery 248
Downey, William 89
Doyle, John 22
Dozier, Nathan J. 32, 144
Dranesville 82, 122
Drewry's Bluff 95–96
Dry Tortugas 234
Dublin 258
Duckworth, William H. 32, 81
Duerson's Mill 136
Duggar, William W. 19–20, 237
Dumas, Aurelius W. 32, 100, 219, 251, 259
Dumfries 90
Dunaway, Benjamin F. 9
Duncan, David U. 29, 31, 226
Duncan, Elisha D. 29, 31, 226, 247
Duncan, Elizabeth E. 235
Duncan, James D. 235
Duncan, James O. 17, 105, 226, 235
Duncan, John Francis 157, 160, 247
Dunlap, Alexander 31, 106, 226
Dunlap, Henry C. 17, 126
Dunn's Creek Cemetery 234
Durrett, Josephus 26, 74
Dykes, John 22

Early, Jubal 94, 162, 179
East Tennessee and Georgia Railroad 41
East Tennessee /and Virginia Railroad 41

Eastland, C. 28
Eatman, Albert 17, 72
Eatman, Francis L. 17, 105
Eatman, Newton J. 15, 17, 144, 235
Eatman, Phelan 17, 235
Ebenezer Presbyterian Church Cemetery 235
Eddings, Leonidus 20, 81
Edmiston, Calvin 14, 105, 158
Edmiston, James 14, 84, 259
Edwards, Perry 23, 226, 241
Eighth Alabama Regiment 75, 83, 94, 96, 102, 104, 108–109, 111, 128, 140, 142, 155, 162–163, 167, 186, 188, 218
Elder, David 20, 94
Eleventh Pennsylvania Cavalry 195
Eleventh Vermont Regiment 193
Ellerson's Mill 102
Ellett, Andrew J. 26, 72
Ellington, William W. 19–20, 106, 126, 188
Elliot's Salient 198
Ellis, Evander C. 16, 188
Elmira Prison Camp 248
Elmore, Pearson 20
Elmore, Robert 20, 100, 178, 226, 237
Elmwood Plantation 17, 238
Emmitsburg Road 150–153, 156
England, Matthew M. 33, 66, 71, 83–84, 116
Englebert, Frank/Frederick 26, 89, 244
Enon Cemetery 248
Eoline 242
Erdman, F.W. 226, 262
Ergle, Jacob M. 31, 84
Erwin, Enoch F. 87, 96
Escatawpa 241
Eskridge, Austin P. 34, 81
Eskridge, Joe N. 158
Eskridge, Joseph A. 9, 74
Eskridge, William 9, 72
Espey, Pilgrim A. 87, 106
Ethel 240
Ethridge, William J. 9, 74
Ethridge, William R. 67, 84, 257
Eubanks, Joseph E. 14, 226
Eufaula 257
Eutaw 4, 11–14, 16, 66, 115, 217, 233–235, 257
Eutaw Cemetery 234
Eutaw House 257
Eutaw Rangers 11
Eutaw Rifles 11–13
Evans, James R. 14, 226
Evans, Mattie 230
Evans, Nathan G. 120
Everett, Joseph E. 31, 106, 226, 247
Ewell, Richard 146, 175, 187, 222
Ezell, Frank M. 34, 158, 226

Faha, James 34
Fairfax Court House 70, 74, 80
Fairfield 149, 161
Fairgrounds, Lynchburg 48
Fairgrounds, Montgomery 38
Fairview Cemetery 253, 256

Faith, James A. 22, 157
Faith, William C. 22, 71, 75, 106
Falk, James J. 32, 188
Falmouth 132
Fannin 241
Fant, John D.L. 29, 31, 258
Farmville 223
Farmville, Battle 221–225
Farrell, Thomas 34, 113
Farrington, Charles L. 26, 106, 139, 146, 192, 244, 259
Fason, Calvin 17, 72, 235
Fayette and Pickens Rifles 31–32, 38, 45–46, 49, 54, 85, 114, 216, 226–227
Fayette Court House 32, 38, 45
Fayetteville 149
Featherston, W.S. 102, 111, 121, 198, 200
Fellowship Church Cemetery 248
Ferguson, Albert 247
Ferguson, Benjamin F. 106, 208, 226, 247
Ferguson, Edward 247
Ferguson, Green 247
Ferguson, H. 28
Ferguson, Homer 247
Ferguson, James P. 27, 31, 192
Ferguson, Lizzie 247
Ferguson, Newton L. 27
Ferguson, Pearl 247
Ferguson, Pin 247
Ferguson, Walter 247
Ferrell, Thomas 164
Fetner, Levi J. 22
Few, William L. 22, 112
Field, Charles W. 176, 180, 202
Field, George W. 10–14, 38, 42, 54, 86, 105, 107, 109, 111–112, 115–116, 233, 258–259, 261
Field, Harriet Wallace 10
Field, Stephen G. 10
Fifteenth New Jersey Regiment 141
Fifth Alabama Regiment 73, 75
Fifth Maine Regiment 141
Finch, Willis 17, 112
Finegan, Joseph 188
Finley, Thomas M. 26, 106, 244
Finn's Point National Cemetery 146–147, 231
First Confederate Congress 6
First Minnesota Regiment 153–154
First New Hampshire Artillery 223
First New Jersey Regiment 141
First New York Sharpshooters 151
First Presbyterian Church Cemetery 245
First Regiment Alabama Volunteers 257
First Rhode Island Artillery 223
Fitts, Oliver 23, 106, 117
Fitzgerald, Martha 247
Fleming, C.K. 193
Fletcher, M.H. 21
Fletcher, Matthew M. 22, 112
Fletcher, Richard J. 21–22, 54, 85, 116, 126, 134–135, 151, 156, 161, 172, 239, 259
Flint Hill 162

Flint Rock 148
Floyd, John H. 87, 224
Fondron, John B. 23, 147, 241
Ford, Henry P. 9, 74
Ford, William N. 26, 113
Forest Church 246
Forkland 14, 73, 237, 257
Forney, D.P. 216
Forney, John H. 66–67, 74, 78, 163, 233
Forney, William H. 211, 216–217, 219, 221
Forniss, William R. 9, 231
Fort Fillmore 78
Forty-First Alabama Regiment 66
Forty-Fourth Alabama Regiment 147
Forty-Third Alabama Regiment 231
Foster, Andrew J. 32, 106
Foster, Elijah J. 31, 106, 144, 226, 247
Foster, Fannie S. 247
Foster, Grace G. 247
Foster, Nannie L. 247
Foster, Sallie S. 247
Foster, Thomas J. 226, 259
Four Mile Run 202
Fourteenth Alabama Regiment 129, 140, 142, 155, 167, 218
Fourth Alabama Regiment 75
Fourth Pennsylvania Reserves 110, 260
Fourth U.S. Artillery 152
Fourth Vermont Regiment 193
Foust, Charles Wesley 167
Fowler, W.H. 12
Franklin, Gillis 23, 122
Franklin, William B. 261
Frankville 237
Frasier, Lafayette W. 157
Frayser's Farm, Battle 107–113, 133, 189, 254, 260
Frazier, William H. 22
Fredericksburg 127, 130–132, 137, 147, 261
Fredericksburg Road 180
Fredericksburg-Spotsylvania Confederate Cemetery 132, 261
Fredrickstown 122–123
Free, Alice 248
Free, Calvin W. 87, 106, 183, 247
Free, Effie 248
Free, Fannie 248
Free, James T. 28
Free, Mary 248
Free, Melvina 248
Free, Willia 248
Freeney, Doc 22
Friend, John W. 14
Friendship Cemetery 249
Frisby, William F. 20, 112, 157, 226
Fritz, A. 19
Front Royal 128, 148, 162
Fuller, James B. 87, 178, 226
Fuller, Thomas E. 14, 112
Funderburk, Jacob J. 29, 31, 144, 158, 248, 259

Gaddy, Raleigh M. 26, 106, 139, 226
Gaines' House 102

Gaines' Mill, Battle 101–107, 113, 134, 238, 241
Gainesville 120, 257
Gallant, Daniel C. 26, 157
Gallant, James Crow 244
Gallant, Leva 226, 244
Gallant, Marion 87, 157, 160, 244
Gallant, Martha 243
Gallant, William 26, 89
Gallion 232, 238
Gallion, Martha Jorge 245
Galloway, Charles 14, 226
Gamble, Joseph 67, 126, 231, 257
Gammill, Benjamin M. 31, 192, 248
Gammill, Mattie J. 248
Gandy, James A. 226, 262
Gandy, James F. 15–16, 202
Gannon, Andrew J. 31, 139, 146, 183
Gardner, Jackson 241
Gardner, John S. 23, 84, 241
Gardner, Margaret 241
Garland, L.C., Dr. 258
Garner, Andrew J. 23, 106
Garner, Brantley W. 23, 140, 226
Garrett, William 7
Garrott, Isham W. 7, 52–53, 229
Gary Springs 36
Gathright, Wilson R. 16, 105, 144
Gausden, Mary Anne 240
Gayle, Dewitt 22, 50
Gee, Jeremiah W. 32, 113
General Hospital, Culpeper Court House 69
General Hospital No. 18 101
Geneva 231
Geneva Presbyterian Cemetery 232
George, James H. 33, 71, 107, 116, 134, 254
Germania Ford 148, 175
Gettysburg 149
Gettysburg, Battle 78, 147, 149–160, 241
Gibbon, John 188, 190–191, 214
Gibson, James S. 14, 178, 204, 262
Gibson, John 26, 72
Gilbert, Alexander S. 14, 160
Gilbert, Benjamin 22, 112
Gilkey, Alda V. 248
Gilkey, Emm Mine 248
Gilkey, L.A. 27
Gilkey, Walter M. 27, 31, 63, 65, 248
Gilkey, William M. 248
Gillis Creek 96
Gillmore, Allen A. 9
Gillmore, Basil N. 9, 143, 165
Gillmore, James M. 67, 72, 257
Gillmore, Thomas J. 87, 143, 147
Girardey, J.B. 203
Given, George W. 34, 113
Glass, Benjamin 67, 231, 257
Glass, Jonathan 231
Glass, Mary 232
Glass, Mike 231
Glass, William 231
Glass, Ft. 231
Glover, Frank L. 20, 116, 128, 133, 164
Goff (Gaff), James W. 34, 106

Golden Springs Church Cemetery 241
Goldsborough 91
Gonzales County 232
Goode's Bridge 222
Goodson, Rufus G. 23, 112
Goodwin, Henry Clay 23, 112
Goodwin, Martin G. 23, 84
Gordo 30, 248
Gordon, Benjamin F. 14, 105, 138
Gordon, James J. 13–14, 85, 115, 133
Gordon, James M. 16–17, 96, 257
Gordon, John B. 98, 182, 218–219
Gordon, Robert H. 15–16, 105, 112, 116, 257, 260
Gordon, Samuel Otterson 257
Gordon, Walter H. 17, 62, 70, 258
Gordonsville 118, 261
Gordy, John A. 209, 239, 257
Gore, Robert F. 31, 74
Goree, Eli W. 26, 72
Goree, Florence 247
Goree, Orlando, H. 15, 17, 112, 131–132
Goss, Carolina L. 241
Goss, Fletcher J. 23, 89, 241
Goss, Florence Rosa Rubel 241
Goss, Helen G. 241
Goss, Henry Laurens 241
Goss, Indiola 241
Goss, James Halstead 241
Goss, Joseph Ray 241
Goss, Maud B. 241
Goss, Samuel Edwin 241
Gossett, William P. 26, 106
Gracie, Archibald, Jr. 53, 71, 74, 79, 86, 92, 96, 101, 230–231, 260
Grant, Lewis A. 193
Grant, U.S. 175, 186–187, 189–190, 192, 202
Gray, Benjamin F. 87, 179, 227
Gray, John A. 87, 113, 226, 254
Gray, Lysander J. 34, 113, 254
Gray, Selina 255
Greaner's Factory Hospital 260
Green, John P. 26, 72, 226
Green, Joseph R. 22, 112, 239
Green, L.P.S. 27
Green, Thomas H. 22, 157
Green, William H. 26, 113
Green, William N. 23, 100
Green Pond 245
Greencastle 149
Greene County 10
Greene County Greys 10–11, 13–14, 35, 38, 41–42, 52, 61, 114, 204, 210–211, 226–227, 259
Greene Springs 30
Greensboro 4, 217, 237
Greensboro Cemetery 229
Greensboro Guards 12
Greenwood, Anderson H. 233, 257
Greenwood, John 17, 112
Greenwood, Nathan K. 14, 70, 233, 257
Greenwood Cemetery 231, 234, 236
Gregg, Francis C. 32, 106, 144, 226
Griffin, Charles H. 87, 122, 204
Griffin, David A. 87, 100, 138, 146

Griffin, John R. 34, 94, 259
Griffin, Robert B. 87, 145, 204, 220, 254, 262
Griffin, Robert H. 34, 107, 145
Griffin, William 23, 157, 206, 208, 241
Griffith, Paula 246
Griffith, Web 246
Griffith, William J. 9, 105, 226
Grimes, Thomas R. 22, 112
Grizzle, David M. 17, 183
Groesbeck 252
Groveton 90, 120
Guild, Lafayette 158, 176
Gullett, Richard B. 19–20, 106
Gulley, John M. 19–20, 112
Gunn, J.W. 22
Gunn, W.F. 22
Gunter, F.A. 27
Guthrie, Allen 254
Guthrie, James Marion 254
Guthrie, John W. 34, 107, 204, 220, 254
Guthrie, Zowie 254

Hagerstown 123, 149, 161
Hagerstown Road 123
Hale, Mary 229
Hale, Stephen F. 3–7, 29–30, 37, 42, 71, 82, 86, 94, 96, 102, 104–105, 116, 229, 257, 260
Hall, George W. 87, 226
Hall, Jordan 14, 126
Hall, Joseph 22, 258
Hall, Margaret C. 243
Halltown 124
Hamburg 33, 240, 242
Hamilton, John D. 164
Hamilton, Mary A. 233
Hamilton, Matthew P. 14, 138, 146, 164, 202, 233
Hamilton, Milton A. 87, 213, 226
Hamilton, Peter H. 233, 257
Hamiter, Annie Maude 248
Hamiter, Frances Eva 248
Hamiter, Joel J. 87, 144, 226, 248
Hamiter, John T. 31, 126, 144, 209, 226, 248
Hamiter, John T., Jr. 248
Hamiter, Lela 248
Hamiter, Mattie 248
Hamiter, William Frederick 248
Hamlet, Robert G. 14, 105, 226
Hamner, Elizabeth 244
Hamner, Thomas W. 26, 106, 139, 146, 157, 244
Hampton, Wade 194, 214
Hampton Road 95
Hancock, W.S. 180, 187, 214
Hankins, James P. 9, 112, 158, 165, 231
Hankins, Nathan Y. 19–20, 100, 106, 213
Hannibal, Benjamin 22, 84
Hannon's ice pond 197
Hanover Junction 183–186
Hanovertown 186
Hardee, W.J. 258
Harden, A.B. 34, 75

Harding, Samuel 23, 72
Hardy, Jacob B. 22, 75, 207
Harkey, Alexander 26
Harkness, James C.B. 15, 17, 133, 164, 211, 216–217, 262
Harkness, William B. 15, 17, 257
Harper, Marcellus E. 34, 113, 117
Harpers Ferry 48, 123–124
Harris, Benjamin F.R. 106
Harris, John C. 87
Harris, Joseph H. 87
Harris, Lemuel 32, 38, 46, 51, 68, 79, 85, 88, 106, 116, 133, 164, 202, 212, 258
Harris, Rufus L. 17, 105, 157, 160, 259
Harrison, William O. 17, 62, 235
Harrison House 181
Hart, Benjamin T. 19–20
Hartley, Quintera Decima 237
Hasty, Benjamin F. 26, 126, 244
Hasty, John 87, 178, 226
Hatcher, John P. 31, 157, 248
Hatcher, Thomas 87, 192
Hatcher's Run 212, 214
Hatcher's Run, Battle 217–219
Hatter, John P. 14, 156–157, 164, 168, 220, 234
Hatter, John P., Jr. 234
Hatter, Joseph William 234
Hatter, Mary Jane 234
Hawkins, Aaron 29–30, 81
Hawkins, Herbert P. 29, 31
Hay, Alabama 255
Hay, Emma 255
Hay, J.P. 255
Hay, John D. 255
Hay, Lenora 255
Hay, Mattie 255
Hay, Milton 255
Hay, William J. 34, 145, 227, 255
Hayes, A.H. 18
Hayes, Charles 12
Hayes, James N. 26, 116, 130, 133, 144, 164, 211–212, 216, 226
Hayes, John A. 9, 105, 213
Hayes, Pleasant L. 26, 178, 226, 244
Hayes, Thomas N. 26
Hayes, William S. 26, 204, 220
Hazel River 148, 162
Heard, Jesse J. 88
Heard, John 67, 257
Heard, Joseph M. 22, 204
Heard, Thomas S. 9, 70
Heath, Henry C. 9
Heath, James L. 87
Heber Springs 251
Hebron Cemetery 247–248
Heidt, Eli A. 34, 258
Hemphill, James S. 31, 106, 226, 248
Henderson 256
Henderson, Frank 226, 262
Henderson, James W. 87, 95
Hendon, Susan 245
Hendricks, T. 19
Henry, A. 27
Henry, Hugh 242
Henry, James W. 226
Henry, John C. 23, 100, 226, 242

Henry, John W. 242
Henry, Julius Goodwin 242
Henry, Mary D. 242
Henry, Patrick C. 23, 112, 122, 242
Henry, Robert 87
Henry, Robert J. 29–30
Henry, William, Jr. 141
Henry, Wirt Shropshire 242
Herman, William F. 34, 94, 259
Herndon, Thomas H. 5, 13, 75
Heth, Henry 176
Hickory Street 197
Higginbotham, Benjamin T. 16, 73, 94, 112, 116, 133–134, 136, 144, 164, 172, 211, 257
Higginbotham, Sarah J. 243
High, Isaiah S. 14, 95
High Bridge 223–224
Hill 258
Hill, A.P. 101–102, 108, 146, 168–169, 175, 179, 185, 187, 189, 192, 208, 221
Hill, Alexander P. 188
Hill, Daniel H. 95–96, 98, 101, 125
Hill, Gabriel L. 14, 89, 258
Hill, Henry 192, 226
Hill, James 38
Hill, James, Jr. 23, 50
Hill, John L. 87
Hill, John T. 17, 112
Hill, S.F. 28
Hill, Samuel M. 15–16, 187
Hill, William M. 28
Hilton, Williamson W. 34, 84
Hilton Head Island 33
Hinson's Ford 119
Hitt, Alexander P. 17, 226
Hitt, James M. 17, 186
Hodge, John W. 31, 74
Hodge, Joseph W. 31
Hodo, James B. 29, 31, 106, 183, 208, 248
Hogan, Archibald 242
Hogan, Marion 87, 112, 242
Hogan, Needham B. 9, 35, 98, 110, 140–142, 157, 231, 260
Hogan, Richard 87, 100, 112, 144, 242
Hogan Springs 35
Hoke, Robert F. 188
Hoke's Bluff 241
Holcomb, Thomas H. 9, 50, 100, 109, 112, 115, 210
Holifield, Robert F. 34, 72
Holland, William T. 31–32, 79, 81
Hollingsworth, Francis M. 32, 157
Hollingsworth, Henry C. 32, 113
Hollingsworth, Thomas G. 32, 106
Holly, Milton 34, 89
Holly Square 257
Hollywood Cemetery 117, 128, 207, 229, 236, 261
Holmes, Theophilus H. 91, 108
Holms, Jordon 23
Honnoll, Ann 173
Hood, John B. 120–121, 129
Hooks, Augustus F. 22, 144, 211, 226, 239
Hooks, Samuel 22, 112, 117, 259

Hooks, William D. 22, 178
Hooppaugh, Andrew F. 17, 226, 259
Hooppaugh, Daniel M. 16, 62, 178
Hopewell 257
Hopewell Pass 119–120
Hopewell Primitive Baptist Church Cemetery 252
Hopkins, Juliet Opic 71
Hopkins, William D. 34, 226, 255
Horn, James F. 34, 183
Horn, Leslie L. 23, 144, 165
Horton, Elam P. 164, 227
Horton, Hugh 262
Horton, James W. 17, 69, 72
Horton, John W. 34, 158, 165
Horton, Samuel H. 32, 183
House, James H. 26, 75, 89
Houston and Davis 11–12
Howard, Alfred 29, 31, 72
Howard, Bettie 44
Howard, Mary E. 243
Howard College 33, 66
Howard's Grove Hospital 262
Howell, John 25
Howell, Roda 32
Howell, Thomas B., Independent Volunteers 34, 255, 258
Howell, Thomas B., Tuscaloosa Rifles 26, 244
Howell, William J. 20
Hubbard and Pollard 12
Huckabee, Lucius 67, 105, 138, 146, 257
Huckaby, R.U. 27
Hudgins, B.A. 28
Hudgins, F.F. 28
Hudson, William C. 22, 71, 75
Huff, William L. 34
Huger, Benjamin 96–97, 107
Hughes, Basil M. 26, 87, 113, 129, 132, 139, 146, 157, 160, 170, 245
Hughes, Charlotte Bell 130
Hughes, Daniel 130
Hughes, Jesse 87, 106, 129, 157, 244
Hughes, John 257
Hughes, John B. 4, 25–26, 116, 126, 129–130, 133, 158, 164, 204, 212, 216, 226, 245, 257
Hughes, Mattie 236
Hughes, William W. 26
Hummell, William H. 19–20, 106
Humphreys, Andrew A. 223
Humphries, Jesse M. 88, 259
Hunsucker, Archie M. 34, 227, 255
Hunsucker, Ebenezer 255
Hunsucker, Effie 255
Hunsucker, Estella 255
Hunsucker, Grover Cleveland 255
Hunsucker, Hezikiah Columbus 255
Hunsucker, Idella Clara 255
Hunsucker, Malachi 255
Hunsucker, Martha 255
Hunsucker, Monroe Harrison 255
Hunsucker, Rebecca 255
Hunsucker, Robert Edward 255
Hunsucker, William P. 34
Hunt 247
Hunter, William L. 14, 226

Huntsville, Alabama 4
Huntsville, Texas 238, 244
Hurlbut, William H. 42
Hurricane Cemetery 244
Hutchinson, J.J. 75

Independent Volunteers 33, 41, 46, 83, 114, 211, 226–227
Inge, Francis J. 14, 74, 234, 257
Inge, Rebecca Eaton 234
Inge, Richard, Dr. 234
Iola 237
Irwin, James 88

Jack, Thomas M. 172
Jackson, Joshua 22
Jackson, Thomas J. 59, 101–102, 107, 119, 121, 128, 136, 146
Jackson, William Thomas 162, 167
James, Absalom H. 87, 106, 242
James, Adam F. 23, 100, 106, 224, 242
James, Charles 22
James, Dan 22, 106, 239
James, Daniel 239
James, John 22, 75, 116, 128, 133, 157, 164, 166, 188, 211
James, John G. 239
James, Margaret 239
James, Mary 239
Jarratt's Station 195
Jarvis, Alexander 115
Jarvis, Carter 23
Jarvis, Mary Elizabeth 115
Jasper 245
Jay, Thomas J. 31, 106
Jefferson 9, 237, 257
Jefferson, Annie 244
Jefferson Cemetery 237
Jeffersonton 119
Jenkins, Micah 108
Jennings, Annie Rebecca Whitaker 245
Jennings Chapel Cemetery 245
Jericho 257
Jericho Mills 185
Jerusalem Plank Road 189–190, 192, 195, 197
Jetersville 223
Johnson, Albert J. 22, 144, 202
Johnson, Alfred A. 9, 105
Johnson, Allen H. 26, 245
Johnson, Cora Arena 235
Johnson, Daniel F. 29, 31, 106, 226
Johnson, Edward 182
Johnson, Elisha D. 31, 226
Johnson (Johnston), Ivan H. 26, 89
Johnson, John W. 23, 106, 138, 146, 224
Johnson, Merrit Morgan 10, 143
Johnson, Oliver C. 23
Johnson, Thomas H. 9, 105, 202
Johnson, Thomas J. 14, 138, 213, 259
Johnson, William G. 34, 130
Johnson, William H. 20, 157
Johnson and Bostick 12
Johnson's Island Cemetery 159
Johnson's Island Prison 160, 221

Johnston, Joseph, Gen. 48, 55, 57, 59–60, 74, 90–91, 95–96, 129, 222
Jolly, Hannah 236
Jolly, John B. 10, 112, 138, 215
Jolly, Juliet 235
Jolly, Matthew A. 17, 71, 96, 236, 260
Jolly, Peter 236
Jolly, Thomas B. 87, 224
Jolly, William 10, 231
Jones, Banbury 20, 104, 106
Jones, David R. 120
Jones, George 22, 157, 160, 226, 259
Jones, J. Clairbon 231
Jones, John A. 22, 106, 144
Jones, John L. 17, 81
Jones, John W. 19–20, 122, 207, 237
Jones, Josiah J. 17, 144, 226
Jones, N. Henderson 14, 75, 89
Jones, Rebecca D. 231
Jones, Richard A. 231
Jones, Wiley P. 10, 231
Jones, William H. 22, 157
Jones, William Henry 231
Jones, William P. 32, 113
Jones Chapel Baptist Church Cemetery 245
Jordan, Benjamin F. 19–20, 100
Jordan, Thomas C. 17, 95, 259

Kautz, August 194
Kautz and Wilson's Raiders, Skirmish 193–195
Keasler, Edward H. 29, 31, 84
Keer, James D. 28
Keeton, James N. 26, 202, 204, 221, 259–260
Keeton, William Jesse 24, 87, 113, 260
Keith, John 22, 72
Kelley, Ferguson 32
Kelly, Herschel 129
Kelly, James M. 10, 143, 158, 160
Kelly, Lemuel H. 17, 126, 126, 144, 261
Kelly, T.A. 19
Kelly's Ford 119, 261
Kemp, Jefferson M. 31
Kemper, James 98, 108
Kennedy, Josiah H. 87, 106
Kennedy, Josiah McNeil 44
Kennedy, Richard M. 15–16, 72–73, 130, 133, 164, 211, 217–220, 226, 236, 257
Kennedy, William L. 14, 73
Kent, James M. 87, 202
Kerr, William J. 31, 126, 204
Kershaw, J.B. 140, 176
Kilpatrick, William 28
Kimbrough, Elizabeth Alston Douthitt 234
Kimbrough, James D. 14, 105, 234
Kimbrough, Marmaduke 234
King, J.H. 142, 171, 208–210, 260
King, John E. 34
King, Margaret Ellwood 251
King, William H. 34, 107
King's Mill 91, 259
Kirk, Felix 34, 107

Kirker, Charles F. 20, 106, 112, 226
Kirkland, Calvin R. 32, 226, 251
Kirkland, James A. 32, 100
Kirkland, William F. 32, 85, 106, 157, 213, 251
Kirksey, Cicero 105
Kizziar, Edward 26, 226
Klingle House 153
Knight, Abner 139, 146, 192, 226
Knight, Thomas J. 14, 112, 117
Knox, Carlos La Fayette 16, 128, 257, 259, 261
Knox, John A. 14, 84
Knox, Samuel P. 14
Knox, Zannie B. 235
Knoxville, Alabama 14, 234
Knoxville, Tennessee 41–43
Kornegy, Barney H. 23, 100
Kosickco Cemetery 240

Lacy, James L. 26, 226
Ladies Soldier's Aid Society of Greensboro 72
Lamb, Robert H. 14, 105
Lampkin Cemetery 252
Land, E.G. 248
Land, Joe H. 248
Land, Joseph M. 31, 248
Land, L.A. 248
Land, Mary E. 248
Landrum, Americus 236
Landrum, Edmund 67, 95, 257
Landrum, Mastin W. 22
Lane, James H. 203
Lane, William F. 32, 158, 206, 208
Lanford, Thomas H.P. 17, 105
Langford, Andrew J. 34
Langhorne, Mary 17
Latham, H.B. 28
Latham, James A. 27
Latham, John B. 27
Latham, Sarah 243
Latham, Wesley E. 23, 157, 191
Law, George W. 19–20, 94, 259
Lawhorn, David 87
Lea, Henry Clinton 34, 107
Lebanon Church 91–92
Lee, E. 27
Lee, Fitz 194
Lee, Fulton M. 23, 224
Lee, J.H. 19
Lee, James E. 27, 31, 144, 209
Lee, James H.B. 10
Lee, James P. 14, 226
Lee, Robert E. 76, 91, 118–119, 122–123, 128, 132, 136, 143, 162–164, 175–176, 180, 184–187, 189, 193, 195, 199, 202, 209, 214–215, 223, 225
Lee's Farm 259
Lee's Mill 92–95
Leesburg 122, 123
Leighton, William S. 19–20, 178
Leon County 235
Leopard, John C. 23, 112
Leopard, William H. 26, 72, 202
Leroy 240
Leroy, First Baptist Church 231
Letcher, John 48

Letterman, Jonathan 160
Levingston, Esqr. C. 32, 74
Lewis, Mary 36
Lewis, Mary A. 237
Lewis, Mary F. 258
Lewis, Paul H. 221
Lewis, William 22
Lewis House 64–71, 259
Lexington 5, 256
Liberty Hill 243
Lieutenant Run 197
Lightsey, Daniel E. 23, 191
Lightsey, David E. 23, 106, 204, 226
Lightsey, Martin N. 23, 204
Lightsey, Moses J. 23, 106, 157
Lincoln, Abraham 3–4, 29
Lincolnton 67
Linden 9–10, 230–231, 257
Linden Academy 9
Linden Court House 9–10
Linden Hotel 7, 257
Lindsey, Jackson 26
Lindsey, Mary Francis 252
Linebarger, Michael H. 31, 213, 248
Lipsey, Mary B. 249
Lipsey, W.L. 28
Lipsey-Hamiter House 248
Little, D. Milton 14
Little River Turnpike 122
Livingston 247
Lockhart, Columbus 20, 89
Lockhart, Harrison C. 171
Lockhart, Robert P. 34, 113, 255
Lomax, Samuel S. 19–20, 237
Long, Ephraim 32, 158, 204, 220, 251
Long, Francis 251
Long, Gorda 251
Long, Julia 251
Long, Liberty 251
Long, Lorenza D. 251
Long, Lucinda 251
Long, Margaret 251
Long, T. Jefferson 251
Long, Tener 251
Long, Tildon 251
Long, William 251
Long Bridge Camp 95
Long Bridge Road 108, 111
Longstreet, James 95–97, 99, 102, 111, 119–120, 122, 125, 128, 130, 146, 162, 176, 178, 221, 260–216
Loper, Allen 22
Loring, W.W. 233
Louden Park Cemetery 165, 249
Love, Henry O. 31, 158, 160, 226, 248
Lovelady, Cumberland F. 88, 94
Lovelady, David C. 88, 192
Lovelady, Noah H. 34, 158
Lovelady, Mary E. 255
Lovelady, William 202
Lowe, David A. 32, 157, 226
Lowe, William J. 32, 113, 157–158, 165
Lowery, John T. 32, 75
Lowry, Charles C. 23, 112
Lowry, Thomas A. 17, 105, 157
Loyd, Margaret L. 234

Loyd, William P. 14, 193, 226, 234
Lucas, Edward R. 34, 134, 164, 213, 216–217, 259
Lucas, Oscar M. 164, 179, 183, 227, 255
Luling 245
Luther Store 232
Lynchburg 30–31, 39, 41–42, 47–52, 207, 225, 227
Lyon, F.S. 171
Lyon, Robert L. 17, 144, 219
Lyon, William H. 19–20

Maben 248
Macon 18–20, 238
Madison Springs 30
Magilton, Albert L 110
Magnolia 238
Magnolia Cemetery 238
Magruder, John B. 91, 95
Mahaffy, John H. 17, 112, 226, 236
Mahone, William 101, 140, 179–180, 186–188, 190, 192–196, 198–199, 205, 214–216, 219, 221–223, 225
Makamson, A. 27
Makamson, Calvin M. 29, 31, 126, 188, 248
Makamson, G.E. 248
Makamson, Hortense 248
Makamson, J.T. 248
Makamson, M.A.L. 248
Makamson, Minnie Lee 248
Makamson, W.J. 248
Manassas Gap Railroad 59, 61, 120
Manassas Junction 11, 55, 59, 61, 63–64, 70, 90
Manassas, Second 120–122, 126
Manley, T.B. 19
Mantua 257
Maplesville 23, 241, 255
Marengo County 7, 231
Marengo Rifles 7, 9–10, 35, 40–41, 43, 100, 114, 210, 226–227, 260
Marion 7, 33, 46, 66, 83, 134, 238–239, 255–256
Marion Cemetery 253, 255–256
Marion Rifles 83
Marler, Benjamin F. 27, 30, 157, 226, 248
Marlow, John 34, 145, 183
Mars 257
Marsh Creek 149–150
Marshall, William T. 10, 74
Martin, John 22
Martin, Thomas 22, 95
Martinsburg 127, 162
Maryland Heights 124
Mashburn, Amanda 241
Mason, J.T. 19
Mason, Joseph M. 22
Mason, Payton B. 20, 237
Mason's Hill 77
Massey, W.P. 87, 95
Massingale, William B. 34, 107, 226
Mathers, Emily Melissa 231
Mathis, William M. 208
Mattapony River 184
Maughan, James 89
Maxwell, John B. 15, 17, 104–105

May, Della 234
May, Lizzie Ann 234
May, Lula Pearl 234
May, Moody H. 14, 204, 234
May, Moody H., Sr. 234
Mayberry, George L. 23, 100
Mayberry, Jacob D. 87, 212, 224, 242
Mayfield, J. 25
McArthur, John D. 23, 106, 131, 138, 146
McCafferty, Margaret Ann 248
McCain, William J./A. 26, 259
McCall, George A. 110–111
McCarroll, James 20
McCauley, William F. 19–20, 183
McClelen, Bailey George 39, 55, 124, 258
McClellen, George 82, 90, 107
McClinton, Benjamin E. 10, 226, 231
McCollum, Elizabeth 251
McCollum, Henry M. 32, 251
McCollum, Josievine 251
McCollum, Lucy 251
McCollum, Neuman 251
McCollum, Tack 251
McCormic (McCormick), John 34, 226
McCoy, Alexander J. 26, 113, 117
McCracken, William E. 14, 189–190, 195, 220
McCrackin, John S.B. 17
McCraw, Betty Bertha 242
McCraw, Inez Mae 242
McCraw, James M. 23, 157, 242
McCraw, Laura Ann 242
McCraw, Letha Orianna 242
McCraw, Mabry Adams 242
McCulley, John S. 14, 138, 204, 220
McCulley, Richard J. 14, 55, 96, 257, 259
McCulley, Robert R. 87, 189–190, 195, 220
McDonald, James T. 10, 202
McDonald Cemetery 250
McDowell, Fergers 27–28
McDowell, Frannie 249
McFarland, James Thomas 87, 215, 231
McGee, Henry 14, 158
McGee, James 26, 106, 202, 226, 245
McGehee, Thomas 87, 128
McGill, William ??
McGraw, James H. 31, 89
McGraw, Washington L. 27, 31, 226, 248
McGuire, Patrick F. 14, 112
McGuire, Wiley 26, 113
McHenry, Ft. 159
McIlvain, Robert 241
McInnis, Bryant L. 34, 50, 71, 255, 259
McIntosh 239
McIntosh, Alexander M. 14, 183, 226
McIntosh, William A.D. 10, 110, 126, 226

McJinsey, Sillman 87, 94
McKenzie, F.M. 22
McKinley 9
McKinney, George A. 31, 113
McKinney, John M. 27
McLane (McClain), Robert H. 17, 89, 259
McLaughlin, William 67, 158, 257
McLaughlin, William B. 34, 89
McLaws, Lafayette 123–125, 130, 136, 140, 261
McMahon, James 87, 178, 245
McMath 26
McMath, Clement Clay 87, 144, 261
McMath, Elisha 24
McMath, Frances Gorman 24
McMath, James H. 24–26, 38, 54, 78, 87, 91, 94–96, 99, 112, 116, 129, 258–260
McMath, Joseph E. 26, 144, 204, 220
McMillian, William A. 17, 112
McMillion, John 23
McNeil Cemetery 231
McNeill, Charles 19–20, 109, 112
McNeill, D. 19
McNeill, William A. 10, 109, 112
McPhatter, Malcom 113
McShan 247, 250, 257
McShan, William C. 29, 31, 113
McTurk, William J. 26, 113
Meade, George G. 167, 192, 194, 214
Mechanicsville 187
Mechanicsville Bridge 102
Mechanicsville Turnpike 96, 101
Medline 254
Medline Cemetery 254
Meggs, Martha A. 241
Melton, Amelia 247
Melvin, Stewart 33, 89
Memphis 247, 252
Meridian 248
Merrill, Frederick A. 140
Merrill, Joseph S. 14, 105, 126, 128
Merriman, Joseph W. 34, 145
Mesopotamia Cemetery 233, 235
Mexican War 4, 6, 9, 11–12, 58, 79, 216, 257
Michael, George 19–20, 188
Michie, Thomas J. 22, 85, 110, 112
Middletown 123
Miles, John W. 32, 126, 251
Milledgeville 7
Miller, Robert P. 31, 106, 259
Miller, Sarah Ann 232
Miller, William B. 34, 158
Miller Park 48–49
Millport 38, 249–250, 257
Millwood 60
Milner, James E. 17, 84
Mine Road 136
Mine Run 169–170
Mineral Springs Cemetery 247–248
Mitchell, Andrew J. 26, 144
Mitchell, Thomas L. 34, 126
Mixon, Benjamin 251
Mixon, Carrie 251
Mixon, John 251
Mixon, John A. 32, 251, 258

Mixon, Minerva 251
Mixon, Richard 251
Mizell, Robert C. 87, 145
Mobile 15, 38–39, 43, 45, 81, 231, 233–236, 238–240, 257–258, 260
Mobile and Ohio Railroad 38
Mobile and Ohio Railroad Depot 46
Mobile Resolutions 4
Mobley, Allen 231
Mobley, Jesse B. 10, 231
Mock, Lee 28
Monroe 248
Monroe, Henry E. 14, 137–138, 146
Monroe, John 87
Monroe, William O. 13
Monroe County 11
Montague County, Texas 230
Montevallo 257
Montgomery 15, 37–38, 41, 43, 45, 86, 236–237, 253, 258
Montgomery, David M. 17, 105, 183, 226, 236
Montgomery, Jennie B. 236
Montgomery, Julia R. 237
Montgomery and West Point Railroad 41
Moody, Carter 7
Moody, James 8
Moody, Sarah 7
Moody, Young M. 7–9, 101, 115, 231, 260
Moore, Albert 87, 137–138, 146, 204
Moore, Andrew B. 7, 11–12, 18–19, 24, 27–28, 31
Moore, Elizabeth 231
Moore, Frances Lavonia 254
Moore, James R. 87
Moore, John A. 31, 258
Moore, John Moses 231
Moore, Martin J. 23, 70
Moore, Moses, M.D. 165, 226, 231
Moore, Robert 14
Moore, Spencer Green 14
Moore, Sydenham 3–7, 11–13, 21, 30, 35, 37, 39, 45, 50, 54, 63, 65, 67–68, 70–71, 73, 75–86, 90–91, 94–101, 104, 227, 229, 257, 259–261
Moore, Thomas 17, 106
Moore, William H. 14, 157, 204
Moorehead, James H. 29–30, 101, 116, 133, 157, 259
Moorehead, Mary 249
Moorehead, Mattie 249
Moorehead, Milus J. 29, 31, 100, 106, 249
Moorehead, Nancy 249
Moore's Bridge 257–258
Morgan, Alfred J. 10, 124, 158, 231
Morgan, Alfred Kirskey 232
Morgan, Alice Eliza 232
Morgan, Ammie Evandice 232
Morgan, Birdie Z. 232
Morgan, Carrie Mae 232
Morgan, Celesta 232
Morgan, Cornelius Mentor 232
Morgan, Daniel A. 31, 113
Morgan, Emma Mae 232
Morgan, Ft. 11–13, 15

Morgan, George Baxter 232
Morgan, Julie S. 232
Morgan, Leon Bowers 232
Morgan, Leona Blanche 232
Morgan, Lizzie Lee 232
Morgan, Mary Eva 232
Morgan, Merrit 67, 148, 213, 231–232, 257
Morgan, Robert Edward Lee 232
Morgan, Robert R. 165, 232
Morgan, Sallie Bertha 232
Morgan, William C. 9–10, 40, 43, 54, 63, 65, 112, 226, 232, 258
Morgan Springs 33
Moring, Sarah Rebecca 231
Morris, William F. 14, 100, 157, 204, 220
Morrison, Jeremiah 26, 81
Morrow, Jefferson J. 87
Morrow, John G. 26, 259
Morrow, William W. 23, 89, 258
Morton 255
Morton, F.M. 88, 100
Morton, George W. 34, 107
Moseley, Robert 22, 89
Moses, John T. 87, 100
Mosley, Mary Lavena 239
Mott, Gershom 190–191, 214
Mott's Run 136
Mounier, H.A. 19
Mt. Airy 17
Mt. Carmel Cemetery 242
Mt. Gilead Church Cemetery 242
Mt. Hebron 16, 235
Mt. Hebron Methodist Church Cemetery 250
Mt. Jackson 165, 232
Mt. Olive Church Cemetery 242
Mt. Sterling 257
Mt. Tabor Cemetery 251
Mt. Vernon Arsenal 53
Mt. Zion Cemetery 254, 262
Mountain Creek 240, 245, 255
Mountain Run 119
Mundy, Frank H. 13–14, 55, 110–111, 115, 127, 133, 157, 159–160, 164, 221, 234, 257, 261
Mundy, Frank Perrin 234
Mundy, Mattie Browning 234
Mundy, Thomas Gustave 234
Munich 236
Munson's Hill 77
Murphy, Mary A. 12
Murphy, James 22, 122
Murphy, John 17, 105, 117, 257, 260
Murphy, Owen 34
Muse, Jackson 79
Muse, Nathaniel, P. 33, 50, 113
Muse, William C. 34, 113, 179, 224
Mustin, William G. 28
Mustion, Jesse W. 20
Myrtlewood 232
Myrtlewood Cemetery 247

Naben, Y.L. 27
Nabers, Horatio G. 106, 157, 160
Nabers, James F. 27
Nabers, John F. 27
Nabors, John 87, 113

Nabors, Thomas J. 26
Nall, Wiley H. 32, 226, 251
Nall Cemetery 252
Nanafalia 9, 257
Nanafalia Baptist Church Cemetery 236
Napier, Lemuel 10, 232, 259
Naruna 248
Neary, Nicholas 14, 138, 146
Neely, Sarah 236
New Baltimore 91
New Kent Court House 95, 260
New Kent Road 95
New Orleans 231
New Prospect 257
Newbern 38
Newbern Presbyterian Church 37
Newby's Cross Roads 162
Newton, Philip M. 32, 81, 252
Newtonville 252, 258
Nichols, A.F. 28
Nichols, Bellzora 247
Nichols, Moses 10, 232
Nichols, Susan Ann 232
Nine Mile Road 95–96, 107
Nineteenth Mississippi Regiment 58, 67, 75, 78, 85
Ninety-Fifth Pennsylvania Regiment 141
Ninety-Sixth Pennsylvania Regiment 141
Ninth Alabama Regiment 58, 65, 67, 77–79, 85, 92, 96, 99, 102, 104, 108, 111, 125, 128, 140, 142, 155, 167, 171, 178, 198, 201, 208–210, 218, 260
Nixon, George 34
Noble, Calvin 20, 202
Noland, Isaac M. 31, 226, 249
Norred, Benjamin 87, 100
Norred, Marshall 260
Norred, Wesley 87, 100
Norris, Francis M. 87, 215, 232
Norris, Martin C. 13–14, 105, 138, 257
North Anna River 184–186
North Port 26, 245
North Port Rifles 25
Norwood, John W. 87
Norwood, Nathaniel 17, 112, 191, 262
Nowell, Kenturah Roxanna Diana Elizabeth 238
Nunn, William H. 32
Nunnalee, Howell 11
Nunnalee, James 234
Nunnalee, Luman 234
Nunnalee, Malinda 11
Nunnalee, Stephen F. 6, 11–14, 63, 85, 89, 234

Oak Grove Franconia Cemetery 249
Oakley, Jordan W. 87, 112, 237, 260
Oakley, Thomas W. 19–20, 100, 260
Oakwood Cemetery 238, 243–244
Oakwood Confederate Cemetery 117, 147, 230–232, 259, 262
Occoquan 75
Octagon 231

O'Daniel, W.D. 27
Odd Fellows Cemetery 249
Odum, Harrison 22, 81
Odum, William 22, 213
Oglesberry, Thomas J. 26
Ogletree, Benjamin H. 112, 226
Ogletree, Daniel S. 112, 226
Ogletree, James L. 10
Ogletree, Thomas J. 10, 258
Old Abilene Cemetery 252
Old Capitol Prison 170
Old Hepzibah Cemetery 244
Old Linden Cemetery 230, 254
Old Spring Hill Cemetery 237
Oldham, Marion 23, 106
Oliver, Ann 252
Oliver, James W. 32, 106, 126, 213, 226, 252
Oliver, Mattie C. 252
Oliver, Sarah J. 252
One Hundred Nineteenth Pennsylvania Regiment 141
One Hundred Twenty-First New York Regiment 141–142
O'Neal, Allie 231
O'Neal, Wooten 22, 164, 204, 261
O'Neal Family Cemetery 231
Orange and Alexandria Railroad 70
Orange Court House 70, 91, 118–119, 162–168, 170, 175, 259
Orion 257
Orleans 119
Osborn, Wyman A. 20, 140, 157
Otey, Thomas S. 26, 74
Our Soldier's Cemetery 165, 232
Owen, T.S. 28
Owen, Thomas M. 11, 238, 244
Owen, Thomas R. 23, 126
Owen, William R. 87, 131
Ox's Ford 185

Palmer, Walter T. 30, 116, 128, 133, 164, 212, 219
Palmetto 32, 38, 251
Pamunkey River 186
Paragould 246
Parham, John P. 14, 217
Paris 236
Parish, J. 19
Parker, Jesse S. 10, 100, 260
Parker, King, Dr. 134
Parker, R.G. 28
Parker, Walter C.Y. 33, 50, 71, 83, 110, 113, 116, 133, 255, 260
Parker County 235
Parker's Store 176
Parks, Levi J. 22, 158
Paschal, James J. 17, 106, 112
Patterson, Ira 237
Patterson, Robert 58–59
Patterson, Robert A. 20, 100, 237
Patton, Abner E. 14, 105, 117
Patton, Martha E. 234
Payne's Chapel Cemetery 250
Payne's Chapel UMC 232
Pearce, Pleasant L. 23, 112
Pearl, James 87
Pearl, Stephen 10
Pearl, Thomas 10, 112, 226

Peck, William R. 218–219
Peeks, Thomas 27
Pegram, John 219
Pegues, Christopher James 237
Pegues, J.B. 20
Pegues, Jennie Decima 237
Pegues, Lila 237
Pegues, Mary Zula 237
Pegues, Ruby Mae 237
Pegues, Wille Grey 237
Pegues, William C. 20, 106, 237, 259
Pegues, William Clyde 237
Pender, W.D. 163
Pendergrass, Amanda Rachel 236
Pendergrass, Ida 236
Pensacola 15
Peoples, Joseph H. 20, 89
Percell, William R. 20, 106, 157
Perkins, John K. 32, 113
Perrin, Abner 175–178, 181, 262
Perry, Arthur M. 14, 187, 193
Perry, Herman H. 17
Perry County 7, 220
Person, James W. 23, 72
Person, Willis D. 24, 165
Petersburg 91, 189, 217, 230, 237
Petersburg and Weldon Railroad 91
Petersburg Pike 189
Petersburg trenches 196, 213
Petty, George 34
Pevy, Raleigh 22
Phares, John W. 14, 234
Pharis, James S. 22, 81
Phelan, James 7
Phifer, Charles H. 10, 112
Phifer, John H. 10, 112
Phifer, Michael 20
Philadelphia 15, 255
Phillip Schoppert House 234
Phillips, Arthur B. 87, 143, 234
Phillips, Benjamin 87, 126
Phillips, Elias E. 224, 240
Phillips, Fannie Artelia 234
Phillips, James E. 31, 72
Phillips, James T. 31, 144, 188
Phillips, John H. 14, 73, 112, 158
Phillips, Martha A. 234
Phillips, Pete 234
Phillips, Thaddeus M. 24, 157, 160, 242
Phillips, Walter 234
Phillips, William A. 34, 100, 139, 146
Phillips, William H.H. 32, 126, 158, 160
Pickens County Guards 27, 29–30, 38, 45, 114, 226–227
Pickensville 247, 249, 251
Pickensville Lower Cemetery 247, 249
Pickett, George E. 108, 129, 155
Piedmont Station 59–62, 67, 70–71
Pierce, Beverly B. 87, 226
Pierce, John G. 17, 53–54, 217
Pierson, George W. 26, 157, 226
Pilgrim's Rest 258
Pine Grove Methodist Cemetery 240
Pinetucky 33, 79, 255

Piper House 125
Pippen, Little Berry A. 17, 157, 204
Pitzer's Woods 150–151
Plank Road 130, 136, 138–143, 169, 175–176, 178
Plaquemine 238
Platt, Bryant 164
Pleasant Grove 257
Pleasant Grove Cemetery 243
Pleasant Ridge 235–236, 257
Pleasant Valley 21, 124
Plum Run 153
Plummer, William A. 26, 113, 117
Po River 179–181
Poe, William T. 25
Poellnitz, Charles A. 20, 237
Poellnitz, James A. 20, 237
Poellnitz, Julius Edwin 237
Point Lookout 203, 220, 227, 254, 262
Pollard 257
Pollard, John T. 34, 89
Ponder, Sarah 242
Pool, John W. 14, 112, 126
Poole, John B.P. 26, 157, 165
Porter, Benjamin F. 22, 126, 144, 211, 215, 240
Porter, Davis 240
Porter, Frank W. 240
Porter, Jimmy Woodfin 240
Porter, John C. 240
Porter, Mary 240
Porter, Mattie 240
Porter, Sank 240
Porter, Thomas Lee 240
Portland 237
Posey, Ella E. 239
Post, George C. 10, 224
Potts, Henry R. 24, 70
Pounds, Isham W. 34, 255
Pounds, John M. 34, 113, 117
Pounds, Lucinda 255
Powell, Eliza 252
Powell, Ezekiel R. 32, 252
Powell, Fannie 252
Powell, Jane 252
Powell, John C. 26, 245, 258
Powell, General Marion 87, 112, 191
Powell, Reuben 252
Powell, Susan A. 241
Powell, Zenomia 252
Prairieville 36, 39, 237
Prater, John A. 32, 113
Pratt, John 28
Prattville 240
Presbyterian Church Cemetery 236
Price, William M. 34, 147
Pridmore, Elijah J. 31, 96
Prince, Belle Eleanor 237
Prince, Emma Boddie 237
Prince, Jennie Moore 237
Prince, John Edmund 237
Prince, John H. 18–20, 36, 50, 53, 112, 116, 133, 164, 211, 216, 221, 226, 237, 257, 259
Prince, Julia Elizabeth 237
Prince, Mary Brown 237
Prince, Oliver Haywood 237
Prince, Richard Knott 237

Prince, Robert Joseph 237
Prince, Sydney Alexander 237
Prince, Thomas M.C. 87, 106, 117
Prince, William M. 17, 112
Propst, Allen H. 32, 106, 157, 226, 252
Prospect Hill 21, 172, 239
Providence 11, 29–30
Providence Cemetery 245
Provisional Congress of the Confederate States of American 3, 5, 6
Pryor, Roger 97, 102, 111, 121, 125
Puckett, J.W. 28
Puckett, Joel H. 27
Pugh, R.M. 22
Pumphry, Jesse 26, 106
Purcell, Jeff 20

Quinn, Chesterfield 87, 209, 242
Quinn, Dovie 242
Quinn, Halsey 242
Quinn, Lula M. Grace 242
Quinn, Maggie Bell 242
Quinn, Martha V. 242
Quinn, Oliver Judson 242
Quinn, Pearl 242
Quinn, Phillip M. 242
Quinn, Robert Chester 242
Quinn, Sarah F. 242
Quinn, Thomas Walter 242
Quinn, Velmer Lee 242
Quinn, Warren Lee 242
Quinn, William Peyton 242
Quinney, James M. 20, 219

Raccoon Ford 119
Ragland House 197
Raiford, James H. 34, 258
Rain, Leslie V. 22, 144, 215
Rains, John B. 9, 115, 133, 142, 164, 210, 216, 259
Rainwater, Edward 22, 96
Rainwater, Moses A. 22, 112
Raleigh 7, 257
Randall, James L. 31, 249, 258
Randall, Joel R. 29, 31, 84
Randall, Sarah Alcanza 252
Randol, Alanson M. 109
Randolph 23, 38, 44, 240
Randol's Battery 109–112, 260
Rapidan Heights 175
Rappahannock River 119, 130–131
Rappahannock Station 119
Rasberry, Newton 24, 112, 243
Rasberry, Richard F. 24
Rasberry, William R. 24, 112, 243
Ratliff, Little S.B.J. 88, 226, 255
Ratliff, William H.H. 34, 145, 158
Ratliffe, John 88
Ravenswood 76
Rawls, Charles Spurgeon 238
Rawls, Connie 238
Rawls, Della 238
Rawls, Georgia 238
Rawls, James Thomas 238
Rawls, Simion Seth 238
Rawls, Simon H. 20, 106, 140, 238
Ray, Frances 241
Ray, James 26, 72

Ray, Joseph J. 26, 106, 117
Ray, Olivia 231
Rayfield, Thomas 24, 112, 226
Rea, Robert M. 34
Read, Hugh K. 31
Read, John B. 257
Ream's Station 194–195
Ream's Station, Battle 208–209, 213
Red Bay 245
Redd, John A. 87, 178, 226
Redd, William W. 87
Reelfoot Lake 246
Reese, Benjamin W. 87, 117
Reeves, Thomas 26
Reform 30, 247–248
Rembert, Mary 237
Rembert Hill Cemetery 237
Renfro, James H. 26, 50, 72
Reves, John C. 226, 259
Reynolds, Gilbert M. 17, 96
Rice's Station 223
Richards, Joseph N. 26
Richardson, Ed 239
Richardson, Erlander M. 15–16, 105, 203, 226, 236, 257
Richardson, Jackson W.J. 32, 72
Richardson, John Addison 236
Richardson, John H. 87, 106, 249
Richardson, Luther H.J. 32, 89
Richardson, Thomas B. 17, 69, 105
Richardson, William H. 15, 17, 127, 133, 157, 164, 172, 181, 183
Richmond 6, 15, 52–55, 70, 91, 100, 184, 207, 217, 258
Richmond and Danville Railroad 52, 222
Ricks, Frances R. 243
Riddell's Shop 189
Ridgeway, John C.J. 14, 55, 111, 152, 156–157, 257
Ried, Francis M. 14, 89
Riggins, James E. 10
Rigsby, John T. 26, 74
Risinger, John C. 24, 258
River Road 95, 136, 138–139
Roane, Curtis R. 20, 170, 238
Roane, Spencer 238
Roanoke 17
Roberson, Mollie 249
Roberts, George 22, 112, 117
Roberts, James 164, 178
Roberts, Martin Van B. 14, 140, 261
Robertson, Elizabeth 250
Robertson, Ella F. 238
Robertson, Jesse J. 24
Robertson, Patsy 250
Robertson, Richard M. 20, 53, 94, 238, 259
Robinson, Jesse 16, 95, 112, 259
Robinson, John J. 87
Robuck, William P. 14, 105, 138, 164, 204, 207, 226
Rodgers, Henry L. 32, 208
Rogers, Francis M. 10, 112
Rogers, George T. 199
Rogers, Hugh 67, 257
Rogers, Martha Ann 232, 253
Rogers, William H. 10, 112, 226
Roger's House 153

Rooney, Bernard 20
Roper, Thomas F. 24, 183
Roper's Farm 148
Roseman, Alice 252
Ross, James N. 32, 113
Ross, Joseph N. 20, 84
Ross, Martha 236
Ross, Thomas F. 10
Ross, William 67, 105
Ross, William C. 126, 226, 257
Ross, William G. 26, 113, 117
Rosser, Francis M. 26, 106
Rowanty Creek 218
Rudd, James E. 29, 31
Ruffin, John E. 20, 238
Ruffin, Roberta 238
Russell, Martha 252
Russell County 234
Rutherford County 4
Ryan, Patrick 109

Sailor's Creek 223
St. Andrew's Church 36, 39, 41
St. Augustine 58
St. James College 161, 261
St. Michaels Cemetery 238
St. Stephens 21, 43
Salem Church 127, 137–147
Salem Church Cemetery 248
Salient 179–183
Salisbury 166
Sanders, Benjamin F. 88, 158, 226, 255
Sanders, Charles Peake 14
Sanders, Charles W. 15, 17, 226
Sanders, Elizabeth Ann 14
Sanders, John C.C. 14–16, 35, 38, 51, 54, 69, 77, 84, 88, 94, 107, 109, 111–112, 115, 118, 122, 125–126, 134–135, 137–138, 140, 142–144, 156, 161–163, 166, 171, 173, 182–183, 186–187, 190, 195–196, 198–201, 203–207, 210, 227, 236, 259
Sanders, John D., Independent Volunteers 88
Sanders, John D., Pickens County Guards 31, 106, 259
Sanders, John W. 27, 30–31, 84
Sanders, Richard A. 10
Sanders, William H., Dr. 15, 17, 38, 54, 64, 68, 71, 73, 77, 79–83, 85, 93–94, 98, 104, 111, 120–122, 128, 134, 162, 169–170, 173, 182, 196, 200, 204–205, 207, 217, 226, 236, 239, 258–260, 262
Sanders, William H.H., Confederate Guards 17, 106, 215, 217, 236
Sanders, William H.H., Pickens County Guards 29, 31
Sandy Chapel Cemetery 241, 243
Sanford, Benjamin F. 23, 81, 106.
Sanford, Martha 240
Sardis Church 231
Saunders, Rebecca A. 255
Savannah, Mary Ann 248
Saxon, W.E. 259
Scarbrough, David P. 13–14, 89
Schirm, John 20, 183
Schoepf, Albin Francisco 146

Schoppert, Phillip 234
Schoppert, Robert P. 13–14, 133, 164, 211, 217, 234
Scott, George W. 180
Scott Station 244
Scottsville 257
Scroggins, William W. 24
Searcy, George W. 22, 84
Searcy, James 22
Second New Jersey Regiment 141
Second Ohio Cavalry 194
Seddon, James 164, 186
Sedgwick, John 137, 143
Seeley, Francis W. 152
Self, Andrew J. 29, 31, 113
Sellick, James B. 34, 258
Selma 38–40, 43, 234, 255
Seminary Ridge 154
Senatobia 251
Sentell, John R. 20–21, 100, 112
Seven Pines, Battle 96–100, 113, 130, 242
Seventh Pennsylvania Regiment 110
Seymore, James I. 31, 106
Shackleford, Jesse H. 87, 139, 146, 245
Shady Grove 179
Shady Grove Methodist Cemetery 248
Shady Grove Road 180, 187
Shamblin, David 26, 202, 245
Sharpe 246
Sharpsburg 124–126, 130, 240
Shaw, James P. 29, 31, 144, 186, 226, 249
Shaw, Paul G. 9, 191, 259
Shaw, Thomas W. 31, 157, 160, 165, 249
Shaw, William J. 31, 183, 215
Shelton, Alice 252
Shelton, John W. 32, 60, 188, 192, 226, 252
Shelton, L.M. 27
Shelton, Rufus H. 32, 85, 106, 116, 133, 158, 164, 252
Shenod, J.C. 27
Shepherd, Andrew Earlie 249
Shepherd, Hiram E. 249
Shepherd, John T. 31, 84, 249
Shepherd, Lula 249
Shepherd, Martha F. 249
Shepherd, Susan Lenorah 249
Shepherdstown 124, 127, 148, 161
Shepperd, H. 27
Shepperd, John T. 27
Sherwood, Benjamin 22, 112
Sherwood, Edwin A. 87, 144, 158, 165
Shevernell, O. 34, 258
Shiloh 9, 232
Shiloh Baptist Cemetery 232
Shinn, Mary Eliza 240
Shivers, Jesse B. 113, 255
Shorter, John Gill 11
Shropshire, Margaret 242
Shultz, Allen 22, 106
Shultz, John R. 22, 112
Shuttlesworth, Joseph R. 26, 144, 177–178

Sigel, Franz 261
Sikes, Arthur 252
Sikes, Elbert 252
Sikes, Ella 252
Sikes, Enoch 164, 226, 252
Sikes, Ginnie 252
Sikes, Harvey 252
Sikes, Lillian 252
Sikes, Mauda 252
Sikes, Oscar 252
Simmons, Burrill 22, 84
Simmons, John F. 21, 72
Simmons, Laura 237
Simpson, A.Y. 22
Simpson, Jackson 22, 106
Simpson, Lewis 22
Sims, Fannie 246
Sims Hill Cemetery 255
Singleton, James S. 157, 257
Singleton, Joseph 67, 89, 257
Sisson, John A. 20–21, 112
Six Mile 257
Sixteenth Massachusetts Regiment 152
Sixteenth New York Regiment 141
Sixth Alabama Regiment 73, 75
Sixtieth Alabama Regiment 195
Sixty-First New York Regiment 180
Sixty-Ninth Pennsylvania Regiment 190
Skates, John W. 14, 204, 220, 234
Skates, William B. 87
Skinner, James L. 20–21, 84
Smelley, E. Lula 242
Smelley, George Bluford 242
Smelley, Henry Clarence 243
Smelley, James David 242
Smelley, Jason E. 242
Smelley, John H. 24, 226, 242
Smelley, M. Columbus 243
Smelley, March C. 242
Smelley, Montera 243
Smelley, R. Walters 242
Smelley, William Jackson 242
Smelley, Wilson 242
Smelly, David W. 164, 223–224, 243
Smelly, James W. 164, 207, 226, 243
Smelly, Simpson 243
Smith, Arthur C. 22
Smith, Benjamin F. 32, 145, 192
Smith, Cadir M. 24, 106, 138, 146
Smith, David C. 31, 84, 259
Smith, Edmund Kirby 48–49, 57–59, 63, 66–67, 258
Smith, Franklin L. 29, 31, 226, 249
Smith, Frederick B. 22, 112, 117
Smith, Gustavus W. 67, 74, 78, 85, 95
Smith, Henry S. 32, 60, 70, 258
Smith, James M. 32
Smith, Jasper 26, 113
Smith, Jeddiah H. 87, 106, 113
Smith, John 34
Smith, John G. 10, 84
Smith, Joseph Lee 58
Smith, N.F. 28
Smith, Robert L. 32, 100, 158
Smith, Thomas J. 17, 112, 144, 226
Smith, W.D. 27

Smith, William M. 22
Smith, Zoe 254
Smitherman, Charles 24, 72
Smitherman, Joseph 243
Smitherman, Martha Jane 242
Smitherman, Newton H. 24, 100, 144, 178
Smitherman, Thomas J. 24, 44, 89, 243
Sneed, David V. 23, 72
Sneed, William J. 24
Snider, David 26, 70
Solley, Frederick E. 10, 104–105, 157, 232
Somerville 252
Sorrel's Brigade 17
South Anna River 186
South Side Railroad 52, 194, 213
Spangler's Woods 150–152
Spear, Samuel D. 195
Speed, Leroy H. 31, 226, 249
Speed, Marianne Caroline 249
Speed, Thomas W. 179, 262
Speed, William A. 31, 113, 226, 249, 259
Speed Mills 247
Spell, T.R. 246
Spinks, Jasper 24, 100
Spinks, Newton 24, 106
Spiva, James 67, 178, 257
Spotsylvania, Battle 179–183
Spotsylvania Court House 178
Spring Hill 238, 248, 257
Spring Hill Cemetery 247
Springfield 14, 231, 234
Springfield, John R. 87, 214
Springle, Robert E. 21, 226
Sprinker, Isaac 109
Sprowl, John M. 28, 30
Sronce, John A. 22, 84
Stacy, Ervin 87, 226
Stafford, James R. 17, 62, 106, 191, 226
Stage Road 208
Stallsworth, Joseph P. 17
Stanifer, Jeff 253
Stanley, Amaritta Alzira 242
Stanley, Asa A. 24, 112, 126, 144, 157, 226
Stansbury Hill 138–140, 143, 145
Stansbury House 138
Stansel, M.L. 27
Staunton 172, 239
Steadman, Jesse H. 10, 157
Steed, Thomas G. 18
Steele, Abner Newton 25–26, 76, 113, 116–117, 259
Steele, Elmore A. 17, 112, 204, 259
Steele, John J. 15, 17, 122
Steele, Richard Griffith 25
Stemson, Zemiah 24
Stephenson, William H.H. 10, 226
Stevensburg 119, 147
Stewart, Charles 87, 96
Stewart, Dubose 238
Stewart, Hannah Holliday 238
Stewart, James H. 20–21, 106, 157, 226, 238
Stewart, John A. 17, 112, 144, 215

Stewart, Josiah G. 31, 106
Stewart, Laura Pierce 248
Stewart, M. Daniel L. 34, 113, 145, 204, 220
Stewart, Martin L. 27, 30, 101, 106, 116, 133, 164, 212, 216, 225
Stewart, Reuben J. 32, 85, 106, 252
Stewart, Tom 28
Stewart, William H. 201
Stockton 257
Stokely, Joseph B. 22, 112, 117
Stoker, Davidson 29, 31, 106, 259
Stoker, E.S. 240
Stoker, James B./S. 23, 226, 240
Stone, C.L. 28
Stone, L.M. 28
Stonewall Cemetery 128, 258
Stony Creek Depot 194
Story, Andrew J. 29, 31, 106, 226, 249
Story, Benjamin Ferdinand 249
Story, Georga Mayes 249
Story, George W. 17
Story, Leila 249
Story, Susan A. 249
Story, Willett Wilson 249
Strasburg 56–57, 236
Strickland, George W. 32, 106, 113
Strickler 252
Strudwick, Edmund L. 21, 84
Strudwick, James W. 19
Strudwick, Osmund L. 20, 116, 128, 133, 144
Strudwick, Shepherd T. 21
Stuart, James E.B. 101
Sudduth, Jabez P. 32, 50, 113, 144, 157
Sudley Springs 122
Suggs, George P. 10, 89
Sullivan, James H. 31–32, 66, 79
Sullivan, Richard S. 87, 170
Sullivan, Thomas 17, 106
Summerdale 239
Summers, Daniel P.M. 32, 113, 132
Summers, William T. 183, 252
Sumter County 233–234
Sumter, Ft. 15
Suttle, James N. 24, 100, 243, 259
Suttle, Sarah Margaret 242
Suttle, William J. 23, 112, 116, 133, 164, 204, 212
Sutton, Emma J. 249
Sutton, George S. 249
Sutton, Jesse E. 249
Sutton, Maggie 249
Sutton, Mary 249
Sutton, Pleasant A. 31, 249
Sweetwater 257

Tadlock, James H. 34, 255
Tadlock, John W. 164, 192, 226
Tadlock, Malcomb D.C. 88, 145, 226, 255, 259
Tadlock, William D. 34, 72
Taggart, Moses W. 31, 157, 160
Talbird, Henry 33, 54–55, 66, 71, 101, 116, 255
Talladega 239
Tallapoosa County 231

Talliaferro, David M. 20, 112
Tannehill, Mary Lavina 25
Tannehill State Park 242
Tarr, Francis B. 17, 183, 226
Tayloe, Catherine 238
Tayloe, Edward 238
Tayloe, George E. 17–20, 39–40, 54, 100, 116, 173, 210–211, 216, 238
Tayloe, George Plater 17
Tayloe, George Willis 238
Tayloe, J.W. 18–19
Tayloe, James Sterling 238
Tayloe, John K. 238
Tayloe, Lomax P. 238
Tayloe, Mary L. 238
Tayloe, Rosa Fielding 238
Tayloe, W.H. 223
Tayloe, William Randolph 238
Taylor, Charles A. 32, 113
Taylor, Florence W. 237
Taylor, George W. 24, 112
Taylor, J.W. 28
Taylor, Jacob J. 87, 106
Taylor, Lewis 24, 106
Taylor, Thomas R. 31, 113
Taylor, W.H. 193, 211, 218, 262
Taylor House, Dr. 130–131, 137–138
Telegraph Road 138, 184–185
Telephone 241
Tenth Alabama Regiment 39, 58, 67, 75, 78, 82, 85, 92, 96, 102, 104, 108, 111, 128, 137–138, 140, 142, 151–152, 155, 167, 216, 218, 221, 262
Tenth Massachusetts Battery 223
Terry, Caroline 243
Terry, James C. 32, 106, 122, 259
Terry, John T. 27
Terry, Mary Elizabeth 256
Terry, Richard C. 100, 122
Thames, James 34, 258
Tharp, Lemuel 14, 126
Thetford, Kennon 235
Thetford, Samuel Lewis 235
Thetford, William F. 14, 138, 183, 235
Thetford, William F., Jr. 235
Third Alabama Hospital 165
Third Alabama Regiment 75
Third Maine Regiment 151
Third Maryland Cavalry 160
Third U.S. Artillery 152
Third Vermont Regiment 193, 195
Thirteenth Alabama Regiment 73, 75, 218
Thirty-Eight Virginia Regiment 58, 67, 78, 82, 85, 94
Thom, Reuben 106, 116, 128, 133, 157, 164, 172, 259
Thomas, B.C. 28
Thomas, Elias M. 24, 112, 186, 226, 243
Thomas, Tristram S. 27, 31, 75, 158, 165
Thomas' Artillery 58, 67, 85
Thomaston 232
Thompson, D.S.P. 20
Thompson, Elias B. 34
Thompson, President F. 20–21, 81

Thompson, Fleming W. 14, 126, 135, 137–138, 146, 149, 156, 164, 166, 168, 170–171, 173, 189, 197, 204, 220
Thompson, James W. 20–21, 81, 202
Thompson, Joseph 34, 183
Thompson, Joseph C. 31
Thompson, Lewis L. "Independence," 21, 112
Thompson, Thomas H. 87, 157
Thompson, William J. 32, 72
Thomson, Eleanor Caroline 25
Thomson, Peter K. 26, 202, 226
Thomson, Randolph 226
Thornrose Cemetery 239
Thornton, E.V.F. 165
Thornton, Edward Levi 252
Thornton, Emily 251
Thornton, Eunice May 252
Thornton, Glen Everett 252
Thornton, James M. 252
Thornton, Lottie E. 252
Thornton, Lucinda B. 252
Thornton, Mary E. 252
Thornton, Nancy E. 252
Thornton, Preston W. 32, 145, 252
Thornton, Susan Florence 252
Thornton, Thomas J. 252
Thornton, William Lee 252
Thoroughfare Gap 119–120
Thrasher, Emanual C.B. 87
Thrasher, Thomas 87
Threat, Jesse 32, 183, 226
Tibbs, David A. 26, 113, 131
Tice, Daniel 10
Tice, William H.F. 87, 157, 226
Tinen, Patrick S. 190
Todd, Bernard 207
Toll Gate 139–140, 142–143, 145
Tombigbee River 236
Trammill, John B. 34, 113
Trammill, Shade C. 34, 62, 84
Trantham, Julie Edwina 248
Traweek, George 31–32, 38, 54, 79–81, 101
Traweek, George L. 32, 85, 158
Traweek, Margaret 32
Traweek, Nelson 32
Traweek, Simon 32, 226
Traweek, Spencer 32
True, John A. 14, 112
True, William L. 14, 112
Trussell's Ferry 13
Tryon 26
Tucker, Henry B. 87, 226, 232
Tucker, James D. 10, 89
Tucker, James J. 21, 81
Tucker, James W. 232
Tucker, Solomon 157, 165
Tucker, Thomas W. 10, 158, 165
Tucker, William H. 232
Tucker Missionary Cemetery 255
Turkey Ridge, Battle 187–188
Turnbull, John G. 152
Turner, Meshack A. 88
Turner, Sam 21, 100
Turnipseed, James A. 31, 89, 249
Turnipseed, John W. 31, 144, 226, 249

Tuscaloosa 14, 24–25, 38, 66, 87, 234, 236, 258
Tuscaloosa Rifles 4, 25–26, 38, 44, 72, 114, 129, 226–227
Tuskegee 237
Tutwiler, Henry 30
Tutwiler, Robert P. 14
Twelfth New Hampshire Regiment 152
Twentieth Alabama Regiment 230
Twenty-Fourth Alabama Regiment 245
Twenty-Third New Jersey Regiment 141, 145

Underwood, John A.B. 34, 256
Union 16
Union Chapel Cemetery 235, 248
Uniontown 39–40, 172, 238, 257–258
United States Ford 136
Upchurch, Robert J. 17, 112, 260
Updegrove, George 34, 113
Ustick, Mary Elizabeth Jarvis 234

Vaile, Jesse M. 32, 100, 139, 146
Van Buren 253
Vance, Philip M. 87, 133, 164, 202, 206, 212, 216, 223–224, 226
Vance, Samuel W. 26, 177
Van Dorn, Earl 81, 85
Vanzant, Samuel H. 29–31, 94, 101, 116
Varner, James H. 10, 112, 117
Varner, Jesse 67, 84, 257, 259
Varner, John R. 10, 226, 232
Varner, Samuel 10, 84, 259
Vaughan, Asa 87, 144, 146, 213
Vaughan Road 218
Vaughn, James I. 17, 187, 236
Verdiersville 169
Vicksburg Cemetery 230
Vienna 236
Virginia and Tennessee Railroad 41
Virginia Military Institute 17

Waco 233, 252
Waddell, Beverly L. 33, 75, 164, 213, 261
Waddell, Thomas J. 21, 75
Wade, Thomas 67, 117, 257
Wade, William 67, 112, 257, 259
Waggoner, James M. 87, 178, 207
Waggoner, Olive Perilee 242
Wait, Richard H. 32, 126, 252
Wake County 7
Walden, Abel A. 32, 66, 71, 79, 106, 116, 133, 164, 202, 206, 208, 212, 216, 252, 259
Walden, George W. 32, 226
Walker, Allen Jones 232
Walker, Amanda Jane 232
Walker, Eli Thomas 232
Walker, George Malone 232
Walker, Jackson Rogers 232
Walker, James Brooks 232
Walker, John 21
Walker, Nathaniel R. 87, 213, 232
Walker, Nathaniel Rogers 232

Walker, Susan Rebecca 232
Walker, William Nathaniel 232
Wall, Annis 240
Wall, Joel 240
Wall, Melvin 240
Wall, Monsfield 240
Wall, Rhoda Ann 240
Wall, Wright 23, 186, 226, 240
Wallace, D.C. 87, 192
Wallace, George 87
Wallace, John B. 34, 192
Wallace, Ruffus B. 34, 145, 256
Waller, Alexander M. 10, 89, 259
Waller, John 67, 147, 257
Waller, Robert L. 17, 106, 202
Walton, William P. 34, 145, 193, 256
War of 1812 231
Ward, John 34, 139, 146
Ward, Needham 21, 224, 238
Ward, Solomon A. 26, 113, 259
Ward, Thomas A. 32, 113
Warren, Aaron 34, 256
Warren, Gouverneur K. 218
Warren, Isaac 256
Warren, John Franklin 256
Warren, Linard 256
Warren, Marion 34, 94, 256, 259
Warren, Mary 256
Warren, Mosely 256
Warren, Sarah J. 256
Warren, William 256
Warrenton 128, 167
Warrenton Springs 91, 119
Warrenton Turnpike 120
Warthen, James E. 20–21, 112, 257
Warwick River 92–93
Washburn, Andrew J. 34, 158
Washington D.C. 4, 146
Washington Sharpshooters 21
Watkins, R.E. 13
Watkins, William W. 87, 226
Watlington, Cornelius 21, 112, 133, 164, 210–211, 215–217, 226, 239
Watson, Alice 245
Watson, Amos 245
Watson, Bazzel 245
Watson, Benjamin 245
Watson, Charlie 245
Watson, Della 245
Watson, Dock 245
Watson, Edward 245
Watson, Finis 245
Watson, James 245
Watson, Jonathan 245
Watson, Joseph 245
Watson, Leroy 245
Watson, Robert A. 87, 204, 221, 245
Watson, S.D. 75
Watson, Samuel O.P. 26, 84
Watts, William 27
Way Hospital 217
Wayne, Alexander F. 10, 105, 158, 226
Weaver, George J.H.T. 26, 113
Weaver, John W. 26, 122
Webb, Columbus 24, 72
Webb, George Willis 14, 112, 144
Weekly, Thomas J. 33, 113
Weigle's Mill 149

Weisiger, D.A. 190, 198
Welborn, David E. 32, 89
Welch, Andrew S. 29, 31, 72
Welch, Jim 9
Weldon 91, 190
Weldon Railroad 192–193, 195, 202, 205, 208
West Blocton 242
West Perry 253, 256
West Point 41, 43, 46
Western and Atlantic Railroad 41–42
Westminster 158
Wheeler, Joseph 3, 7
White, A.D. 34, 258
White, Henry C. 14, 62, 121, 262
White, John A. 17, 122
White, John G. 26
White, Marion F. 87
White, Mary Ann 234
White, Oran 32, 106
White Oak Swamp 107
White Oak Swamp Bridge 189
White Plains 119, 261
White Post 148
White's Ford 122
White's Tavern, Battle 202–204, 211–213
Whiteside, Elenora 168
Whiteside, John N. 168
Whiteside, Joseph C. 17, 168, 226
Whitfield, Needham G. 20–21, 43, 258
Whitley-Whitson-Strong Family Cemetery 244
Whitlock, Hesperia Laventine 239
Wier, A. 28
Wier, James D. 27
Wier, John W. 27, 106
Wier, Samuel M. 31, 89
Wier, Thomas A. 27, 31, 82, 113, 226
Wier, W.K. 28
Wier, W.S. 27
Wiggins, John W. 27
Wilcox, Cadmus M. 65–67, 78, 82, 92–93, 97–101, 104, 108–111, 118–123, 127–132, 135–140, 149, 151–156, 160–163, 171, 176, 185, 259–261
Wilcox Farm 195, 262
Wilcox Farm, Battle 188–192
Wilderness, Battle 175–179, 183
Wilkins, Eliza 249
Wilkins, Jasper 32, 113, 126, 158
Wilkins, John 249
Wilkins, John A. 31, 60, 249

Wilkins, Robert 249
Wilkins, Tanin B. 249
Wilkinson, James 67, 226, 257
Williams, Charles W. 20–21
Williams, D.W. 87, 106
Williams, Elihu E. 34, 113
Williams, G. 20
Williams, George W. 87, 144, 224
Williams, Henry T. 32, 170
Williams, James E. 29, 31, 204
Williams, John Martin 23
Williams, Joseph J. 10, 112, 140, 202, 226
Williams, L. 226, 262
Williams, Tescharner 17, 69
Williams, William C., Confederate Guards 17, 69, 81
Williams, William C., Marengo Rifles 10, 112
Williams, William J. 31, 84
Williamsburg 91, 95
Williamsburg Road 95–96
Williamson, Carroll D. 21, 226
Williamson, Henyard T. 26, 113, 116, 130, 133, 164, 202, 212
Williamson, William H. 21, 100
Williford, Joseph G. 87, 109, 112
Williford, Meady M. 14, 226, 259
Willingham, W.C. 20
Willis, Delia 17–18, 173, 238
Willis, George Sallie 17
Willis, John B. 23
Willis Church Road 189
Willoughby's Run 150
Wilson, B.F. 28
Wilson, Burr 252
Wilson, Charles S. 31, 113, 226, 249
Wilson, Francis C. 17, 226
Wilson, James H. 17, 112, 194, 226
Wilson, Jason 31, 50, 226
Wilson, William 87, 113, 252–253
Wilson, William F., Confederate Guards 17
Wilson, William F., Pickens County Guards 31, 84
Wilson, William J. 87, 224–225
Wimberly, Thomas J. 32, 106, 145
Winchester 55–59, 70, 127–128, 162, 258, 261
Windham Cemetery 249
Winn, Thomas W. 17, 157, 183, 202
Winn, Walter E. 19–20, 71, 94, 104, 116, 142, 164, 171–172, 182, 191–192, 221
Winn's Chapel Congregational Methodist Church Cemetery 242

Winship, Lucius A. 23, 116, 133
Winstanley, Walter 22, 100
Witherspoon, James M. 232
Witherspoon, Thomas M. 9, 128, 133, 164, 210, 217, 232, 259
Witherspoon, William D. 226
Wolf, George 160
Womack, Lowndes 14
Wood(s), David S. 34, 89
Wood, John R. 224, 259
Wood Park 17
Woodfin, George W. 33
Woodlawn Cemetery 230, 248
Woodruff, George F. 24, 100, 157
Woods, Elisha 14, 105
Woods, John R. 29, 31, 84, 249
Woods, Wiley B. 31, 106, 113
Woods Family Cemetery 250
Woodson, Reavis, B. 9, 121
Woodstock 26, 242
Woodward, George W. 23, 112
Wooley, Green B. 24, 89
Wooten, Jasper W. 29, 31, 187
Wooten, Joseph E. 14, 186
Worrell, J. Thomas 34, 72
Worsham, Pleasant L. 23, 112, 240
Worthington, William 67, 105, 226, 257
Wright, Ambrose R. 190, 198
Wright, Clairborn 226, 259
Wright, Franklin 106, 259
Wright, Horatio 190, 192–193
Wright, Ignicious 32, 113, 158
Wright, P. Simpson 202
Wynne's Mill 92

Yancey, William L. 79
Yancey Rifles 21, 41, 43, 68, 114, 211, 226–227
Yateman, John W. 87, 192, 219, 250
Yeager, Louisa Ann 244
Yearby, Alexander F. 32, 252
Yearby, Arthur Frank 253
Yearby, Thomas Adley 253
York 255
Yorktown 91–95
Yorktown Road 95
Yorkville 30, 249
Young, Levi 87, 95
Young, Strudwick 21, 106, 165
Young, William B. 9, 17, 35, 105, 115, 133, 164, 210, 226
Young Men's Christian Association 167

Zion Cemetery 237

www.ingramcontent.com/pod-product-compliance
Ingram Content Group UK Ltd.
Pitfield, Milton Keynes, MK11 3LW, UK
UKHW050540150426
5217IPUK00026B/2017